Microeconomics, Macroeconomics and Economic Policy

Microeconomics, Macroeconomics and Economic Policy

Essays in Honour of Malcolm Sawyer

Edited by

Philip Arestis
University of Cambridge and University of the Basque Country

First published 2011 by
PALGRAVE MACMILLAN

Palgrave Macmillan in the UK is an imprint of Macmillan Publishers Limited, registered in England, company number 785998, of Houndmills, Basingstoke, Hampshire RG21 6XS.

Palgrave Macmillan in the US is a division of St Martin's Press LLC, 175 Fifth Avenue, New York, NY 10010.

Palgrave Macmillan is the global academic imprint of the above companies and has companies and representatives throughout the world.

Palgrave® and Macmillan® are registered trademarks in the United States, the United Kingdom, Europe and other countries.

ISBN 978–0–230–29019–8

This book is printed on paper suitable for recycling and made from fully managed and sustained forest sources. Logging, pulping and manufacturing processes are expected to conform to the environmental regulations of the country of origin.

A catalogue record for this book is available from the British Library.

Library of Congress Cataloging-in-Publication Data
Microeconomics, macroeconomics and economic policy: essays in honour of Malcolm Sawyer/edited by Philip Arestis.
p. cm.
Includes index.
ISBN 978–0–230–29019–8 (alk. paper)
1. Microeconomics. 2. Macroeconomics. 3. Economic policy.
I. Sawyer, Malcolm C. II. Arestis, Philip, 1941–
HB172.M5985 2011
330—dc22   2011011740

10   9   8   7   6   5   4   3   2   1
20   19   18   17   16   15   14   13   12   11

Printed and bound in Great Britain by
CPI Antony Rowe, Chippenham and Eastbourne

Contents

List of Tables

List of Figures

Notes on the Contributors

Philip Arestis is Honorary Senior Departmental Fellow, Cambridge Centre for Economics and Public Policy, Department of Land Economy, University of Cambridge, UK; Professor of Economics, Department of Applied Economics V, University of the Basque Country, Spain; Distinguished Adjunct Professor of Economics, Department of Economics, University of Utah, US; Senior Scholar, Levy Economics Institute, New York, US; Visiting Professor, Leeds Business School, University of Leeds, UK; Professorial Research Associate, Department of Finance and Management Studies, School of Oriental and African Studies (SOAS), University of London, UK; and holder of the British Hispanic Foundation 'Queen Victoria Eugenia' British Hispanic Chair of Doctoral Studies. He is Chief Academic Adviser to the UK Government Economic Service (GES) on Professional Developments in Economics. He has published as sole author or editor, as well as co-author and co-editor, a number of books, contributed in the form of invited chapters to numerous books, produced research reports for research institutes, and has published widely in academic journals.

Andrew Budd received a BS in Economics and Computer Science from Trinity College (Hartford) in 2008, and a Masters of Business Administration from the Sloan School of Management at MIT in 2010. His research interests include Post Keynesian economics, agent-based simulation, data mining and visualisation. He is now employed as a Senior Project Manager in the Technology Innovation group at ESPN, where he oversees the development of novel statistical analysis systems.

Keith Cowling is Professor of Economics at the University of Warwick where he has spent most of his professional life. He has published over a wide area of industrial economics and political economy. His publications include a considerable number of books including *Monopoly Capitalism*, his most important central publication. His papers include contributions to the *Journal of Political Economy*, the *European Economic Review*, the *Economic Journal*, *Kyklos*, *Economica*, and the *International Journal of Industrial Organisation*. He was previously President of the European Association for Research in Industrial Economics (EARIE) and editor of the *International Journal of Industrial Organization (IJIO)*.

His present research interests revolve around the deficiencies of monopoly capitalism and the formation of appropriate industrial strategies for addressing this world, including the global imbalances, which have recently become evident.

Teresa García del Valle is Associate Professor of Statistics at the University of the Basque Country, in Bilbao, Spain. She has a PhD from the University of the Basque Country. Her research interests are in the area of applied statistics. This expertise finds wider application in economics, as this is applied especially in the area of public economics. She has published a number of articles on those topics in books, edited books and in refereed journals. The latter include the *American Journal of Economics and Sociology*, the *Journal of Post Keynesian Economics* and *Revista de Economía Mundial*. She has participated and contributed to a number of conferences in her areas of expertise. She has been invited as Visiting Professor by a number of Latin American universities, including Universidad Autónoma Juan Misael Saracho (Tarija, Bolivia), Universidad Nacional Autónoma de México (México, D.F.) and Universidad del Salvador (El Salvador).

Amitava Krishna Dutt received his PhD in economics from MIT and is Professor of Economics and Political Science at the University of Notre Dame. His areas of specialization are macroeconomic theory, development economics, international economics and political economy and his current research focuses on global uneven development, growth and distribution, and consumption and happiness. He is the author or editor of several books, including *Growth, Distribution and Uneven Development* (1990), *International Handbook of Development Economics* (coeditor, 2008), and *Economics and Ethics* (co-author, 2010) and is the author of over 150 papers published in edited volumes and economics journals, including the *American Economic Review*, the *Cambridge Journal of Economics*, the *International Review of Applied Economics*, the *Journal of Development Economics*, the *Journal of Development Studies*, the *Journal of Post Keynesian Economics*, the *Oxford Economic Papers*, the *Review of Political Economy*, and *World Development*. He is a co-editor of the international journal, *Metroeconomica*.

Gerald Epstein is Professor of Economics and a founding Co-Director of the Political Economy Research Institute (PERI) at the University of Massachusetts, Amherst. He has written articles on numerous topics, including financial regulation, alternative approaches to central banking for employment generation and poverty reduction, and capital account management and capital flows. He has worked with UN organisations, including the United Nations Development Program and the International Labour Organization in the areas of pro-poor macroeconomic policy in Madagascar, South Africa, Ghana, Cambodia and Mongolia, and with UN-DESA on developing alternatives to inflation targeting monetary policy. Most recently his research has focused on the impacts of financialisation (editor, *Financialization and the World Economy*, 2005) and alternatives to inflation targeting (co-editor with Eric Yeldan, *Beyond Inflation Targeting: Assessing the Impacts and Policy Alternatives*, 2009) and work on financial reform issues with SAFER.

Jesus Ferreiro is Associate Professor in Economics at the University of the Basque Country, in Bilbao, Spain, and an Associate Member of the Centre for Economic and Public Policy, University of Cambridge. His research interests are in the areas of macroeconomic policy, labour markets and international financial flows. He has published a number of articles on those topics, in edited books, and in refereed journals such as the *American Journal of Economics and Sociology*, *Economic and Industrial Democracy*, *Économie Appliquée*, *Ekonomia*, *European Planning Studies*, the *International Journal of Political Economy*, the *International Labour Review*, the *International Review of Applied Economics*, and the *Journal of Post Keynesian Economics*.

Giuseppe Fontana is Professor of Monetary Economics at the University of Leeds, UK and Associate Professor at the Università del Sannio (Italy). He has recently been awarded the 2008 G.L.S. Shackle Prize, St Edmunds' College, Cambridge, UK. He is a Life Member Fellow at Clare Hall (University of Cambridge, UK), a Visiting Research Professor at the Centre for Full Employment and Price Stability (University of Missouri Kansas City, USA), and an Associate Member of the Cambridge Centre for Economic and Public Policy (University of Cambridge, UK). He has authored and co-authored over twenty book chapters, and over thirty international journal papers including publications in the *Cambridge Journal of Economics*, the *International Review of Applied Economics*, the *Journal of Economic Psychology*, the *Journal of Post Keynesian Economics*, *Metroeconomica*, *Revue Economie Politique*, and the *Scottish Journal of Political Economy*. He has recently published *Money, Time, and Uncertainty*.

Carmen Gomez is Associate Professor in Economics at the University of the Basque Country, in Bilbao, Spain. Her research interests are in the areas of macroeconomic policy, labour market and foreign direct investment. She has published a number of articles on those topics, in edited books, and in refereed journals such as the *American Journal of Economics and Sociology*, *Economic and Industrial Democracy*, *Économie Appliquée*, and the *Journal of Post Keynesian Economics*.

Ilene Grabel is Professor at the Josef Korbel School of International Studies at the University of Denver. She has been a Research Scholar at the Political Economy Research Institute of the University of Massachusetts since 2007. Grabel has worked as a consultant to the United Nations Development Programme (UNDP)/International Poverty Centre, the United Nations Conference on Trade and Economic Development (UNCTAD)/Group of 24, the UN University's World Institute for Development Economics Research, and with Action Aid and the NGO coalition, 'New Rules for Global Finance'. She has published widely on financial policy and crises, the political economy of international capital flows to the developing world, the relationship between financial liberalisation and macroeconomic performance in developing countries, central banking, exchange rate regimes, and the political economy of remittances. Grabel is co-author (with Ha-Joon Chang) of *Reclaiming Development: An Alternative Policy Manual* (2004). Grabel also blogs for the Triple Crisis (http://www.triplecrisis.com/).

Geoffrey C. Harcourt was born in Melbourne, Australia in June 1931 and educated at the University of Melbourne and Cambridge. Half of his teaching life was spent at the University of Adelaide, and the other half at the University of Cambridge. He has authored or edited 25 books, including *Some Cambridge Controversies in the Theory of Capital* (1972); *The Structure of Post-Keynesian Economics* (with Prue Kerr, 2006), *Joan Robinson* (2009), seven volumes of selected essays, and about 240 papers in journals and books. He is Emeritus Reader in the History of Economic Theory, Cambridge (1998), Emeritus Fellow, Jesus College, Cambridge (1998) and Professor Emeritus, Adelaide (1988). Currently he is Visiting Professorial Fellow, UNSW (2010–13).

Peter Kriesler was born in Sydney, Australia in 1956. He was educated at the University of Sydney and the University of Cambridge, where he also taught before moving to a full-time position at the University of New South Wales, where he is currently an Associate Professor. He is an executive editor of the *Economic and Labour Relations Review*, and on the board of the *Australian Journal of Human Rights*, the *Cambridge Journal of*

Economics and the *History of Economics Review*. He organises the Annual Australian Society of Heterodox Economists Conference (SHE), which is now in its ninth year. He has published on the Australian, Asian and European economies, as well as on Marxian, Kaleckian and Post Keynesian economics, the history of economic theory, issues related to path determinacy, monetary economics, labour economics and human rights. He has authored and edited eight books, and published over seventy papers.

Julio López received his BA in economics at the Universidad de Chile, and later took his PhD in economics at the University of Warsaw. He is currently professor of macroeconomics at the Universidad Nacional Autonoma de Mexico. He has been invited professor at the Universidad Autonoma de Barcelona; Ecole des Hautes Etudes en Sciences Sociales, Paris; and Universidade Federal do Rio de Janeiro. He has published extensively in the scientific journals of Latin America, Europe and the USA. His latest book, *Michal Kalecki*, co-authored with Michael Assous, was published by Palgrave Macmillan, in 2010.

John McCombie is Director, Cambridge Centre for Economic and Public Policy, Department of Land Economy, University of Cambridge, UK; Fellow and Director of Studies in Economics, Downing College; Cambridge; Director of Studies in Land Economy, Downing College, Christ's College and Girton College, Cambridge. He did both his undergraduate degree and his PhD at the University of Cambridge. He was recently Specialist Advisor to the House of Lords and consultant to the World Bank and the Asian Development Bank. He was an editor of *Regional Studies* and is currently an editor of *Spatial Economic Analysis*. His a co-editor or co-author of 15 books, author of over 100 chapters in books and articles in journals such as the *Cambridge Journal of Economics*, the *Economic Journal*, *Oxford Economic Papers*, the *Journal of Regional Science*, the *Journal of Post Keynesian Economics*, and the *Manchester School*. His main areas of research include regional economics, economic growth, and the balance-of-payments constraint, critiques of the aggregate production function, and Keynesian economics.

William Milberg is Professor of Economics and Chair of the Economics Department at the New School for Social Research in New York and a Research Fellow at the New School's Schwartz Centre for Economic Policy Analysis. He is currently a Research Coordinator for the DFID project, 'Capturing the Gains from Globalization'. He has served as a consultant to the UNDP, the ILO, the UNCTAD and the World Bank, and is the author of *The Making of Economic Society*, 13th edition (2011, with Robert Heilbroner), *The Crisis of Vision in Modern Economic Thought* (1995, with Robert Heilbroner).

Maureen Pike read German and Economics for the BA at Kingston Polytechnic. She subsequently received a Masters in Economics from Queen Mary College, University of London, followed by a PhD at the London School of Economics. She was a member of the Departments of Economics at the University of Hull and Queen Mary College, University of London. She is currently Principal Lecture in Economics at Oxford Brookes University. She has been a Visiting Scholar at the University of Wisconsin-Milwaukee and University of Colgate in the United States and at Swinburn, University of Technology, Australia. She is an Associate Member of the Cambridge Centre of Economic and Public Policy, University of Cambridge. Her main research interests are in the economics of the labour market and in economic methodology. She is the author (with Richard Perlman) of the book *Sex Discrimination in the Labour Market: The Case for Comparable Worth.*

Robert Pollin is Professor of Economics and founding co-director of the Political Economy Research Institute (PERI) at the University of Massachusetts-Amherst. His research centres on macroeconomics, conditions for low-wage workers in the USA and globally, the analysis of financial markets, and the economics of building a clear-energy economy in the USA. His books include *A Measure of Fairness: The Economics of Living Wages and Minimum Wages in the United States* (co-authored, 2008); *Contours of Descent: US Economic Fractures and the Landscape of Global Austerity* (2003); and the edited volume *The Macroeconomics of Saving, Finance, and Investment* (1997). Most recently, he co-authored *Green Recovery* (September 2008), *The Economic Benefits of Investing in Clean Energy* (June 2009) and *Green Prosperity* (June 2009) exploring the economics of building a clean-energy economy in the USA. He is currently consulting with the US Department of Energy on the economic analysis of clean energy investments.

Lauren Schmitz is Research Assistant at the New School's Schwartz Center for Economic Policy Analysis and a PhD candidate in the Department of Economics at the New School.

Felipe Serrano is Professor in Economics at the University of the Basque Country, in Bilbao, Spain He is the head of the Department of Applied

Economics V at the University of the Basque Country. His research interests are in the areas of social security, the welfare state, labour market, innovation and economic policy. He is the author of a number of articles on those topics, in edited books, and in refereed journals such as *Economies et Sociétés, Ekonomia, European Planning Studies*, the *Industrial and Labor Relations Review*, the *International Labour Review*, the *International Review of Applied Economics*, and *the Journal of Post Keynesian Economics*.

Mark Setterfield is Professor of Economics in the Department of Economics at Trinity College, Hartford, Connecticut, Associate Member of the Cambridge Centre for Economic and Public Policy at Cambridge University, and Senior Research Associate at the International Economic Policy Institute, Laurentian University. His research interests are macro-dynamics and Post Keynesian economics. In addition to authoring one book and editing six volumes of essays, he has published in a variety of peer-reviewed journals, and currently serves on the editorial boards of the *Review of Political Economy*, the *Journal of Economic Education, Circus: Revista Argentina de Economía*, and INTERVENTION: *European Journal of Economics and Economic Policies*.

Nina Shapiro is Professor of Economics at Saint Peter's College, New Jersey, and a member of the managerial board of editors of *Journal of Post Keynesian Economics*. She received her PhD from New School for Social Research, New York, and taught for a number of years at Rutgers University, where she directed the graduate study in the history of economic thought. Her work spans the fields of macroeconomics and microeconomics, with her most recent publications on the macroeconomic effects of competition and its imperfection. She has edited, with Tracy Mott, a volume on the economics of Josef Steindl: *Rethinking Capitalist Development* (2005); and is currently working on a book on the firm in economic thought.

David A. Spencer is Senior Lecturer in Economics at Leeds University Business School, the University of Leeds, UK. His main research interests lie in the areas of the economics and political economy of work and labour. He has written on the nature and development of ideas on work in economics as well as on issues of labour supply, employment and unemployment, and work organisation. His research incorporates an interdisciplinary element and aims to explore ways by research on work and labour issues might be integrated. He has also undertaken theoretical and empirical research on the quality of work. His research has been published in international journals, including the *Cambridge Journal of Economics*, *Economic and Industrial Democracy*, *Labor History*, the *Review of Political Economy*, and *Work, Employment and Society*. He is author of *The Political Economy of Work* (2009).

Jan Toporowski studied Economics at Birkbeck College, University of London, and the University of Birmingham. He has worked in fund management and international banking. In 2004 and 2005 he was Leverhulme Fellows and Official Visitor in the Faculty of Economics and Politics, University of Cambridge. In 2005 he was a Research Fellow at the Bank of Finland. Jan Toporowski is currently Reader in Economics and Chair of the Economics Department of the School of Oriental and African Studies, University of London. His most recent book is *Why the World Economy Needs a Financial Crash* and *Other Critical Essays on Finance and Financial Economics* (2010). Jan Toporowski is working on an intellectual biography of Michal Kalecki.

Emilio Caballero Urdiales is a Professor of Economics at Mexico's National University. His publications include *Los Ingresos tributarios de México* (2009), *Los Ingresos Tributarios del Sector Público de México* (2006) and *El Tratado de Libre Comercio entre México, Estados Unidos Y Canadá: Ventajas y Desventajas* (1991).

Malcolm Sawyer: An Appreciation

Philip Arestis

The essays in this volume are put together to celebrate the work of Malcolm Sawyer. They are very much related to the work of Malcolm, highlighting the various areas in which he has made substantial contributions to economics. These span from microeconomics to macroeconomics, including to a very large extent economic policy aspects in both areas of economics. Needless to say in no way do they cover the totality of the phenomenal and original work of Malcolm Sawyer. The obvious and justified constraints of publishing such a volume do not allow full coverage, which would probably not be possible even in the absence of such constraints.

Malcolm was born in Oxford in January 1945. He studied Mathematics for his first degree at Balliol College, University of Oxford, 1963–66, gaining a BA (Oxon.) in Mathematics in 1966. He then pursued a postgraduate course at the London School of Economics, 1966–68, where he gained the MSc in Economics, with Distinction.

Malcolm was then appointed as a Lecturer in Economics at University College, University of London, where he stayed until 1977. While at University College, Malcolm was a tutor to students of economics, 1970–74, and also worked for a year, 1974–75, as Administrator at the Organisation for Economic Co-operation and Development (OECD) in Paris. Malcolm also worked as a consultant to the OECD on public expenditure and income maintenance as well as health provision, where he made substantial contributions to OECD's Public Expenditure on Income Maintenance in 1976, Public Expenditure on Health in 1977, and on income and wealth distribution as part of their Social Indicators Programme. Over the period 1977–78, Malcolm acted as a consultant to the European Economic Community (EEC) on industrial matters and also consultant to the Royal Commission on the Distribution of Income and Wealth.

In 1978, Malcolm moved to the University of York. He was Reader in Economics until being promoted to Professor of Economics in 1984. In 1991 he moved to the University of Leeds as Professor of Economics, where he remains to this day. Malcolm has been extremely active at the University of Leeds, and prior to that at the University of York. At the University of Leeds he was twice appointed Head of the Economics Division (1991–96 and 1998–2002). He was Deputy Chair of the School of Business and Economic Studies, 1994–95, Postgraduate Tutor also at the School of Business and Economic Studies, 1993–96. Director, Centre for Industrial Policy and Performance, University of Leeds, 1998–2001, Associate Dean, Personnel and Support Services, Leeds University Business School, 2000–02 and Pro-Dean for Learning and Teaching, Faculty of Business, University of Leeds, 2005–09. All of these positions clearly testify to a clear recognition by the University of Leeds of Malcolm's enormous abilities not merely as a researcher but also as an academic administrator and teacher. He was a member of Council of the Royal Economic Society, 1998–2002, and a member of the Steering Committee, Conference of Heads of University Departments of Economics, 2003–05. He has taken up a number of visiting appointments such as Guest Research Fellow, International Institute of Management, Berlin 1985; Visiting Scholar, New School, New York, 1997; Research Fellow, Jerome Levy Economics Institute, USA, 1997; and Senior Visiting Fellow, 1998– today; distinguished Visiting Fellow, La Trobe University, Melbourne, Australia, March/April 2002; Visiting Lecturer, Korea University, Seoul, Korea, May/June 2002; Visiting Professor, University of Missouri Kansas City, USA, September/November 2002; and visiting researcher Political Economy Research Institute, University of Massachusetts Amherst.

Further recognition of Malcolm's academic qualities is his very active involvement in terms of acting as referee for numerous journals, too many to enumerate here. Malcolm has also been very active in terms of editorial roles. Most important of all is his position as Managing Editor of the *International Review of Applied Economics*, a role he has been very active at since 1986 to date. As editor of this journal, Malcolm has been extremely effective in steering this journal to high quality so that the demand for space is extremely high. Despite the very short life of this journal, it has actually become one of the most important 'open-minded' economic journals. Malcolm is also a member of the editorial board of the *Journal of Post Keynesian Economics*, 1998–today, and founding and managing co-editor of the *International Papers in Political Economy*. Also over the same period, he has been the editor of the *New Directions in Modern Economics* for Edward Elgar Publishing Ltd. He has also been a member of the editorial board of the *Journal of Income Distribution*, 2000–06, and a joint editor of the same journal, 2003–06; a member of the editorial board, *Review of Political Economy*, 1988–93; a member of the editorial board of the *Zagreb International Review of Economics and Business* 1998–today; a member of the editorial committee of the *Problemas del Desarrollo*, 2001– today; and a member of the scientific board of the *Intervention: European Journal of Economics and Economic Policies*, 2004–today.

Malcolm has been not only an extremely active supporter of research, but also a highly productive and effective researcher and a very popular teacher. At University College London, the main lecture courses which he gave were in the areas of microeconomic analysis (second year), industrial economics (third year), labour economics (second year) and contributions to graduate course on the economics of public policy. At the University of York, Malcolm taught graduate courses in advanced macroeconomics and in organisation of firms and industries and undergraduate courses in macroeconomics, industrial economics, alternative perspectives in economics and current UK macroeconomic problems. At the University of Leeds, he has taught on a range of courses including graduate courses in economic theory, economics of globalisation, industrial economics and public sector economics. Malcolm has also been involved in the teaching of undergraduate courses in the economics of European integration, macroeconomics of the UK economy, management economics, economic analysis and applied economics. In all these courses, Malcolm has been an extremely open-minded teacher in that he has sought to make sure that students are taught a range of paradigms in economics. This approach has also been very much in place in terms of his involvement with postgraduate supervision. Malcolm has been the main supervisor for really a huge number of PhD theses, in topics over a wide range from the macroeconomics of Victorian Britain through the Post Keynesian analysis of money to analysis of the changing nature of work organisation. It is little surprise that he was asked to serve as Teaching Quality Assessor, Wales, in 1997, and Subject Reviewer in Economics, QAA, England 2000–01. Many of his students are now well established academics and policy makers around the world.

All of these activities have been accompanied by the usual demands of external examining, for both undergraduate and graduate courses as well as PhDs, practically everywhere in the UK university sector. These duties have been carried out not just in the UK, but elsewhere too; for example, Malcolm has been external supervisor for PhD students at the European University Institute, Florence, and also for CNAA degrees. Additionally, Malcolm has served as external assessor for appointments and promotions at numerous UK universities. He has also been external assessor for staff appointments and promotion at other universities outside the UK.

Malcolm's research activities have been very rich in terms of both depth and breadth. Throughout his academic life Malcolm has been concerned with what might be called an 'open-minded' approach to economics. Such an approach has its focus on a specific paradigm, and in the case of Malcolm this is a Post Keynesian/Kaleckian one, but at the same time not ignoring other paradigms. His early work was in the area of industrial economics, where he wrote significant textbooks on Theories of the Firm and on Economics of Industries and Firms. In later work he sought to draw on industrial economics in the formulation of approaches to macroeconomics where the analysis of imperfect competition is a major component of the microeconomics of macroeconomics (1, 2, 3, 6, 7, 8, 9, 10, 11, 12, 13, 41, 42, 43, 44, 50; where the numbers refer to entries in the 'Selected Bibliography' below). It has evolved into a more general consideration of the political economy of market socialism and the possibilities for different forms of economic organisation, where distributional aspects are paramount (4, 12, 13, 30, 59, 61). This has been followed by a more focused approach on Post Keynesian Price Theory (11, 30, 46). At the same time more or less, but even today, another important area in which Malcolm has been a main contributor is in 'The Economics of Michal Kalecki' (20, 21, 45, 47, 52). More recently, Malcolm's work on this tradition has paid particular attention and reference to the Kaleckian analysis of money and inflation (5, 20, 21, 31). This approach led to the development of his and others' ideas on the role of endogenous money in an industrialised economy (18, 20, 55, 60). A comprehensive critique of the traditional idea that money is exogenously determined by the decisions of the central bank has been developed by Malcolm's contributions along with a more pragmatic approach that treats money as an endogenous variable determined essentially by the liquidity preference of the banking sector (21, 31, 35). A related issue where Malcolm has been very active in contributing is monetary policy, especially so as it relates to what has come to be known as the New Consensus Macroeconomics (25, 28, 30, 33, 35, 36, 46, 55, 57, 58, 60) but also in terms of the potential of different and more Keynesian-based monetary policy type after the 'great recession' (16, 37, 39). Another important contribution of Malcolm is his work on the so-called third-way approach to economic policy in particular. Analysis of the economics of the 'third way' and the economic policies of the (UK) 'new' Labour government was such interest in the long list of Malcolm's research concerns, where an important and effective critique has been developed (32, 34, 56, 57, 58).

A further area of Malcolm's research interests relates closely to the intellectual and institutional obstacles to full employment (9, 14, 17, 43, 51, 53, 54, 63, 64). In this research Malcolm seeks to identify the constraints on the achievement of full employment (23, 30, 44, 54), and from that to suggest policies to help in reaching full employment (30, 33, 63). Within this general area a critical evaluation of the concept of non-accelerating inflation rate of unemployment (NAIRU) has been developed (23, 47), especially in terms of the importance of aggregate demand and economic policies influencing NAIRU (33). The latter contribution is very important in terms of the New Consensus Macroeconomics, which assumes NAIRU as purely supply determined.

Developments in Europe has been a major concern in Malcolm's work. Not merely what used to be the EEC and now is the EU, but also in terms of developments ever since the creation of the European common currency; even before January 1999, Malcolm had been heavily committed to an alternative to what has come to be known as the euro. Malcolm has been very critical of both the institutional and theoretical underpinnings of these arrangements. Particular attention and focus on a possible alternative policy framework for the euro has been a very fruitful area of research in Malcolm's list (15, 19, 22, 24, 49, 59).

The development of Post Keynesian macroeconomics, and within this the particular concern with the relationship between imperfect competition and macroeconomic analysis and the synthesis of different views on pricing and investment (18, 40, 43, 53, 63). In all this work economic policy considerations are of crucial importance, especially so in the area of fiscal policy. Concern with the latter is of particular current significance. In a series of contributions Malcolm demonstrated the effectiveness of fiscal policy. And all that well prior to the current 'great recession', a time when the New Consensus Macroeconomics supporters and others completely downgraded the importance of fiscal policy as a stabilisation tool. Recent initiatives on the fiscal policy front, which turned the possibility of a 'great depression' into only a 'great recession' and more, if only certain governments were more responsible on this front, have vindicated beyond any doubt Malcolm's research findings (27, 29, 32, 38, 48, 43, 62).

On top of all these activities, Malcolm has been an extremely active organiser of, and participant in, important conferences, not merely in the UK but also in Europe and in the USA. As a result of these latter activities, a good number of journal special issues and edited books have materialised and included as well as referred to in this appreciation of his work.

Selected Bibliography

Articles

1. 'Concentration in British manufacturing industry', *Oxford Economic Papers* (vol. 23, 1971).

2. 'The earnings of manual workers: A cross-section analysis', *Scottish Journal of Political Economy* (vol. 20, 1973).
3. 'Mergers, growth and concentration' (with S. Aaronovitch), *Oxford Economic Papers* (vol. 26, 1975).
4. 'Income distribution in OECD countries', *OECD Economic Outlook*, Occasional Studies (July 1976).
5. 'Models of inflation in the United Kingdom' (with S.G.B. Henry and P. Smith), *National Institute Economic Review* (August 1976).
6. 'The variance of logarithms and industrial concentration', *Oxford Bulletin of Economics and Statistics* (vol. 41, 1979).
7. 'Monopoly welfare loss in the United Kingdom', *Manchester School* (vol. 50, 1980).
8. 'On the specification of structure–performance relationships', *European Economic Review* (vol. 17, 1982).
9. 'Collective bargaining, oligopoly and macro-economics', *Oxford Economic Papers* (vol. 34, 1982).
10. 'The influence of cost and demand conditions on the rate of change of prices' (with S. Aaronovitch and P. Samson), *Applied Economics* (vol. 14, 1982).
11. 'Price change and oligopoly' (with S. Aaronovitch), *Journal of Industrial Economics* (vol. 30, 1982).
12. 'The nature and role of markets', *Social Concept* (vol. 6, no. 2, 1993 (reprinted with revisions in C. Pitelis (ed.), *Transactions Costs, Markets and Hierarchies* (Oxford: Blackwell)).
13. 'Reflections on the nature and role of industrial policy', *Metroeconomica* (vol. 43).
14. 'Overcoming the barriers to full employment in capitalist economies', *Economie Appliquée* (vol. 48, 1995).
15. 'Unemployment and the independent European System of Central Banks: Prospects and some alternative arrangements' (with P. Arestis), *American Journal of Economics and Sociology* (vol. 56(3), 1997).
16. 'How many cheers for the Tobin Financial Transactions Tax?' (with P. Arestis), *Cambridge Journal of Economics* (vol. 21(6), 1997).
17. 'Keynesian policies for the new millennium', *Economic Journal* (with P. Arestis) (vol. 108, 1998).
18. 'Post Keynesian economics and its critics' (with P. Arestis and S. Dunn), *Journal of Post Keynesian Economics* (vol. 21(4), 1999).
19. 'An alternative stability pact for the European Union' (with P. Arestis and K. McCauley), *Cambridge Journal of Economics* (vol. 25(1), 2001).
20. 'Kalecki on imperfect competition, inflation and money', *Cambridge Journal of Economics* (vol. 25(2), 2001).
21. 'Kalecki on money and finance', *The European Journal of the History of Economic Thought* (vol. 8(4), 2001).
22. 'Explaining the euro's initial decline' (with P. Arestis, I. Biefang-Frisancho Mariscal, A. Brown), *Eastern Economic Journal* (vol. 8(1), 2002).
23. 'The NAIRU, aggregate demand and investment', *Metroeconomica* (vol. 53(1), 2002).
24. 'The euro: Reflections on the first three years' (with P. Arestis, A. Brown, K. Mouratidis), *International Review of Applied Economics* (vol. 16(1), 2002).

25. 'The Bank of England macroeconomic model: Its nature and implications' (with P. Arestis), *Journal of Post Keynesian Economics* (vol. 24(2), 2002).
26. 'Post Keynesian price theory' (with Nina Shapiro), *Journal of Post Keynesian Economics* (vol. 25(3), 2003).
27. 'Reinventing fiscal policy' (with P. Arestis), *Journal of Post Keynesian Economics* (vol. 25(4), 2003).
28. 'Can monetary policy affect the real economy?' (with P. Arestis), *European Review of Economics and Finance* (vol. 3(3), 2004).
29. 'On fiscal policy and budget deficits' (with P. Arestis), *Intervention. European Journal of Economics and Economic Policies* (vol. 1(2), 2004).
30. 'Aggregate demand, conflict and capacity in the inflationary process' (with P. Arestis), *Cambridge Journal of Economics* (vol. 29(6), 2005).
31. 'The nature and role of monetary policy when money is endogenous' (with P. Arestis), *Cambridge Journal of Economics* (vol. 30(6), 2006).
32. 'Fiscal policy matters' (with Philip Arestis), *Public Finance* (vol. 54, 2006).
33. 'The relationship between capital stock, unemployment and wages in nine EMU countries' (with P. Arestis and M. Baddeley), *Bulletin of Economic Research* (vol. 59(2), 2007).
34. 'Fiscal policy under New Labour', *Cambridge Journal of Economics* (vol. 31(6), 2007).
35. 'A critical reconsideration of the foundations of monetary policy in the New Consensus Macroeconomics Framework' (with Philip Arestis), *Cambridge Journal of Economics* (vol. 32(5), 2008).
36. 'Fiscal and interest rate policies in the "New Consensus Framework": A different perspective', *Journal of Post Keynesian Economics* (vol. 31(4), 2009).
37. 'What monetary policy after the crisis?' (with P. Arestis), *Review of Political Economy* (vol. 22(4), 2010).
38. 'The return of fiscal policy' (with P. Arestis), *Journal of Post Keynesian Economics*, (vol. 32(3), 2010).
39. 'Crises and paradigms in macroeconomics', *Intervention* (vol. 7(2), 2010).
40. 'Labour supply, employment and unemployment in macroeconomics: A critical appraisal of orthodoxy and an heterodox alternative', *Review of Political Economy* (vol. 22(2), 2010).

Books

41. *Theories of the Firm* (Weidenfeld and Nicolson and St Martin's Press, 1979).
42. *Economics of Industries and Firms: Theories, Evidence and Policy* (Croom Helm and St Martin's Press, 1981; second edition 1985).
43. *Macro-economics in Question* (Wheatsheaf Books and M.E. Sharpe, 1982).
44. *Business Pricing and Inflation* (Macmillan and St Martin's Press, 1983).
45. *The Economics of Michal Kalecki* (Macmillan and M.E. Sharpe, 1985).
46. *The Challenge of Radical Political Economy* (Harvester Wheatsheaf and Barnes & Noble, 1989).
47. *Unemployment, Imperfect Competition and Macroeconomics: Essays in the Post Keynesian Tradition* (Edward Elgar Publishing Ltd, 1995).
48. *Re-examining Monetary and Fiscal Policies in the Twenty First Century* (with P. Arestis) (Aldershot: Edward Elgar, 2004).

49. *The Euro: Evolution and Prospects* (with P. Arestis and A. Brown) (Aldershot: Edward Elgar, 2001).
50. *A Future for Public Ownership* (with K. O'Donnell) (London: Lawrence & Wishart, 1999).

Edited books

51. *The UK Economy* (Oxford University Press, 15th and 16th editions).
52. *The Legacy of Michal Kalecki* (2 volumes, Edward Elgar Publishing Ltd, 1999).
53. *The Relevance of Keynesian Policies Today* (with P. Arestis) (Palgrave Macmillan, 1997).
54. *The Political Economy of Economic Policies* (with P. Arestis) (Palgrave Macmillan, 1998).
55. *The Political Economy of Central Banking* (with P. Arestis) (Edward Elgar Publishing Ltd, 1998).
56. *The Economics of the Third Way* (with P. Arestis) (Edward Elgar Publishing Ltd, 2001).
57. *Neo Liberal Economic Policy: Critical Essays* (with P. Arestis) (Edward Elgar Publishing Ltd, 2004).
58. *The Rise of the Market: Critical Essays on the Political Economy of Neo Liberalism* (with P. Arestis) (Edward Elgar Publishing Ltd, 2004).
59. *Alternative Perspectives on Economic Policies in the European Union* (with P. Arestis) (Palgrave Macmillan, 2006).
60. *A Handbook Of Alternative Monetary Economics* (with P. Arestis) (Edward Elgar Publishing Ltd, 2007).
61. *Critical Essays on the Privatisation Experience* (with P. Arestis) (Palgrave Macmillan, 2008).
62. *Current Thinking on Fiscal Policy* (with J. Creel) (Palgrave Macmillan, 2008).
63. *21st Century Keynesian Economics* (with P. Arestis) (Palgrave Macmillan, 2010).
64. *Socialist Economic Review 1982* (with D. Currie) (London: Merlin Press, 1982).

Part I
Microeconomics

1
The Function of Firms: Alternative Views

Nina Shapiro

1 Introduction

Why are firms formed? What function do they perform? These questions continue to elude economics, which, in spite of the discarding of the 'black box' conception of the firm, and growth of a voluminous literature on the subject, is still 'in search of a theory of the firm' (Garrouste and Saussier, 2005).

This search has been constrained by the preconceptions of the discipline and dominance of neoclassical views. These frame the discussion, centring the analysis on the resource allocation concerns of neoclassical economics. The problem of the firm is that of the choice of resource allocation devices, with firms identified with their 'internal' organisation, and explanations of their existence sought in the efficiencies of that resource allocation. Firms must improve, in some way, the resource allocations of the economy for their formation to be 'rational', and the theory of the firm identifies the conditions under which its resource allocations are optimal.

The limitations of this neoclassical perspective on the firm are discussed below, with its development being examined along with alternative conceptions. Both classical and Post Keynesian economics have a quite different view of the firm – one that highlights its importance in economic growth and development – and these conceptions will be contrasted with the neoclassical view.[1]

2 The neoclassical conception

Neoclassical treatments of the nature of the firm take their direction from Coase's 1937 work on the subject. They address its questions about the existence of firms, viewing, as Coase does, their presence in the economy as problematic, and asking, as Coase (1937) put it, 'why a firm emerges at all in a specialized exchange economy' (p. 390).[2]

That 'puzzle' was not addressed in the traditional neoclassical theory, which took the existence of firms for granted. It assumed their presence, attributing to them the activities of production. Firms employed and combined the productive factors of the economy, deciding their uses, yet no reason was given for why firms directed them. Could not the factors employ themselves?

Production can be organised outside of firms, through the market, and, indeed, economics assumes that it is so. The economic system, as Coase says, is 'supposed to work itself'. Its operations are coordinated through its prices, and there is no need for any regulation other than that provided by those prices. These correct production mistakes, falling when product supply exceeds demand, and rising when demand exceeds supply. Price changes align the production and consumption of products, while price levels indicate the profitability of different lines of production. Economic agents can decide their production without knowledge of the plans and actions of others, for all they need to know to make the best use of their resources are prices.

Yet, if production can be coordinated through prices, and that market coordination works as well as the traditional theory assumes, why do we have the firm's 'visible hand'? Why are resources allocated within firms when they could be allocated, and allocated efficiently, through the market?

Coase's own answer (1937) to this question is well known – it has to do with the costs of using markets. They can coordinate production, but they cannot do this without the costs of acquiring information on prices and negotiating and settling production contracts. Producers have to discover the 'relevant prices', and effect separate contracts with each of their suppliers. These transaction costs limit the operations of markets, creating space for those of the firm, and the firm emerges in a market economy because it reduces transaction costs.

The employees of a firm do not have to contract separately with each other, as would be the case if their production were coordinated through the market. They need to effect only one contract – the employment contract with the firm. That substitution of a 'single contract' for a 'series of separate contracts' reduces the contracting costs of production (Coase, 1937), making it cheaper to contract through firms than through markets. And while firms are not costless either – they have to be managed, and there are 'diminishing returns' to management – the cost of coordinating production within a firm can be less than the cost of coordinating the same set of activities through market transactions.

Firms are formed when and where their administration of production costs less than its market coordination. They 'supplant' markets when they can effect transactions more efficiently, when the internalisation of transactions reduces their costs. And although the transaction costs that explained the development of firms in Coase (1937) are not the ones highlighted in the transaction cost literature – here the emphasis is on the costs of enforcing and renegotiating contracts rather than those of effecting them – the conception of the firm is the same. The firm is a substitute for the market, an alternative contracting mode or 'governance structure' (Williamson, 1985). It differs from the market not in terms of its function, but in the way it performs that resource allocation.

Both the firm and market allocate resources among competing ends, and both are understood and evaluated in terms of the efficiency of their resource allocations. That allocative efficiency is essential; the scarcity of resources demands it. Since resources are limited, and there are not enough of them, we must make the most of the ones we have, allocating them to their most valuable uses. This resource allocation is the central problem – indeed, neoclassical economics recognises no other – so that the critical question about the firm is the nature of its resource allocation, and the firm and market distinguished by their allocation mechanisms.

Whereas markets allocate resources 'unconsciously', without express intent, firms allocate them purposively, in accordance with a plan. Their operations are administered, and organised hierarchically, with resource allocations effected through 'fiat' or 'command' (Williamson, 1994). Employees of firms are directed by their management, rather than by the impersonal forces of the market. Their work is supervised rather than self-directed, dictated by the requirements of the firm, and serving its objectives, and that 'supersession' of market directives and incentives is the distinguishing mark of the firm (Coase, 1937).

Firms are administrative units rather than units of production – 'hierarchies' rather than 'production functions' (Williamson, 1975). They centralise production, vertically integrating its operations, and develop not for technological reasons, but for governance ones (Williamson, 1985). It is not the indivisibilities or scale economies of production that explain the firm's presence, but the opportunism and 'bounded rationality' of economic agents. These impede market transactions, for, when contracts cannot cover all possible eventualities, and economic agents are opportunistic, one or the other party to the transaction can take advantage of the other. They can provide lower-quality goods or services than were expected, or threaten to withhold them unless a more favourable contract is negotiated. Firms can control this opportunism more effectively than markets – they have greater regulatory powers – and the theory of the firm identifies the transactions most subject to that opportunism. Its unit of analysis is 'the transaction', and objective, explaining the division of transactions between firm and market 'governance mechanisms' (ibid.).

But while a firm is not a market, and cannot be understood as a 'nexus of contracts',[3] it is also the case that firms produce for the market. They are profit-making enterprises, organised for profit, and, indeed, if they were not, their decisions would not be affected by transaction costs. Their profit objective connects their development to that of the market, making it impossible to envision them in the absence of money and commerce. Firms could not operate without markets, nor would these be the same without them. Firms develop and expand markets as well as 'supplant them', commercialising products, standardising them, and increasing their uses. They affect markets just as markets affect them, and neither their presence nor importance in the market can be understood in abstraction from their profit objective.

3 The capitalist firm

The importance of profit in the operation of firms was highlighted in classical economics, where the pursuit of profit was the distinguishing mark of the firm. It was not just an employer, it was the capitalist employer, and while it supervised the labour it employed, that direction of production was not the function of the firm. Firms were needed not to coordinate or regulate production, but to expand it. They were the central agents of economic growth and development.

The firms of classical economics were expansive. They invested profits, and reinvested them, increasing profits rather than 'maximising' them. Their profit pursuit was boundless, and investment constrained only by their past profits. 'Accumulate, accumulate! – That was Moses and the prophets' (Marx, 1965, p. 595), and while the investment of profits came at the expense of consumption, consumption was not the reason profits were made or firms owned. For, unlike the enterprise owners of neoclassical economics, those of classical economics – the 'capitalists' – were interested in wealth alone.

The capitalist had the 'greed of the miser', his passion for riches (Marx, 1965). Profit, for him, was not a mere source of income. Making it was a vocation; it was all that he worked for and desired, and it was 'only in so far as the appropriation of ever more and more wealth' was the 'sole motive' of his actions that he acted as a capitalist: 'Use-values must therefore never be looked upon as the real aim of the capitalist; neither must the profit on any single transaction. The restless never-ending process of profit-making alone is what he aims at' (ibid., p. 152)

Profit was an end in itself – the capitalist had no other. He was the agent of his enterprise, the 'personification of capital'. He devoted his life to his enterprise, identifying its value with his own, and while he drew an income from the enterprise, and this income was much higher than that of his employees, it was not the purpose of his firm. Firms were formed not to live off their earnings, but to invest them. Capital accumulation was the reason for the firm.

The importance of the firm was the importance of capital, and in classical economics, capital was essential – nations could not be wealthy without it. Their wealth was produced by labour, but capital was needed for increases in the productivity of labour. Neither the division of labour that improved the 'skill and dexterity of the laborer', nor the machinery that 'abridged and facilitated' his labour, could be increased without an increase in capital (Smith, 1936, p. 326).

While Smith's division of labour was 'limited by the extent of the market', exchange was not its only requisite. It required not only a market large enough for the sale of the products of separate trades, but, also, a capital great enough for their establishment. The specialisation of labour had to be financed, and businesses established for their revenues to cover costs, and operations internally financed.

A worker could not specialise his labour, become, for example, a 'baker' or 'weaver', without the 'materials and tools' of the trade, or the goods required for his subsistence during the time of the production and sale of its products. Both production and sale of products took time – customers had to be found and products made – so that while the worker could purchase the means of his employment with the proceeds from the sale of his product, he could not do so until his production was completed, and product sold, and thus, as Smith notes, 'a stock of goods of different kinds must be stored up somewhere sufficient to maintain him, and to supply him with the materials and tools of his work, till such time, at least, as both these events can be brought about' (Smith, 1936, p. 259). The worker could not specialise his labour without that 'prior accumulation of stock', and the division of labour depended as much on the capital available for the employment of labour as it did on the extent of the market for its product: 'As the accumulation of stock must, in the nature of things, be previous to the division of labour, so labour can be more and more subdivided in proportion only as stock is previously more and more accumulated' (ibid., p. 260).

Greater subdivisions of labour required greater capital investments, for the division of labour in any 'branch of business' was limited by the number of workers within it, and their numbers could not increase without an increase in the capital that funded their production. The 'wage fund' would have to increase for their numbers to rise, and the workers provided with the requisite means of their production. These, as Smith says, have to be sufficient for the 'constant employment' of the workmen (Smith, 1936, p. 260) – their labour could not be productive otherwise. Some, or all, of them would be idle for part of their working time, and the economies made possible by the increase in their numbers, and the greater specialisation it allowed, would not be realised.

Just as the division of labour was limited by the availability of capital, so was the employment of the machinery that facilitated labour. The mechanisation of production had to be financed also, as did machinery improvements. Thus, it was, as Smith notes, 'by means of an additional capital only', that the 'undertaker of any work' could 'provide his workmen with better machinery' (Smith, 1936, p. 326), and the machinery he could 'invent', like the machinery he could 'afford to purchase', depended on the extent of his capital (ibid., p. 260).[4]

While productivity improvements required the accumulation of capital, its accumulation 'naturally' led to their adoption. The person who employs his stock as a capital, Smith argues, 'necessarily wishes' to employ it in the most productive manner possible. He 'endeavours, therefore, both to make among his workmen the most proper distribution of employment, and to furnish them with the best machines which he can either invent or afford to purchase' (Smith, 1936, p. 260). His desire for profit ensures the introduction of whatever innovations his capital allows, and the industry of a nation not only increases with its capital, but, 'in consequence of that increase, the same quantity of industry produces a much greater quantity of work' (ibid., p. 260).

Whereas the importance of the profit objective in the adoption of innovations is emphasised in Smith (1935), its importance in their development is emphasised in Marx (1965). Here, the capitalist desire for profit not only ensures the productive employment of labour, but also increases in the productivity of labour. That development of the 'productive powers of labor' was 'the historical task and justification of capital' (Marx, 1966, p. 259).

For Marx, as for Smith, profit was made through the employment of labour – it was part of labour's product. The capitalist's share of the product, its profit margin, depended on the cost of labour. The lower the labour cost of a product, the higher could be the profit from it, and productivity improvements reduced labour costs. They decreased the amount of labour needed for the production of the product.

While process innovations reduced product prices as well as labour costs, they did not do so until they became the prevalent methods of production. The value of a product depended on the labour requirements of its production, but these were not the labour requirements of any individual producer, but the 'socially necessary ones' (Marx, 1965, p. 39). Thus, as long as the process innovations of a producer were not carried out by competitors, and during the time in which they were not, they would reduce labour costs without reducing the price of the product, and productivity improvements would increase profit (ibid., 317).

Innovations gave firms cost advantages over competitors, allowing them not only to enlarge their market share, but also to enlarge their profit margin.[5] Firms that introduced them made more profit than others, an 'extra profit', and since their desire for profit was unlimited, and competition a competition for profits, there was a race to innovate. Firms tried to innovate faster than competitors, developing their own innovations rather than just adopting those of others, and productivity increased as their innovations were diffused and each tried to improve on the cost reductions of others. Competition was fought through the 'cheapening of commodities', and commodities cheapened through 'heightening the productiveness of labor' (ibid., p. 319).

This is not to say that the pursuit of profit was all that was needed to secure advances in productivity. The technologies of industries also mattered, as did the scientific and technical know-how of society. Yet while these limited the innovations of firms, they did not fix their methods of production, or limit them to a 'choice' among existing ones. Firms exploited the technological opportunities of industries, improving the production processes they coordinated, and designing better ways of organising them. They divided, and subdivided, the labour of production, and mechanised the instruments. Firms devised both better means and methods of production, and while their profit provided the capital needed for these innovations, their profit objective provided the incentive.

Profit was the cost of growth, and the firm its engine. It institutionalised the acquisitive drive, legitimising wealth acquisition, and making it the end of production. With the development of the firm, profit becomes the sole purpose of production, with products produced not for consumption, or to exchange them for others, but for – and only for – the money that can be made from them. Profit, and profit alone, decides production, while the amount made measures its value, and it was because firms produced for profit that their development advanced the wealth of nations.

While it is true that products and production processes can be improved for reasons other than profit, and innovations financed with funds other than profits, it is difficult to imagine the innovations of modern industry occurring in the absence of profit. And this is not only because of the difficulty of raising funds for innovation – it is risky[6] – or because of the effectiveness of the profit incentive – it is 'high-powered'. It is also because the profit objective frees production from the constraints of past practices, making innovations possible.

Although the profit objective limits the choices of producers, it does not prescribe them. Any product can be produced as long as its production is profitable, and not only are many products profitable, but many more can become profitable. Producers need not produce the products produced in the past, with the methods used in the past. They can produce and develop new products, redesign them and their production processes, and develop and employ new technologies. Both the products and processes of production are changeable, and neither would be if the traditions of industries, or culture of a society, determined production practices, and producers were not free to produce whatever products, or use whatever methods, they expected to be most profitable.

The profit objective of firms is essential to the innovation that makes nations wealthy. Wealth production, as the classical economists emphasised, is capitalist production, and, while its profit can be a personal end as well as an organisational objective, the profit that can be made by individuals working on their own is limited. It is limited by their particular knowledge and skills as well as their life spans, whereas the profit end, as Marx emphasises, is inherently unlimited. There is no amount of profit that can satisfy the desire for it, for profit is a monetary sum, and, as Marx says, 'one sum of money is distinguishable from another only by its amount' (1965, p. 150). A million dollar profit is profit, but so is a billion dollar profit, and a trillion dollar profit. Profits can always be greater than they are, so that when profit is sought for its own sake – when it is an end rather than a means to another (such as consumption), the pursuit of it is endless.

Making profit is not like baking a cake. It is not a task, with a beginning and an end, but an interminable process. That 'restless never-ending process' cannot be carried out by individuals; it requires organisations dedicated to its purpose – for profit firms. These, by their very nature, have no end other than profit, and while the profit firms can make is also limited, and they can make no more than a finite amount at any given time, unlike individuals, they can increase profits over time, producing more and more, and in their corporate form, at least, they can make them forever. They are 'infinitively lived'.

Firms can make greater profits than individuals can. They can employ many individuals, with various knowledge and skills, utilising the human capital of many, not just that of a single individual. They can increase the number they employ, and increase the kinds of labour they employ, increasing profits through both diversification and expansion. And while the economies of specialisation are open to both individuals and firms, only firms can realise the economies of organisation and cooperation.

Markets can coordinate the operations of production, but they cannot 'think' about them, about their interconnections and shortcomings of their organisation. That consideration of work design, of what is done and how it is done is a function of management.[7] It is performed within firms, by their engineers and other technical personnel, and can be effected through them only. It is only in so far as the operations of production are performed together, in an organisation that their interconnections can be assessed, and the knowledge learned from the performance of any one of them utilised in the design of the others. And it is precisely because they are performed together in firms that these can rationalise the production they coordinate, dividing and realigning its operations.

This 'organized cooperation', as Richardson (1999) calls it, is especially important in the production of new products. These, by their very nature, have to be designed, and their production planned out, while their improvement requires the assessment and adjustment of the operations of their production. Their development requires the expertise of many different specialities, and firms organise the labour of those with the requisite capabilities, just as they organise the labour required for the products' production.

Firms unite the knowledge and efforts of many, combining their labour through its organisation.[8] This combination of labour frees it from the constraints of individual labour, creating, as Marx emphasises, a new productive power – 'the collective power of the masses' (Marx, 1965, p. 326). What can be done within firms is much more, both qualitatively and quantitatively, than can be done by individuals working on their own, and it is because it is that firms appeared in markets, becoming the dominant form of capitalist production. Their productive capabilities is the reason 'why it might be profitable to form a firm' (Coase, 1937).[9]

4   Megacorps

The organisational advantages of firms, and especially large firms, are a central theme of the Post Keynesian theories of Galbraith (1967) and Eichner (1976). These share the classical economists' concern with the requisites of economic growth and development, and have the same view of the importance of capital accumulation. The economic problem for them is not allocative efficiency, but dynamic efficiency – how to advance the wealth of nations – and firms undertake the investment and innovation that advance it.

In *The New Industrial State* and other works, Galbraith takes issue with the traditional conception of the ideality of the market. This 'conventional wisdom' is strikingly at odds with reality, with the operation and performance of capitalist economies. And this is not only because of the absence in these economies of 'perfect competition' – industries are concentrated and firms large – but also because of the absence of the assumed consequences. The inefficiencies traditionally associated with monopoly – restricted output and costly production – are not evident in the American economy, 'which, on grounds of sheer physical performance, few are inclined to criticize', and whose leading industries are not those closest to the competitive ideal, but oligopolies:

> The American farmer, the producer who most closely approaches the competitor of the model, does almost no research on his own. It was the foresight of genius that caused this to be recognized at an early stage in our history, with the result that technical development within this field has been almost completely socialized. ... The other industries which are distinguished by a close approach to the competitive model are also distinguished, one can almost say without exception, by a near absence of research and technical development. The bituminous coal industry ... the clothing industry, the lumber industry and the shoe industry do very little research. ... no one would select them as a showpiece of American industrial achievement. The showpieces are, with rare exception, the industries which are dominated by a handful of large firms. (Galbraith, 1952, pp. 95–6)

This discrepancy between economic theory and reality is explained by the 'imperatives of technology', which are not recognised in the traditional theory. This theory might be applicable to the early stages of technical development, when the 'application of science and technology to industry' could be done by entrepreneur-inventors, with no more than a practical understanding of its operations, and the capital that could be raised through personal connections or family relations. But, 'technical development has long since become the preserve of the scientist and the engineer', and 'most of the cheap and simple inventions have ... been made' (ibid., p. 91). The knowledge and capital needed for product and process innovation have increased with the advancement of technology, as has the time needed for their development. The development of modern technologies, their products and processes, requires the resources of the large industrial concern, and its success is the result of the demands of technology.

Technology is 'the systematic application of scientific or other organized knowledge to practical tasks'. It requires the 'division and subdivision' of these tasks into their component parts, for it is only through this simplification of them that 'organized knowledge can be brought to bear on their performance' (Galbraith, 1967, p. 11).[10]

There is, as Galbraith emphasises, 'no way' that organised knowledge 'can be brought to bear' on the production of a product as a whole. Metallurgical knowledge, for example, 'can be used in the design of the cooling system or engine block' of an automobile, and chemistry in decisions 'on the composition of the finish and trim', but neither can be 'applied to the manufacture of the whole vehicle'. For technology to improve its production, it has to be broken down into tasks 'coterminous with some established area of scientific or engineering knowledge' (ibid., p. 11), the relevant knowledge applied to them, and the adjusted operations combined into the manufacture of the finished product. This dividing, redesigning, and realigning of the operations of a product's production increases the time of its development, and the greater is the application of technology, the greater the time required.

Increases in the time needed for product development raises its cost, increasing working capital requirements, as do increases in the knowledge required. This knowledge can be supplied only by those with the requisite expertise so that scientists, engineers, and other highly educated personnel have to be hired. And when the application of their knowledge requires new or different machinery, which is typically so in the case of new products and product models, that machinery will have to be developed or acquired, and this, also, raises the costs of product development.

As technology advances, the cost of technical progress increases, and while the entrepreneur-inventor cannot afford the increased cost, the large industrial enterprise can. Its scale of production, along with its market power, generates sufficient finance. The capital requirements of innovation can be met out of its profits, while the entry barriers that protect them reduce the risks of long-term investments. That enterprise can undertake the 'large commitments in time and capital' needed for product development, and while the costs and risks of this innovation can be reduced through subcontracting, the machinery, materials, or parts it requires cannot be contracted out before they are known, their properties specified, and the interconnections among them worked out. These tasks cannot be done by the market, nor, as Galbraith emphasises, can the market be relied on for the labour that can do them.

This specialised labour has to be recruited, and its procurement planned. It is not readily available in the market, like 'ordinary' (unskilled) labour is. Its supply, as well as that of other technical personnel, is arranged through the planning procedures of the corporation, by production managers, human labour specialists and others hired for that purpose. Their job is the procurement and retention of the required labour – that which the corporation requires – while the job of others is its organisation. That organisation, as Galbraith emphasises, is essential – 'the inevitable counterpart of specialization'. It is 'what brings the work of specialists to a coherent result'; and 'if there are many specialists', as there are, and must be, in the modern industrial corporation, this organisation 'will be a major task'. Indeed, so complex will be the job of organising specialists that 'there will be specialists on organization and organizations of specialists on organization' (ibid., p. 14).

The labour that organises and performs the varied, specialised tasks of the modern corporation is its 'technostructure'. This technostructure is responsible for the industrial achievements of that enterprise, and it is called 'the technostructure' because it, like the large enterprise it is part of, is the inevitable outcome of technical progress. Even 'more perhaps than machinery, massive and complex business organizations are the tangible manifestation of advanced technology' (ibid., p. 15). And while this technology is not always beneficial, and, as Galbraith says, it might be possible to make 'a case against technical progress', no case can be made for the possibility of this progress in the absence of the capital and organisation of the modern corporation (ibid., p. 30). The large industrial concern is 'an almost perfect' instrument of technical progress.

The large industrial enterprise is also essential for growth in Eichner (1976). For him, as for Galbraith, growth depends not only on the development of firms – as it did in classical economics – but on the development of firms of a certain kind – those with the attributes of 'megacorps'. These, and only these, can sustain the expansion of economies, for only they have the requisite finances and incentives.

The megacorp is distinguished by both its size and ownership structure. Its large size and accompanying market power gives it sufficient and secure finances, both of which, as Galbraith argued, are critical for long-term investment. The corporate organisation of the firm is also critical to this investment; it separates its operation from the life circumstances of its owners, freeing its expansion from the 'human limitations' of limited interest and life (Eichner, 1969).

The megacorp does not have the limited life span of the owner-operated enterprise, nor is its management dependent on the personal interests or capabilities of its owners. It is professionally managed, by those interested in management, trained in its principles, and experienced in its practices. And while these also have limited life spans, and some might retire or seek positions elsewhere, others can be hired. Their positions can be filled through promotions and new appointments so that while managers (and other employees) of the corporation come and go, and its shares change hands, the corporation remains.

The megacorp can operate indefinitely, making profit endlessly. It can 'accumulate, accumulate'– as did the firms of classical economics – and that growth is its end. Its pricing power is used in the interests of growth, with mark-ups on products set with the requisites of growth in mind, and these requirements decide all the operations of the enterprise, from the products it invests into its profit distributions and investment financing. Growth is the overriding objective, with the firm 'maximising' its growth through maintaining its position in the industries it dominates, and using the profits earned, and technology developed, in them to diversify into new, higher-growth industries (Eichner, 1976, 1987).

The objective of the owner-operated firm – the 'neoclassical proprietorship' – is quite different. Whereas the megacorp seeks an ever-increasing profit, that neoclassical firm seeks a 'maximum' one. That short-run profit maximisation reflects the interests of its management, which are the same as those of its owners. These live off the earnings of the firm; their income fluctuates with its profit, so they are naturally interested in the amount made at any point in time. And while that interest in the short-term profit of the firm does not preclude an interest in the long-term profit, any increase in the latter that requires a decrease in the former, such as a product improvement that increases costs, would come at the expense of their income, as would any reinvestment of profits. They are thus reluctant to sacrifice the profit of the short run for the more uncertain profit of the long run, and given the financial frailty of their enterprise – it is a small, 'perfectly' competitive firm – this short-run profit maximisation is not 'irrational' (Eichner, 1976, p. 21).

The megacorp is neither financially frail nor owner-operated. Investment in its future will most likely be the best use of profits, and that reinvestment of profit does not come at the expense of the income of its managers either. Indeed, quite the contrary, for their salaries depend on the performance of the enterprise, and insofar as investment improves its performance, increasing its profit and/or growth prospects, it increases the salaries of its managers along with their job security, promotion possibilities, and professional standing. They can manage the megacorp in its own best interests without hurting their own, and while these might not be the same as those of its owners, they are not in control.

The owners of the megacorp are owners in name only; they are 'passive rentiers', with no active involvement in its affairs or real knowledge of them. They could not run the firm even if they wanted to – they do not have requisite knowledge – and their interest in its operations is a limited as their knowledge of them. Their shares are liquid and investments diverse, so that while they are keenly interested in the dividends of the corporation and market price of its shares, they have little interest in its long-term growth or survival.

The shareholders of the megacorp are just one of its 'several constituencies'. They are no more important to the enterprise than its other constituencies (such as its creditors or workforce), and its interests cannot be identified with any one of them. The megacorp has to be 'viewed as having a life – and interests – entirely of its own, separate and distinct from that of any individual or group of individuals' (ibid., p. 22). It was not a 'property' – an asset or production facility – but an organisation, and organisations have purposes, those for which they are formed. They have ends of their own.

While all firms pursue profit, not all seek and make the same amount. The profit of owner-operated firms is limited by their structure; they can make no more profit than their owners want them to make, and no more than can be made with the productive capacity that their owners themselves can manage. The megacorp faces no such limits on its profit. It can operate many plants simultaneously and expand its productive capacity with the profit from its past investments. Profit can be retained and invested, increasing profit and providing more for investment, and while that firm cannot make an infinite profit, it can, as Marx would say, make ever and ever more.[11]

5   Firm and market

The profit incentive of markets requires more than markets. Profit has to be legitimated for individuals to devote themselves to its pursuit, and production geared to its requirements. Profit has to become the norm of production, the measure of its efficiency and value, and this is not possible without the institutionalisation of profit in the for-profit firm.

The importance of this enterprise is highlighted in classical economics, where firms were 'capitals', and market economies dynamic because they were capitalist. Markets were possible in the absence of firms, as was market production. Products could be produced for sale for the purposes of purchasing others, those that individuals could not produce, or produce efficiently, themselves. Yet, that 'simple commodity economy' could not achieve the productivity advances of a capitalist economy, and it could not achieve them precisely because it had no capitalist firms.

These firms increased the productivity of labour, creating a new productive power, the 'collective power of the masses'. Their development developed that productive power, while the 'imperatives of technology', along with the profit end of these firms, drove their expansion. Firms outgrew, as Galbraith and Eichner emphasised, the capabilities of their owners, just as they outgrew those of individual workmen, taking on the attributes of the modern corporation, and becoming the central agents of economic growth and development.

Notes

1. This discussion draws on previous work with Malcolm Sawyer on market structure (Sawyer and Shapiro, 2010) and is greatly indebted to our discussions on the issues.
2. Coase's importance is widely recognised in the literature on the firm. See Williamson and Winter (1993) for the views of major contributors to that literature, and chapter 5 of that work for Coase's own view of his influence.
3. This is the conception of Alchian and Demsetz (1972) and other economists of the neoclassical school, who take issue with the Coasian differentiation of the firm from the market, arguing that the firm is nothing more than a 'nexus of contracts'.
4. The capital requirements of modern industry are emphasised in Chandler's (1977) account of its development.
5. They could, of course, do both, for prices would not have to be reduced in proportion to costs for the price reduction to stimulate sales, and market share of the firm rise. For an extended discussion of the effect of process innovation on the profits of firms, see Steindl (1952).

6. The importance of profits in the financing of innovations is highlighted in Chandler's account (2001) of the evolution of the consumer electronic and information technology industries. See also his account (2005) of the development of the chemical and pharmaceutical industries.

7. This function is emphasised in Levine's discussion (2010) of organisations, where their development is connected to the necessity and legitimacy of thinking about work rather than taking its products and operations for granted, and this 'planning and designing' is 'the activity typical of the modern organization'.

8. The ability of firms to unite the knowledge of many is highlighted in Lazonick (2002), where firms are viewed as overcoming the 'bounded rationality' of economic agents, and the collective and cumulative learning they make possible a central advantage of their organisation.

9. The productive capabilities of firms are the focus of the 'competence' and 'resource-based' conceptions of the firm, which explain its profit, and the profitability of different firms, in terms of the distinctiveness of their 'organizational capabilities'. See Teece (2007) and Ghoshal, Hahn, and Moran (1999), and for the differences between these capabilities views and the transaction cost view see Hodgson (1998) and Winter (1993). Also see Penrose (1959), which inspired much of this literature.

10. Smith (1937) also noted the importance of the simplification of tasks for their technological improvement, as did Marx (1965), where the division of labour of 'manufacture' was the foundation for the technological advances of 'modern industry'.

11. This is not to say that the profits of megacorps will be reinvested, or that they will be run in their own best interest. Their managers can be opportunistic as well as incompetent; they can run the firm in their own personal interests, profiting at its expense and hurting the interests of its other employees and constituents, as has been more than evident in the current era of 'finance capital'. Yet while that behaviour is certainly unprofessional, and may also, as Galbraith suggests, be fraudulent, it is entirely in keeping with the profit ethos of the enterprise. For an extended discussion, see Levine (2010).

References

Chandler, A.D. (1977) *The Visible Hand*, Cambridge, MA: Harvard University Press.

Chandler, A.D. (2001) *Inventing the Electronic Century*, New York: Free Press.

Chandler, A.D. (2005) *Shaping the Industrial Century*, Cambridge, MA: Harvard University Press.

Coase, R. (1937) 'The nature of the firm', *Economica*, 4, 386–405.

Coase, R. (1993) 'The nature of the firm: Influence', in O.E. Williamson and S.G. Winter (eds), *The Nature of the Firm*, Oxford: Oxford University Press, pp. 61–74.

Eichner, A. (1969) *The Emergence of Oligopoly: Sugar Refining as a Case Study*, Baltimore, MD: John Hopkins University Press.

Eichner, A. (1976) *The Megacorp and Oligopoly*, New York: M.E. Sharpe.

Eichner, A. (1987) *The Macrodynamics of Advanced Market Economies*, Armonk, NY: M.E. Sharpe, Inc.

Galbraith, J.K. (1952) *American Capitalism: The Concept of Countervailing Power*, Boston, MA: Houghlin Mifflin Company.

Galbraith, J.K. (1967) *The New Industrial State*, Boston, MA: Houghton Mifflin.

Garrouste, P. and S. Saussier (2005) 'Looking for a theory of the firm: Future challenges', *Journal of Economic Behavior & Organization*, 58, 178–99.

Ghoshal, S., M. Hahn, and P. Moran (1999) 'Management competence, firm growth and progress', *Contributions to Political Economy*, 18, 125–50.

Hodgson, G. (1998) 'Competence and contract in the theory of the firm', *Journal of Economic Behavior & Organization*, 35, 179–201.

Lazonick, W. (2002) 'Innovative enterprise and historical transformation', *Enterprise & Society*, 3, 3–47.

Levine, D.P. (2010) *Object Relations, Work and the Self*, London: Routledge.

Marx, K. (1965) *Capital*, vol. 1, Moscow: Progress Publishers.

Penrose, E. (1959) *The Theory of the Growth of the Firm*, Oxford: Basil Blackwell & Mott, Ltd.

Richardson, G.B. (1999) 'Mrs. Penrose and neoclassical theory', *Contributions to Political Economy*, 18, 23–30.

Sawyer, M. and N. Shapiro (2010) 'The macroeconomics of competition: Stability and growth questions', in M. Lavoie, L. Rochon and M. Seccareccia (eds), *Money and Macrodynamics*, New York: M.E. Sharpe.

Smith, A. (1937) *The Wealth of Nations*, New York: Modern Library Edition.

Steindl, J. (1952) *Maturity and Stagnation in American Capitalism*, Oxford: Basil Blackwell.

Teece, D.J. (2007) 'Explicating dynamic capabilities: The nature and microfoundations of (sustainable) enterprise performance', *Strategic Management Journal*, 28, 1319–50.

Williamson, O.E. (1975) *Markets and Hierarchies*, New York: Free Press.

Williamson, O.E. (1985) *The Economics Institutions of Capitalism*, New York: The Free Press.

Williamson, O.E. and Winter, S.G. (eds) (1993) *The Nature of the Firm*, Oxford: Oxford University Press.

Winter, S.G. (1993) 'On Coase, competence, and the corporation', in O.E. Williamson and S.G. Winter (eds), *The Nature of the Firm*, pp. 179–95.

2
Industrial Structure and the Macro Economy

Keith Cowling and Philip R. Tomlinson

1   Introduction

In this chapter, we consider the nature of modern capitalist structures and trace its implications for macroeconomic performance and for broader issues of democracy and freedom. Our central proposition is that modern capitalist structures are monopolistic or oligopolistic, and that, consequently, they are inherently unstable and prone to economic crises. Moreover, the dominance of large transnational corporations generally impedes the democratic process to the detriment of the wider public interest. In taking this line, our approach follows that of Baran and Sweezy (1966), Kalecki (1971), Cowling (1982) and Cowling and Sugden (1994, 1998) and draws upon both orthodox and heterodox perspectives.

The chapter is organised as follows. We will begin by briefly outlining the extent of monopoly power in modern capitalist economies (section 2). We will then explore the implications of a rising degree of monopoly power for income distribution and aggregate demand (section 3). Finally, section 4 considers the broader implications of monopoly capitalism for democracy and freedom.

2   Modern capitalist structures

Modern capitalism is characterised by large, usually transnational, corporations operating in oligopolistic markets. Indeed, wherever we look we tend to observe 'competition among the few' (Fellner, 1949). Thus we expect to observe the use of monopoly power both at the level of the individual markets for goods and services and at the aggregate level, where economic and political power have become inextricably entwined. Moreover, in national contexts, the large transnational corporations have become the dominant actors and are a 'powerful interest group' (Rothschild, 2005, p. 445).

In exploring the evidence for this view, it is appropriate to consider the degree of market concentration. However, such data are often problematic and can be difficult to interpret. For instance, most measures assume that import penetration reduces domestic industrial concentration, but such measures ignore the impact of imported goods from transplants of transnational corporations with operations in the domestic economy. Adjusting for such discrepancies generally leads to the conclusion that imports lead to a lesser rather than a greater degree of competition (Cowling et al. 2000; Pryor, 2001). Further more, while Census of Production data may indicate a large number of production units in any industrial country, such (smaller) units are often operating under the strategic ambit of a few large corporations and are thus unable to determine their own long-term strategic orientation (Cowling and Sugden, 1998). Despite reservations with regards to standard measures of industrial concentration, the recent evidence points towards a significant rise. For the US, Pryor provides strong evidence of rising industrial concentration since the early 1980s (having adjusted for imports) in manufacturing, which he attributes largely to increased merger activity. In US services, there are difficulties in defining activities within the sector due to structural changes over time – yet where the structure of the services sector is held constant, Pryor (p. 314) again points to a 'significant upward trend in concentration' (something he attributes to the emergence and growth in national (service) chains). In addition, there was anecdotal evidence during the 1990s suggesting that concentration levels rose in transportation, communications, public utilities as well as finance, insurance and real estate: again, merger activity appeared the primary reason (ibid., 314–15). Furthermore, US concentration has been supplemented by a rising number of strategic alliances and partnerships (often the cover for cartels) which strengthen monopoly power.

On the global stage, we also observe growing concentration in the communications, information technology (IT) and media industries, together with important merger/consortia activity in recently privatised public utilities. It is often claimed that these sectors have been opened up to the forces of global competition through the emergence of new technologies, yet there is increasing evidence that a few major corporations are emerging as dominant players in these industries at the global level. For example, the servicing of global IT networks as run by global players in a variety of industries appears to have become the exclusive preserve of two or three service providers. In addition, Microsoft's dominance in software and computer operating systems has long been a source of friction for both US and EU anti-trust authorities, while recent concerns have been raised over Google's monopoly position as the global internet search engine (see *Financial Times*, 26 January 2010). We have also witnessed significant developments in telecommunications with global consortia emerging – in the late 1990s, there were a number of prominent mergers and strategic alliances involving the world's major telecommunication companies (see Jamison, 1998). These developments are particularly significant since IT was considered, by many observers, to be a means of nullifying the effects of monopoly power. Furthermore, in their study of online markets, Daripa and Kapur (2001) conclude that claims that e-commerce will lead to more (price-) competitive environments are overstated and that in many online markets, industrial structures are likely to become more concentrated (see also Pryor, 2001). Indeed, recent discussions of the possible monopoly control of the internet could completely undermine its democratic base (see Sugden, Te Velde and Wilson, 2009).

3 Oligopoly, income distribution and aggregate demand

Oligopolistic structures generally prevail at some stage of the global production process: obviously a myriad of small production units exist, but they do so within a system dominated by relatively few giants. It goes without saying that such structures will obviously have implications for the nature of competition and strategic rivalry. This has been the subject of much consideration in industrial economics, although generally we will tend to observe a mixture of strategic entry-deterrence, collusion and a general divergence of prices from the competitive level and a rise in the degree of monopoly power (see Cowling and Tomlinson, 2005). Such a scenario has implications for the broad distribution of income between capital and labour and ultimately the performance of the macroeconomy (see Kalecki, 1938, 1971; Cowling, 1982).

In general, the monopolisation of markets results in an increase in the share of profits. In some cases, this may be absorbed within the corporate hierarchy as pay bonuses and their managerial expenses, and a decline in the share of wages. However, that increase in the general degree of monopoly may create problems in the aggregate demand of the economy; although the supply side may dictate a growth in profit shares, as a potential, the lack of aggregate demand may leave problems associated with the realisation of these profits. Indeed, a system that changes the balance between capital and employment income may have aggregate demand effects which have often been ignored in recent economic debate, but which were previously seen as central elements of macroeconomic debate. Rising income inequalities are likely to depress domestic consumption levels and while consumption may be temporarily maintained by induced reductions in the household propensity to save combined with increases in household debt levels, such measures are unlikely to be sustainable in the long run. Indeed, rising household debt levels are likely to exacerbate any realisation crisis, as evident in the economic downturn in the US and the UK during the early 1990s and also in the present economic crisis. If we expect the aggregate propensity to consume to fall as the income flow switches away from wages towards profits, then what happens to investment spending and government demand become central issues.

In his survey of empirical investment functions, Chirinko (1993, p. 1909) concluded with the observation that 'the response of investment to price variables tends to be small and unimportant relative to quantity variables', and to this extent the effect of the rise of monopoly power on product prices relative to wages is not going to have much impact. The key issue is to ensure capacity utilisation is maintained at a high level. However, despite this evidence, things appear to be changing – domestic investment may be increasingly disconnected from domestic demand. Firms are increasingly serving global markets from least-cost locations, so that the location of investment and wage rates at that location, are now significant issues: local investment will be connected with local costs rather than local demand. In a world where transnational corporations increasingly dominate investment decisions, the location of investment has to be modelled in the context of the firm as a (potential) global entity. This has not been done in the past, although some recent econometric studies have attempted to do so. In the case of the UK, Young (1999) found that UK average costs relative to those in OECD countries were a significant factor in explaining UK investment, suggesting that international cost differentials are a significant factor. This study receives support in Hatzius (2000), which finds – for both the UK and Germany – that the elasticity of investment with respect to unit labour costs has risen significantly since the liberalisation of FDI in the 1970s. Finally, Tomlinson (2002) found evidence that investment in Japan's domestic machinery industries is sensitive to changes in foreign wage costs. Such evidence may suggest that traditional investment functions are misspecified and Chirinko's conclusions may no longer be appropriate. Investment demand in the national economy is determined by transnational forces managed by transnational corporations and as such, becomes more unstable.

If investment is problematic, then perhaps other factors can sustain aggregate demand: for instance, foreign demand and demand by government. In the case of net exports, the empirical results are ambiguous: as concentration increases exports may grow, but there is usually a counter rise in imports (Koo and Martin 1984). The budget deficit could be seen as a way of resolving a potential demand crisis: in the short run a demand deficiency can be remedied by an expansionary fiscal policy, but such policies will be politically contestable and unsustainable. During the Golden Age following the Second World War, there appeared to be a commitment to full employment on the part of all political parties, which was supported by international agreements such as Bretton Woods. Yet a full employment policy had dynamic consequences: it led to a shift in the balance of power favouring labour. Whereas before, the threat of dismissal had been an effective discipline in bargaining with labour, the commitment to full employment nullified this threat, which in turn led to accelerating wage inflation and a shift of income from profits to wages.

In response, the corporate sector retreated from Keynes, and pursued a campaign for a more liberal policy agenda at both national and global levels. Following the gradual abandonment of full employment policies, governments were faced with various social welfare constraints, which created in turn a crisis for the public finances: an unplanned consequence of general stagnation. The conclusion has to be that there is no easy way out of a realisation crisis via state intervention in demand. This is not to say that demand management is not an important tool of policy, indeed one that is becoming more important in a globalised world economy (see Krugman 1999), but it is incomplete. Globalisation tendencies render demand management more problematic, in so far as they tend to be based on the nation-state. For instance, an expansionary policy will tend to generate balance of payments deficits more quickly and fiscal crises more generally, since any domestic expansion in aggregate demand can be satisfied by transnationals using global outsourcing: a scenario that was experienced in the US during the 1990s, where the growth in output was not paralleled by a growth in employment. So while the nation-state bears the cost of demand expansion, it receives only a fraction of the benefits. Governments quickly learn that fiscal stimulus can lead to fiscal problems and consequently refrain from expansionary fiscal policy. There is a weakening of the commitment to full employment. This can be seen quite clearly in the case of the Japanese economy during the 1990s, where fiscal stimuli led to fiscal crises, while Japan's large transnationals expanded their global operations causing the 'hollowing out' of Japan's industrial base (Cowling and Tomlinson, 2000, 2002).

This does not mean that Keynesian policy is ineffective, but the world has to be reorganised for such policies to be feasible. This is a long way off, and for the present reliable tools for alleviating demand-side crises appear significantly diminished.[1]

Are there any remaining features of monopoly capitalism that appear capable of saving the day and avoiding a realisation crisis? Well, consumer behaviour may be harnessed to the task of providing a more reliable response to the production plans of the corporate sector. To the extent that the household propensity to save can be reduced the potential demand-side crisis, associated with the growth of monopoly power and the implied redistribution of income, coupled with a retreat from Keynesianism, is reduced and delayed. We observe a low propensity to save among households: saving only takes place to finance the consumption of household durables (Ruggles 1993), and we must ask, has this resulted from the behavioural characteristics of monopoly capitalism? We need an explanation of the Marglin phenomenon, that household equilibrium marginal propensity to consume is equal to one (Marglin, 1974), for which there is considerable empirical evidence: he simply refers to the character of our culture, meaning American culture. We turn first to James Duesenberry for a very perceptive, but long-lost, theory of aggregate consumption.[2]

Duesenberry's theory is based on interdependent preferences. The individual is the product of society, people tend to emulate the decisions of others: there is a 'demonstration effect' (Duesenberry 1967). His problem was to determine why people work such long hours, even as real income increases, and why the savings of households are so low, in the face of so much insecurity. So why the drive to higher levels of consumption? Duesenberry offers the 'demonstration effect', but that presupposes its existence. Emulation can go either way – yuppy (high) or hippy (low), conspicuous consumption or conspicuous non-consumption. Duesenberry relies on 'the character of our culture' (as with Marglin), but is this endogenous to the present corporate economy? Perhaps this matter is not left to the individual. It may be seen by powerful interests as being too important for that.

Advertising and product innovation could provide the key, as with the related phenomenon of the elasticity of demand at the individual market level. Duesenberry, however, devotes just 12 lines to this (p. 105), concluding 'it seems doubtful advertising explains the phenomena before us'. Nevertheless, we can see the purpose of advertising as creating continuing dissatisfaction with present consumption and also bending consumption in favour of the market and away from public consumption.

But we need to look at the evidence to see how significant this effect actually is and there has been only limited investigation of this phenomenon, essentially because economists generally have not seen advertising as a major influence in the macroeconomy. However, where investigations have been made (for example, Taylor and Weiserbs 1972; Keir 1993), the results are reasonably clear: within a well-specified consumption function, advertising has a significant positive impact on the propensity to consume and there has been in general a rising volume of advertising over the course of the twentieth century. However, whilst advertising can be seen as a way of resolving demand-side problems, because it tends to move pro-cyclically, in line with investment in general, the pressure to consume tends to fall in recession and slump, thus reducing the usefulness of advertising in this macroeconomic role.

More fundamentally, advertising, like other mechanisms we have discussed for resolving demand-side issues, contains its own contradictions: state intervention provokes a change in the balance of power between labour and the corporations, which leads to a corporate response and a deepening debt burden; increases in net exports have to be paid for by the rest of the world and are therefore not generally sustainable; increases in corporate consumption will lead to strategic action by profit recipients to curtail such expenditures; and increased advertising will serve to re-pose all the problems originally posed by increases in monopoly power which it in turn helps to create and sustain. It also produces rising expectations among parts of the population where these cannot fulfilled, leading to the possibility of social disintegration.

Our general conclusion must be that if economic development is driven by powerful corporate interests we cannot be sanguine that the demand side of the system will be capable of sustaining the full employment of resources and this position cannot simply be achieved or regained on any sustainable basis by Keynesian reflation measures because those corporate interests that guide the processes of economic development will oppose the necessary policies. To sustain full employment equilibrium will require more radical strategies.

4   Monopoly capitalism, democracy and freedom

We would now like to explore the compatibility of democracy and freedom within systems of monopoly capitalism. Throughout our analysis, we have demonstrated that the global economy is dominated by large transnational corporations. These corporations often operate in their own strategic interests, excluding others from the democratic process. Democracy is on the retreat, as the concentration of economic power has grown. The question is whether this diminution of democracy is required for economic efficiency. We will argue that rather than there being a trade-off between these two desirable ends, greater real democracy (and freedom) can contribute to the attainment of superior economic performance. In exploring this line, we point towards some institutional changes to secure an extension of democracy.

There are some who argue that democracy is feasible only under conditions of capitalism. Despite the variable meaning given to democracy by those who take this view, the one constant feature is the lack of participation. This echoes the views of much of contemporary political theory and political sociology. In such an analysis political equality is simply equated with universal suffrage. Participation is ruled out by 'the facts of political life' – the problems of scale in modern industrial society and the apathy of the citizens. It is also seen to be undesirable because of the instability it would create – the experience of Weimar Germany is cited, as is the then generally observed lack of attachment to democracy of the apathetic masses who would be asked to participate. As Lively (1975) points out, the unspoken assumption is that stability is impossible at a greater level of democracy than is currently observed, and indeed that what is being stabilised is itself desirable.

All this is in sharp contrast to those theorists who give a deeper meaning to political equality and require participation by the people in all aspects of society as the precondition of democracy. Rousseau, for instance, saw economic equality and economic independence as necessary preconditions for political equality, and participation ensured political equality was made effective. The greater the participation of the individual the better able she is to do so. John Stuart Mill saw participation as providing 'good' government but also better individuals. He also came to see the importance of participation in the workplace, but it was G.D.H. Cole who more fully developed the ideas of participatory democracy in a modern industrial society. For democracy to exist a participatory society must exist, not simply for its direct contribution to democracy via participation within that particular sphere of activity, for example, the workplace, but also because of the indirect effect on the democratic process in general. The elimination of authoritarianism in one sphere contributes to its elimination elsewhere. This also means that greater democracy within the political arena would be expected to lead to demands for democracy elsewhere. If this is not forthcoming then stable democracy is not possible, assuming congruence is not achieved by less democracy in government! It would suggest, however, that 'greater participation would enhance rather than detract from the stability of democratic regimes' (Lively 1975, p. 86). The fact of ignorance, apathy and alienation is an argument *for* participation, rather than against it. Extending participation within the economy is therefore of crucial significance for democracy in its broadest sense, but it is precisely at this point that the incompatibility between democracy and capitalism emerges.

Equal participation of all involved in an economic enterprise would undermine the essence of a capitalist firm. It is not the market which is the essence of a capitalist system – a feature which tends to be emphasised by those equating capitalism with freedom and democracy – since it is possible to envisage a non-capitalist market system consisting of independent producers or workers' co-operatives. Rather it is the subordination of labour within the production process. Whilst some degree of participation by workers in decision making within the capitalist enterprise will always be present it can never approach the level of equal participation without transforming social relations within the firm. Again this does not mean that non-capitalist production cannot exist within a capitalist system, rather the point is that non-capitalist production cannot be dominant without transforming such a system.

Thus, full democracy implies equal participation for all in every aspect of society and capitalism must deny this within the economic arena. A fundamental antagonism therefore exists between capitalism and democracy, which is obscured by the existence of universal suffrage. This does not mean that gaining universal suffrage was an insignificant event in the march towards a full democracy, nor that further gains cannot be made within the capitalist system. It suggests rather that further gains will be strongly resisted and that ultimately further democratic advance will require a transformation of the system. Some may argue we already have a 'mixed economy', with the public sector assuming an important role, so that the system is already transformed. Without getting into detailed argument it seems clear that capitalist enterprise retains a dominant position in the economy and that public enterprise has retained a form of organisation as authoritarian as that of the capitalist sector, so that the existence of a 'mixed economy' appears not, as yet, to have enhanced the democratic polity.

Whilst the incompatibility of democracy within capitalist organisation is a feature of any capitalist system, this incompatibility increases as economic power becomes more concentrated. Equal participation within the economic enterprise will always be inconsistent with capitalism but so long as capitalist enterprise remains small-scale in nature its power to subvert the system of political democracy remains circumscribed. Clearly, so long as any degree of economic inequality exists then political equality will generally not exist; the two are inter-related. Capitalism's evolution has led to the concentration of control over economic resources. Consequently, many communities have lost their economic independence and some degree of control over their direction; others have had some degree of autonomy taken away from them, and centres of economic power have grown up, capable of sub-verting the political process.

There are also parallel changes in the organisation of big business which has undermined democracy. Two tendencies which stand out in this regard are transnationalism and centripetal developments. At one and the same time the dominant centres of economic power, the major corporations, are internationalising production and drawing the control of the use of an ever-increasing share of the world's economic resources into the ambit of the key cities of the world (see Hymer, 1975). These twin developments pose problems for the democratic control of work and the strategy of the firm for democratic control within the evolution of the city or region and will ultimately undermine the autonomy of the nation-state itself. The other characteristic of central importance for democratic control which arises with the growth of giant corporations is the underlying centripetal tendency inside such organisations. Within the advanced industrial countries the giant firm has emerged largely as a result of merger activity. Large numbers of small firms have, over some-times extended periods of time, become agglomerated into large multi-plant firms. This sort of transformation of the industrial structure has, in many cases, led to the loss of a degree of local and regional autonomy, and in some cases where the acquirer is a foreign-based corporation, a loss of national autonomy. This is not to say the system of relatively small firms, with a local base, which characterised earlier industrial structures, represented a thriving democracy in microcosm; but there was nevertheless an element of local control which disappeared following merger. Higher-level strategic decision making and associated higher-level occupations have been pulled to the centre and the periphery has developed all the characteristics of a branch plant economy. Strategic decisions with major implications for many local and regional (and even national) communities are being made elsewhere. For an increasing proportion of people control over their lives is being eroded by such centralising economic forces.

But not only is this leading to a reduction in local autonomy. The same centralising forces imply a siphoning off of resources to the centre which reduces the capacity of the periphery to sustain its own economic, political and cultural development on which future self-determination is based. For a largely autonomous local or regional economy, the community will receive not only the wage share of the income generated but also most of the profit share. As the economic base of the area is taken over by outside interests so the profit share is extracted for use at the centre and lost to the local community. Now, of course, it was always the case that only a small fraction of the community had a direct claim on the profit share, and it is also the case that at least part of the profit share after takeover will be returned for reinvestment. Nevertheless, it was probably generally true that the philanthropy of the local rich made a contribution to the cultural development of the local community which has been lost in the centralising process. Generally, the growth of economic dependency has stunted the broader development of a local, regional or national community and therefore imperilled its future hopes of self-determination.

Thus, democratic control suffers in two respects: control over higher-level decisions is being lost, as is control over the resources required for community self-determination. The almost inevitable outcome is the outmigration of the educated, leading to further decline in the cultural development of the community. Centripetal economic tendencies become centripetal political and cultural tendencies and the community enters a vicious circle of relative decline. Thus, whole communities lose effected control over their own lives – the essence of true democracy. It is also the case that such communities cannot easily break out of these processes of cumulative causation by supply-side adjustments, such as investing in education – which might be a typical, democratic response, so long as the demand side remains outside their control. If such supply adjustments are made the most likely outcome would be speeding up of the rate of outmigration and thus an increase in the rate of relative decline. Increasing educational investment would only contribute to the economic and cultural resurgence of the community if parallel action were taken to secure control of production, employment and investment.

Whilst the increasing concentration of economic power is a matter of general concern for democracy, perhaps the most direct and pervading influence on the effective functioning and growth of a democracy will be felt in the case of the communications sector. Despite a communications revolution, ownership and control is highly concentrated and diversity is more apparent than real. The sector is characterised by a highly concentrated structure *within* each form of communication – press, television, sound broadcasting, cinema, books and the internet; but also interlocking ownership and control patterns *across* forms of communication – national and local newspapers; newspapers and television; newspapers and local radio; newspapers and books; and vertical links *between* production and distribution, as in the cinema and the use of the internet. As Raymond Williams (1966) once commented, 'The extension of communications has been part of the extension of democracy. Yet, in this century, while the public has extended, ownership and control of the means of communication have narrowed … In the modern trend towards limited ownership, the cultural conditions of democracy are in fact being denied: sometimes ironically in the name of freedom.'

Williams's views are as true today as they were in the mid-1960s. Moreover, the communications sector offers an example, albeit a particularly telling one, of the significance and centrality of corporate governance for policy making. The recognition there are varied interests in a corporation's activities, and that these are reflected in different strategies, means that corporate governance must be a central issue for public policy. As we have seen, the modern corporation is governed by a small subset of those with a significant interest in its activities. This group governs in pursuit of its own ambitions and objectives, opting for strategies that others would not wish to follow. This raises a serious problem if it is seen to be desirable that these activities serve the interests of people more generally. The problem is a particular case of a more general concern that we have identified as strategic failure: the concentration of strategic decision-making power implies a failure to govern in the public interest. In focusing on the public interest, we follow the analyses of Dewey (1927) and Long (1990), but in a different context: we see it as also appropriate for much of economics. Long argues that the 'consequences of private parties' actions create a public as that public discovers its shared concern with their effects and the need for their control. The public's shared concern with consequences is a public interest' (p. 171). We see the public interest in corporate activities, particularly strategic, as agreed, and evolving concerns among all those significantly affected by those activities and strategies. To avoid strategic failure we have to design ways of achieving democratic governance. Such a governance-centred approach to policy is at odds with present practice with its foundation in market failure, where the emphasis is on the benefits of markets and market competition. When governance is raised it is normally in the context of private versus public ownership. We see the democratisation of strategic choice as not being reducible to one of ownership.

We recognise that the market-centred approach can be seen to serve the public interest. One argument underlying such a view can be seen in Arrow–Debreu type general equilibrium models (see Debreu 1959; Arrow and Hahn 1971): the presence of ubiquitous perfect competition ensures Pareto-optimal outcomes. The takeover process in competitive capital market may be seen as a less extreme way of serving the public interest. By contrast, the strategic failure analysis is founded on the significance of *imperfect competition* which, we have argued, is pretty ubiquitous within the modern capitalist economy. The central objective in the governance-centred approach is not reducible to Pareto optimality and stands in sharp contrast to the aim of a market-centred approach. Whether or not something is in the public interest must always be determined by democratic processes: the identification of objectives is the most fundamental of strategic decisions and it is not for those unaffected to determine them and not for those affected to be excluded from those decisions (see Sugden and Wilson (2002) for an analysis of strategic decision-making in economic development). Without the democratic process taking place the outcome remains unclear and unknown.

Whilst the prime objective of the strategic failure approach is to ensure democratic decisions, including the determination of objectives, the effectiveness by which they can be achieved remains important but an assessment of effectiveness can only be made in the context of specified objectives and those objectives can only be determined through democratic choice. The contrast between a governance-centred approach and a market-centred one is classified when we consider the use of 'exit' and 'voice'. Hirschman (1970), in his seminal contribution, identifies exit as central to market processes and voice as crucial to democracy. He argues that exit is 'neat', 'impersonal' and 'indirect': his view is that democratic process, of its essence, entails 'the digging, the use, and hopefully the slow improvement' of channels of voice, 'essentially an art constantly evolving in new directions' (Hirschman 1970, pp. 17 and 43). Voice is at the heart of strategic failure analysis. The policy aim of the governance-centred approach is to design a policy that both recognises and nurtures the evolving art so vividly described by Hirschman, and maintains a judicious mix and balance of both voice and exit processes.

This brings us to the related issue of freedom. Whilst freedom has been implicit (and sometimes explicit) in much of our discussion of monopoly capitalism, it is important to bring out more directly its central features in concluding our chapter given its fundamental significance in human development – economically, socially and politically. Berlin's (1969) essays – which seek to distinguish positive and negative aspects of freedom – offer a good starting point (and have already been mentioned in the context of free trade). Many, of course, would begin with Milton Friedman's (1963) celebration of *Capitalism and Freedom*, but he is clear that he is talking about competitive capitalism, having examined arguments and evidence for the existence of monopoly capitalism and found them wanting. In contrast we have concluded that the present ubiquitous nature of monopoly capitalism raises concerns for our fundamental freedoms.

For Berlin, negative freedom means the absence of constraints on behaviour imposed by others: he saw the restriction of choice as the greatest change to freedom. In contrast, positive freedom concerns the ability to be 'a doer – deciding, not being decided for, self-directed ... conceiving goals and policies on (one's) own and realising them' (Berlin, 1969). Both concepts were seen as valid by Berlin, but he stressed the historical argument for the perversion of the positive concept: such distortions come when the positive concept is transformed from a concept of individual self-mastery to one of harmonious collective self-direction (see Bailey and De Ruyter, 2007). However, he later recognised that 'positive liberty is as noble an ideal as negative liberty' (see Lukes, 1997).

The recognition of the different dimensions of freedom and the dominance of negative freedom within mainstream economic analysis becomes apparent, with market transactions seen as an expression of negative freedom (see Dasgupta, 1986). Buchanan (1986) rejects positive economic freedom: 'whether or not the individual has the ability or power to undertake the activity is a separate matter', but Sen (1999) rejects such an extreme position, and sees 'substantive freedom' as embodying not just freedom from hunger and access to health care and education, but also 'freedom participation in the social, political and economic life of the community' (see also Christensen, 2009). Sen sees the processes of participation as not only a means to development, but also constituting part of development, in themselves (Bailey and De Ruyter, 2007): Frey and Stutzer (2001) see participation as contributing directly to happiness and present some interesting supporting evidence.

5 Concluding thoughts

Modern capitalist structures are highly monopolistic and carry intrinsic contradictions that lead to endemic crises and strategic failure.

Moreover, the ubiquity of strategic failure demands policies much broader, and deeper, than existing monopoly and merger policies; something reflecting the systemic nature of the present deep crisis of capitalism. Our analysis points to the need for public oversight of critical strategic decisions in the evolution and development of the economy, locally, regionally, nationally and transnationally. This is not the place to develop the detail of such oversight but we can provide some general pointers for the crucial sectors. Partly it is a matter of the economic and social importance of the sector, but partly it is a matter of whether control is vested in particularly few hands. In this regard, finance and IT would seem fundamental: finance underpins every transaction and IT underpins every modern technology. The private control of finance has been at the centre of debate and publications in the recent turmoil of the financial system which can be seen as reflecting a strategic failure of mammoth proportions in that sector, which has an effect on the whole global system. It lies at the innovatory core of the new economy, also impinging importantly on finance.

It might be considered obvious that a strategy for the fundamentals of the economy should be directed by the public interest. The present situation demonstrates the significance of when they are not. However, it is another matter entirely to design policies by which the public interest can be realised and sustained. Nevertheless, the difficulty of the project should not deter the public from seeking after such a design. At the same time it is important to stress that the public interest in corporate governance goes much deeper than laws and regulations. Democracy in essence requires a change in the nature of corporate governance from within, impossible by legal decree or regulations from without. It is important to nurture a society where people are able to penetrate the processes of governance which direct their lives. Such citizens can demand and assure that good governance prevails. As we have already argued, more effective, participatory governance can be achieved by changes in corporate law and regulation: Branston et al. (2006) examine some possibilities. The key point is that various possibilities emerge for more democratic corporate governance arrangements as soon as they allow for positive freedoms to exist (Bailey and De Ruyter, 2007). Free markets could exist but through ways which avoid strategic failure: creating free markets in a positive and negative sense by widening participation in strategic decisions. This is a democratic view of freedom, a freedom for the many rather than the few.

Notes

1. This can also be seen in demand-stimulating policies followed by governments in the present economic crisis.
2. Dominant mainstream theories appear inconsistent with the evidence (see Ruggles, 1993).

References

Aaronovitch, S. and Smith, R. (1981) *The Political Economy of British Capitalisation*, London: McGraw-Hill.

Arrow, K.J. and Hahn F. (1971), *General Competitive Analysis*, San Francisco: Holden-Day.

Bailey D. and A. De Ruyter (2007), 'Globalisation, economic freedom and strategic decision making', *Policy Studies*, 283(4), 383–98.

Baran, P.A. and Sweezy, P.M. (1966) *Monopoly Capital*, New York: Monthly Review Press.

Berlin, I. (1969) *Four Essays on Liberty*, Oxford: Oxford University Press.

Branston, J.R., Cowling, K. and Sugden, R. (2006) 'Corporate governance and the public interest', *International Review of Applied Economics*, 20(2), 189–212.

Buchanan, J.M. (1986), *Liberty, Market and State, Political Economy in the 1980s*, Brighton: Wheatsheaf Books.

Chirinko, R.S. (1993) 'Business fixed investment spending: Modelling strategies, empirical results and policy implications', *Journal of Economic Literature*, 31, 1875–911.

Christensen, J. (2009) 'Reframing economic development: thing or mystery', *International Review of Applied Economics*, 23(6), 723–41.

Cowling, K. (1982) *Monopoly Capitalism*, London: Macmillan.

Cowling, K., and Sugden, R. (1994) *Beyond Capitalism: Towards a New World Economic Order*, London: Pinter.

Cowling, K., and Sugden, R. (1998) 'The essence of the modern corporation: Markets, strategic decision-making and the theory of the firm', *The Manchester School*, 66(January), 59–86.

Cowling K. and Tomlinson P.R. (2000) 'The Japanese crisis – A case of strategic failure?', *Economic Journal*, 110(June), F358–F381.

Cowling, K. and Tomlinson, P.R. (2002) 'Revisiting the roots of Japan's economic stagnation: the role of the Japanese corporation', *International Review of Applied Economics*, 16(4), 373–90.

Cowling K. and Tomlinson, P.R. (2005) 'Globalisation and corporate power', *Contributions to Political Economy*, 24, 33–54.

Cowling, K., Yusof, F.M. and Vernon, G. (2000) 'Declining concentration in UK manufacturing? A problem of measurement', *International Review of Applied Economics*, 14, 45–54.

Daripa, A. and Kapur, S. (2001) 'Pricing on the Internet', *Oxford Review of Economic Policy*, 17, 202–16.

Dasgupta, P. (1986) 'Positive freedom, markets and the welfare state', *Oxford Review of Economic Policy*, 2(2), 25–36.

Debreu, G. (1959) *Theory of Value*, New York: John Wiley.

Dewey, J. (1927) *The Public and its Problems*, Denver, CO: Holt; page numbers refer to the reproduction in J.A. Boydston (ed.) (1988), *John Dewey. The Later Works Volume 2*: 1925–1927, Carbondale, IL: Southern Illinois University Press.

Duesenberry, J.S. (1967). *Income, Saving and the Theory of Consumer Behaviour*, Oxford: Oxford University Press.

Fellner, William J. (1949) *Competition Among the Few*, New York: A.A. Knopf.

Friedman, M. (1963) *Capitalism and Freedom*, Chicago and Phoenix: University of Chicago Press.

Frey, B.S. and Stutzer, A. (2001) *Happiness and Economy*, Princeton, NJ: Princeton University Press.

Hatzius, J. (2000) 'Foreign direct investment and factor demand elasticities', *European Economic Review*, 44, 117–43.

Hirschman, A.O. (1970) *Exit, Voice, and Loyalty: Responses to Decline in Firms, Organisations and States*, Cambridge, MA: Harvard University Press.

Hymer, S.H. (1975) 'The multinational corporation and the law of uneven development', in H. Radice, *International Firms and Modern Imperialism*, New York: Penguin, pp. 38, 50.

Jamison, M.A. (1998). 'Emerging patterns in global telecommunications alliances and mergers', *Industrial and Corporate Change*, 7(4), 695–713.

Kalecki, Michal (1938) *Essays in the Theory of Economic Fluctuations*, London: George Allen and Unwin.

Kalecki, Michal (1971) *Dynamics of the Capitalist Economy*, London: Cambridge University Press.

Keir, T. (1993) 'The aggregate advertising – consumption relationship revisited', MSc. Econ. dissertation, University of Warwick.

Koo, A.Y.C. and Martin, S. (1984) 'Market structure and US trade flows', *International Journal of Industrial Organisation*, 2(3), 173–97.

Krugman, P. (1999) *The Return of Depression Economics*, London: Penguin.

Lively, J. (1975) *Democracy*, Oxford: Basil Blackwell.

Long, N.E. (1990) 'Conceptual notes on the public interest for public administration and policy analysts', *Administration and Society*, 22(2), 170–81.

Lukes, S. (1997) 'Berlin's century: interview by Steven Lukes and Isaiah Berlin', *Prospect*, October, pp. 46–53.

Marglin, S. (1974) 'What do bosses do? The origins and functions of hierarchy in capitalist production', *Review of Radical Political Economics*, Summer.

Pryor, F.L. (2001) 'New trends in US industrial concentration', *Review of Industrial Organisation*, 18, 301–26.

Rothschild, K.W. (2005) 'New worlds–new approaches. A note on future research strategies', *Kyklos*, 58, 439–47.

Ruggles, R. (1993) 'Accounting for saving and capital formation in the United States 1947–1991', *Journal of Economic Perspectives*, 7(2), 3–17.

Sen, A. (1999) *Development as Freedom*, Oxford: Oxford University Press.

Sugden, R. and Wilson, J.R. (2002) 'Economic development in the shadow of the consensus: a strategic decision-making approach', *Contributions in Political Economy*, 21, 111–34.

Sugden, R., Te Velde, R. and Wilson, J.R. (2009) 'Economic development lite: Communication, art and ICTs in a globalised economy', in Silvia Sacchetti and Roger Sugden (eds), *Knowledge in the Development of Economies: Institutional Choices under Globalisation*, Cheltenham: Edward Elgar, pp. 205–28.

The Financial Times (2010) 'Is Google now a monopoly?', *Financial Times Ltd*, London, 26 February.

Taylor, L.D. and Weiserbs, D. (1972) 'Advertising and the aggregate consumption function', *American Economic Review*, September.

Tomlinson, P.R. (2002) 'The real effects of transnational activity upon investment and labour demand within Japan's machinery industries', *International Review of Applied Economics*, 16(2), 107–29.

Williams, R. (1966) *Communications*, London: Chatto & Windus.

Young, G. (1999) 'The influence of foreign factor price and international taxation on fixed investment in the UK', *Oxford Economic Papers*, 51(2), 355–73.

3
Unemployment, Power Relations, and the Quality of Work

David A. Spencer

1   Introduction

The writings of Malcolm Sawyer have posed a significant challenge to mainstream economic thinking. Among other things, they have highlighted the failure of established macroeconomics to offer an adequate account for the existence and persistence of unemployment. They have also called for a different theoretical and policy agenda aimed at the restoration of full employment. Sawyer has drawn upon the work of Michał Kalecki to expose the barriers (intellectual as well as political and economic) to lower unemployment and has set out some of the fundamental reforms required to regain and sustain full employment in society. His work provides an enduring source of insight into real world economic problems (for example, unemployment) and the ways to overcome them.

   This chapter focuses upon the effects of unemployment upon power relations and the quality of work. The issue of unemployment and its relationship to the balance of power between capital and labour has long been analysed in economics. Some early ideas found in the writings of Marx see unemployment as functional to the achievement of low inflation and high productivity under capitalism. Unemployment acts to bear down on the pretensions of the working class and to moderate wage inflation and keep order and discipline in the workplace. This Marxian theme was later re-emphasised by Kalecki. Modern economics has also considered the negative effects of unemployment on the bargaining power of workers: for example, versions of the Phillips curve relationship assume that lower unemployment will give workers the confidence and power to push for higher wages, leading to higher price inflation. But there is another dimension to the nexus between unemployment and power relations and this relates to the influence which unemployment has on the quality of work. It can be argued that unemployment is a barrier to a higher quality of work via its negative impacts on the ability of workers to realise their needs and interests for rewarding and meaningful work. Unemployment matters then not just because it consigns some people to enforced idleness but also because it prevents the improvement in the quality of work.

The chapter aims to elaborate on the above point. It is divided into four main parts. The first part highlights how unemployment imposes heavy costs (economic as well as social and psychological) on the unemployed. In doing so, it draws upon and evaluates the nascent literature on 'happiness' in economics, which, in contrast to much mainstream economics, recognises the costs of unemployment. The second part deals with the impact of unemployment on those in work. Unemployment is associated with increased job insecurity and potentially increased work intensity as well as longer work hours. A high and rising level of unemployment shifts the balance of power in the workplace towards employers and makes it more difficult for workers to promote and achieve their interests. The argument will be made that higher unemployment is associated with a lower quality of working life, a fact that strengthens the case for its resolution. The third part of the chapter is concerned with questions of policy. It is argued that while policies must aim to eliminate unemployment they must also be focused upon the protection and promotion of a high quality of work. A 'jobs at any price' strategy is to be resisted, in particular, because of the adverse effects that the imposition of low-quality jobs have on the well-being of workers. A criticism of some conventional Keynesian policy interventions is that they have promoted employment growth without much attention to the quality of jobs to be created. This criticism applies to both traditional 'make-work' schemes and modern-day job guarantee proposals. The fourth part suggests the need for a policy agenda that combines the pursuit of full employment with the advancement of job quality.

2 The costs of unemployment

The idea that unemployment is something that reduces the well-being and happiness of people would seem a matter of common sense. When asked to think about the experience of unemployment, most people would rate it as an unhappy state. The fact that the prospect of job loss and redundancy is so dreaded by most people confirms this point. Yet, in much mainstream economic thinking, unemployment is presented as something that people wish to pursue and for which they gain some subjective reward. Take the example of New Classical economics. It represents unemployment as a 'leisure activity' that people choose or volunteer to partake in when the real wages on offer are too low relative to what they expect them to be in the future. According to this approach, the unemployed 'enjoy' their time out of work and face no economic compulsion to take paid work; rather they are seen to opt in and out of work at their own volition. Unemployment is simply time not spent working and is assumed to be a source of utility.

Such a picture of workers' choices and of the experience of unemployment is a gross distortion of reality. The unemployed are not utility-maximising agents simply waiting for a rise in real wages to occur. They are people suffering severe costs due to their exclusion from work. The unemployed suffer not only the distress of a loss of income and consumption but also the loss of social connection with colleagues at work and the loss of opportunities to use and develop their competencies and talents through work. People value work for non-economic ends and their experience of unemployment is made worse through their inability to do and be things they value while at work (see Spencer, 2009). The costs of unemployment are also magnified by the social stigma attached to being unemployed and the psychological distress caused by the loss of self-esteem and self-worth. The idea that people gain enjoyment from unemployment and can switch between work and non-work as and when they like contradicts the realities of the world in which we live. Most people must work in order to live and when not in work they incur high economic and non-economic costs.

Heterodox economists have long been critical of the approach to unemployment found in mainstream economics (see Sawyer, 1995a). Their criticisms have taken several forms. One line of critique is to highlight the absence from mainstream economics of a proper explanation of the involuntary nature of unemployment. The idea that people may be without work 'through no fault of their own' has been a key theme in heterodox macroeconomics. Post Keynesian economists have placed particular stress on the role of deficient aggregate demand in denying workers the opportunity to work: this distinguishes their approach from 'sticky wage' or 'sticky price' explanations of involuntary unemployment contained in New Keynesian macroeconomics. Another line of critique is to pinpoint the failure of mainstream economics to uncover the costs attached to unemployment and to stress the need for coordinated policy interventions to achieve and maintain full employment.

On this second point, there has been increased recognition within mainstream economic debates that the human costs of unemployment are high. The nascent 'economics of happiness' represents one notable development where the subjective costs of unemployment are directly recognised (Frey and Stutzer, 2002; Layard, 2005). This new perspective focuses on the measurement of the subjective well-being of individuals using the results of social surveys. It challenges the conventional economic idea that utility is non-measurable and non-comparable across individuals. Instead it argues that utility or happiness can be read off from the responses that people give to social surveys that ask them to rank their satisfaction with different aspects of their lives. A key finding is that unemployment is associated with low reported subjective well-being. Unemployed workers are shown to report much lower levels of subjective well-being than those in work, a result not entirely explained by the loss of wages (Clark et al., 2001).

Richard Layard, a leading proponent of happiness economics, questions the mainstream economics representation of unemployment as 'chosen leisure'. He describes unemployment as a 'disaster: it reduces income but it also reduces happiness directly by destroying the self-respect and social relationships created by work. When people become unemployed, their happiness falls much less because of the loss of income than because of the loss of work itself. Economists almost always ignore this reality, and some even allege that extra leisure must be a benefit to the unem-ployed' (Layard, 2005, p. 67). Layard reports evidence that people suffer greater unhappiness from unemployment than from non-employment (for example, being a discouraged worker who has given up looking for work). He also suggests how the unhappiness caused by unemployment persists over time. People do not habituate to unemployment (although Layard notes how the personal costs of unemployment are lessened where others are unemployed) and they continue to suffer the ill effects of unemployment even after they return to work. The 'scarring' effects of unemployment on individual subjective well-being in this case are long lasting and difficult to erase (see also Clark et al., 2001).

Layard suggests that the costs of unemployment are felt not just by the unemployed but also by the employed. He writes that

> even when in work, people fear unemployment and when unemploy-ment goes up, it has a major impact on the happiness of everybody including those in work. Thus if unemployment rises, it has two effects. First, there is the direct effect, because more people are unemployed. Then there is the indirect effect on everyone. So low and stable unem-ployment must be a major objective of society. (Layard, 2005, p. 68)

It has also been found that rises in unemployment have a greater negative impact on subjective well-being than rises in inflation (see Di Tella et al., 2001). Such a finding reinforces the view that the reduction of unemployment should be a central priority of government policy making.

But where does unemployment come from and how exactly should it be lowered? Layard's answers to these particular questions reveal his continued commitment to mainstream macroeconomics. He suggests that unemployment is a product of imperfections or inflexibilities in the labour market: he is concerned in particular about issues relating to the conditionality of unemployment benefits and the flexibility of wages. His view is that unemployment can only be successfully lowered by the reform of the labour market. Writing about the 'consensus' view in mainstream economics, Layard states that 'you cannot permanently reduce unemployment by increasing aggregate demand for a country's output, because this will only produce inflation. Instead, you have to alter the structure of the labour market' (Layard, 2005, p. 172). Such sentiments fit with those outlined by Layard and co-authors back in the early 1990s (Layard et al., 1991). Layard, in essence, subscribes to the NAIRU (non-accelerating inflation rate of unemployment) framework. According to this framework, there is a unique rate of unemployment at which the inflation rate is stable. In policy terms, Layard suggests that the NAIRU (as a supply-side determined equilibrium) can be reduced by the encouragement of a welfare-to-work programme and flexible wages (Layard, 2005, pp. 172–4).

However, Layard is willing to accept that the labour market might be made less flexible, by the implementation of rules concerning the hiring and firing of labour. Such rules are seen as important in terms of enhancing job security and thereby the subjective well-being of workers. Layard rejects the idea that workers should be given the freedom to negotiate with employers on an individual basis. As he writes,

> if an individual worker asks his employer for more security in return for a lower wage, it casts doubt on his willingness to work. So collective action (including legislation) to provide reasonable job security is an important element of a civilised society. Of course workers should be sacked for bad behaviour, which is currently quite difficult in countries like Italy. But workers also should be entitled to proper notice and compensation for redundancy, and redress if wrongfully dismissed. (Layard, 2005, p. 175)

The essential idea is that labour protection policies add to happiness levels in society by counteracting the problem of job insecurity.

Layard's support for collective measures to protect and promote the interests of workers is to be welcomed. Yet there is a sense in which his approach lacks some vital aspects. Specifically, he does not give any credit to the barriers to full employment that arise on the demand side of the economy. He is too much concerned with the structure of the labour market to give attention to possible demand constraints on the achievement of full employment.

A different and more rounded approach to the explanation of unemployment is to be found in the work of Sawyer and other Post Keynesian economists. Such economists see unemployment as the product of a lack of aggregate demand (Sawyer, 1995a, b). Unemployment is seen to arise where firms are unable to increase output and employment to accommodate the available supply of labour. Those who suffer unemployment may be prepared and willing to work, but they will be unable to secure work because of a sheer lack of available jobs. Here it can be noted how even the most work-ready and flexible workers may fail to obtain work: their failure to find work is not a symptom of their own personal faults or unwillingness to accept work at prevailing wages; rather it is a product of there being too few jobs to meet the available labour supply. The recent economic crisis has pointed to the weaknesses of a supply-side approach: it cannot be plausibly argued that the rises in unemployment in the wake of the economic crisis were down to a sudden increase in the inflexibility of the labour market.

The wider point to make is that while one can recognise the costs of unemployment one also needs an adequate theory to understand the causes and solutions to unemployment. Happiness economics may offer the former, but it is not yet clear whether it offers the latter. The argument advanced here is that more established heterodox economic perspectives inclusive of Post Keynesian economics offer a better explanation of the barriers to lower unemployment and the ways to resolve them.

3   Unemployment and job quality

Kalecki (1943) wrote famously of the political obstacles to full employment under laissez-faire capitalism (see Sawyer, 2009). He argued that unemployment would be favoured by employers to avoid political instability and to keep 'discipline in the factories'. The threat of the sack provided a useful weapon for employers in their quest to secure the consent of workers. Kalecki suggested that employers would resist full employment policies in order to maintain their power over workers. While full employment benefited employers in terms of higher aggregate demand and hence higher profitability, its achievement and maintenance promised an upsurge in working-class militancy that could not be tolerated by them.

Kalecki implied that job quality would suffer as a result of the high unemployment required by employers to maintain order in the workplace. Workers, on the one hand, would face job insecurity, because of their fear of unemployment. On the other hand, they would be required to work more intensively and for a longer period of time, because of their vulnerability to job loss. Unemployment, in short, meant a harsh and unhappy life for those in work.

Kalecki's ideas on unemployment were shaped by those of Marx, and in particular his notion of a 'reserve army of labour'. According to this notion, a surplus or reserve army of unemployed workers is required by employers to moderate and curb the desires and expectations of the active or employed workforce. Kalecki, following Marx, showed how the fear and threat of unemployment acted as a barrier to the achievement of the material as well as non-material interests of workers.

Unlike Marx, however, Kalecki implied that capitalism could be reformed to achieve full employment. 'Full employment capitalism', in Kalecki's view, required the development of 'new social and political institutions which will reflect the increased power of the working class. If capitalism can adjust itself to full employment, a fundamental reform will have been incorporated in it' (Kalecki, 1943, p. 331). The 'fundamental reform' that Kalecki had in mind included a number of distinct elements (see Sawyer, 2009). For example, it entailed the move to a co-ordinated system of wage bargaining based on the establishment of consensus over the distribution of income between wages and profits: this had the particular advantage of accommodating inflationary pressures at full employment. Other reforms included the reorganisation of work including the introduction of some form of worker participation. The democratisation of the workplace was seen to help secure high productivity without the back-up threat of unemployment.

The idea of unemployment as a device for disciplining workers has resurfaced in modern economics via the theory of efficiency wages. In the influential model of Shapiro and Stiglitz (1984), high unemployment is seen as necessary and indeed unavoidable to prevent 'shirking' by workers. This model bears only a superficial resemblance to the approach of Kalecki and Marx, however. Thus, in the Shapiro and Stiglitz model, the reason for unemployment is linked to the natural sloth of workers: the genetic disposition of workers to 'shirk' is assumed to necessitate the use of high unemployment as a disciplinary device (the model developed in Bowles (1985), although presented as 'Marxian' in nature, shares much the same analytical content as the model of Shapiro and Stiglitz and thus can be classified as a part of the 'shirking' variant of efficiency wage theory). Kalecki's approach, with its origins in Marx, offers a quite different perspective by highlighting the role of class conflict as a factor in the creation of barriers to full employment. Unemployment is not required because workers are lazy as such but rather because employers need to maintain their control in the workplace. Here it is argued that the barriers to full employment are political in origin, and not the product of some aberrant human frailty to avoid hard work (Spencer, 2002).

The idea that unemployment affects job quality through its impacts on the balance of power between workers and employers can be used to explain actual trends in job quality. In Britain, for example, the period of falling unemployment from the late 1990s to the mid-2000s can be seen to have been favourable to workers in terms of the progress of their interests and needs at work. The available evidence on reported job quality over the above period does indeed confirm this (for further detailed discussion, see Brown et al., 2007). On various measures, job quality as perceived by workers improved between 1998 and 2004. Perceptions of the climate of employment relations and of achievement at work showed positive changes. The reason for such improvement can be linked to the low and falling unemployment achieved in Britain over this period. Against the background of tighter labour markets, employers faced greater pressure to offer better terms and conditions of work in order to retain and recruit workers. Such concessions reflected on shifts in power relations at work: effectively, there was a modest shift in the balance of power towards labour. It can be argued that policy changes under the New Labour government were not the most crucial factors behind the gains in job quality. Some policies, such as the minimum wage, were undoubtedly beneficial. However, in general, employment policies were diluted in the interests of business: for example, the minimum wage was set at a relatively low rate, and statutory rights to flexible working were rejected in favour of 'right to request' policies. The more significant factor behind the gains in job quality was the strengthening in the bargaining position of British workers caused by a reduction in unemployment.

The recent reversal in the fortunes of the British economy and the return of higher levels of unemployment are likely to wipe out these gains. High and rising unemployment creates a more insecure and fearful workforce. Workers who face the threat of the sack are likely to be under greater pressure to accept reduced wages, higher work intensity, and less autonomy over work. They are also less likely to be able to secure flexible forms of working and to strike a balance between work and home life. The fact that workers in Britain remain less unionised and less protected by the law than in the past can be expected to add to the malaise at work due to the economic crisis.

At an international level, the rise in unemployment across nations promises an upsurge in social unrest and strike activity. Those in work can expect to face downward pressure on their real incomes and cuts in their terms and conditions of work. With the spectre of unemployment hanging over them, many workers are likely to feel more insecure about work and to be more prone to work-related anxiety and stress. A recent ILO report showed that workers' perceptions of the quality of work had been adversely affected by the depressed state of the labour market (ILO, 2010). The 'age of austerity' looks set to bring about an even bleaker work life for many millions of workers around the world. The costs of a lower quality of work, in this case, are to be added to those of higher unemployment.

4   Jobs count

Unemployment is a bad thing. It is associated with the loss of economic output. It is also associated with the loss of human potential and with human misery and unhappiness. But how should it be resolved? Should the sole focus be on the growth of the quantity of jobs in the economy? Here the argument would be that unemployment is so costly that any jobs (even bad ones) will do, as long as they provide opportunities for the unemployed to return to work (see Layard, 2003, who seems to suggest that any job is better than no job, from the perspective of promoting subjective well-being in society). But should there also be a concern for the quality of jobs to be created? It will be argued below that, in looking to reduce unemployment, policy should focus on ensuring that jobs meet the needs of people as workers, rather than just as wage-earners.

J.M. Keynes (1936) argued in the *General Theory* that the key limit on employment creation was the level of aggregate demand. High unemployment was the result of low aggregate demand. If aggregate demand was depressed in the economy, then action was required to increase it, in order to create the jobs needed for the unemployed to be hired. Keynes seemed to suggest that any kind of job creation scheme would do, as long as it added to spending power in the economy. He suggested that even apparently 'wasteful' activities and events (for example, pyramid-building, earthquakes, and wars) could prove of use in promoting the increased spending power required to stimulate the economy and to lower unemployment (Keynes, 1936, p. 129). Keynes was not, of course, suggesting that pyramids be built or wars be encouraged: rather his point was that aggregate demand needed to be stimulated in some way to move the economy back to full employment and that the methods to achieve this goal were less important than the achievement of the goal itself.

Keynes felt that the state could take the lead in creating jobs, for example, via public works programmes. Once again, it did not matter what kind of jobs the state sought to create. The state, for example, might look to pay the unemployed to bury bottles in the ground (Keynes, 1936, p. 129). This would add spending power to the economy, which – as a result of the multiplier effect – would help to generate additional output and employment. Indeed, it would be much better if the bottles that workers buried in the ground were filled with money and private firms were offered contracts to unearth them. For, in that case, the rise in spending power and the accompanying economic boost to the economy would be that much greater.

Obviously, it would be far better if the state looked to encourage activities other than hole-digging. 'It would, indeed, be more sensible', Keynes (1936, p. 129) wrote, 'to build houses and the like; but if there are political and practical difficulties in the way of this, the above [hole-digging] would be better than nothing.' The point was that the form which public investment took was incidental to the process of job creation. Of much greater importance was the impact which this investment had on the level of aggregate demand since this was what ultimately determined the level of employment.

Keynes's position as outlined here was later criticised by Joan Robinson, who observed that Keynes had not focused sufficiently on the content of the employment to be created through the pursuit of higher spending power. Robinson (1962, p. 91) wrote that 'if employment is an end in itself no questions can be asked about its content'. But it is a matter of concern what kind of employment is generated in the economy. If additional employment is created through the increase in military expenditure, for example, then the reduction in unemployment and move to full employment may not be viewed as an unmitigated success. There is the more specific question of the quality of jobs to be created. Providing the unemployed with jobs such as hole-digging may help to create jobs and boost spending power in the economy, but it fails to offer employment opportunities that are rewarding and meaningful. The lack of available job opportunities of any kind is no greater a scourge on society than the proliferation of jobs which require workers to spend their time and effort performing useless and demeaning tasks which have little or no social benefit in output terms. Problems are magnified in this case where the state is seen to impose these types of tasks on the unemployed seemingly against their will.

Keynes was optimistic that the state would eventually come to adopt more socially responsible policies. 'It is not unreasonable', he wrote, 'that a sensible community should be content to remain dependent on such fortuitous and often wasteful mitigations when once we understand the influences upon which effective demand depends' (Keynes, 1936, p. 220). Here Keynes implied that the force of reason would lead the state to concentrate its spending on socially useful activities. Robinson (1962, p. 92) challenged this optimistic view, referring to the case of 'military Keynesianism' as an example of the use of Keynesian principles for wasteful and destructive (literally!) ends. The critical problem for Robinson was Keynes's failure to make any form of normative statement in relation to the type and nature of employment which ought to be encouraged by the state. For Robinson, Keynes overlooked the political aspects of demand management policies: 'he falls into the fallacy of supposing that there is some kind of *neutral* policy that a Government can pursue, to maintain effective demand in general, without having any influence upon any particular demand for anything' (ibid.: emphasis in original). Keynes should have been more precise about the kind of things that the state should look to target its spending upon, if only to avoid the false charge that he was in favour of job creation schemes based on the promotion of hole-digging.

Keynes was confident that capitalism could be reformed and was sceptical in relation to the case for collective planning and socialism. Commenting on the employment problem, he wrote the following:

> To put the point concretely, I see no reason to suppose that the existing system seriously misemploys the factors of production which are in use. There are, of course, errors of foresight; but these would not be avoided by centralising decisions. When 9,000,000 men are employed out of 10,000,000 willing and able to work, there is no evidence that the labour of these 9,000,000 men is misdirected. The complaint against the present system is not that these 9,000,000 men ought to be employed on different tasks, but that tasks should be available for the remaining 1,000,000 men. It is determining the volume, not the direction, of actual employment that the existing system has broken down. (Keynes, 1936, p. 379)

The above quote indicates Keynes's somewhat relaxed attitude to the allocation of workers to jobs in society. There was no concern that there might be a need to reallocate jobs by state intervention: for example, there was no indication of the need for greater public ownership of productive assets. Rather the concern was with the deficit of employment relative to the available supply of labour. As Keynes puts it, the chief failure of the system was the low volume of employment, rather than the misemployment of workers.

At the time Keynes wrote the *General Theory*, the shortage of available jobs was the pressing economic problem and the case for job creation was a compelling one. However, there is a sense in which achieving full employment should be about more than just boosting the number of available jobs. There is also the issue of ensuring that the jobs which are created meet certain basic criteria. Firstly, jobs should be socially useful: they should not be of the hole-digging variety, but rather should meet some economic and social need. Secondly, jobs should be rewarding for workers to do; that is, they should provide opportunities for them to meet their material and non-material needs through work (see Green, 2006). Keynes, while cognisant of the need to provide socially valuable jobs, could have done more to bring out the importance of progressing the quality as well as quantity of available jobs.

The above points chime with the critical comments made by Sawyer (2003, 2005) about modern-day 'employer of last resort' (ELR) schemes, which seek to provide the unemployed with guaranteed jobs at minimum wages. He criticises these schemes among other things for imposing low-quality jobs on the unemployed. ELR schemes require the unemployed either to take jobs or to lose their benefits. They are coercive in this sense. They are also designed to provide quick access to work for those made unemployed in economic downturns. In order to be available as and when required, jobs offered by ELR schemes must be low skilled as well as temporary in nature to allow movement to non-ELR jobs when demand in the economy picks up. Sawyer (2003, 2005) implies that ELR proposals recreate something like the workhouse schemes of Victorian Britain: that is, they seek to force the unemployed (irrespective of their talents and competencies) to undertake low-paid and low-skilled jobs. The imposition of low-quality jobs as a way out of unemployment is seen by Sawyer as a regressive step and as inferior to a policy approach aimed at increasing employment via an expansion of the public sector.

The broader point made by Sawyer is that jobs should not be created for their own sake. Here he departs from the kind of 'make-work' schemes sometimes associated with the work of Keynes (see above). Rather he suggests that some consideration must be given to the economic and social worth of jobs (see Sawyer, 2005). Jobs should be encouraged that are worthwhile both in terms of the creation of valuable economic output and in terms of enabling workers to achieve well-being at work. This particular point is developed further in the next section.

5   Fully employed and fully flourishing at work

The conquest of unemployment is important not just in providing the unemployed with access to wages but also in allowing them the scope to participate in potentially intrinsically rewarding activities. Here one needs to consider work both as a means to an end and an end in itself. Economists, including Keynes, have tended to see work from the perspective of its income-generating potential (Spencer, 2009). The case for full employment in this sense is made on the basis of giving the unemployed an income that would otherwise be denied to them. It is also argued that the reduction of unemployment generates additional output that can be consumed by society. However, in this approach, the merits of work are judged by the extrinsic gains from work. What tends to get neglected is the potential part played by work in developing the faculties and competences of people.

As we have seen already, unemployment is a barrier to higher work quality. Its existence and persistence tilts the balance of power towards employers and makes it more difficult for workers to secure improvements in the pecuniary and non-pecuniary rewards of work. It can be argued here that the reduction in unemployment would be of benefit in terms of the improvement of job quality. The move to full employment would empower and embolden workers to secure reforms in the workplace that improve their welfare. One point to make is that the case for full employment can be defended on the basis of its positive effect on the ability of people to improve their lives at work. Full employment eliminates the human misery of unemployment and simultaneously helps to create a work environment in which workers are better able to meet their needs.

What of the impacts of lower unemployment on productivity? One argument could be that lower unemployment will undermine productivity as workers seek to reduce their performance at work. This is based on the assumption that workers must be coerced to work by some form of threat – in this case, the threat of unemployment. Such an assumption is made in the 'shirking' model of Shapiro and Stiglitz (1984). This model rules out the possibility of full employment on the basis that the latter is incompatible with 'no shirking'. One objection here is that workers are not preordained to resist work but rather are led to resist work through the circumstances they face. Workers may be resistant to work under conditions where their interests are left unmet but they may consent and cooperate where the organisation of work is more reflective of their needs. The point missed in the model of Shapiro and Stiglitz is that the preferences of workers are endogenous rather than exogenous: they depend on – and can be altered by – the nature and organisation of work (much the same criticism can be applied to the model of Bowles (1985), which although professing to take account of endogenous preferences, is based on the standard assumption of the disutility of work: see Spencer, 2002). By moving beyond the false and biased assumption that each and every worker is a 'shirker', one can begin to see how high productivity can be achieved without the need for the creation of a climate of fear and threat in the workplace. As we saw above, Kalecki's 'fundamental reform' of capitalism involved the search for a form of work organisation that could realise a high level of productivity in the absence of the threat of job loss.

There is also the point that the threat of unemployment is an inefficient way of achieving productivity gains. The issuing of threats of dismissal helps to secure the compliance of workers, but it does not secure from them the type of consummate performance that is needed by employers to achieve successful production. Workers' ingenuity and creativity is repressed and stifled by the fear of unemployment. Their willingness to innovate and take risks is also dampened where they fear the sack. Note how workers use 'work-to-rule' tactics as a way to get back at employers: such tactics may be expected to increase under circumstances where employers gain compliance through the threat of dismissal. In short, it can be argued that unemployment is a barrier to the harnessing of the potentialities of workers and indeed leads to a situation where the performance of workers is less than what it could be under alternative circumstances where the threat and fear of unemployment is absent.

The argument to be made here is that there is a need both to eliminate unemployment and to promote higher job quality. There should never be a trade-off between these two goals. Rather they should be treated as compatible goals, requiring not only policies to encourage higher aggregate demand in the economy, but also measures to reform the institutions and structures of the workplace to provide for more meaningful forms of work. With these policies and measures in place, one could envisage moving to a situation where the available labour supply is fully employed in jobs that are extrinsically as well as intrinsically rewarding.

6 Summary and conclusions

This chapter has argued that there is a connection between unemployment and the quality of work. This connection can be understood in terms of the power relationship between workers and employers. Unemployment strengthens the ability of employers to resist improvements in job quality. It also encourages them to use methods such as increased work intensity and longer work hours to achieve higher profitability. The move to full employment, by contrast, enables workers to better meet their interests and needs at work. It offers them the scope to resist so-called 'low routes' to higher profitability based on sweated labour and to achieve progressive changes in the workplace. While there remain severe institutional barriers to higher job quality, it can be argued that the reduction of unemployment can help the efforts of workers to secure for themselves a better quality of work. Traditionally, the case for full employment has been made on the basis of the negative influence of unemployment on economic output and on the well-being of the unemployed. This chapter has suggested that a further argument in support of full employment is its positive influence on the ability of those in work to achieve higher well-being.

One key conclusion of the chapter is that the goal of full employment should be extended to include the encouragement of higher-quality work. The objective should be to create not just any jobs but jobs that meet with the needs of workers. Higher-quality jobs would be those that offer high pay, job security, high levels of discretion, and reasonable hours of work. There should be no sacrifice of job quality for the sake of creating jobs; rather there should be an attempt to achieve more fulfilling work for all.

The recent crisis has brought about a return to high unemployment. It has also led to erosions in job quality. If full employment and high job quality are to be promoted and restored in future, then this will require a fundamental change of economic theory as well as ideology and policy. For those who are concerned to achieve such a change, the economics of Malcolm Sawyer remain an important source of insight and illumination.

References

Bowles, S. (1985) 'The production process in a competitive economy: Walrasian, Marxian, and neo-Hobbesian models', *American Economic Review*, 76(1), 16–36.

Brown, A., Charlwood, A., Forde, C. and Spencer, D. (2007) 'Job quality and the economics of New Labour: A critical appraisal using subjective survey data', *Cambridge Journal of Economics*, 31(6), 941–71.

Clark, A., Georgellis, Y. and Sanfey, P. (2001) 'Scarring: The psychological impact of past unemployment', *Economica*, 68, 221–41.

Di Tella, R., MacCulloch, R. and Oswald A. (2001) 'Preferences over inflation and unemployment: Evidence from surveys of happiness', *American Economic Review*, 91, 335–41.

Frey, B. and Stutzer, A. (2002) *Happiness and Economics*, Princeton, NJ: Princeton University Press.

Green, F. (2006) *Demanding Work: The Paradox of Job Quality in the Affluent Society*, Princeton, NJ: Princeton University Press.

ILO (2010) *World of Work Report 2010: From One Crisis to the Next?*, Geneva: International Labour Organisation.

Kalecki, M. (1943) 'Political aspects of full employment', *Political Quarterly*, 14(4), 322–31.

Keynes, J.M. (1936) *The General Theory of Employment, Interest and Money*, London: Macmillan.

Layard, R. (2003) 'Good jobs and bad jobs', *Centre for Economic Performance Occasional Paper*, no. 19.

Layard, R. (2005) *Happiness: Lessons from a New Science*, London: Penguin Books.

Layard, R., Nickell, S. and Jackman, R. (1991) *Unemployment: Macroeconomic Performance and the Labour Market*, Oxford: Oxford University Press.

Robinson, J. (1962) *Economic Philosophy*, Harmondsworth: Penguin.

Sawyer, M. (1995a) *Unemployment, Imperfect Competition and Macroeconomics: Essays in the Post Keynesian Tradition*, Aldershot: Edward Elgar.

Sawyer, M. (1995b) 'Overcoming the barriers to full employment in capitalist economies', *Economie Appliquée*, 48, 185–218.

Sawyer, M. (2003) 'Employer of last resort: Could it deliver full employment and price stability?', *Journal of Economic Issues*, 37(4), 881–908.

Sawyer, M. (2005) 'Employer of last resort: A response to my critics', *Journal of Economic Issues*, 39(1), 256–64.

Sawyer, M. (2009) 'Kalecki on the causes of unemployment and policies to achieve full employment', in Philip Arestis and John McCombie (eds), *Unemployment: Past and Present*, Basingstoke: Palgrave Macmillan, pp. 7–28.

Shapiro, C. and Stiglitz, J. (1984) 'Equilibrium unemployment as a worker discipline device', *American Economic Review*, 74(2), 433–44.

Spencer, D. (2002) 'Shirking the issue? Efficiency wages, work discipline, and full employment', *Review of Political Economy*, 14(3), 313–27.

Spencer, D. (2009) *The Political Economy of Work*, London: Routledge.

4
The Problem of Young People Not in Employment, Education or Training: Is There a 'Neet' Solution?

John McCombie and Maureen Pike

1 Introduction

For a long time Post Keynesians have argued convincingly that national unemployment rates, together with their accompanying regional variations, are not due to labour market rigidities such as the real wage being too high. The primary cause is the lack of effective demand and the absence of jobs. But this does not mean that the supply side can be neglected. Long periods of unemployment lead to deterioration of skills and lack of motivation, such that even if demand picks up, the efficiency of these workers will have been greatly eroded. But what is of even greater cause for concern is the rapid growth in the UK of the number of young people who are likely never to have held a job since leaving school. This would not be so much of a problem if they had been in training or education, but there has also been a rapid rise in the last few years of young people who are inactive and not enrolled in education or training. These are the so-called 'Neets'. The danger is that they may well never adapt to the routine and the structure of the working day and have few of the minimum skills that are demanded by employers. There is the real danger of the development of an underclass of people, primarily in the depressed regions and the inner cities, who will never have held a job and will be literally unemployable.

As Philip Arestis notes in 'Malcolm Sawyer: An Appreciation' at the beginning of this festschrift, one of Malcolm's areas of research relates to the 'institutional obstacles' that prevent the achievement of full employment and the policies that should be introduced to overcome these. In this chapter, we investigate one current area of concern, namely, the reasons for the rise and persistence in the number of Neets in the UK. This is not merely a consequence of the credit crunch of 2007, as the rise predates this by several years.

We begin by examining some of the recent developments in the youth labour market and seek to identify the extent of the Neet problem. Neets are not a random sample of the age group in question and thus we examine their characteristics and discuss why this group is of concern. We then seek to investigate the causes of the Neet problem and conclude that they have little, or nothing, to do with such commonly advanced explanations such as the national minimum wage or immigration from the EU. They are to be found in the high degree of social deprivation that affects young people even before they start school and hence require carefully targeted social policies to offset this.

2 Why are the Neets a cause for concern?

Across the whole of the OECD countries, youth employment has been hit particularly hard by the recession of 2008–09. But as far as the UK is concerned, two facts stand out. The first is that the ratio of youth to adult unemployment is much higher in the UK compared with the majority of other countries. The second is that the deterioration in the job prospects for youths began before the 2007 downturn commencing around 2004 and, while exacerbated by the subprime crisis, has not been entirely caused by it. As the Low Pay Commission (LPC, 2010, p. 131) commented: 'despite high total employment levels, it is unclear why young people's employment prospects have deteriorated in the recent past compared with other groups'. This trend is perplexing given that these were the years of relative prosperity and when other age groups show no such adverse developments. This pattern in youth unemployment is mirrored by the trend in youth economic inactivity rates where the deterioration set in even earlier, and the increase in education rates was not sufficient to offset this deterioration. Indeed, the UK ranks only 24th out of 30 OECD countries in terms of the proportion of 17-year-olds staying on in education.

The Neet problem reached crisis level in 2009, when newspaper headlines proclaimed the fact that the number of Neets had topped the million mark for the first time. This was notwithstanding the fact that the previous Labour government had set itself a Public Services Agreement target to reduce the proportion of 16–18-year-old Neets from 9.6 per cent in 2004 to 7.6 per cent in 2010. Even had the last administration survived until the end of 2010, it is almost certain that the target would not have been met.

There are two key important factors which appear to be connected to the risk of becoming Neet. The first is the level of qualifications obtained while in school and the second is family and household circumstances. According to the OECD (2008), about a fifth of 16–24-year-olds without an upper secondary qualification (at least 5 GCSEs at A* to C level, or their vocational equivalent) were Neet, which was double the rate of those with such qualifications. The importance of qualifications for employment is also borne out by Barham et al. (2009) and DCSF (Department of Children, Schools and Families) (2007).[1] The OECD (2008) reports that in the UK, one year after leaving education, under a half of young people who left school without an upper secondary qualification were employed. The report also highlights that between 2001 and 2005, low-skilled youths not in education were twice as likely to experience persistent unemployment or inactivity than 16–24-year-olds not in education on average and the relative degree of this disadvantage had increased since the 1990s. It is also apparent that the employment premium associated with educational qualifications is also greater in the UK. While highly qualified youths do better in the UK than their counterparts elsewhere, low-skilled youths perform below the OECD average. Rennison et al. (2005) find that exiting from the Neet category is also more difficult for those with no qualifications.

The second major distinguishing characteristic of Neets is their socio-economic background. The differences in family and household circumstances between the Neets and non-Neets are striking, suggesting the likelihood of a vicious circle for the Neets. Barham et al. (2009) find that 41 per cent of 16–17-year-old Neets live in a one-parent family compared with 25 per cent of non-Neets. There are also big differences in their economic circumstances. While 38 per cent of 16–24-year-old Neets live in households without work, this condition affects only 8 per cent of non-Neets. Those who are Neet at 16 are also much more likely to have parents with no or low qualifications. Research by the DCFS (2005) also found that children of parents who had a positive attitude towards education and who had been closely involved in their children's decisions about their post-16 options were much less likely to be Neet (see also Casson and Kingdon, 2007).

Besides low qualifications and socioeconomic disadvantages, there are a number of other risk factors arising from being Neet. These include various health and personal issues. Thus female Neets are 22 times more likely to be teenage mothers than the average (CBI, 2008) and in 2007, 14 per cent of all 16–24-year-old Neets were lone parents compared with only one per cent of non-Neets (Barham et al., 2009).

Children who have been in care and those with mental and physical health issues are also more likely to be over-represented. Being in care is highly correlated with low educational achievement. Coles et al. (2002) report that three-quarters of care leavers have no academic qualifications of any kind. Youth Access (2009) research indicates that mental health problems are far more common among 18–24-year-old Neets, as are stress-related illnesses.

Perhaps unsurprisingly, there are regional variations in the proportion of young people who are Neet. DfE (2010a) data indicate that 18.3 per cent of 16–24-year-olds are Neet in the North-East of England, compared to just 12.3 per cent in the South-East. This regional disparity of approximately six percentage points has been relatively stable since the end of the previous recession in 2002. This disparity mirrors regional disparities in unemployment rates typically associated with longer-term structural economic change. While it is no surprise that unemployment among 16–24-year-olds in areas such as the North-East is higher, this begs the question as to why then a higher proportion of this group do not chose to remain in education, if only *faute de mieux*.

The adverse consequences arising from being Neet for the individual youth and society in general are both economic and social. There is significant evidence (see OECD, 2010) that for disadvantaged youths with low educational qualifications, a spell of unemployment on first entering the labour market will increase the likelihood of future unemployment spells and/or damage future earnings prospects. This so-called 'scarring' effect can be predicted using the standard human capital model, which suggests that, during periods of unemployment, skills are likely to atrophy and that opportunities for learning on the job are sacrificed.

Signalling effects may also be important in that periods of unemployment are interpreted as a negative signal of innate low productivity by potential employers. Gregg and Tominey (2005, p. 487) suggest that 'scarring' is a serious problem – there was a 'large and significant wage penalty, even after controlling for educational achievement, region of residence and a wealth of family and individual characteristics'. Thus at age 42, those who had suffered a period of unemployment of six months or more while young were likely to earn 8–10 per cent less than those who had never been unemployed. The reduction in earnings rose to 12–15 per cent if repeated unemployment spells were experienced.

As well as long-term individual costs, being Neet also has wider consequences for society. Research on social exclusion by the Prince's Trust (2007) estimates the cost of youth unemployment in terms of

Jobseeker's Allowance as £20 million per week, but that this is dwarfed by the productivity loss to the economy which they estimate as £70 million per week.[2] There is also a strong link between being Neet and becoming involved in criminal activity. The above report puts the total cost of youth crime for Great Britain as in excess of £1 billion in 2004. Godfrey et al. (2002) estimate that Neets aged 16–18 are three times more likely to have been involved in crime between the ages 17 to 30.

To conclude this section, being Neet creates both substantial personal and social costs. Given the characteristics associated with being Neet, there is also likely to be the potential for the problem to be self-perpetuating, spreading from one generation to the next through a cycle of social deprivation and exclusion in a Myrdal-type (1944) process of adverse cumulative causation. It is thus important that we understand the reasons why this problem arises and persists.

3   Are there any obvious culprits for the rise in the number of Neets?

The most popular culprits are increased job competition from immigrants and the national minimum wage. Let us consider each of these possible causes in turn.

3.1   Increased job competition

Immigration to the UK rose steadily from 1999 to 2008, with the largest increase taking place in 2004, following the accession of the A8 countries to the EU. (The A8 countries are the Czech Republic, Estonia, Hungary, Latvia, Lithuania, Poland, Slovakia, and Slovenia.)

Taking emigration into account, net immigration reached a high point with more than 200,000 entering the UK in 2004. Large inflows continued right up to and into the recession years, albeit at lower rates of increase than in 2004. The beginning of the rapid influx of immigrants also coincided with the rise in youth unemployment noted above. This coincidence led to a number of accusatory headlines in the national dailies such as '100,000 lose out to immigrants in hunt for work' (*Daily Telegraph*, 18 December 2007).

The perception of a causal link between youth unemployment and recent immigration has been strengthened by the fact that a significant proportion of immigrants are young. Blanchflower et al. (2007) report that between May 2004 and September 2006, 82 per cent of immigrants were aged 18–34 and 43 per cent were in the 18 to 24 age group. They were, on average, better educated than their UK counterparts and this educational advantage has been rising with more recent waves of immigrants.

Current economic research gives no straightforward answers regarding the impact of immigration on wages and employment. The supposition that an influx of labour will lead to downward pressure on wages ignores the possibility that in addition to a shift in the supply curve of labour, a shift in the demand curve is also likely, as immigrants add to the demand for goods and services. The impact will also be dependent on the extent to which the skills of immigrants are complementary or substitutable for those of indigenous workers. Finally, as shown by Dustmann et al. (2008), it is crucial to model how the supply of capital interacts with the supply of different skill groups. If the price of capital is fixed in international markets, then, theoretically, immigration may have a positive effect on average wages if the skill composition of immigrants differs from that of native-born workers.

Theoretically, the impact of immigration on unemployment is even less clear-cut. The assumption that an increased flow of immigrants will lead to a reduction in the employment of native workers derives from the 'lump of labour' theory. This assumes that there is a fixed number of jobs and if more people seek work, then unemployment must result. This is a fallacy which reflects a misunderstanding of the nature of job creation. The number of jobs depends on the level of aggregate demand and there is thus a complex interaction between the increased demand the immigrants bring with them, including multiplier effects and the state of the labour market. Given excess capacity, it is unlikely that net immigration has any significant adverse effect on indigenous unemployment.

Based on an extensive survey of studies covering a number of countries, Blanchflower et al. (2007, p. 18) conclude that 'the empirical evidence from around the world suggests that, even when there have been large flows of migrants which are greater in magnitude than the one's the UK has experienced from the A8, that there have been few if any impacts on native outcomes'.

The previous UK Labour government commissioned a number of studies on the impact of immigration on the labour market and relied on the findings to support its then relatively open immigration policy. Thus a study by Gilpin et al. (2006) focused on the impact of migration from the A8 countries on the claimant count of the unemployed. This covers those in receipt of Jobseeker's Allowance, a benefit mainly available to those aged 18 and over. The study, in line with the international evidence referred to above, concludes that there is 'no discernible statistical evidence which supports the view that the influx of A8 migrants is contributing to the rise in claimant unemployment in the UK' (p. 49). However, as noted in a subsequent House of Lords (2008) enquiry into the impact of immigration, a number of expert witnesses questioned the interpretation of the conclusions in the report and pointed to several methodological problems arising from such studies.

Riley (see House of Lords, 2008, volume 1, para. 82, p. 29) pointed to the problem that the study had been unable to account for the possibility of migration of resident workers to other parts of the UK in response to the inward immigration from abroad. This is also an issue raised by Hatton and Tani (2005) who, while also finding small wage and employment effects in their own study, indicated that there is evidence that interregional mobility is important. They point out that induced migration may result in a downward bias in the estimated impact of immigration on native employment outcomes.

In evidence to the House of Lords, Rowthorn (see House of Lords, volume 1, para. 83, p. 29) also criticised the government's interpretation that the finding in the Gilpin study of a statistically insignificant effect of immigration on unemployment necessarily implied that such effects are small. While statistically insignificant, some of the results reported in Gilpin indicate the possibility of quite large quantitative effects, with most of the long-run coefficients being at least 0.6, indicating that in the long-run for every 100 immigrants who enter a region, 60 or more existing workers will be displaced. Rowthorn emphasises that the fact they are statistically insignificant does not mean they are small, only that there is too much noise in the system to be able to estimate them accurately. The House of Lords report thus concluded that there was a need for further research to enable more definitive conclusions to be drawn.

The Gilpin study has been updated by Lemos and Portes (2008). Their report tries to improve on the previous work in a number of ways, including covering a longer time span and using occupational data to examine whether migration had differential effects on different occupational and demographic groups. The econometric analysis covers the period May 2004 to May 2006 and this is extended by descriptive analysis of the data for the period to September 2007. Controlling for both the possibility that inward migration from abroad may induce internal migration by natives from the regions affected and for the possible endogeneity associated with the fact that regions with higher growth rates and higher levels of employment may attract more immigrants, their results show small but statistically insignificant effects of immigration on unemployment, regardless of the level of geographical aggregation. Thus, data at the county level suggest that a one-percentage point increase in the proportion of A8 countries' immigrants in the working population would increase the claimant unemployment rate in the UK by only 0.057 percentage points. When the analysis is repeated for various demographic subgroups, the coefficients remain small, without a consistent sign (depending on the regional aggregation level) which, in most cases, is statistically insignificant.

In summary, the majority of studies on immigration find either no, or a small, negative impact of increased immigration on youth unemployment. While there is thus little or no evidence of a displacement effect, this does not tell that those already displaced prior to the increase in immigration have not found it harder to reintegrate themselves into the labour market post-2004. Unemployment is also an imperfect measure of displacement, as some of those who may lose their jobs may enter inactivity rather than unemployment. To the extent that displacement has taken place, it also raises the question as to why those whose labour market opportunities may have become more constrained turned to unemployment and inactivity as opposed to education. We thus need to seek answers to this elsewhere.

3.2 The possible effect of the minimum wage

In 1999 the government introduced the national minimum wage which, over the period 1999 to 2004, rose at a rate that exceeded the average earnings index, before falling until it matched the growth of the latter. Could this be the explanation for the rise in youth unemployment and, hence, in the number of Neets?

The mainstream view based upon the assumption of a competitive labour demand suggests that this would have the effect of youths being priced out of the labour market. Support for this argument can be found in empirical work in the US carried out in the 1970s and summarised in Brown et al. (1982). But the conventional view was challenged by a series of studies carried out in the early 1990s by Card (1992) and Katz and Krueger (1992). In a symposium published in the *Industrial and Labor Relations Review* these authors, using a monopsony model complete with market frictions found either a zero, or even a small positive, effect of an increase of the national minimum wage (NMW) on teenage employment. These results were highly influential on the decision to introduce the NMW in the UK as it was considered that this could partly resolve the problem of low pay without adverse employment effects.

Nevertheless, the methodology (the so-called 'natural experiment' or difference in differences approach) and the data collection methods involved in these and subsequent studies by these authors have been subjected to considerable criticism by neoclassical economists (see Ehrenberg, 1995). In the UK, the monopsony model and the US results has received support from the work of Stewart (2004) and Dickens and Draca (2005).

Turning next to the impact of the NMW on the numbers undertaking education and training, the result is again ambiguous and depends in part upon the economic approach taken in the analysis. As a NMW generally raises the opportunity cost of not being in employment, it is predicted that there will be a reduction in participation rates in education. However, if we follow the logic of the competitive model, if the NMW leads to an increase in unemployment, then for some, the opportunity cost of staying on in education will fall. From an a priori perspective the net effect is not clear-cut.

When we consider the supply of training, then, following Becker (1964), it is generally expected that employers will not pay for general training and such training will be mainly financed by employees who 'pay' by accepting wages lower than their marginal productivity during training. If the NMW exceeds the latter wage, then the worker will be prevented from 'paying' for training and the acquisition of skills will be negatively affected. If training is instead specific to the firm, the standard prediction is that training costs will be shared between employer and employee. During training the employees are paid a wage above their marginal product, but after training they receive a higher wage which is below their now higher marginal product. If the NMW exceeds the wage that would have been paid while training, the employer can recoup this by further reducing the post-training wage. In this way the impact of a NMW can be mitigated.

The predictions above are based on the assumption that training is supplied in a perfectly competitive labour market. However, if the market is characterised by substantial frictions caused by transaction, search, and information costs, then it has been shown (see Acemoglu and Pischke, 2003) that firms may be willing to pay for general training as post training the firm can pay a wage less than the marginal product without the fear that employees will leave. Furthermore in the presence of such monopsony imperfections, the gap between the wage paid and the worker's marginal product will rise with the level of skill. For workers whose marginal product is then below the imposed minimum, the employer's monopsony rent will be eliminated and there is thus an incentive to restore this by increasing the skill level of such workers through increased training. However, it should be noted that this conventional analysis depends upon the usual neoclassical assumptions underlying the labour market.

The evidence on the effect of the NMW on education and training is also mixed. Neumark and Wascher (2008) report their earlier work found an adverse effect with some evidence of those induced to leave school displacing the less able teenagers already employed. Pacheco and Cruickshank (2007) find that when the NMW was first introduced in New Zealand, it increased the school enrolment rate, but further increases reduced enrolment. Their interpretation of this is that the introduction of the minimum wage induces the less able teenager, faced with lower employment probabilities post minimum wage introduction, to stay on in school, but that subsequent increases in the minimum encourage more able teenagers out of school and into the labour market. Frayne and Goodman's (2004) simulation analysis for the UK suggests that while the increases in wages do tend to induce teenagers to shift out of school into the labour market, the numbers involved are insignificant. De Coulon et al. (2010), using data from local authority areas differentially affected by the introduction in the youth rate, find no effect. Their study suggests that staying on rates are driven mainly by personal and family characteristics, rather than local wage rates.

Turning to training, for US data Acemoglu and Pischke (2003) find no evidence of an adverse effect, whereas Neumark and Wascher (2008) report contrary results, especially for workers in their early twenties. Arulampalam (2004) finds that in the UK the incidence of training increases: a one-percentage point increase in the NMW increasing training by 8 to 11 percentage points.

In this section we have examined the most commonly cited reasons for the poor showing in the youth labour market. It is difficult to place the blame squarely on either increased job competition or minimum wages. We therefore now turn to what we see as the root cause of the Neet problem: the failure of the UK education system.

4   The failure of the education system

In the last few decades there has been a rise in the demand for skills driven mainly by skill-biased technological change. In the UK, this manifested itself through a large rise in wage inequality and an increase in the 'education premium'. This shift in demand against the unskilled has substantially weakened the low-skilled labour market. While this secular rise in demand has occurred in many other countries, its consequences for those at the bottom end of the labour market have not been so disastrous, because their education systems have enabled more effective reskilling to take place in response to skill-biased demand shifts. According to Nickell (2003, p. 8) 'The comparison with Northern European countries is very telling and suggests that, relative to the UK, their education systems have managed to raise a higher proportion of young people above a decent minimum threshold.'

What is clear is that at the bottom end of the scale where the Neets are, education attainment is inadequate, in terms of both basic literacy and numeracy (Rashid and Brooks, 2010; National Employers' Survey, 2010). The surprising thing is that this is at a time when general educational standards have been rising (McNally and Vaitilingam, 2010). This paradox has led some to question the role of target attainment levels which have been introduced in recent years throughout the UK schooling system.

Casson and Kingdon (2007) claim the problem with the target of five A*–C passes at GCSE is threefold: it encourages schools: (i) to avoid taking on those likely to miss the target; (ii) to concentrate resources on students who can be helped to turn Ds into Cs, thus disadvantaging both low and high performers. Finally, (iii) it makes it difficult to establish vocational education as an effective alternative. The target has become a good example of Goodhart's Law, namely when a measure becomes a target, it ceases to be a good measure. McNally and Vaitilingam (2010) also raise concerns about the extent to which the apparent rise in educational attainment in recent years is simply a reflection of 'teaching to the test', rather than real knowledge imparted (Mansell, 2008, and Ofsted, 2008).

Criticisms of the UK's poor offering in vocational education are well documented (see Steedman and West, 2003; and Steedman, 2005). While the weakness of vocational education has long been recognised and has resulted in a plethora of government initiatives, none of these have succeeded in a wholesale transformation of the system. Just such an overhaul was recommended by the Tomlinson Report which advocated the scrapping of existing qualifications and their replacement with a unified framework of qualifications to cover both academic and vocational education. The report was shelved by the then government in favour of piecemeal tinkering, such that A levels still remain as the 'gold standard'. Other measures such as the 14–19 Diplomas in 2008 have raised criticisms.

In a recent speech on the urgent need for reform, Michael Gove, Secretary of State for Education, said '... the problem is our failure to provide young people with a proper technical and practical education of a kind that other nations can boast. ... there have been a series of failed governmental interventions, too numerous to list, none of which got to the heart of the matter' (DFE, 2010b). During the speech, Gove announced the setting up of an independent review of pre-19 vocational education. The Wolf Review is due to report in 2011.

5   Tackling disengagement – the way forward

Reform of the school system for 14–19-year-olds and its shortcomings for low-achievers may go some way to tackling the disengagement of young people who are most at risk of becoming Neet. However, it is a necessary, but not sufficient condition, for solving the Neet problem.

In addition to the education reforms such as the New Diplomas, previous governments have introduced a raft of measures to try and alleviate the Neet problem. These include the New Deal and its 2009 successor, the Flexible New Deal; the 2008 September Job Guarantee; a revamping of the National Apprenticeship Service; and the introduction of Education Maintenance Allowances (see DCSF, 2009). But the Neet problem has proved intractable. Why? Our contention is that all of the policies deal with the consequences of disengagement but do not tackle the real issue, which is the underlying cause of disengagement.

There is substantial evidence that the risk factors associated with being Neet – educational underachievement, poor attitudes to education and behavioural problems in school – are already present in pre- and primary school. Sodha, the author of a new report on children's disengagement from education (Sodha and Margo, 2010), finds evidence that one in ten children lack the basic tools to engage with education even before they get to school. These 'nursery Neets' display the kind of behavioural and communication problems which have been strongly linked to subsequent underachievement and exclusion from school. In some disadvantaged areas up to 50 per cent of children are starting school without adequate language and communication skills. This claim is also borne out by research from the charity I CAN (2010) which links this lack of development in speech, language and communications skills to subsequent social exclusion. Disadvantage in pre-school attainment is then perpetuated in primary school. Thus in England, 8 per cent of 11-year-olds leave primary school with reading and/or maths skills below those of the average 7-year-old. Sodha aptly describes the government's previous approaches to the Neet problem of concentrating resources on helping pupils with post-16 training and jobs as 'shutting the stable door after the horse has bolted'.

We have seen that another risk factor closely associated with being Neet is family socioeconomic circumstances. Using data from the Millenium Cohort Study, Goodman and Gregg (2010) show that educational deficits emerge early in children's lives and even by the age of three there is a considerable gap in the cognitive, social, and emotional development of children from different income groups.

The case for early intervention to prevent the apparent deficits in cognitive skills is made very convincingly by James Heckman.[3] His research on the economics of child development draws on both the theory of human capital and recent developments in neuroscience. In contrast to arguments based on equity, Heckman and Masterov (2007) build their case for early intervention to help disadvantaged children on a purely economic argument, resting on the claim that investing in this group of pre-school children leads to large private and social benefits. Skill formation is seen as a life-cycle process beginning in the womb (maternal health makes a difference to future child outcomes) and continuing into the workplace. In this view, the acquisition of skill is a dynamic, synergistic process: skills acquired in one stage of the life cycle influence the initial conditions and subsequent learning at the next stage of the life cycle. Since skill begets skill, early deficits in skill acquisition produce later disadvantages that are very costly to remedy. Heckman's research draws on evidence from a number of US studies of early intervention programmes targeted at disadvantaged children. He concludes that a cost–benefit analysis of these programmes gives rates of return of 16 per cent: 4 per cent for the participants and 12 per cent for the rest of society.

His work also views skill formation as being multidimensional: human capital is only one aspect of successful skill formation – and not necessarily the most important one. Families are viewed as the cornerstone of skill formation – schools have to work with what families give to them. Dysfunctional families (and his research attests to an increase in recent decades in those that fall into this category) produce children with deficiencies relating not just to ability, but also social deficits. Skills themselves are often viewed as one-dimensional, that is, cognitive, but work on the economics of child development emphasises that non-cognitive skills are equally important as determinants of future child outcomes. In the UK, work by Carneiro et al. (2007), using data from the National Child Development Survey, confirms Heckman's claim. The development of non-cognitive skills in early childhood is empirically important for a host of later outcomes, including whether an individual plays truant at school, stays on at school post-16, their subsequent employment and earnings history, and even their subsequent involvement in criminal activity.

Thus, based on the above research, there are huge potential gains from programmes which target resources on children in disadvantaged families. As suggested by Heckman, if your child participates in such a programme, the majority of the benefits accrue to society. Such positive externalities provide the classic case for government intervention to promote such programmes. Improving the early home and learning environments of disadvantaged children is a clear example of a policy which does not face an equity/efficiency trade-off. Such a policy also provides us with a potential answer to the question of 'Do we have a Neet solution?'.

Unfortunately, the UK lags behind most other European countries in terms of its investment in resources on pre-school children. OECD (2008) notes that the intention of the UK Government to extend early childhood education and care (ECEC) for 3–4-year-olds from the existing 12.5 hours per week to 20 hours per week by 2010 fell short of practice elsewhere, as does the number of nursery places available. Even this intention never reached fruition as the entitlement currently remains at 15 hours per week. For children aged 0–3, there is no entitlement to ECEC, although this is due to change under recent announcements in the 2010 Comprehensive Spending Review.

In the UK, early years services are principally provided under the auspices of Sure Start Children's Centres (SSCCs), which have been rolled out across the nation since 2006. These centres are modelled on programmes such as Head Start in the US and seek to provide an integrated range of services including early education, child care, health care and parenting support for families with children under five. Funding in 2010 was for SSCCs is £1.14 billion per year. This pales into insignificance compared to the annual estimated costs of the Neet problem. As noted by the House of Commons (2010), evidence on whether or not such expenditure is a cost-effective way of reaching disadvantaged families is difficult to assess, since there is no standardised data collected on a national basis. However, evidence from programmes such as Head Start (see OECD 2008) emphasise that the success of such programmes depends crucially on programme quality, linked specifically to the availability of adequate funding and well-trained specialist staff. The 2010 CSR announced that over the course of this parliament that funding for SSCCs was to be protected in cash terms. What this means, however, is a cut in real terms of approximately 9 per cent by 2014–15. Such a cut in funding can only jeopardise the long-term gains from early intervention.

If the government is serious about finding a Neet solution, this is one cut too many. Sodha and Margo's (2010) report on children's disengagement from education is aptly subtitled 'a generation of disengaged children is waiting in the wings ...'. Unfortunately, recent government policy pronouncements give us no reason to believe that the current generation of disadvantaged under-fives can expect a different fate from that of today's 16–24-year-old Neets.

To conclude, that standard neoclassical arguments that the Neet problem is caused by the introduction of the NMW or is the consequence of net immigration is not supported by the evidence. The Post Keynesian argument of the necessity of an increase in effective demand is a necessary, but not sufficient condition, for reducing the number of Neets. The problem lies mainly in the satisfactory early development of children. In other words, it reflects supply-side characteristics, but not the 'supply side' as in the neoclassical schema. To understand and hence reduce, if not solve, the problem requires a multidisciplinary approach to which Post Keynesians, with their pluralist outlook have much to contribute.

Notes

1. Neets are also more likely to have had difficult experiences such as exclusion from school and to have engaged in truancy in year 11. Persistent truants are seven times more likely to be Neet at age 16.
2. The annual cost is thus approximately £4.6 billion.
3. Heckman won the Nobel Prize for Economics in 2000.
4. All internet references accessed 26 October 2010.

References[4]

Acemoglu, D. and Pischke, J.S. (2003) 'Minimum wages and on-the-job training', *Research in Labor Economics*, 22, 159–202.

Arulampalam, W., Booth, A.L. and Bryan, M.L. (2004) 'Training and the New Minimum Wage', *Economic Journal*, 114(494), C87–C94.

Barham, C., Walling, A., Clancy, G., Hicks, S. & Conn, S. (2009) 'Young people and the labour market', *Economic & Labour Market Review*, 3(4), 17–29.

Becker, G.S. (1964) *Human Capital: A Theoretical and Empirical Analysis, with Special Reference to Education*, Chicago: University of Chicago Press.

Blanchflower, D., Saleheen, J. and Shadforth, C. (2007) 'The impact of the recent migration from Eastern Europe on the UK economy', https://www.bankofengland.co.uk/publications/speeches/2007/speech297.pdf.

Brown, C., Gilroy, C. and Cohen, A. (1982) 'The effect of minimum wages on employment and unemployment', *Journal of Economic Literature*, 20, 487–528.

Card, D. (1992) 'Do minimum wages reduce employment? A case study of California, 1987–1989', *Industrial and Labor Relations Review*, 46(1), 38–54.

Carneiro, P., Crawford, C., and Goodman, A. (2007) 'The impact of early cognitive and non-cognitive skills on later outcomes', CEE DP92, Centre for Economics of Education, University of London.

Casson, R. and Kingdon, G. (2007) 'Tackling low educational achievement', Joseph Rowntree Foundation, http://www.jrf.org.uk/sites/files/jrf/2063-education-schools-achievement.pdf.

CBI (2008) 'Towards a Neet solution: Tackling underachievement in young people', http://www.cbi.org.uk/pdf/CBI-NEET-Oct08.pdf.

Coles, B., Hutton, S., Bradshaw, J., Craig, G., Godfrey, C. and Johnson, J. (2002) 'Literature review on the costs resulting from social exclusion among young people aged 16–18', DfES Research Report, RR347.

DCFS (2004) '14–19 curriculum and qualifications reform. Final report of the Working Group on 14–19 reform'. http://www.dcsf.gov.uk/14-19/documents/Final%20Report%20Summary.pdf.

DCFS (2005) 'Young people not in education, employment or training: Evidence from the Education Maintenance Allowance Pilots Database', Research Report RB628, http://www.education.gov.uk/research/data/uploadfiles/RR628.pdf.

DCFS (2007) 'Reducing the number of young people not in education, employment or training (Neet)', http://www.dcsf.gov.uk/14-19/documents/neet_strategy_0803.pdf.

DCFS (2009) 'Investing in potential', http://www.dcsf.gov.uk/14-19/documents/8537-DCSF-Investing%20in%20Potential-WEB.pdf.

De Coulon, A., Meschi, E., Swaffield, J., Vignoles, A. and Wadsworth, J. (2010). 'Minimum wage and staying-on rates in education for teenagers'. Research report for the Low Pay Commission. January, Institute of Education, University of London; University of York; and Royal Holloway, University of London.

DfE (2010a) 'Neets quarterly brief', August http://www.dcsf.gov.uk/rsgateway/DB/STR/d000950/NEETQB2_2010.pdf.

DfE (2010b) 'It's not simply an academic question – Why we need radical reform of vocational education', http://education.gov.uk/inthenews/speeches/a0064364/michael-gove-to-the-edge-foundation.

Dickens, R. and Draca, M. (2005) 'The employment effects of the October 2003 increase in the National Minimum Wage', Research Report for the Low Pay Commission, Centre for Economic Policy, Discussion Paper No. 693.

Dustmann, C., Glitz, A. and Frattini, T. (2008) 'The labour market impact of immigration', *Oxford Review of Economic Policy*, 24(3), 478–95.

Ehrenberg, R.G. (1995) 'Myth and measurement: The new economics of the Minimum Wage', *Industrial and Labor Relations Review*, 48(4), 827–49.

Frayne, C. and Goodman, A. (2004) 'The impact of introducing a National Minimum Wage for 16 and 17 year olds on employment and education-outcomes', http://www.lowpay.gov.uk/lowpay/research/pdf/institute-fiscal-studies.pdf.

Gilpin, N., Henty, M., Lemos, S., Portes, J. and Bullen, C. (2006) 'The impact of the free movement of workers from Central and Eastern Europe on the UK labour market', Department of Work and Pensions Working Paper, No. 29.

Godfrey, C., Hutton, S., Bradshaw, J., Coles, B., Craig, G. and Johnson, J. (2002) 'Estimating the cost of being "Not in Education, Employment or Training" at age 16–18', DFES Research Report, RR346.

Goodman, A. and Gregg, P. (eds) (2010) 'Poorer children's educational attainment: How important are attitudes and behaviour?', http://www.jrf.org.uk/sites/files/jrf/poorer-children-education-full.pdf.

Gregg, P and Tominey, E. (2005) 'The wage scar from youth unemployment', *Labour Economics*, 12(4), 487–509.

Hatton, T.J. and Tani, M. (2005) 'Immigration and inter-regional mobility in the UK, 1982–2000', *The Economic Journal*, 115(507), F342–F358.

Heckman, J.J. and Masterov, D.V. (2007) 'The productivity argument for investing in young children', http://jenni.uchicago.edu/human-inequality/papers/Heckman_final_all_wp_2007-03-22c_jsb.pdf.

House of Commons (2010) 'Sure Start Children's Centres, Fifth Report of Session 2009–10', Children, Schools and Families Committee, Volume I, http://www.publications.parliament.uk/pa/cm200910/cmselect/cmchilsch/130/130i.pdf.

House of Lords (2008) 'The economic impact of immigration', vol.1 Report, and vol.2 Evidence. London: The Stationery Office Limited.

I CAN (2010) 'Language and social exclusion', Talk Series 4, Issue 4, http://www.ican.org.uk/en/sitecore/content/Home/DVDs%20and%20Books/ICTalk%204.aspx.

Katz, L.F. and Krueger, A. (1992) 'The effect of the Minimum Wage on the fast-food industry', *Industrial and Labor Relations Review*, 46(1), 6–21.

Lemos, S. and Portes, J. (2008) 'New Labour? The impact of migration from the new European Union Member States on the UK labour market', Department for Work and Pensions, Working Paper 52.

Low Pay Commission (2010) National Minimum Wage: Low Pay Commission 2010 Report, http://www.lowpay.gov.uk/lowpay/lowpay2010/commissioners.shtml.

Mansell, W. (2008) *Education By Numbers*, London: Politico/Methuen.

McNally, S. and Vaitilingam, R. (2010) 'Has labour delivered on the policy priorities of "Education, Education, Education"?', Centre for Economic Performance, LSE http://cep.lse.ac.uk/briefings/pa_education.pdf.

Myrdal, G. (1944) *An American Dilemma: The Negro Problem and Modern Democracy*, New York: Harper & Bros.

National Employer Skills Survey for England 2009: Key Findings Report (2010) UK Commission for Employment and Skills, http://www.ukces.org.uk/tags/report/national-employer-skills-survey-for-england-2009-key-findings-report.

Neumark, D. and Wascher, W.L. (2008) *Minimum Wages*, Cambridge, MA: MIT Press.

Nickell, S.J. (2003) 'Poverty and worklessness in Britain', http://eprints.lse.ac.uk/20038/1/Poverty_and_Worklessness_in_Britain.pdf.

OECD (2008) *Jobs for Youth: United Kingdom*, Paris: OECD.

OECD (2010) 'Rising unemployment during the crisis: How to prevent negative long-term consequences on a generation', OECD Social, Employment and Migration papers, No. 106. Paris: OECD.

Ofsted (2008) *Mathematics: Understanding the Score*. London: Ref. No. 070063.

Pacheco, G.A. and Cruickshank, A.A. (2007) 'Minimum wage effects on educational enrollments in New Zealand', *Economics of Education Review*, 26(5), 751–83.

Prince's Trust (2007) 'The cost of exclusion', http://www.princes-trust.org.uk/PDF/Princes%20Trust%20Research%20Cost%20of%20Exclusion%20apr07.pdf.

Rashid, S. and Brooks, G. (2010) 'The levels of attainment in literacy and numeracy of 13–19 year olds in England, 1948–2009', National Research and Development Centre for Adult Literacy and Numeracy, http://www.nrdc.org.uk/publications_details.asp?ID=181#.

Rennison, J., Maguire, S., Middleton, S. and Ashworth, K. (2005) 'Young people not in education, employment or training: Evidence from the Education Maintenance Allowance Pilots Database'. Nottingham: DfES Publications.

Sodha, S. and Margo, J. (2010) 'Ex curricula', *Demos,* http://www.demos.co.uk/publications/excurricula.

Steedman, H. (2005) 'Skills for All', *Centrepiece*, Winter, pp. 24–7.

Steedman, H. and West, J. (2003) 'Finding our way: Vocational education in England', CEP Occasional Paper CEPOP, 18. London: Centre for Economic Performance, London School of Economics.

Stewart, M. (2004) 'The impact of the introduction of the UK Minimum Wage on the employment probabilities of low-wage workers', *Journal of the European Economic Association*, 2(1), 67–97.

Youth Access (2009) 'The impact of recession on young people and on their needs for advice and counselling services', Policy Briefing, July, http://www.youthaccess.org.uk/resources/publicatio's/upload/The-impact-of-the-recession-on-young-people-and-on-their-needs-for-advice-and-counselling-services.pdf.

5
The Business of Macro Imbalances: Comparing 'Gluts' in Savings, Money and Profits

William Milberg and Lauren Schmitz

1 Introduction

The large imbalances in international payments that emerged in the 2000s are widely presumed to have contributed to the financial collapse and worldwide recession that began in 2008. Portes (2010, p. 40) states that the macro imbalances were 'the fundamental cause of the crisis'.[1] Even now, with the immediate threat of financial collapse behind us, there are prominent voices claiming that the return of global imbalances puts the international financial system at great risk of a new collapse. According to Cline and Williamson (2009), '[L]arge external imbalances can only aggravate not moderate, fragility in the financial system'.[2] The recent IMF effort to broker a USA–China agreement to reduce imbalances by targeted amounts over the next five years gives an indication of the perceived importance of such rebalancing.

Payments imbalances are understood as a reflection of imbalances in macroeconomic conditions, specifically between saving and investment. In one version of events, the current macro imbalances are the result of a 'savings glut', notably in China, but also in other East Asian and developing countries.[3] In another version, the problem has been excessively loose US monetary policy, resulting in extremely low interest rates and thus heightened borrowing and consumption by American households.[4] We refer to this version of events as the 'money glut' explanation.

In this chapter, we propose an alternative microeconomic explanation of the imbalances that focuses on the outsourcing strategies of firms and the contribution of outsourcing to, on the one hand, trade deficits, wage stagnation and rising corporate profits and, on the other hand, a rise in household borrowing and financial speculation. We call this the 'profits glut' explanation of the payments imbalances, since its fundamental feature is a rise in corporate profit rates (cost mark-ups) and the profit share, due to successful corporate strategies in the 2000s.

Key to our analysis is the view that the current account imbalance is not simply the passive inverse of the capital account imbalance but is driven by autonomous microeconomic forces, including firm strategies. Our focus is on lead-firm governance of global value chains, which have resulted directly in a steady increase in the US import share. Indirectly, these strategies have resulted in higher cost mark-ups, depressed labour demand in the US and a higher profit share. This heightened inequality has contributed to the current account deficit since stagnant real median wages over a long period in the USA created the need for American house-holds to borrow heavily in order to maintain consumption standards. Thus the 'profits glut' has contributed directly to deteriorating macroeconomic imbalances but was also a contributing cause of the crisis through the fall in median income and the subsequent rise in income at the top end.

This chapter connects macroeconomic change to forces at the level of specific firms and industries and is thus a tribute to Malcolm Sawyer. Over the decades Sawyer's research has spanned across industrial economics, Kaleckian theory, and Post Keynesian macroeconomics and thus his latest work in macroeconomics is imbued with a keen appreciation for the importance of also understanding industrial change.

The chapter contains six sections. Section 2 presents the basic data on the US and Chinese foreign balances. In section 3 we review the three glut theories. Section 4 delves into some sectoral and firm-level evidence on the relation between USA–China imports and profits. In section 5 we discuss some policy implications of the profits glut compared to the other glut explanations. Section 6 summarises and concludes.

2   The US and Chinese imbalances

The US trade deficit is not new, and in previous eras, like this one, the deficit has also been related to major economic changes. The trade deficit first emerged in the 1960s and the persistence of the deficit, and the associated run on the US dollar, was the immediate cause of the col-lapse of the Bretton Woods Agreement in 1975.[5] In the post-Bretton Woods era it was presumed that flexible exchange rates would facilitate current account adjustment. Nonetheless, the US trade deficit has been persistent and it began to grow significantly in the 2000s, reaching almost 6 per cent of GDP in 2006 (Figure 5.1). It improved in 2008 as imports collapsed more than exports, but has declined again in the first three quarters of 2010 to 3.8 per cent of GDP.

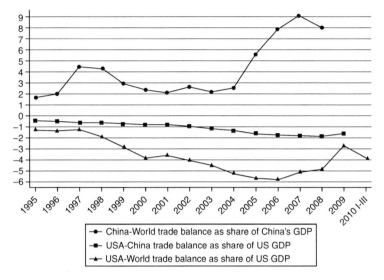

Figure 5.1   Trade balances as share of GDP for USA–World, USA–China, and China–World, 1995–2010 I–III
Source: Own illustration. Data: World Development Indicators, The World Bank, US Census Bureau, Foreign Trade Division, and Bureau of Economic Analysis, National Income and Product Accounts.

As the US trade deficit grew, other countries, first in Germany and Japan, then in China, developed substantial trade surpluses. Figure 5.1 shows the dramatic increase in China's trade surplus from 1.6 per cent of China's GDP in 1995 to 9 per cent of GDP in 2007. These surpluses facilitated the growing demand for capital imports from current account deficit countries, especially the USA. Recently, the current macroeconomic imbalances debate has focused on the US bilateral trade balance with China. The balance has deteriorated steadily since 1985 and the deterioration accelerated beginning in 2001. Since 1985, US imports from China rose from $3.86 billion to $296.4 billion in 2009, while exports rose from $3.85 billion to $69.5 billion, or from a position of near balanced trade to a deficit that approaches 2 per cent of US GDP (Figure 5.1).

The booming exports to the USA have generated a rapid accrual of foreign currency reserves in China and their subsequent investment in the USA. China's foreign reserves have quintupled since 2002, reaching $1.4 trillion by September of 2007. Accumulation of US Treasury securities rose from a stock of $59.5 billion in October of 2000 to $938.3 billion in October of 2009.[6] These foreign currency reserves, like those funds of the nonfinancial corporations in industrialized countries, must be invested with concern for return and risk. Thus one attraction of US assets for the Chinese is the safety of US Treasury securities. Another apparent goal of recycling surpluses into US capital markets has been to prop up the value of the dollar, which in turn sustains the competitiveness of Chinese exports.

3 Explaining persistent imbalance: a tale of three gluts

3.1 The savings glut

What are the causes of the enormous payments imbalance between the USA and China? There are two competing explanations. The first, made famous in a speech by Federal Reserve Chairman Ben Bernanke, is that a 'savings glut' in several rich countries with ageing populations and more recently in the developing world, particularly China, has translated into a massive excess of saving over investment, and resulting current account surpluses according to the standard macroeconomic identity:

$$GNP = C + I + G + CA = C + S + T \tag{1}$$

where GNP is gross national product, I is private investment, C is private consumption, G is government spending, T is government tax revenue, S is private saving, and CA is the current account balance.
Rearranging gives:

$$CA = (S - I) + (T - G) \tag{2}$$

This is the standard representation of the identity that the current account is the sum of private and public saving minus spending. Figure 5.2 shows gross national savings and domestic investment rates in the USA and China. The current account surplus in China rose to historic highs as savings skyrocketed over investment after 2004, while the US current account deficit expanded as national savings fell to historic lows relative to investment rates over the past decade.

Lim (2010) surveys the literature on high savings rates in East Asia and points to four main factors. One is demographics, in particular the decline in fertility rates as the working age population has grown leading to a low dependency ratio and high household savings. Second, and related to the first, is high precautionary savings for retirement income, health care and children's education, since social provision

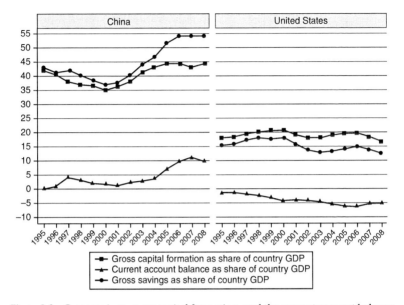

Figure 5.2 Gross savings, gross capital formation, and the current account balance as share of GDP in China and the United States, 1995–2008
Source: Own illustration. Data: World Development Indicators, The World Bank, National Income and Product Accounts, Bureau of Economic Analysis.

of these is limited. Third is the high cost of housing, which promotes saving. Fourth is an inefficient financial sector with low rates of return that require high levels of saving if income of savings is to support, say, retirement.

A curious feature of this list of determinants of the high savings rate in East Asia is that they would seem to be relatively insensitive to changes in the exchange rate, which has been the focus of the policy debate around rebalancing. This raises the idea of altering US saving behaviour instead of that in China. While the savings glut hypothesis places the blame for the imbalances on the East Asians, and especially the Chinese, the view that the blame lies in the extremely low levels of saving in the USA is closely related since it is based on the same identity given in (2) but from the perspective of the USA. It is difficult, in fact, to determine which of these positions is correct, since the identity given in (2) provides no insight into the direction of causality. Since government expenditure and revenue is sometimes considered driven more by exogenous forces than S and I, identity (2) also supports the 'twin deficits' view of the US current account deficit, whereby a fall in (T-G) translates directly into a deterioration of the CA. Chinn and Ito (2008), strong proponents of the twin deficits view, find that across industrial countries, a 10 per cent deterioration in the fiscal balance is associated with a worsening current account deficit (as a share of GDP) of between 1 and 4.9 per cent. The authors conclude that fiscal factors might be as important as excess savings arising from East Asia in explaining global imbalances (Chinn and Ito, 2007, p. 479).

The problem with the twin deficits argument in the case of the USA is that it is not supported by the facts. In the post-Bretton Woods period the two deficits often move in opposite directions. Most stark is that over the period 1992–2000 the fiscal stance moved from a 6 per cent deficit to a 2 per cent surplus while the trade balance worsened from a 1 per cent to 4 per cent deficit as a share of GDP. During the 2000s, and prior to the economic crisis of 2008, the deficits did move together, however as is clear in Figure 5.2 above, the current account decline in this period is part of a long-term deterioration. Blecker (1992, 2009) has argued that the weakness of the twin deficits argument is due to its presumption that changes in (T-G) have no effect on S and I and thus are fully translated into changes in the current account. If this *ceteris paribus* presumption does not hold, then changes in the fiscal position can have little effect on the current account.

3.2   The money glut

A second, if less popular, explanation is that the imbalances are the result of excessively loose monetary policy leading to what we refer to as a 'money glut'. In this view, the Federal Reserve ran excessively loose monetary policy that led to very low interest rates, which in turn encouraged consumers in the USA to borrow and spend, both domestically and abroad. Low interest rates are said to reduce the rate of saving, leading to an increase debt (domestic and foreign) and deterioration in the current account. More specifically, the low rates are attributed with driving up real estate prices, which then, through a wealth effect, raise consumption and imports. According to Aizenman (2010), there was a ripple effect of the low rates in the private and public sectors. He writes, 'Had the US been in financial autarky, the real interest rate during the 2000s would have been higher, mitigating the increase in real estate valuation, and forcing a combination of higher private saving, lower investment, and fiscal adjustment' (p. 27). Aizenman (op. cit., p. 29) argues further that low real rates contribute to the persistence of global imbalances for an additional reason – they give a false sense that deficits can be financed at low cost and that associated fiscal imbalances can be sustained. A second dimension of the money glut argument is that low rates and the associated high asset prices encourage a quest for higher-return assets. In this sense, the low rates led to an undervaluation of risk (Portes, 2010, p. 41).

Taylor (2007) also traces the 'money glut' process as largely working through the housing market. Low rates drove up demand for housing and increased not only housing prices, but also the expectation of future increases in housing prices. Taylor continues that,

> With housing prices rising rapidly, delinquency and foreclosure rates on subprime mortgages also fell, which led to more favorable credit ratings than could ultimately be sustained. As the short-term interest rate returned to normal levels, housing demand rapidly fell, bringing down both construction and housing price inflation. Delinquency and foreclosure rates then rose sharply, ultimately leading to the meltdown in the subprime market and on all securities that were derivative from the subprimes. (p. 465)

The traditional view of the money glut is captured in Figure 5.3. A shift in money supply is associated with a lower equilibrium exchange rate that translates into a current account deterioration at lower levels of saving and higher levels of investment.

The money glut hypothesis is supported by those at both ends of the political spectrum. John Taylor is an orthodox monetary economist, who served as economic advisor to President Bush in the 2000s. From

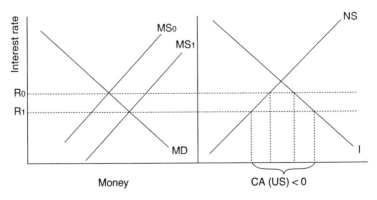

Figure 5.3 The 'money glut' with interest-sensitive saving and investment
Source: Own illustration.

a Marxian perspective, Lapavitsas (2009) writes that, 'Loose monetary policy in the early 2000s compounded both domestic macroeconomic imbalances in the USA and global imbalances' (p. 1). That is, low US rates fed into excessive borrowing and encouragement of investment in more risky assets, contributing to both the degree of financial fragility and the capital account surplus and current account deficit.

3.3 The profits glut

Here we offer an alternative explanation of the imbalances, which we call the 'profits glut' because it is motivated by the successful drive for profits growth by US and Chinese corporations. The premise of the profits glut hypothesis is that the current account deficit has an autonomous dimension, independent of the capital account and driven by the corporate strategies of individual firms and specifically by corporate offshore sourcing strategies. This hypothesis emphasises corporate strategy in the 1990s and 2000s with its focus on mass customisation, core competence, offshoring of production of parts and components and a reduced commitment to long-term employment relations and secure worker pensions. The profits glut hypothesis can be simply put: Expanded offshoring by US firms in China contributed directly to the trade deficit and to higher mark-ups over cost, and indirectly to the US imbalance through its contribution to wage stagnation in the USA through depressed demand for labour.

Economists generally presume that the capital account determines current account movements, but the transmission channel from one to the other is rather unclear. Presumably capital inflows lead to exchange rate appreciation that in turn drives a current account deterioration. Specifically, in the ongoing debate about whether the current account drives the capital account or vice versa, firm-level considerations (which are likely to be behind the current account) are typically considered subsidiary to macroeconomic forces. As Dorman (2007) writes,

> It is a serious mistake to conflate accounting identities and equilibrium relations. The equality between the current account and the surplus of net national savings over investment is strictly one of accounting and has no implications for equilibrium... The commonly encountered expression that capital account surpluses 'suck in' imports qualifies as mystification, since the availability of funds on the capital account does not drive trade flows... (p. 50)

Dorman notes that there are two types of transmission mechanisms from the macro to the micro in terms of global imbalances. One is through interest rates and exchange rates (Mundell–Fleming and portfolio-balance models) and the other through income (Thirlwall's model of balance of payments constrained growth). The problem with invoking the former is that exchange rates are notoriously unpredictable and thus any theory relying on a systematic relation between imbalances and exchange rates is likely to be empirically very weak. The problem with invoking the income-based model is that it considers the issue precisely in the opposite direction, which is to say that the imbalance leads to a particular constraint on the rate of growth, not the other way around.

Dorman (2007) and Blecker (1992, 2009) are among the few economists to have questioned the orthodox reasoning that the capital account drives the current account, insisting instead that international competitiveness has autonomous and firm-level elements. Blecker (2009), for example, includes 'the deterioration in U.S. competitiveness' among the various causes of the trade deficit, noting that, 'it is difficult for the U.S. to engineer a reduction in its overall trade imbalance while the manufacturing sector has been restructured in ways that make it more dependent on imports' (p. 3). This view departs clearly from the orthodoxy, according to which the S–I imbalance determines the size of the current account deficit and comparative advantage determines the commodity composition of trade. In the 1990s, Paul Krugman (1994) attacked the notion of international competitiveness (as opposed to comparative advantage) as a 'dangerous obsession'. Nonetheless, Blecker, Dorman and a few others have maintained the heretical view, often drawing on the Schumpeterian tradition, in which technology gaps are persistent and innovation is more important than price competition in international trade.[7]

The profits glut hypothesis goes one step further in the treatment of competitiveness (and profits), since we link them to imports rather than exports. In the neoclassical (Heckscher–Ohlin) trade model, capital-abundant countries would be expected to experience a rise in the profit rate with trade liberalisation and an expansion of exports and imports. Similarly, in the tradition of both Keynes and Kalecki, profits are expected to rise with exports, not with imports, as we are claiming here. In Kalecki's balance sheet relationship equating national income and expenditure:

$$P + W + T = C_k + C_w + I + G + (X - M), \qquad (3)$$

where P = Profits, W = Wages, T = Tax revenue, C_k = Capitalists consumption, C_w = Workers consumption, and the rest is as specified above.

Blecker (1999) derives the profit multiplier, which shows the effect of an improved balance of trade on profits, as follows:

$$\Delta P = \frac{1}{1 - C_r} \ \Delta (X - M), \tag{4}$$

where C_r is capitalists' propensity to consume out of profits. The intuition behind (4) is that an increase in exports implies a rise in sales and an increase in profits. We can broaden the Kaleckian analysis, however, to capture the distinction between different types of imports. Kalecki wrote in the 1930s about an economy like the UK where imports were heavily oriented towards primary commodities and exports were largely manufacturers and services. Competitive imports will lower both profits and wages in domestic competing firms. Non-competitive imported inputs would depress wages or employment, while boosting profit rates and the profit share.

The implication is that when imports are not competitive imports (that is, they do not compete with a domestic producer), then the trade deficit can have a different impact on profits and the profit share than envisioned in the Kaleckian framework. A mechanical way to think about this is that if imports do not constitute competition with domestic producers then such imports do not lower industrial concentration ratios. Cowling et al. (2000) do precisely this calculation for the case of the UK motor vehicles sector (that is, cars, vans, trucks and buses). Traditional measures of concentration show a steady decline in concentration beginning in the mid-1970s through 1995. When they recalculate the concentration figures to account for non-competitive imports (by adding a certain percentage of the imports to the sales of the top five firms) they find that concentration ratios in all product categories returned in the 1980s and 1990s almost to the levels of the early 1970s.

> UK imports of manufactures should not be construed as independent of the domestic structure of production... Previous measures of concentration, which have adjusted domestic concentration ratios for imports, have been made, for the most part, under the assumption that all imports are competitive. In a world of transnationally organized production and trade, where dominant domestic producers may act to control imports strategically, this can no longer be considered an acceptable working assumption. (Cowling et al. 2000, pp. 47, 52)

There is a growing body of research on the issue of the impact of offshoring on profits, with estimates of the cost reduction ranging between 20 and 40 per cent. The evidence is not unambiguous. Milberg and Winkler (2010b) show that the effects vary by country and in particular depending on the labour market institutions in place. Görg and Hanley (2004), using a sample of 12 Irish electronics manufacturers, find that firm-level profits are directly related to offshoring for large firms (in employment terms) and not significantly related for the small firms in the sample. In a study of small and medium-sized Japanese firms, Kimura (2002) found no relation between subcontracting and profitability. In a study of German manufacturing firms, Görzig and Stephan (2002) found offshoring of materials to be associated with higher profits but offshoring of services to be associated with lower profits.

The motives for firm offshoring range from the pursuit of greater flexibility to diversification of location in order to reduce risk to the lowering of production costs. All of these goals support company profitability. Over the past 20 years US corporate profits have risen and the profit share of national income has reached a 40-year high. At the same time, US corporations faced price competition in product markets and thus slow-rising product prices at home. To maintain cost mark-ups and profits, firms shifted their corporate strategy to control of costs, in part by expanding their global production networks. Such offshoring accounts for up to 27 per cent of goods input purchases in some US industries, 50 per cent or more of US imports, and provides reported cost savings of 20 to 60 per cent.

Figure 5.4 shows US corporate profits for the period 1995–2009. The acceleration is marked in the pre-crisis 2000s. Figure 5.5 shows the US corporate profit share (measured by corporate profits as a percentage of gross corporate value added), imports from low-income countries, and investment as a share of GDP for the period 1970–2006/07, along with import trends discussed above. After falling from post-Second World War highs in the mid-1960s, the profit share recovered from the mid-1990s. It has been higher during the last two business cycles than at any time since the 1960s. Imports from low-income countries – a broad measure of offshoring – has also risen steadily from the mid-1980s onwards. Investment as a share of GDP has shown a declining trend around expected cyclical movements.

If we break saving and investment into household and corporate saving and investment, then (2) can be rewritten as follows:

$$CA = (S_h - I_h) + (S_b - I_b) + (T - G) \qquad (5)$$

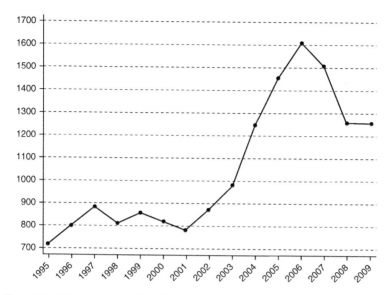

Figure 5.4 US corporate profits with inventory valuation and capital consumption adjustments, 1995–2009 (billions of USD)
Source: Own illustration. Data: US Bureau of Economic Analysis, National Income and Product Accounts, Tables 6.16 C & D.

Where the subscript *h* refers to the household sector and *b* to the business sector. In this formulation, the rise in corporate savings, or profits, is associated with an improvement in the current account balance. However, if, as we have seen, the rise in corporate profits is also associated directly with more imports and, indirectly, with lower household savings, then the positive relation between profits and the current account breaks down.

In regression analysis for the 29 US sectors over the period 1998–2006, Milberg and Winkler (2010a) find that offshoring is negatively and significantly related to the labour share of national income. Mahoney et al. (2007) find a similar relation in an econometric study of US services.

The profits glut explanation of macro imbalances is depicted in Figure 5.6. Key is that the heightened offshoring is part of an array of corporate practices, including a narrowing of focus on core competence, a retreat from human resource practices of long-term employment and defined benefit pensions. Lazonick (2010) refers to this as the 'new economy business model'. He emphasises how the model is also linked to greater pressure for short-term stock price performance, or 'shareholder value maximisation'. This has brought a wave of financialisation of

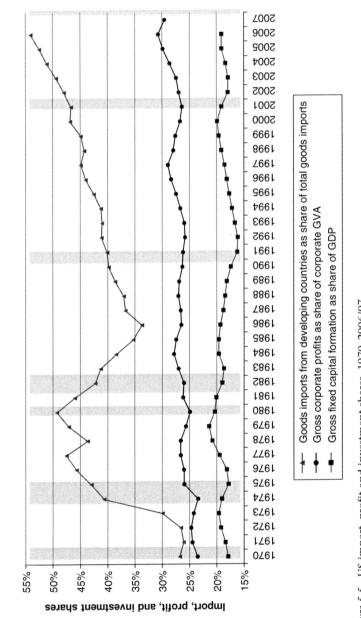

Figure 5.5 US import, profit and investment shares, 1970–2006/07

Source: Milberg and Winkler (2010a). Data: US Bureau of Economic Analysis, National Income and Product Accounts; UNCTAD *Handbook of Statistics.*
NB: Gross profits are calculated by adding net operating surplus and consumption of fixed capital. Their sum is divided by gross value added. Grey bars correspond to US business cycles recessions according to the definition of the NBER.

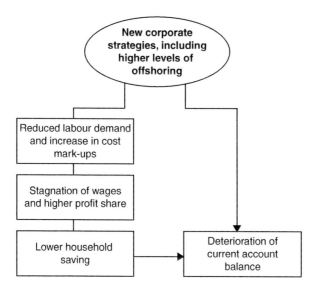

Figure 5.6   The 'profits glut'
Source: Own illustration.

non-financial corporations, especially through the use of share repurchases aimed at reducing the supply of outstanding shares in order to raise the price per share.

4   Profits and the macro imbalance: sectoral and firm-level analysis

4.1   Business savings and the balance of trade

There is unfortunately very little available firm-level data on international trade. Bernard et al. (2007) have analyzed firms in trade using the LFTTD database, but there is extremely restricted access and we were unable to use it for this project. One result from Bernard et al. (2007) is that only a very small share of US firms are involved in export, and a high percentage of the firms that export are also involved in importing. This implies that the standard notion that exports are the source of profits (derivable both within a neoclassical Heckscher–Ohlin framework and an open economy Kaleckian framework) may be supported in the data by a spurious correlation since imports too would be correlated with profits.

A few recent studies of individual firms support our argument. A close analysis of Apple's 2005 30 GB fifth-generation video iPod shows that of the $299 retail price, the cost of inputs is $144.60. Apple's profit on the item is realized in its worldwide sales. Its ability to import the fully assembled item from China results in a much lower cost and thus higher mark-up than if the assembly were handled in the USA. Imports contribute to profitability, especially in a monopoly or oligopoly product market since cost savings are not passed through fully to consumers. Note also that since China assembles the iPod using mostly imported components (from companies headquartered in Japan, the USA, Taiwan and Korea who themselves do some offshore production in China, Singapore and Taiwan), the export and import data do not accurately capture the national identity of the problem in any specific case.[8]

A second example is Wal-Mart, which alone imported $27 billion in goods from China in 2006 and was responsible for 11 per cent of the growth in the USA–China trade deficit between 2001 and 2006 (Scott, 2007, p. 1). Wal-Mart's profits in 2006 were $11.23 billion – a 78.4 per cent increase in profits compared to 2001.[9] Wal-Mart undertook $62 billion in dividends and share buybacks in 2006, equivalent to 74 per cent of its net income.[10] Wal-Mart's reliance on low-cost imports and low pay standards (for example, health insurance benefits) for its domestic (US) workforce has become one of the lightning rods for attacks on the new economy business model.

IBM provides a third example of successful globalization with a high foreign content to their production. As they have shifted over from being a manufacturer of mainframe and then personal computers to being an IT services provider, they have shifted operations increasingly overseas and have changed their employment practices in the USA. IBM's profitability has grown as its foreign employment as a share of its total employment has increased.

4.2   Profits and USA–China trade at the sector level

To address the issue of business saving and the balance of trade more systematically, we look at sectoral data. Table 5.1 shows the 2008 USA–China trade balance by commodity, along with the profit share (gross operating surplus as a share of value added) for the related industry, and the growth in the share of imports in gross sector output in each industry. Data are for three-digit NAICS sectors and their growth rates are over the period 2002–08. The top importing industries in 2008 were in the Computer and Electronic Product Manufacturing subsector, which reported a trade deficit with China of more than $94 billion, profit share growth of 43 percent, and import share growth of 20 per cent. Other sectors with high deficits with China and relatively rapid growth in the

Table 5.1 USA–China average annual industry import share and profit share growth rates by NAICS commodities, 2002–2008

Commodity by NAICS Sector	2008 Trade Balance (US-China)	Profit Share Growth	Import Share Growth (US-China)
334 Computer & Electronic Products	−$94,110,552,099	42.57%	20.19%
339 Miscellaneous Manufactured Commodities	−$37,884,745,023	2.02%	7.44%
315 Apparel & Accessories	−$26,132,657,713	−2.72%	26.06%
335 Electrical Equipment, Appliances & Components	−$21,541,908,062	2.44%	11.00%
316 Leather & Allied Products	−$20,394,304,346	−2.72%	13.85%
337 Furniture & Fixtures	−$14,582,743,545	−0.90%	13.71%
332 Fabricated Metal Products, Nesoi	−$13,540,365,762	2.36%	14.01%
326 Plastics & Rubber Products	−$9,270,337,303	0.69%	16.38%
333 Machinery, Except Electrical	−$9,205,091,226	4.07%	14.47%
331 Primary Metal Mfg	−$7,600,007,475	12.02%	42.97%
314 Textile Mill Products	−$7,257,486,494	24.84%	25.84%
327 Nonmetallic Mineral Products	−$4,579,563,446	−3.79%	7.87%
325 Chemicals	−$3,474,390,339	1.30%	28.63%
321 Wood Products	−$2,537,106,912	−0.42%	16.22%
323 Printed Matter And Related Products, Nesoi	−$2,135,069,189	−0.65%	16.12%
336 Transportation Equipment	−$1,844,897,123	−1.33%	22.17%
322 Paper	−$1,443,274,645	3.64%	19.68%
114 Fish, Fresh/Chilled/frozen & Other Marine Products	−$1,287,144,871	−2.21%	13.26%
313 Textiles & Fabrics	−$923,348,258	24.84%	24.41%
211 Oil & Gas	−$498,041,607	1.97%	27.10%
311 Food & Kindred Products	−$368,457,332	−1.48%	20.42%
312 Beverage & Tobacco Products	$848,045	−1.48%	−2.78%
511 Newspapers, Books & Other Published Matter, Nesoi	$22,789,373	−0.64%	−3.45%

(*continued*)

Table 5.1 Continued

Commodity by NAICS Sector	2008 Trade Balance (US-China)	Profit Share Growth	Import Share Growth (US-China)
324 Petroleum & Coal Products	$102,356,265	5.55%	0.28%
112 Livestock & Livestock Products	$117,368,051	1.15%	10.65%
113 Forestry Products, Nesoi	$135,062,485	-2.21%	9.47%
212 Minerals & Ores	$538,817,745	2.34%	4.30%
111 Agricultural Products	$8,788,536,815	1.15%	8.89%

Source: Own calculation. Data: U.S. Bureau of the Census: Foreign Trade Division, USA Trade Online and Industry Product Accounts, Bureau of Economic Analysis. Table is ranked by the 2008 US-China trade balance. Import share growth is average growth of the US-China NAICS commodity import value as a share of gross industry output from 2002–2008. Profit share growth is average growth of the gross operating surplus as a share of industry value added from 2002–2008.

profit share were Miscellaneous Manufactured Commodities, Primary Metal Manufacturing, Textile Mill Products, and the Textile & Fabric subsector. Interestingly, retail industry suppliers, including the Apparel & Accessories, Leather & Allied Products, and Furniture & Fixtures subsectors, are characterised by high trade deficit and import share growth, but negative profit share growth, indicating that profits in these manufacturing subsectors are possibly being passed through to larger retail firms.

Table 5.2 shows the Kendall rank-correlation coefficients in each NAICS subsector for the year-to-year industry profit share and the corresponding sector's share of imports as a percentage of their gross output from China, both over the period 2002–08.[11] Certain subsectors with a high Chinese trade deficit exhibit strong positive and significant correlations, including Computer and Electronics (0.81), Miscellaneous Manufactured Commodities (0.71), Fabricated Metal Products (0.71) and the Machinery, Except Electrical (0.71) subsector. Two sectors show a significant negative correlation (Petroleum & Coal Products and Forestry Products) and both are sectors in which imports are raw materials as opposed to manufacturers.

5 The politics of macro imbalances

What are the policy implications of our analysis? Most of the policy debate – from both the left and the right – has been about the overvaluation of the renminbi vis-à-vis the dollar. This is the most direct response to the problem only if the interpretation of the imbalance is that of micro to macro, with the current account driving the capital account. However, as we have seen, of the three different 'glut' explanations, only the profits glut adopts this as the direction of causality. Blecker (2009), to his credit, emphasises dollar devaluation as an important part of the solution to what he calls the US 'deficit trap'. Some US politicians have also called for tariffs against Chinese imports, which of course would also be a very direct response on the current account side. The savings glut theory would seem to support the Keynesian position that an increase in China should increase domestic consumption and recycle the surplus with a greater domestic and import demand. Alternatively, it implies that the USA should raise its rate of saving relative to the rate of investment. McKinnon (2010) is consistent in this regard, writing that, 'One cannot presume that US net saving will rise when the dollar is devalued' (p. 82). The money glut view would indicate that the USA should have avoided the loose monetary policy that kept interest rates too low.

Table 5.2   Kendall tau-b rank-correlation coefficients for the NAICS industry profit share and the US-China NAICS commodity import share, 2002–2008

Commodity by NAICS Sector	Correlation Coefficient
111 Agricultural Products	−0.14
112 Livestock & Livestock Products	0.43
113 Forestry Products, Nesoi	−0.71**
114 Fish, Fresh/Chilled/frozen & Other Marine Products	−0.62*
211 Oil & Gas	0.33
212 Minerals & Ores	0.43
311 Food & Kindred Products	−0.24
312 Beverage & Tobacco Products	0.05
313 Textiles & Fabrics	−0.05
314 Textile Mill Products	−0.05
315 Apparel & Accessories	−0.24
316 Leather & Allied Products	−0.24
321 Wood Products	−0.43
322 Paper	0.71**
323 Printed Matter And Related Products, Nesoi	0.24
324 Petroleum & Coal Products	−0.81**
325 Chemicals	0.52
326 Plastics & Rubber Products	0.05
327 Nonmetallic Mineral Products	−0.52
331 Primary Metal Mfg	0.62*
332 Fabricated Metal Products, Nesoi	0.71**
333 Machinery, Except Electrical	0.71**
334 Computer & Electronic Products	0.81**
335 Electrical Equipment, Appliances & Components	0.05
336 Transportation Equipment	−0.05
337 Furniture & Fixtures	−0.05
339 Miscellaneous Manufactured Commodities	0.71**
511 Newspapers, Books & Other Published Matter, Nesoi	0.33

Observations per industry = 7
P-values: p*<0.1, p**<0.05.

Source: Own calculation. Data: U.S. Bureau of the Census: Foreign Trade Division, USA Trade Online and Industry Product Accounts, Bureau of Economic Analysis. Table is ranked by NAICS sector. Industry profit share is gross operating surplus as a share of industry value added. Import share is the value of US-China NAICS commodity imports in each industry as a share of gross output.

The profits glut hypothesis may explain why renminbi revaluation has not been pushed more forcefully by the US government over the course of the past two administrations. If imports are important for profitability in important sectors, then the establishment of a strong dollar is in the national interest. The rise of offshoring and the emergence of sophisticated global production networks led by US transnational corporations have consequently altered the political dynamics of international trade. Traditionally, management and labour unions came to Washington as a team, lobbying for trade protection. Today, free trade and a strong currency is more beneficial to profits than it is to wage income, and so management increasingly supports trade liberalisation and a strong dollar, leaving labour unions alone seeking protection, or the blockage of free trade agreements with developing countries, or dollar depreciation.

Mancur Olson's *The Logic of Collective Action* provides a useful framework for explaining this shift in political economy. He writes, 'Unless the number of individuals in a group is quite small... *rational, self-interested individuals will not act to achieve their common or group interests*' (1965, p. 2; emphasis in original). Typically, this argument is seen as the reason that labour unions argue for trade protection and consumers who benefit from the lower prices that free trade brings were too diffuse a group to organise on behalf of trade liberalisation. Today, the calculus is reversed. Profits accrue to a relatively small part of the population – increasingly small, if the trends in US income distribution are an indication, and the losses to labour income from the strong dollar are diffused across the rest of the economy. Or, 'Where small groups with common interests are concerned, then, there is a systematic tendency for 'exploitation' of the great by the small!' (Olson, 1965, p. 29).

6 Summary and conclusions

When asked in a 1989 interview if he would 'like to be remembered as the accountant of the economics profession' Sir John Hicks replied, 'I would not mind in the least. No I would not.'[12] There is a lot to be said for accounting foundations of economics, especially in contrast with the anachronistic behavioural assumptions rooted in the eighteenth-century utilitarianism that underpin most orthodox economics. But in the area of the global macroeconomic imbalances that have received enormous attention from economic policy makers over the past five years, accounting is helpful but not decisive in the analysis of the causes and solutions. The problem is that endogeneity is rampant, and therefore causality is extremely hard to decipher. Writing precisely about the current global imbalances, Aizenman (2010) remarks, 'Causal associations in macroeconomics are conjectural, at best' (p. 27).

We have presented three alternative explanations of the global imbalances, each of which identifies a different exogenous factor in the determination of the immutable accounting identity shown in (2).

Given the conjectural nature of the causation involved in producing the macro imbalances, the overwhelming support by economists for the savings glut and the money glut theories is troubling. We have proposed in this short chapter that it is equally plausible that issues of firm competitiveness, and corporate strategies more generally, may directly be driving the current account imbalances, which in turn require capital imbalances for financing. We have focused on corporate offshoring strategies, which have raised firm mark-ups, depressed labour demand and wages, and contributed to a rising profit share in the USA.

The profits glut hypothesis is as consistent with (2) as any of the other theories. The profits glut view also contributes to the growing support for the view – recently offered in popular writings by Madrick (2010) and Reich (2010) – that the unsustainably high levels of household borrowing are the result of the long-term increase in income inequality experienced in the USA and elsewhere. As Papanikolou and Madrick (2010) point out, the real issue is not inequality per se but the long-term stagnation of real wages. American households borrowed in order to maintain increases in consumption during a period when real wages were stagnant, while high-income households supported the speculative activity of investment banks that led to the immediate crisis in financial markets. In light of this view, promotion of an institutional framework of regulation, social protection and state support may be as vital to ensuring the future stability of global imbalances as any other macro-level adjustment.

Notes

1. Also see Portes (2010), Obstfeld and Rogoff (2009), Horn et al. (2009).
2. Cited in Suominen (2010, p. 88).
3. Bernanke (2005, 2007).
4. Taylor (2007).
5. Block (1985) and Eichengreen (2006).
6. From the US Dept of Treasury: http://www.ustreas.gov/tic/mfhhis01.txt.
7. See Dosi et al. (1990).
8. Linden et al. (2007). See Ma and Van Assche (2010) for an analysis of China's 'process trade'.
9. From CNN Money.com: http://money.cnn.com/magazines/fortune/fortune 500/2006/snapshots/1551.html
10. Milberg (2008).
11. We use Kendall's coefficient both because we have relatively few observations per subsector and the data used are not normally distributed – the profit

share measures are right-skewed, while the import share has a large number of values around zero and is therefore also right-skewed. Unlike Spearman's coefficient, Kendall's coefficient is also robust to ties, allowing for identical industry profit shares between some of the subsectors.
12. Klamer (1989).

References

Aizenman, J. (2010) 'On the causes of global imbalances and their persistence: Myths, facts and conjectures', Chapter 3 in S. Claessens, S. Evenett and B. Hoekman (eds), *Rebalancing the Global Economy: A Primer for Policymaking*, London: CEPR and VoxEU.org.

Bernanke, B. (2005) 'The global saving glut and the U.S. current account deficit'. Speech delivered for the Sandridge Lecture at the Virginia Association of Economists, Richmond, 10 March. Available at www.federalreserve.gove/boarddocs/speeches/2005/200503102/default.htm.

Bernanke, B. (2007) 'Global imbalances: Recent developments and prospects', Bundesbank Lecture, Berlin, 11 September. Available at www.federalreserve.gov/newsevents/speech/berhanke20070911a.htm.

Bernard, A., Jensen, B., Redding, S., and Schott, P. (2007) 'Firms in international trade', *Journal of Economic Perspectives*, 21(3), 105–30.

Blecker, R. (1992) *Beyond the Twin Deficits*, Armonk, NY: M.E. Sharpe.

Blecker, R. (1999) 'Kaleckian models for the open economy', in J. Deprez and J. Harvey (eds), *Foundations of International Economics: Post Keynesian Perspectives*, London: Routledge.

Blecker, R. (2009) 'The trade deficit trap: How it got so big, why it persists and what to do about it', *EPI Working Paper*, No. 284, July.

Block, F. (1985) *The Origins of International Economic Disorder*, Berkeley: University of California Press.

Chinn, M. and H. Ito (2008) 'Global current account imbalances: American fiscal policy versus East Asian savings', *Review of International Economics*, 16(3), 479–98.

Claessens, S., Evenett, S., and Hoekman, B. (eds) (2010) *Rebalancing the Global Economy: A Primer for Policymaking*, London: CEPR and VoxEU.org.

Cline, W. and J. Williamson (2009) 'Equilibrium exchange rates', *VoxEU.org*, June 18.

Cowling, K., Yusof, F., and Vernon, G. (2000) 'Declining concentration in UK manufacturing? A problem of measurement', *International Review of Applied Economics*, 14(1), 45–54.

Dorman, P. (2007) 'Low savings or a high trade deficit? Which tail is wagging which?', *Challenge Magazine*, July–August, 49–64.

Dosi, G., Pavitt, K. and Soete, L. (1990) *Technology and International Competitiveness*, New York: NYU Press.

Eichengreen, B. (2006) *Global Imbalances and the Lessons of Bretton Woods*, Cambridge, MA: MIT Press.

Görg, H., and A. Hanley (2004) 'Does outsourcing increase profitability?', *The Economic and Social Review*, 35(3), 267–88.

Görzig, B., and A. Stephan (2002) 'Outsourcing and firm-level performance', *Discussion Paper No. 309*, Berlin: DIW.

Horn, G., Joebges, H., and Zwiener, R. (2009) 'From the financial crisis to the world economic crisis (II)', *IMK Report No. 40* (English Version), Dusseldorf: Macroeconomic Policy Institute (IMK).

Kimura, F. (2002) 'Subcontracting and the performance of small and medium firms in Japan', *Small Business Economics*, 18, 163–75.

Klamer, A. (1989) 'An accountant among economists: Conversations with Sir John R. Hicks', *Journal of Economic Perspectives*, 3(4), 167–80.

Krugman, P. (1994) 'Competitiveness: A dangerous obsession', *Foreign Affairs*, 73(2), 28–44.

Lapavitsas, C. (2009) 'The roots of the global financial crisis', SOAS/CDPR *Development Viewpoint*, No. 28, April.

Lazonick, W. (2010) *Sustainable Prosperity in the New Economy?*, Kalamazoo, MI: The Upjohn Institute.

Lim, L. (2010) 'Rebalancing in East Asia', Chapter 4 in S. Claessens, S. Evenett and B. Hoekman (eds), *Rebalancing the Global Economy: A Primer for Policymaking*, London: CEPR and VoxEU.org.

Linden, G., Kraemer, K. and Dedrick, J. (2007) 'Who captures value in a global innovation system? The case of Apple's iPod', *UC Irvine: Personal Computing Industry Center*. Available at http://www.escholarship.org/uci/item/1770046n.

Ma, A. and A. Van Assche (2010) 'The role of trade costs in global production networks: Evidence from China's processing trade regime', mimeo, University of San Diego.

Madrick, J. (2010) 'American incomes: soaring or static?', *The Nation*, 19 July.

Mahoney, M., Milberg, W., Schneider, M. and von Arnim, R. (2007) 'Dynamic gains from US services offshoring: A critical view', Chapter 5 in E. Paus (ed.), *Global Capitalism Unbound: Winners and Losers from Offshoring*, London: Palgrave Macmillan.

McKinnon, R. (2010) 'Why exchange rate changes will not correct global imbalances', Chapter 12 in S. Claessens, S. Evenett and B. Hoekman (eds), *Rebalancing the Global Economy: A Primer for Policymaking*, London: CEPR and VoxEU.org.

Milberg, W. (2008) 'Shifting sources and uses of profits: Sustaining US financialization with global value chains', *Economy and Society*, August 37(3), 420–51.

Milberg, W. and Winkler, D. (2010a) 'Financialization and the dynamics of offshoring', *Cambridge Journal of Economics*, 34(2), 275–93.

Milberg, W. and D. Winkler (2010b) 'Outsourcing economics', mimeo, the New School for Social Research, Department of Economics.

Milberg, W. and D. Winkler (2010c) 'Economic insecurity in the new wave of globalization: Offshoring and the labor share under varieties of capitalism', *International Review of Applied Economics*, 24(3), 285–308.

Obstfeld, M. and Rogoff, K. (2009) 'Global imbalances and the financial crisis', *Federal Reserve Bank of San Francisco Conference*, 18–20 October.

Olson, M. (1965) *The Logic of Collective Action*, New Haven: Yale University Press.

Papanikolou, N. and Madrick, J. (2010) 'The stagnation of male wages in the US', *International Review of Applied Economics*, 24(3), 264–75.

Portes, R. (2010) 'The cost of global imbalances', Chapter 5 in S. Claessens, S. Evenett and B. Hoekman (eds), *Rebalancing the Global Economy: A Primer for Policymaking*, London: CEPR and VoxEU.org.

Reich, R. (2010) *Aftershock: The Next Economy and America's Future*, New York: Alfred A. Knopf.

Scott, R. (2007) 'The Wal-Mart effect: Its Chinese imports have displaced nearly 200,000 jobs', *EPI Issue Brief*, No. 235, Washington, DC: The Economic Policy Institute.

Suominem, K. (2010) 'This time will be different? Addressing the unsound post-crisis drivers of global imbalances', Chapter 13 in S. Claessens, S. Evenett and B. Hoekman (eds), *Rebalancing the Global Economy: A Primer for Policymaking*, London: CEPR and VoxEU.org.

Taylor, J. (2007) 'Housing and monetary policy', *Housing, Housing Finance and Monetary Policy*, Symposium Sponsored by the Federal Reserve Bank of Kansas City, Jackson Hole, Wyoming, 30 August–1 September.

Part II
Macroeconomics

6
A Critical Appraisal of the New Consensus Macroeconomics

Philip Arestis

1 Introduction[1]

Malcolm Sawyer has been one of the earliest critics of what we now know as the New Consensus in Macroeconomics (NCM in short). It has been a great privilege to have had the opportunity to work with Malcolm Sawyer all these years, not merely on this aspect of macroeconomics, but also on many others. It is, therefore, a real pleasure to contribute to this particular volume and elaborate further on the vast amount of research that Malcolm Sawyer has successfully undertaken over the years (as, for example, in Sawyer, 2009; see, also, Arestis and Sawyer, 2003, 2004a, 2004b, 2006, 2008a, 2008b).

NCM has emerged over the recent past and has become highly influential in terms of current macroeconomic thinking. In addition, the policy implications of the NCM paradigm are particularly important for this aspect of macroeconomics.[2] Price stability can be achieved through monetary policy since inflation is a monetary phenomenon; as such it can only be controlled through changes in the rate of interest. Goodfriend (2007) argues that this particular proposition has been backed by actual monetary policy experience in many countries around the globe, following the abandonment of money supply rules in the early 1980s. Academic contributions also helped the foundations of the NCM on both theoretical and empirical grounds; for example, 'The Taylor Rule became the most common way to model monetary policy' (Goodfriend, 2007, p. 59; see, also, Orphanides, 2007).

The discussion and assessment of the NCM in this contribution is in the context of an open economy (see, also, Arestis, 2007b). In section 2, following this introduction, we consider the open economy aspect of the NCM, which enables some attention to be given to the exchange rate channel of the transmission mechanism of monetary policy in addition to the aggregate demand channel and the inflation expectations channel. In the context of this extended model of NCM its policy implications are examined in the same section. We critically appraise NCM and its policy implications in sections 3 and 4; finally, section 5 summarises and concludes.

2 An open economy New Consensus Macroeconomics and policy implications

We begin this section by discussing an open economy NCM model first, followed by its policy implications.

2.1 The open economy NCM model

Drawing on Arestis and Sawyer (2008a, 2008b) and Arestis (2007b, 2009; see also Angeriz and Arestis, 2007), we utilise the following six-equation model for this purpose.

$$Y^g_t = a_0 + a_1 Y^g_{t-1} + a_2 E_t(Y^g_{t+1}) + a_3[R_t - E_t(p_{t+1})] + a_4(rer)_t + s_1 \quad (1)$$

$$p_t = b_1 Y^g_t + b_2 p_{t-1} + b_3 E_t(p_{t+1}) + b_4[E_t(p_{wt+1}) - E_t\Delta(er)_t] + s_2 \quad (2)$$

$$R_t = (1 - c_3)[RR^\star + E_t(p_{t+1}) + c_1 Y^g_{t-1} + c_2(p_{t-1} - p^T)] + c_3 R_{t-1} + s_3 \quad (3)$$

$$(rer_t) = d_0 + d_1[[(R_t - E_t(p_{t+1})] - [(R_{wt}) - E(p_{wt+1})]] + d_2(CA)_t + d_3 E(rer)_{t+1} + s_4 \quad (4)$$

$$(CA)_t = e_0 + e_1(rer)_t + e_2 Y^g_t + e_3 Y^g_{wt} + s_5 \quad (5)$$

$$er_t = rer_t + P_{wt} - P_t \quad (6)$$

The symbols have the following meaning. a_0 is a constant that could reflect, inter alia, the fiscal policy stance, Y^g is the domestic output gap and Y^g_w is world output gap, R is nominal rate of interest (and R_w is the world nominal interest rate), p is rate of inflation (and p^w is the world inflation rate), p^T is inflation rate target, $RR^\star$ is the 'equilibrium' real rate of interest, that is the rate of interest consistent with zero output gap, which implies from equation (2) a constant rate of inflation; (rer) stands for the real exchange rate, and (er) for the nominal exchange rate, defined as in equation (6) and expressed as foreign currency units per domestic currency unit, P_w and P (both in logarithms) are world and domestic price levels respectively, CA is the current account of the balance of payments, and s_i (with $i = 1, 2, 3, 4, 5$) represents stochastic shocks, and E_t refers to expectations held at time t. The change in the nominal exchange rate, as it appears in equation (2), can be derived from equation (6) as in $\Delta er = \Delta rer + p_{wt} - p_t$.

Equation (1) is the aggregate demand equation with the current output gap (the difference between current out output and trend output) determined by past and expected future output gap, the real rate of interest and the real exchange rate (through effects of demand for exports and imports). Trend output prevails when prices are perfectly flexible without any cyclical distortions in place; it is, thus, a long-run variable, determined by the supply side of the economy. Equation (1) emanates from intertemporal optimisation of expected lifetime utility that reflects optimal consumption smoothing subject to a budget constraint (see, for example, Blanchard and Fischer, 1989, chap. 2).[3] The intertemporal utility optimisation is based on the assumption that all debts are ultimately paid in full, thereby removing all credit risk and default. This follows from the assumption of what is known technically as the transversality condition, which means in effect that all economic agents with their rational expectations are perfectly creditworthy. There is, thus, no need for a specific monetary asset. All fixed-interest financial assets are identical so that there is a single rate of interest in any period. There is, thus, no need for financial intermediaries (commercial banks or other non-bank financial intermediaries) and even money (see, also, Goodhart, 2007, 2008; Buiter, 2008).[4]

Equation (2) is a Phillips curve with inflation based on current output gap, past and future inflation, expected changes in the nominal exchange rate, and expected world prices (and the latter pointing towards imported inflation). The model allows for sticky prices, the lagged price level in this relationship, and full price flexibility in the long run. It is assumed that $b_2 + b_3 + b_4 = 1$ in equation (2), thereby implying a vertical Phillips curve. The assumption of a vertical long-run Phillips curve implies no voluntary unemployment. This is clearly not acceptable, as some contributors have pointed out (see, for example, Blanchard, 2008). The latter assumption implies no voluntary unemployment. This is clearly not acceptable, as some contributors have pointed out (see, for example, Blanchard, 2008). The way to introduce unemployment into the NCM model is still to be undertaken. The real exchange rate affects the demand for imports and exports, and thereby the level of demand and economic activity. The term $E_t (p_{t+1})$ in equation

(2) captures the forward-looking property of inflation. It actually implies that the success of a central bank in containing inflation depends not only on its current policy stance but also on what economic agents perceive that stance to be in the future. If a central bank can credibly signal its intention to achieve and maintain low levels of inflation, then expectations of inflation will be lowered and this term indicates that it may be possible to reduce current inflation at a significantly lower cost in terms of output than otherwise. In this way monetary policy operates through the expectations channel. The view that credibly anchoring inflation expectations, which produces a more favourable trade-off between inflation and economic activity, has been criticised as failing to explain persuasively why it is so important. It fails to demonstrate whether price setters change their decisions on the basis of what their expectations of inflation would be in the future (Blanchard, 2008, p. 21).

Equation (3) is a monetary-policy rule, where the nominal interest rate is based on expected inflation, output gap, deviation of inflation from target (or 'inflation gap'), and the 'equilibrium' real rate of interest. The lagged interest rate represents interest rate 'smoothing' undertaken by the monetary authorities. Equation (3), the operating rule, implies that 'policy' becomes a systematic adjustment to economic developments in a predictable manner. Inflation above the target leads to higher interest rates to contain inflation, whereas inflation below the target requires lower interest rates to stimulate the economy and increase inflation. In the tradition of Taylor rules (Taylor, 1993, 1999, 2001), the exchange rate is assumed to play no role in the setting of interest rates (except in so far as changes in the exchange rate have an effect on the rate of inflation which clearly would feed into the interest rate rule). This treatment of the exchange rate has been criticised (see, for example, Angeriz and Arestis 2007). The monetary policy rule in equation 3 embodies the notion of an equilibrium rate of interest, labelled as RR*. Woodford (2003) defines RR* as the 'equilibrium real rate of return when prices are fully flexible' (p. 248).

Equation (4) determines the exchange rate as a function of the real interest rate differentials, current account position, and expectations of future exchange rates (through domestic factors such as risk premiums, domestic public debt, the degree of credibility of the inflation target, and so on). Equation (5) determines the current account position as a function of the real exchange rate, domestic and world output gaps; and equation (6), which expresses the nominal exchange rate in terms of the real exchange rate. There are six equations and six unknowns:

output, interest rate, inflation, real exchange rate, current account, and nominal exchange rate defined as in (6). Exchange rate considerations are postulated (as in equation 3) not to play any direct role in the setting of interest rates by the central bank.

2.2 NCM policy implications

It is worth emphasising two key assumptions made in the context of the NCM model: the first is that price stability is the primary objective of monetary policy. However, the experience since the credit crunch of August 2007 does not seem to validate this claim. The second is that inflation is a monetary phenomenon and as such it can only be controlled by means of monetary policy, this being the rate of interest under the control of the central bank. This should be undertaken through interest rate manipulation. Monetary policy is thereby upgraded but at the same time fiscal policy is downgraded. This raises the issue of whether deflation is maniputable through changes in interest rates since the latter cannot fall below zero.

The major economic policy implication of the NCM is that monetary policy has been upgraded in the form of interest rate policy. This policy is undertaken through Inflation Targeting (IT). An important assumption that permits monetary policy to have the effect that it is assigned by the NCM, is the existence of temporary nominal rigidities in the form of sticky wages, prices and information, or some combination of these frictions. Accordingly, the central bank by manipulating the nominal rate of interest is able to influence real interest rates and hence real spending in the short run. A further important aspect of IT is the role of 'expected inflation' embedded in equation (3). The inflation target itself and the forecasts of the central bank are thought of as providing a strong steer to the perception of expected inflation. Given the lags in the transmission mechanism of the rate of interest to inflation, and the imperfect control of inflation, inflation forecasts become the intermediate target of monetary policy in this framework where the ultimate target is the actual inflation rate (Svensson, 1997, 1999). Under these circumstances, 'The central bank's forecast becomes an explicit intermediate target. Inflation targeting can then be viewed as a monetary policy framework under which policy decisions are guided by expected future inflation relative to an announced target' (Agénor, 2002, p. 151). Furthermore, the target and forecasts add an element of transparency seen as a paramount ingredient of IT. Consequently, inflation forecasting is a key element of IT. It is, indeed, argued that it represents a synthesis of simple monetary rules and discretionary monetary policy, and as such it constitutes an improvement over targeting monetary aggregates and weaker versions of IT (Woodford, 2007). This inflation-forecast IT, however, entails a serious problem, which is due to the large margins of error in forecasting inflation; this can damage the reputation and credibility of central banks.[5]

3 Assessing the NCM theoretical and policy framework

A number of arguments have emerged from previous assessment exercises of the NCM framework and of the IT policy as implemented in a number of countries. It is worth summarising the arguments that relate to this contribution. Low inflation and price stability do not always lead to macroeconomic stability (Angeriz and Arestis, 2007, 2008). Insufficient attention is paid to the exchange rate (Angeriz and Arestis, 2007). There is insufficient evidence for a long-run vertical Philips curve (Juselius, 2008). There is insufficient evidence that NAIRU is unaffected by aggregate demand and economic policy (Arestis et al., 2007) and by flexible labour markets (Arestis and Sawyer, 2007). Countries that do not pursue IT policies have done as well as the IT countries in terms of the impact of IT on inflation and locking-in inflation expectations at low levels of inflation (Angeriz and Arestis, 2007, 2008a). There is insufficient evidence either to downgrade fical policy (Angeriz and Arestis, 2009) or to show that the NCM propositions are validated by the available empirical evidence (Arestis and Sawyer, 2004b, 2008a). The IT policy framework can only pretend to tackle demand-pull inflation but not cost-push inflation (Arestis and Sawyer, 2008b). Malcolm Sawyer has contributed on the important link between changes in the rate of interest and the rate of change of prices (rather than the level of prices). In Sawyer (2009) it is concluded that such a link is weak on empirical grounds. A further conclusion of this contribution is that changes in the rate of interest do not have the assumed impact on inflation via the exchange rate, as in the NCM theoretical framework – see equations 1–6 above. Sawyer (2010) provides another indictment on the NCM policy framework in that the Phillips curve of equation (2) above lacks firm theoretical foundations. Yet this relationship has been tightly link to developments on central bank independence and inflation targeting.

Three further criticisms have been highlighted in Arestis (2009): the absence of banks and monetary aggregates in the NCM theoretical framework; the use of the equilibrium real rate of interest as in equation (3) above; and related aspects with monetary policy. There is also a serious critique in terms of the treatment of fiscal policy, which is completely downgraded. We devote a separate section on this important aspect after we have briefly discussed the three issues raised in Arestis (op. cit.).

As explained above, the NCM model is characterised by an interest-rate rule, where the money market and financial institutions are typically not mentioned, let alone modelled. The explicit non-appearance of nominal money in the model is justified on the assumption that the central bank allows the money stock to be what is necessary to achieve the desired real rate of interest. Money is thereby a residual (see Woodford, 2008, for a recent contribution). This downgrading of monetary aggregates in NCM models has gone too far even for non-monetarists (see, for example, Goodhart, 2007, 2008). It is also the case that in the NCM model there is no mention of banks in the analysis. It has been noted that in the major text of Woodford (2003) banks make no appearance in the index (Goodhart, 2004). But, then, banks and their decisions play a considerably significant role in the transmission mechanism of monetary policy. It is also the case that in the real world many economic agents are liquidity constrained. They do not have sufficient assets to sell or the ability to borrow. Their expenditures are limited to their current income and few assets, if any. Consequently, this perfect capital market assumption, which implies the absence of credit rationing (meaning that some individuals are credit constrained), means that the only effect of monetary policy would be a 'price effect' as the rate of interest is changed. At the end of the day Friedman (2003) is correct to argue that without 'integrating the credit markets into both the theoretical and the practical analysis of monetary policy is going to be harder' (p. 6).

We turn our attention next to the equilibrium real rate of interest, which plays a crucial role in the NCM. The discrepancy between actual and the equilibrium rate of interest has been termed the real interest rate gap and can be used to evaluate the stance of monetary policy. It is thereby a useful theoretical concept in the analysis of the relationship between the independence of monetary policy and economic fluctuations (Weber et al., 2008). In terms of the six equations above, and equation (3) in particular, it is clear that the equilibrium real rate of interest secures output at the supply equilibrium level (zero output gap) consistent with constant inflation. It is also the case that the use of RR* in NCM models with the emphasis on price stability provides an important benchmark for monetary policy analysis in the context of models with a single rate of interest, with no banks and no monetary aggregates. Under these assumptions, the reaction of the interest rate policy instrument to movements in RR* can ensure price stability.

Wicksell's (1898) natural rate of interest thesis, however, recognises the existence of different interest rates that can determine aggregate demand. For example, loan rates are important when bank credit is the main source of financing for firms. Under such circumstances where the rate of interest on bank loans differs from the policy rate of interest, RR* may not be a useful indicator for monetary policy. De Fiore and Tristani (2008) show that under such circumstances, and on the assumption of asymmetric information and of credit treated in nominal terms in an otherwise NCM model, RR* is heavily model dependent. It reacts differently to aggregate shocks depending on the underlying model assumptions. The crucial distinguishing assumption in this context is whether markets are frictionless or not. Indeed, in markets characterised by friction, a further implication is that monetary policy exerts real effects even in the long run. Consequently, 'it might be difficult for a central bank that is uncertain about the true model of the economy to identify its movements and to use it as regular indicator for the conduct of monetary policy' (p. 33).

Furthermore, the real equilibrium rate of interest should be readily computable from actual economic data. Such data should be available with sufficient precision and whenever the need arises. Weber et al. (2008) demonstrate persuasively that although the real rate of interest could play an important role in the conduct of current monetary policy there are serious problems with it. There is the problem with the interest rate gap that 'is not a sufficient *summary variable reflecting the overall pressure on inflation* in the sense that it captures all possible determinants of price changes' (p. 13). Cost-push shocks is a significant source to inflation and an important element of inflation information to monetary policy makers; but it 'is not mirrored by the natural rate of interest' (p. 13). Furthermore, the empirical estimates for RR* are extremely imprecise, so that the real equilibrium rate of interest 'is not readily computable from observable economic data' (p. 13). This problem is prevalent whichever method might be used for estimating the real equilibrium rate of interest. In Arestis and Chortareas (2008) a more theory-oriented approach is pursued, which attempts to quantify the US RR* as it emerges from a Dynamic Stochastic General Equilibrium (DSGE) framework. Here again a time-varying measure of the equilibrium real interest rate is arrived at; this rate responds to preferences and technology shocks and as such it is time varying. In view of the difficulties that relate to the real rate of interest as just discussed, two serious propositions emerge. The first is what follows from the Weber et al. (2008) analysis, namely 'the natural rate cannot be a surrogate for a detailed analysis of the real and monetary forces relevant to the identification of risks to price stability' (p. 13). The second problem is that in view of the problems identified in this section, a great deal of discretion should be applied in the conduct of monetary policy. But, then, the degree of discretion required might not be compatible with the IT theoretical principles.

Finally in this section we examine monetary policy issues. The NCM theoretical framework relies heavily on the 'efficient markets hypothesis' (EMH), which assumes that all unfettered markets clear continuously thereby making disequilibria, such as bubbles, highly unlikely. Indeed, economic policy designed to eliminate bubbles would lead to 'financial repression', a very bad outcome in this view. The experience with financial liberalisation is that it caused a number of deep financial crises and problems unparalleled in world financial history, culminating to the financial crisis of August 2007. The argument is then that such focus and outright acceptance of the EMH leads to serious mistakes in terms of monetary policy. Asset price targeting may be necessary after all (see Wadhwani, 2008 for a recent restatement). We would go further than merely targeting asset prices and agree with Arestis and Karakitsos (2009), who suggest that targeting net wealth of the personal sector, as a percentage of disposable income, is a more important monetary policy option.

Another serious omission by the NCM supporters is the role of what Keynes (1936) described as 'animal spirits'.[6] Keynes (op. cit.) refers to animal spirits in chapter 12. Addressing instability due to speculation, Keynes (op. cit.) also refers to

> the instability due to the characteristic of human nature that a large proportion of our positive activities depend on spontaneous optimism rather than on mathematical expectation, whether moral or hedonistic or economic. Most, probably, of our decisions to do something positive, the full consequences of which will be drawn out over many days to come, can only be taken as a result of animal spirits – of a spontaneous urge to action rather than inaction, and not as the outcome of a weighted average of quantitative benefits multiplied by quantitative probabilities. Enterprise only pretends to itself to be mainly actuated by the statements in its own prospectus, however candid and sincere... if the animal spirits are dimmed and the spontaneous optimism falters, leaving us to depend on nothing but a mathematical expectation, enterprise will fade and die. (pp. 161–2)

In the concluding paragraph of the same section as the quote just cited, Keynes (1936) goes on to explain that not everything 'depends on waves of irrational psychology' (p. 162). Far from it, for

> the state of long-term expectations is often steady, and, even when it is not, the other factors exert their compensation effects. We are merely reminding ourselves that human decisions affecting the future, whether personal or political or economic, cannot depend on strict mathematical expectation, since the basis for making such calculations does not exist; and that it is our innate urge to activity which makes the wheels go round, our rational selves choosing between the alternatives as best we are able, calculating where we can, but often falling back for our motive on whim or sentiment or chance. (pp. 162–3)

Failure to recognise the importance of 'animal spirits' in monetary policy can lead to wrong conclusions. For under such circumstances, monetary policy can become ineffective. Witness the experience since August 2007, over which period interest rates have been reduced substantially but have had a very feeble effect. In addition, the idea that recapitalising the banks should allow them to lend again has not worked. Once 'confidence' evaporates banks refuse to lend, however well capitalised they may happen to be. So much so that quantitative easing whereby the government guarantees assets acquired by the central bank may be necessary; but here again the reasons alluded to by Keynes (1936), quantitative easing may not work. Indeed, full-scale nationalisation of the banking sector should not be ruled out either.

4   Fiscal policy issues

Equation (1) is actually very revealing in terms of fiscal policy. There is no explicit mention of fiscal policy, although changes in the fiscal stance could be seen as reflected in a change in a_0. The normal argument is that the use of discretionary fiscal policy should be seen as the exception rather than the rule. The norm for fiscal policy should be to let automatic stabilisers to operate in an environment of balanced budgets over the business cycle, and the operation of those stabilisers may be reflected in the coefficients a_1 and a_2. Automatic stabilisers are

> those elements of the tax and spending regime which 'automatically' tend to stabilise the economy over the cycle. For example, during an

upswing, incomes will rise and tax receipts will increase tending to dampen the cycle. Similarly, in a downturn, unemployment benefit payments will rise tending to moderate the slowdown. (HM Treasury, 2003, p. 4)

A number of arguments have been put forward to make the case against the use of discretionary fiscal policy and of long-term budget deficits. The most important, and more widely accepted, are those of crowding out, the Ricardian Equivalence Theorem (RET) and what has been labelled as 'institutional aspects of fiscal policy' (Hemming, Kell and Mahfouz, 2002). The latter arguments can be briefly summarised. Model uncertainty, in that longer and more uncertain lags prevail than it was thought previously; there is the risk of pro-cyclical behaviour in view of cumbersome parliamentary approval and implementation; increasing taxes or decreasing government expenditure during upswings may be politically unrealistic, and this may very well generate a deficit bias; spending decisions may be subjected to irreversibility, which can lead to a public expenditure ratcheting effect; and there may be supply-side inefficiencies associated with tax-rate volatility.

The NCM approach combines the optimising general equilibrium framework with short-run nominal price stickiness. Fiscal policy can have demand implications if it affects the expectations of economic agents concerning their future income and wealth (demand-side effects). It could also have supply-side effects to the extent that it helps to enhance labour market efficiency and labour supply along with the competitiveness of the economy. The latter effects, in their turn, affect the non-accelerating inflation rate of unemployment (NAIRU). Agents in this theoretical framework are expected to be forward-looking and not be liquidity constrained; they are assumed to form expectations in terms of how future developments in government budgetary policies and public finances will affect their lifetime income and wealth.

The introduction of expectations as we have just highlighted, along with the acceptance of the RET, implies that expectational and wealth effects might outweigh the Keynesian type of multiplier effects. An increase in government deficit, for example, that is perceived as permanent by agents, would imply an increase in the future tax burden and a permanent decrease in their expected income and wealth. Agents would decrease their current consumption and save more in anticipation of lower future income. Higher lump-sum taxes would decrease household and worker wealth. It is the case that the initial increase in public spending generates a larger decrease in current consumption.

Labour supply would decrease as a consequence of the negative wealth effects and so would production. The latter comes about in view of the expected increase in future taxes, which induces expectations of lower production as a result of the distorting effects of higher taxation. There are also other supply-side effects in that the increase in public employment reduces private sector labour supply, exerting an upward pressure on wages, which decreases the present discounted value of the future stream of profits. This affects investment adversely. The latter is also affected by higher interest rates in view of the increased deficit (the usual crowding-out effect). It should also be noted that the main theoretical property of RET is the irrelevance of the government's financing decisions vis-à-vis taxes and debt. For example, a fiscal expansion prompts expectations of future fiscal contractions regardless of the way financing is undertaken. Private savings increase to compensate for the reduction in government saving, in the expectation of future tax increases, with the multiplier effect of the fiscal expansion brought to zero in the limit (Barro, 1974).

In the rest of this section we focus on recent developments, and show that this theoretical construct entails a number of assumptions, which may or may not be validated in the real world. This makes it imperative that we also look at the extent of these assumptions being empirically validated. In general terms, the early empirical studies on the effectiveness of fiscal policy within the confines of the NCM concluded that it was ineffective. The rationalisation of this proposition relied essentially on three assumptions: that households optimised intertemporally, that households were not subject to any liquidity constraints, and that households were able to anticipate intertemporal financial constraints (Hemming, Kell and Mahfouz, 2002, survey the theoretical arguments along with the empirical findings of the literature on this approach). However, more recently that unfavourable empirical evidence on fiscal policy has been questioned (see, for example, Van Aarle and Garretsen, 2003), and, in addition, studies have shown results that are contrary to the NCM propositions on the issue of the effectiveness of fiscal policy (Hjelm, 2002). There have also been studies that advocate greater emphasis on fiscal policy as a key economic policy tool in macroeconomic stabilisation and that fiscal policy is more effective than previously thought (Wren-Lewis, 2000). We explore these more recent contributions in what follows.

Arestis and Sawyer (2003) deal further with these issues and conclude that the case for fiscal policy as in the NCM theoretical framework is not supported by the available evidence and theoretical arguments. Even if the institutional factors just alluded to were shown to be theoretically and empirically pertinent, this should not detract from the fact that fiscal policy is still effective. Wren-Lewis (2000) makes this point and proceeds to utilise a simple calibrated model and a more complex econometric macroeconomic model to conclude that 'changes in government spending, income transfers, and indirect taxes can still have an important impact on demand in the short run' (p. 104). Three related studies strengthen the argument. Hemming, Kelly and Mahfouz (2002), when reviewing the literature on the issue, conclude that 'There is little evidence of direct crowding out or crowding out through interest rates and the exchange rate. Nor does full Ricardian equivalence or a significant partial Ricardian offset get much support from the evidence' (p. 36). Another relevant study (Hemming, Mahfouz and Schimmelpfennig, 2002) summarises the argument along similar lines:

> Estimates of fiscal multipliers are overwhelmingly positive but small. Short-term multipliers average around a half for taxes and one for spending, with only modest variation across countries and models (albeit with some outliers). There are hardly any instances of negative fiscal multipliers, the exception being that they can be generated in some macroeconomic models with strong credibility effects (p. 4)

A more recent study (Briotti, 2005) is also supportive of these results; it actually concludes that

> Although many empirical studies strongly reject the full Ricardian Equivalence, the behaviour of private consumption may still be consistent with a partial Ricardian effect. However, empirical evidence is somewhat mixed and no clear conclusions can be reached about the existence and size of the Ricardian effect. A major difficulty stems from measurement problems and methodological issues that greatly affect the estimation of parameters. (p. 21)

5   Summary and conclusions

This contribution has dealt with an area to which Malcolm Sawyer has made substantial and successful contributions during the recent period. This is the critical perspective on the New Consensus Macroeconomics. We have attempted to highlight critically the main characteristics of this particular theoretical framework. The term Consensus is very interesting for it pinpoints a rare level of agreement among economists of the traditional persuasion on macro issues has been achieved. Such a consensus has not been witnessed since the late 1960s/early 1970s when the first consensus was in place, the neoclassical synthesis with its focus on the IS/LM model.

NCM has been generally analysed under the assumption of a closed economy. This chapter has dealt with the open economy NCM where the role of the exchange rate provides an additional channel of monetary policy. Not only has this chapter attempted to clarify the main features of the NCM but it has also focused on its main policy implications.

In doing so the chapter has also critically raised a number of issues with both the NCM's theoretical foundations, and also its monetary policy, which is of course the IT framework. On both accounts, we find that a number of problems and weaknesses are present. In particular, four such weaknesses have been stressed. Two emanate from the absence of money and banks in the NCM model, and from the way the equilibrium real rate of interest is utilised in the same model. A further weakness refers to the efficient markets hypothesis, a very important aspect in view of the recent 'great recession' experience. The fourth weakness refers to the absence of 'animal spirits' in the NCM monetary policy dimension, which we have argued could potentially lead to wrong conclusions. We have also looked at fiscal policy, which is downgraded substantially by the NCM. We find that there are no grounds for such a downgrade. Our overall conclusion is, then, that NCM is based on weak theoretical foundations. This suggests that a great deal more research is necessary to tackle the issues raised in this contribution.

Notes

1. The author gratefully acknowledges support for this work from the Basque Government (Consolidated Research Group GIC10/153).
2. The NCM framework, and its implications for monetary policy, was suggested initially by Goodfriend and King (1997) and Clarida et al. (1999). For an extensive theoretical treatment see Woodford (2003).
3. Woodford (2009) suggests that the 'intertemporal general-equilibrium foundations', which used to be a contentious issue among macroeconomists, is now so widely accepted that it has become an important element of current macroeconomic analysis.
4. There is of course the role of money as a unit of account. However, in view of real money balances being a negligible component of total wealth there are no wealth effects of money on spending. Although monetary policy is central in NCM, money plays no role other than being a unit of account (Galí and Gertler, 2007, pp. 28–9).
5. It is the case that among those central banks that have relied on inflation forecasts, the record has been rather poor. In the UK, for example, the Bank of

England inflation forecasts are always assumed to converge to the target in two years. This, however, fails statistically to materialise in a number of cases.
6. I am very grateful to John King for pointing out to me the difference between animal spirits as in Keynes (1936) and the way Akerlof and Shiller (2009) treat the notion. The latter use the notion 'animal spirits' to indicate the possibility that individuals act irrationally and for non-economic reasons, very different from Keynes' (op. cit.) interpretation as highlighted in the text.

References

Agénor, P. (2002) 'Monetary policy under flexible exchange rates: An introduction to inflation targeting', in N. Loayza and N. Soto (eds), *Inflation Targeting: Design, Performance, Challenges*, Santiago, Chile: Central Bank of Chile.

Akerlof, G.A. and Shiller, R.J. (2009) *Animal Spirits: How Human Psychology Drives the Economy, and Why it Matters for Global Capitalism*, Princeton, NJ and Oxford: Princeton University Press.

Angeriz, A. and Arestis, P. (2007) 'Monetary policy in the UK', *Cambridge Journal of Economics*, 31(6), 863–84.

Angeriz, A. and Arestis, P. (2008) 'Assessing inflation targeting through intervention analysis', *Oxford Economic Papers*, 60(2), 293–317.

Angeriz, A. and Arestis, P. (2009) 'The consensus view on interest rates and fiscal policy: Reality or innocent fraud?', *Journal of Post Keynesian Economics*, 31(4), 586.

Arestis, P. (ed.) (2007a) *Is There a New Consensus in Macroeconomics?*, Basingstoke: Palgrave Macmillan.

Arestis, P. (2007b) 'What is the New Consensus in macroeconomics?', chapter 2 in P. Arestis (2007a).

Arestis, P. (2009) 'New Consensus Macroeconomics and Keynesian critique', in E. Hein, T. Niechoj and E. Stockhammer (eds), *Macroeconomic Policies on Shaky Foundations: Wither Mainstream Macroeconomics?*, Marburg: Metropolis.

Arestis, P., Baddeley, M. and Sawyer, M.C. (2007) 'The relationship between capital stock, unemployment and wages in nine EMU countries', *Bulletin of Economic Research*, 59(2), 125–48.

Arestis, P. and Chortareas, G. (2008) 'Atheoretical and theory-based approaches to the natural equilibrium real interest rate', *Eastern Economic Journal*, 34(3), 390–405.

Arestis, P. and Karakitsos, E. (2009) 'Subprime mortgage market and current financial crisis', in P. Arestis, P. Mooslechner and K. Wagner (eds), *Housing Market Challenges in Europe and the United States – Any Solutions Available?*, Basingstoke: Palgrave Macmillan.

Arestis, P. and Sawyer, M. (2003) 'Reinstating fiscal policy', *Journal of Post Keynesian Economics*, 26(1), 3–25.

Arestis, P. and Sawyer, M. (2004a) *Re-examining Monetary and Fiscal Policies in the Twenty First Century*, Cheltenham: Edward Elgar Publishing Limited.

Arestis, P. and Sawyer, M.C. (2004b) 'Can monetary policy affect the real economy?', *European Review of Economics and Finance*, 3(3), 3–26.

Arestis, P. and Sawyer, M. (2006) 'Fiscal policy matters', *Public Finance*, 54(3–4).

Arestis, P. and Sawyer, M. (2007) 'Can the Euro area play a stabilizing role in balancing the global imbalances?', in J. Bibow and A. Terzi (eds), *Euroland and the World Economy: Global Player or Global Drag*, Basingstoke: Palgrave Macmillan.

Arestis, P. and Sawyer, M.C. (2008a) 'A critical reconsideration of the foundations of monetary policy in the New Consensus Macroeconomics framework', *Cambridge Journal of Economics*, 32(5), 761–79.

Arestis, P. and Sawyer, M. (2008b) 'New Consensus Macroeconomics and inflation targeting: Keynesian critique', *Economia e Sociedade*, 17, (Special Issue), 629–54.

Barro, R.J. (1974) 'Are government bonds net wealth?', *Journal of Political Economy*, 82(6), 1095–117.

Blanchard, O.J. (2008) 'The state of macro', *Working Paper Series No. 08-17*, Department of Economics, Massachusetts Institute of Technology, Cambridge, MA, USA.

Blanchard, O.J. and Fischer, S. (1989) *Lectures on Macroeconomics*, Cambridge, MA and London: The MIT Press.

Briotti, M.G. (2005) 'Economic reactions to public finance consolidation: A survey of the literature', *Occasional Paper Series No. 38*, Frankfurt: European Central Bank.

Buiter, W.H. (2008) 'Central banks and financial crises'. Paper presented to the Federal Reserve Bank of Kansas City Symposium on *Maintaining Stability in a Changing Financial System*, Jackson Hole, Wyoming, 21–3 August 2008. Obtainable from: http://www.kc.frb.org/publicat/sympos/2008/Buiter.09.06.08.pdf.

Clarida, R., Galí, J. and Gertler, M. (1999) 'The science of monetary policy: A new Keynesian perspective', *Journal of Economic Literature*, 37(4), 1661–707.

De Fiore, F. and Tristani, O. (2008) 'Credit and the natural rate of interest', *ECB Working Paper Series*, No. 889, European Central Bank: Frankfurt am Main, Germany.

Friedman, B.M. (2003) 'The LM curve: A not-so-fond farewell', *NBER Working Paper Series*, No. 10123, Cambridge, MA: National Bureau of Economic Research.

Galí, J. and Gertler, M. (2007) 'Macroeconomic modelling for monetary policy evaluation', *Journal of Economic Perspectives*, 21(4), 25–45.

Goodfriend, M. (2007) 'How the world achieved consensus on monetary policy', *Journal of Economic Perspectives*, 21(4), 47–68.

Goodfriend, M. and King, R.G. (1997) 'The new neoclassical synthesis and the role of monetary policy', in B.S. Bernanke and J.J. Rotemberg (eds), *NBER Macroeconomics Annual: 1997*, Cambridge, MA: MIT Press.

Goodhart, C.A.E. (2004) Review of *Interest and Prices* by M. Woodford, *Journal of Economics*, 82(2), 195–200.

Goodhart, C.A.E. (2007) 'Whatever became of the monetary aggregates?', The Peston Lecture delivered in honour of Maurice, Lord Peston, Queen Mary, University of London, 28 February.

Goodhart, C.A.E. (2008) 'The continuing muddles of monetary theory: A steadfast refusal to face facts'. Paper presented to the 12th Conference 'Macroeconomic Policies on Shaky Foundations – Wither Mainstream Economics?' of the Research Network, *Macroeconomics and Macroeconomic Policies* (RMM), 31 October–1 November.

Hemming, R., Kell, M. and Mahfouz, S. (2002) 'The Effectiveness of Fiscal Policy in Stimulating Economic Activity: A Review of the Literature', *IMF Working Paper 02/208*, Washington, DC: International Monetary Fund.

Hemming, R., Mahfouz, S. and Schimmelpfennig, A. (2002) 'Fiscal Policy and Economic Activity in Advanced Economies', *IMF Working Paper 02/87*, Washington, DC: International Monetary Fund.

Hjelm, G. (2002) 'Is private consumption higher (lower) during periods of fiscal constructions (expansions)?', *Journal of Macroeconomics*, 24(1), 17–39.

HM Treasury (2003) *Fiscal Stabilisation and EMU*, HM Stationery Office, Cmnd 799373, Norwich. Available on www.hm-treasury.gov.uk.

Juselius, M. (2008) 'Testing the new Keynesian model on US and Euro area data', *Economics: The Open-Access, Open-Assessment E-Journal*, 2(1), 1–26.

Keynes, J.M. (1936) *The General Theory of Employment, Interest and Money*, London: Macmillan.

Orphanides, A. (2007) 'Taylor rules', in L. Blum and S. Durlauf (eds), *The New Palgrave: A Dictionary of Economics*, Basingstoke: Palgrave Macmillan.

Sawyer, M. (2009) 'Interest rates and inflation: What are the links?', *Intervention: European Journal of Economics and Economic Policies*, 6(1), 81–96.

Sawyer, M. (2010) 'Phillips curve, independence of central banks and inflation targeting', in G. Fontana, J. McCombie and M. Sawyer (eds), *Macroeconomics, Finance and Money: Essays in Honour of Philip Arestis*, Basingstoke: Palgrave Macmillan.

Svensson, L.E.O. (1997) 'Inflation forecast targeting: Implementing and monitoring inflation targets', *European Economic Review*, 41(6), 1111–46.

Svensson, L.E.O. (1999) 'Inflation targeting as a monetary policy rule', *Journal of Monetary Economics*, 43(3), 607–54.

Taylor, J.B. (1993) 'Discretion versus policy rules in practice', *Carnegie-Rochester Conference Series on Public Policy*, December, 195–214.

Taylor, J.B. (1999) 'A historical analysis of monetary policy rules', in J.B. Taylor (ed.), *Monetary Policy Rules*, Chicago: Chicago University Press.

Taylor, J.B. (2001) 'The role of the exchange rate in monetary-policy rules', *American Economic Review*, 91(2), 263–7.

Van Aarle, B. and Garretsen, H. (2003) 'Keynesian, non-Keynesian or no effects of fiscal policy changes? The EMU case', *Journal of Macroeconomics*, 25(2), 213–40.

Wadhwani, S. (2008) 'Should monetary policy respond to asset price bubbles? Revisiting the debate', *National Institute Economic Review*, No. 206, 25–34.

Weber, A., Lemke, W. and Worms, A. (2008) 'How useful is the concept of the natural real rate of interest for monetary policy?', *Cambridge Journal of Economics*, 32(1), 49–63.

Wicksell, K. (1898) *Geldzins und Güterpreise*, Frankfurt: Verlag Gustav Fischer. English translation in R.F. Kahn (1965), *Interest and Prices*, New York: Kelley.

Woodford, M. (2003) *Interest and Prices: Foundations of a Theory of Monetary Policy*, Princeton, NJ: Princeton University Press.

Woodford, M. (2007) 'The case for forecast targeting as a monetary policy strategy', *Journal of Economic Perspectives*, 21(4), 3–24.

Woodford, M. (2008) 'How important is money in the conduct of monetary policy?', *Journal of Money, Credit and Banking*, 40(8), 1561–98.

Woodford, M. (2009) 'Convergence in macroeconomics: Elements of the new synthesis', *American Journal of Economics – Macroeconomics*, 1(1), 267–79.

Wren-Lewis, S. (2000) 'The limits to discretionary fiscal stabilisation policy', *Oxford Review of Economic Policy*, 16, 92–105.

7
Bringing Together the Horizontalist and the Structuralist Analyses of Endogenous Money

Giuseppe Fontana

1 Introduction*

In the introductory chapter of this book, Philip Arestis maintains that throughout the course of his academic career Malcolm Sawyer has adopted an 'open-minded' approach to economics, which had led him first to revive and then make ground-breaking contributions to Kaleckian economics from the 1970s onwards. This chapter supports this view. In his early academic career Malcolm published important empirical papers on the nature of modern capitalist economies (see, for instance, Aaronovitch and Sawyer, 1975a, 1975b; Henry et al., 1976; and Sawyer, 1971, 1976, 1979). This empirical work soon led him to question the dominant macroeconomics theories of the time, namely the *IS-LM* Keynesian theory (hereafter Keynesian theory) and the monetarist theory (Sawyer, 1982). In his view, for all their differences Keynesian and monetarist theories committed the same sin. Keynesian and monetarist theories were based on ad hoc hypotheses, with very little empirical support.

Malcolm singled out two main problems with Keynesian and mon-etarist theories. First, these theories assumed atomistic competition, when in the real world oligopoly was the norm in both product and capital markets. Secondly, they assumed an exogenous money supply, when actually it is the demand for loans by the public that determines the quantity of money that is injected into the economy. The unsatisfac-tory state of macroeconomics together with an 'open-minded' approach to economics led Malcolm to look for an alternative theory that could

---

*This chapter is a revised and updated version of Fontana (2011). The author is grateful to Philip Arestis, Geoff Harcourt and Aurelie Charles for comments on an earlier draft of the paper. The usual disclaimer applies.

be reconciled with his view. The work of Michał Kalecki seemed to provide that opportunity. It included some of the most important ideas put forward by Keynes, such as the principle of effective demand, and the importance of investment in determining the level of output and employment in a country. Yet it also brought to the fore the conflict between different groups of economic agents. According to Malcolm, the conflict between different groups of agents was at the heart of the explanation of many economic problems of the time, including the high level of inflation and unemployment (for example, Sawyer, 1982, Ch. 4; 1983, Ch. 4). In terms of the theoretical dimension of this approach, and especially the different and possibly conflicting roles that groups of agents play in modern economies are at the heart of the endogenous money theory. This is precisely the focus of this chapter.

The main tenet of the latter theoretical contribution is that the supply of money is determined by the demand for loans, and the latter originates within the economic system in order to finance the production and accumulation process or the upsurge of speculative purchases. The main policy implication of the theory is that money and monetary policy is not neutral either in the short or the long run: money is needed for, and has the purpose of, financing the core activities of capitalist economies. While these propositions are now widely accepted by most, if not all non-mainstream economists, there are several details in the theory of endogenous money that are still contentious.[1] The debate between what are usually labelled horizontalists and structuralists is based around the following three arguments. First, there is disagreement over the degree of accommodation by central banks to the demand for reserves of commercial banks. Are central banks always willing to supply the required reserves at the going short-run nominal interest rate? Or could they attempt resisting this demand by changing the interest rate? Secondly, there is a discussion about the meaning and relevance of the liquidity preference of commercial banks. Is the liquidity preference theory consistent with endogenous money? And, if so, does this mean that there is an upward-sloping supply curve for loans? Thirdly, there is a controversy over the implication of the liquidity preference of the non-bank public sector. Are the preferences of the final recipients of bank deposits (that is, wage-earners) necessarily consistent with the preferences of the first recipients of these deposits (that is, firms)? And, if not, is there a mechanism that reconciles the different preferences?

There are two main objectives of this chapter. The first is to review the controversial issues debated by horizontalists and structuralists with the help of an original four-panel diagram (Fontana, 2003; see, also, Palley,

1994), which presents – in a simple and concise way – the nature and origin of the differences between horizontalists and structuralists.

The second objective of this chapter is to encompass the horizontalist and structuralist analyses in a general theory of endogenous money (Fontana, 2004a, 2009). Building on the work of Hicks (1956, 1982), the horizontalist and structuralist analyses are interpreted in the light of an original time framework grounded on the distinction between a single-period analysis and a continuation analysis. A single-period analysis is based on the tacit assumption that within the period under consideration economic agents involved in the money supply process hold constant expectations. However, one of the features of the latter is the possibility of affecting the expectations of all agents involved in it. Therefore, the effects of changes in the state of expectations of central banks, commercial banks, firms, financial intermediaries, and wage-earners are the main concern of a continuation analysis.

2   Controversial issues

The core argument of the endogenous money theory is that the supply of money is determined by the demand for loans, and the latter originates within the economic system in order to finance the production and accumulation processes or the upsurge of speculative purchases. This means that any representation of the endogenous money theory requires at the minimum three markets and four groups of economic agents, namely a central bank, commercial banks (banks for short), firms, and wage-earners. In the following the debate between horizontalists and structuralists is therefore presented in terms of the controversial arguments surrounding the potentially conflicting behaviour of these groups of agents in the reserve market, the credit or loans market, and the financial markets, respectively.

2.1   The reserve market

The first controversy between horizontalists and structuralists is over the relationship between the central bank and banks. In the endogenous money theory central banks set the short-run nominal interest rate (for example, the federal funds rate in the USA, and the official bank rate in the UK) and supply monetary reserves on demand. The short-run nominal interest rate is thus the control instrument used by central banks to affect the lending activity of banks, and thereby the entire economic process. For instance, changes in the short-run nominal interest rate prompt banks to modify base rates (for example, personal loan rates and mortgage rates) at which they lend to their customers. These rates *ceteris paribus* have an important role in influencing the level of investment and consumption, and hence the level of aggregate demand, which in turn affects the volume of output and employment.

The differences between the two analyses of endogenous money can be introduced in terms of a short-run reaction function measuring the elasticity of the nominal interest rate with respect to changes in the demand for reserves. Horizontalists argue for an infinitely elastic reaction function in the time period between revisions of the short-run nominal interest rate (for example, Moore, 1991, 1995), whereas structuralists defend a less-than-perfectly elastic function (for example, Pollin, 1991).

The four-panel diagram in Figure 7.1 shows the contentious description of the reserves market.[2] The focus of the analysis is upon flows, namely changes in the supply of money, and how these changes arise from the flow of new bank loans to borrowers. The upper left panel describes the reserves market. The supply of reserves is represented by a step function, with each horizontal segment representing a different interest rate policy (e.g. i_0, i_1). The horizontal parts of the schedule show the accommodative behaviour on the part of the central bank, while the upward trend (from right to left in the diagram) reflects the structuralist view that central banks have a less-than-perfectly elastic

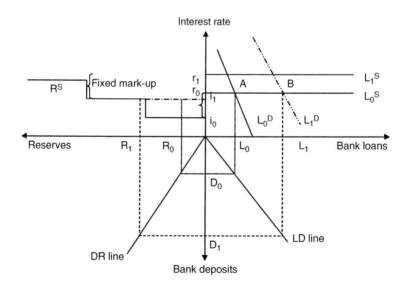

Figure 7.1 A general endogenous money analysis of the reserve market

reaction function. The upper right panel shows the credit market, where banks and firms negotiate terms and conditions of the supply of new loans. Since the debate over the slope of the supply curve of loans is postponed to next section, the curve is represented by a perfectly elastic schedule at a base rate (e.g. r_0), determined as a fixed mark-up over the short-run nominal interest rate (e.g. i_0) set by the central bank. The demand for loans (e.g. L_0^D) is a decreasing function of the base rate (r), and together with the supply of loans (e.g. L_0^S), it determines the total volume of credit (e.g. L_0).

The lower panels are used to describe two main insights of the endogenous money theory, namely 'loans create deposits' (*LD* line), and 'deposits make reserves' (*DR* line), respectively. The equilibrium in the credit market determines via the *LD* line the supply of new deposits (e.g. D_0 in the lower right panel. Note that the *LD* line represents the balance sheet constraint of banks and, for the sake of making the graphical exposition feasible, it is drawn on the assumption that banks hold their liabilities, like time or demand deposits, in a given proportion. The supply of reserves (e.g. R_0) associated with the supply of new bank deposits (e.g. D_0) is shown via the *DR* line in the lower left panel. The *DR* line represents the total demand for reserves.

The four-panel diagram illustrates the underlying sequential analysis that characterises the endogenous money theory, as well as the controversial issues related to the reaction function of the central bank. Expansionary shifts of the demand for bank loans (e.g. L_1^D) cause – via the *LD* line and the *DR* line – increases in the level of bank deposits (e.g. D_1), and of reserves (e.g. R_1), respectively. But, as a result of the new higher level of reserves, the central bank might, although it does not need to, decide to tighten conditions in the reserve market by moving to an (i_1) interest rate policy. This change in the policy stance of the central bank is then likely to affect the lending policy of banks in the credit market (e.g. L_1^S).

Note that this representation of the reserve supply curve is not inconsistent with the neo-Chartalist view that most of the central bank actions are defensive in nature, and are mainly undertaken in order to smooth out the imbalances in the pattern of money flows between the government's accounts on one hand, and banks on the other (Wray, 1998, Ch. 5; also Lavoie, 2006). The central bank supplies the reserves which the banking system as a whole needs in order to achieve balance by the end of each settlement day. However, at any time the central bank chooses the price of these reserves, and hence it can change the price, if it thinks is appropriate or necessary to do it.

Furthermore, it is important to reiterate that for banks the reserve market has been relatively more important than the wholesale market. It is only in the former that liquidity is created, whereas the role of the latter is to circulate existing liquidity between banks. The infamous run on Northern Rock, the fifth-biggest mortgage lender in Britain, in September 2007 is a case in point (*Economist*, 2007). When on the back of problems in the subprime mortgage market in the USA, British banks increased their liquidity preference and avoided lending to each other on the wholesale market, Northern Rock was unable to refinance its business (Chick, 2008). The Bank of England did not intervene by providing the much-needed new liquidity, and panic spread. Whatever the evaluation of the behaviour of the Bank of England, it is clear that outside normal circumstances only the central bank could save a bank from insolvency. The central bank is the bank of banks, in the sense that it is the ultimate maker of liquidity for the economy. The reserve market is still relevant for the money supply process, though many countries including Canada, Sweden, Australia and New Zealand have now no compulsory reserve requirements.

More generally, this simple example suggests that central banks play a very active role in the money supply process. By adjusting the short-run nominal interest rate, they are able to affect lending conditions in the credit market, and, more generally, to control the cost and availability of liquidity in the economy. This power of central banks is recognised by both horizontalists (for example, Lavoie, 1992, pp. 186–9), and structuralists (for example, Howells, 1995, pp. 12–17). Their main difference lies in the assumptions regarding the state of expectations of central banks during the money supply process. Horizontalists discuss the supply curve of reserves associated with a constant state of expectations, whereas structuralists allow for the effects of changes in the state of expectations. Therefore, while the former prefer to discriminate between different stances of monetary policy, and focus only on the freely managed short-run nominal interest rate stance (Lavoie, 1996, p. 279; Moore, 1988, p. 265, n.9), the latter are more inclined to consider complex reaction functions of central banks (Wray, 1992, p. 307; Palley, 1996, pp. 592–3). In terms of Figure 7.1, by the particular time nature of their models, structuralists are prone to consider the overall upward-sloping step function representing the supply of reserves (i.e. R^S), whereas horizontalists focus on each single horizontal part of it (i.e. either i_0 or i_1 policy line).

2.2 The credit market

A more controversial argument between horizontalists and structuralists relates to the behaviour of banks in the credit or loans market. Whether or not reserves are forthcoming at a constant short-run nominal interest rate, structuralists hold that, as a result of an increase in the lending activity, price and non-price terms of credit would rise. Price terms are base interest rates like the standard mortgage rate, whereas non-price terms mainly refer to the income and assets collateral requirements (Wolfson, 1996, pp. 456–7).

Drawing on Minsky's analysis of corporate financial behaviour (Minsky, 1975, Ch. 5 and Ch. 6), most structuralists argue that banks raise their base interest rates at the peak of the business cycle (for example, Wray, 1995, pp. 278–80).[3] As lending increases, banks become increasingly concerned about their own portfolio balance (usually measured by the ratio of loans to equity, and the ratio of loans to safe assets), as well as the liquidity level of their customers (usually indicated by the ratio of debt to equity of firms). Similarly, structuralists maintain that in these circumstances banks often impose restrictions on their lending activity. They conclude that if price and non-price terms are properly considered, the supply of loans is best represented by an upward-sloping curve (Dow, 1996, pp. 498–504; 2006, pp. 43–9).

On their part, horizontalists argue for a horizontal supply curve in the interest–loans space. However, they acknowledge that banks may impose quantitative restrictions on their customers (Moore, 1988, p. 24). Similarly, horizontalists accept that the liquidity ratios of banks and customers play a role in determining base rates over the trade cycle. However, they object to the contention that the supply of loans is necessarily upward sloping in the long run (Lavoie, 1996, pp. 286 and 289; 2006, p. 23). Horizontalists prefer to discuss the effects of changing liquidity ratios in terms of initial restrictions on the borrowing activity of customers. They argue that banks do not curtail credit by marginal variations of the mark-up, although they do change over time the requirements for the identification of sound customers (non-price terms for new loans), and the base rate of their credit offer (price terms for new loans). Therefore, at all times banks only accommodate the so-called solvent or effective demand for loans. More importantly, the supply of loans is a truncated horizontal line: beyond some point, the supply curve simply vanishes (Lavoie, 1996, p. 288). Changed conditions in the credit market are thus best represented by a shift in the demand curve, and a new horizontal supply curve.

Figure 7.2 shows the differences between the horizontalist and structuralist analyses of the credit or loans market. The significant difference from Figure 7.1 is the assumption of a perfectly elastic schedule for the supply of reserves, meaning that only a single monetary policy stance

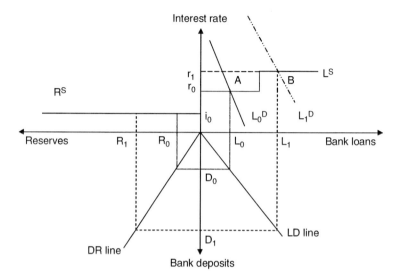

Figure 7.2 A general endogenous money analysis of the credit market

is considered (for example, an i_0 interest rate policy). More importantly, the loans supply schedule is now a function of the liquidity ratios of banks, and their customers. During an economic expansion banks are most likely going to experience a reduction in the level of liquidity. Illiquidity comes from increasingly risky new loans, and from outstanding loans being perceived as more risky. As the peak of the cycle is approached, some banks become aware of the objective fragility of the system, and anxious about the illiquidity of their balance sheets. They are then likely to tighten the requirements for new credit, and to raise their base rates (e.g. r_1). Similarly, as customers take on more debt, banks become concerned about the solvency of their borrowers. As in the previous case, it is likely that banks will revise their requirements upward, and raise the base rates (e.g. r_1). Thus, in these circumstances the supply of loans (L^S) is better represented by a step function. Banks set their base rate, and this determines the height of the loans supply curve (i.e. the relevant horizontal line of the L^S). Their perception of the state of the economy explains the length of the horizontal parts of the curve, i.e. how long banks hold constant the supply price of loans (Fontana, 2003).

In short, the main difference between horizontalists and structuralists lies in the different assumptions about the behaviour of banks in the credit market. Horizontalists look at the credit market under the assumption that during the money supply process banks are not affected by changes, if any, in their own liquidity ratios, and the liquidity ratios of their customers. Structuralists allow for the possibility that over the business cycle banks revise price and non-price terms of credit.

2.3   The financial markets

Another controversy between horizontalists and structuralists is related to the relationship between the different recipients of deposits. In endogenous money theory, the demand for loans mainly originates with firms, while the deposits created by this lending are eventually held by wage-earners. Firms are deficit units involved in income–expenditure decisions. They negotiate with banks the amount of loans necessary for purchasing capital and labour services, and once collateral requirements are satisfied, they own the resulting deposits. These deposits are then exchanged with the owners of the inputs necessary for the production and accumulation processes, in return for their capital and labour services. If transactions between firms are ignored, that is, if the purchasing of capital services is considered an internal transaction of the firms sector, labour services are the only inputs to buy. The supply of new loans is therefore equal to the flow of new deposits transferred from firms to wage-earners.

Wage-earners use these bank deposits to buy commodities in the goods market, and securities in the financial markets. In the simple case in which the public sector and the foreign sector are ignored, firms issue all securities available for purchase in the financial markets. Therefore, the amount of deposits that wage-earners spend in the goods market and in the financial markets is a measure of all new deposits returning to firms. Firms use these deposits to repay banks for their initial loans. This is what in the literature has been labelled the Kaldor–Trevithick reflux mechanism (Kaldor and Trevithick, 1988). Horizontalists use this mechanism to explain how 'excess' deposits for wage-earners are extinguished from the money supply process (Lavoie, 1999, pp. 105–8).

Structuralists usually acknowledge the importance of the Kaldor–Trevithick reflux mechanism (for example, Arestis, 1988, p. 65). However, they argue that the reflux mechanism does not automatically extinguish all newly created deposits (Chick, 1992, p. 205; Cottrell, 1986, p. 17; Dalziel, 2001, p. 144, n. 2; Palley, 1991, p. 397). Wage-earners spend part of these deposits in the goods market, and save the remainder for precautionary or speculative purposes. The consequent allocation of deposits between securities and liquid balances is a portfolio choice, and for this reason it cannot be divorced from changes in interest rates differentials, which are bound to have important repercussions in the loans market (Arestis and Howells, 1996, pp. 540–4). Structuralists thus maintain that the portfolio choice of wage-earners between securities and liquid balances is an important component of the money supply process. It demonstrates the relevance of feedback effects between the credit market, and the financial markets.

Figure 7.3 shows the differences between the horizontalist and structuralist analyses of the financial markets.[4] The significant changes from previous figures are the different slopes of the *LD* line, and their effects on the credit market. For the sake of simplicity, the supply of reserves (R^S) is assumed to be perfectly elastic, meaning that only a single monetary policy is considered. As in the previous figures, the demand for loans (L_0^D) together with the supply of loans (L_0^S) determines the flow of new loans (L_0), and via the LD_0 line the flow of new deposits (D_0). Importantly, the LD_0 line is drawn for a given portfolio choice of wage-earners between securities and liquid balances. Therefore, it cannot be excluded that the flow of new loans (L_0) creates an expansion of new deposits (D_0), which exceeds the willingness of wage-earners to hold them. Wage-earners will then modify their portfolios, attempting to hold fewer deposits (e.g. D_2) by exchanging some of the new deposits (D_0) with securities. The price of securities will rise and the yields will fall.

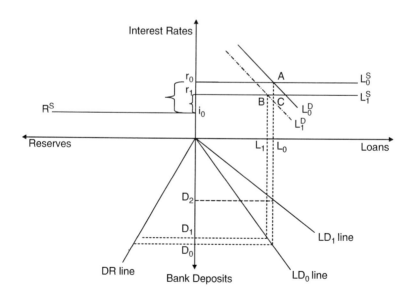

Figure 7.3 A general endogenous money analysis of the financial markets

The LD_0 line rotates anti-clockwise (e.g. LD_1 line). This also means that firms are now able to recover on the financial markets a greater proportion of the initial flow of new deposits (D_0), which in turn reduces their outstanding debts towards banks. The demand for new loans will thus shift inwards (e.g. L_1^D). At the same time, the fall in the yields on securities means that wage-earners are now willing to hold a greater proportion of new deposits (e.g. D_1 rather than D_2). Similarly, it is likely that the fall in the yields on securities will also have an effect on the supply of new loans. Banks will lower their base rate (e.g. r_1), and the supply of new loans shifts downwards (e.g. L_1^S). To prevent cluttering Figure 7.3, and on the assumption of a constant monetary policy, the effects of these changes in the reserve market are not explored here.

In short, horizontalists have examined the two-way relationship between the credit market and the financial markets under the assumption that the ultimate impact of an expansion in the supply of loans has no effects whatsoever on the portfolios of wage-earners. Structuralists have considered the possibility of portfolio choices changing as a result of the supply of new deposits. How portfolio adjustments in the financial markets affect future conditions in the credit market is of the utmost importance in their understanding of the money supply process (Arestis and Howells, 1999, p. 118; also Cottrell, 1988, p. 296; Goodhart, 1989, pp. 32–3; Wolfson, 1996, pp. 458–61).

3 A general theory of endogenous money: a single-period–continuation time framework

The foregoing account of the reserve market, the credit market, and the financial markets suggests that horizontalists and structuralists have in mind two distinct classes of models of the money supply process. These models share the same methodological and theoretical framework, but they differ in terms of the particular assumptions made about the state of expectations of central banks, banks, firms and wage-earners. The purpose of this section is to give precise meaning to this idea. The Hicksian distinction between a single period and a continuation theory of money is used to explain rigorously the limits to the domains of relevance of the horizontalist and structuralist analyses of endogenous money (Fontana, 2003). This argument is offered in a reconciliatory spirit. The final aim is to encompass these analyses into a more general theory of endogenous money.[5]

Horizontalists and structuralists concur that the general aim of the endogenous money theory is to explain the process of creation and circulation of money. They recognise that calendar time normally elapses between the moment in which central bankers, banks, firms, and wage-earners make decisions, and the ultimate outcome of these decisions. During this time, disappointment or new opportunities play a central role in shaping and constraining the behaviour of these groups of agents. Accordingly, these agents continuously revise their plans for and expectations of the future course of events.

Having acknowledged the relevance of calendar time and expectations, horizontalist and structuralist analyses seem to differ in terms of alternative assumptions about the state of the expectations of agents involved in the money supply process, and their influence on the working of the reserves market, the credit market, and the financial markets. From this perspective, horizontalists have proposed what along Hicksian lines could be labelled a single-period analysis of endogenous money, whereas structuralists have proposed a continuation analysis of endogenous money (Hicks, 1982, p. 223).

A single period is the minimum effective unit of economic time for the analysis of agents involved in the money supply process. The length of this period is such that changes in expectations never occur within it, but rather at the junctions of one single period to the next. A single-period theory of endogenous money is thus built on the simple assumption that the state of expectations of central banks, banks, firms, and wage-earners is given. It is given in the sense not of being unique, but rather of being assumed constant. This assumption allows the specification of simple and stable functional relationships that continuously changing expectations would have made it difficult or impossible to study. It is a realistic attempt to specify the fundamental relationships of the money supply process, without ignoring the possibility that changes in the state of expectations may affect the behaviour of agents involved into this process.

Notwithstanding these positive features, the previous section has shown the limitations of a single-period analysis of endogenous money. The possibility that central banks may adopt new monetary stances in response to conditions in the credit market, that over the trade cycle banks may revise price and non-price terms of credit, or that the changes in the portfolios of wage-earners may affect the lending activity of banks has no place in a single-period analysis. This should not come as a surprise. The formal features of a single period narrow the issues that can be investigated within such time framework. In a single period expectations can be disappointed, but their effects are not allowed to alter the current course of events. The effects of changes in the state of expectations have to wait for the next single period.

There are interesting lessons when expectations are allowed to affect the course of events. The actual path followed by the sequence of activities that describes the money supply process is in fact explained by the interactions between what agents plan to do, and what they discover they ought to have planned to do. This is the primary purpose of the continuation analysis of money, which is concerned with the effects of the events of a period upon the expectations that determine the events of the following periods. A continuation analysis is thus the natural complement to a single-period analysis. It is the analysis of a dynamic sequence of single periods. It deals explicitly with linkages between successive periods, and these linkages are an essential step in moving beyond the boundaries of self-contained single periods.

The time framework of a continuation analysis explicitly allows for the fact that the general state of expectations may change in the light of realised results. Inconsistencies between plans of agents come to the centre of the analysis as do all sorts of mechanisms to reconcile them. For example, if central bankers realise that the actual outcome of monetary policy is not what they had expected, they would attempt to do something before it is too late. As their expectations interact with the realised level of demand for monetary reserves, the short-run nominal interest rate is likely to change to reflect the new conditions in the economy. The base interest rates would then be affected, as would be the demand for loans, and the holding of deposits. Thus, the new aggregate supply of reserves would be responding to conditions in the credit market, and the financial markets. Policy reactions from the reserve markets would finally feed back to these markets, creating a complex network of interactions between all agents involved in the money supply process.

These interactions, policy reactions, and feedback effects are an important feature of a continuation analysis, and mark a major difference from a single-period analysis. Keeping with the same example, the latter would show that demand and supply conditions in the reserve market affect the credit market. A single period would then continue for a sufficient length of time such that the loans supply process works itself out completely. During this period, central banks may be disappointed by the results of their policy, banks may experience new opportunities and unexpected problems, or wage-earners may prefer to change their portfolios. Yet the formal features of the single period imply that disappointments, new opportunities or preferences would not have any effect on the state of expectations, and hence on the behaviour of the groups of agents operating in the reserve market, credit market, and financial markets. It is only in the next period that the reserve market, the credit market, and the financial markets would record new demand and supply conditions.

4 Concluding remarks

In the last forty years Malcolm has made ground-breaking contributions to Kaleckian economics, including the development of an original analysis of the nature and role of money and finance in the work of Kalecki and his followers (see, for a recent synthesis of this analysis, Sawyer, 2001; Arestis and Sawyer, 2005). Early in his academic career Malcolm maintained that in modern capitalist economies the supply of money is largely endogenous. 'The money supply is not predetermined but can be varied by the banks over a considerable range at their own discretion in response to the demand by the public for loans' (Sawyer, 1982, p. 11). This idea was intimately related to the results of his empirical research on industrial economics and business pricing, which highlighted the oligopolistic nature of the modern markets. All this soon led him to reject the dominant macroeconomic theories of the time, namely the *IS-LM* Keynesian theory and the monetarist theory in favour of the primitive endogenous money analyses put forward by Nicky Kaldor (Kaldor and Trevithick, 1981), and Basil Moore (1979).

> Money is largely credit money, part of which has been created by the government but most of which has been created by the private banking system. Whilst we cannot be sure what are the institutional assumptions made by the Keynesian/monetarist orthodoxy since they are not spelt out, we would suggest that they are approximately as follows. Markets are approximately perfectly competitive, with households as net savers and firms as net dissevers. Finance for investment is largely raised by the issue of bonds and by indirect borrowing for households with banks acting as intermediaries. Money is exogenously determined or enters the system through government deficits. (Sawyer, 1982, p. 12)

This chapter has looked at the modern features of the endogenous money theory. The core of the theory is that the supply of money in modern economies is determined by the demand for loans, and that this in turn responds to the need for financing production and accumulation, or speculative purchases. Beyond a widespread agreement over the idea that 'loans create deposits' and 'deposits make reserves', there is much controversy. Do central banks accommodate the demand for reserves at the going short-run nominal interest rate? Does the supply of loans slope upwards? Do wage-earners make portfolio choices that affect the future availability of credit?

This chapter has proposed an original four-panel diagram to review the controversial issues between horizontalist and structuralist analyses of endogenous money, before showing that there is a time framework within which these analyses can be made compatible.[6] This time framework is general enough to be used for the analysis of specific institutional settings or specific historical instances. The disagreement between horizontalists and structuralists arises from the particular assumptions made about the general state of expectations of economic agents. Horizontalists rely upon a single-period analysis that is built on the assumption that the state of expectations of all agents involved in the money supply process is given. This assumption allows the specification of stable functional relationships that continuously changing expectations would make very laborious to specify. In contrast, structuralists depend on a continuation framework that explicitly takes account of the fact that the state of expectations of agents may change in the light of realised results. In this way, structuralists are able to tackle controversial issues related to shifting monetary policies, the liquidity preference of banks, and the loans–deposits nexus that are overlooked by horizontalists. The conclusion of this paper is that the horizontalist and structuralist analyses together form a more general theory of endogenous money.

Notes

1. For critical surveys of the endogenous money theory, see Cottrell (1994), Dalziel (2001, Ch. 3), Dow (2006), Fontana (2003), Fontana and Realfonzo (2005), Hewitson (1995), Howells (1995), Lavoie (2006), Rochon (1999), Rochon and Rossi (2003).
2. The author is indebted to Dow (1996, 1997), Howells (1995), Lavoie (1996), Palley (1994, 1996), Pollin (1996), and Sawyer (1996) for early representations of a similar diagram. Howells (2009) uses a similar diagram to explore the effects of introducing key features of the endogenous money theory into the mainstream New Consensus Macroeconomics model.
3. Recently, some structuralists have accepted that this need not necessarily be the case (for example, Howells, 1995, p. 20; Dow, 2006, p. 46). For instance, they acknowledge the point made by Lavoie (1996, pp. 285–90) to the effect that over the business cycle, loans are being taken out, profits earned, and loans repaid (out of profits, and out of borrowing), such that the ratio of loans to profits or to equity does not necessarily rise during the business upswing.

4. The author is indebted to Peter Howells for comments and suggestions on the graphical representation of the controversial issues surrounding the behaviour of economic agents in the financial markets.
5. For a discussion of the encompassing principle as an appropriate characterisation of the Post Keynesian way of thought, see Fontana and Gerrard (2002). For an example of the encompassing principle in practice, see Fontana and Palacio-Vera (2002, 2003).
6. Fontana and Setterfield (2009) use this time framework in order to explain the financial crisis in 2007, and the related recession and policy responses.

References

Aaronovitch S. and Sawyer, M. (1975a) 'Mergers, growth and concentration', *Oxford Economic Papers*, 26, 136–55.

Aaronovitch S. and Sawyer, M. (1975b) *Big Business: Theoretical and Empirical Aspects of Concentration and Mergers in the United Kingdom*, London: Macmillan.

Arestis, P. (1988) 'Post Keynesian theory of money, credit and finance', in P. Arestis (ed.), *Post-Keynesian Monetary Economics*, Aldershot: Edward Elgar.

Arestis, P. and Howells P. (1996) 'Theoretical reflection on endogenous money: the problem with convenience lending', *Cambridge Journal of Economics*, 20, 539–51.

Arestis P. and Howells, P. (1999) 'The supply of credit money and the demand for deposits: a reply', *Cambridge Journal of Economics*, 23, 115–19.

Arestis, P. and Sawyer, M. (2005) 'Aggregate demand, conflict and capacity in the inflationary process', *Cambridge Journal of Economics*, 29, 959–74.

Arestis, P. and Sawyer, M. (eds) (2006) *A Handbook of Alternative Monetary Economics*, Cheltenham: Edward Elgar.

Chick, V. (1992, orig. 1986) 'The evolution of the banking system', in P. Arestis and S. Dow (eds), *On Money, Method, and Keynes: Selected Essays of Victoria Chick*, Macmillan, London.

Chick, V. (2008) 'Could the crisis at Northern Rock have been predicted? An evolutionary approach', *Contributions to Political Economy*, 27, 115–24.

Cottrell, A. (1986) 'The endogeneity of money and money-income causality', *Scottish Journal of Political Economy*, 33, 2–27.

Cottrell, A. (1988) 'The endogeneity of money: reply', *Scottish Journal of Political Economy*, 35, 294–7.

Cottrell, A. (1994) 'Post-Keynesian monetary economics', *Cambridge Journal of Economics*, 18, 587–605.

Dalziel, P. (2001) *Money, Credit and Price Stability*, London: Routledge.

Dow, S.C. (1996) 'Horizontalism: a critique', *Cambridge Journal of Economics*, 20, 497–508.

Dow, S.C. (1997) 'Endogenous money', in G.C. Harcourt and P.A. Riach (eds).

Dow, S.C. (2006) 'Endogenous money: Structuralist', in P. Arestis and M. Sawyer (eds).

Economist (2007) 'The great Northern run', 384, no. 8547, September, 96.

Fontana, G. (2003) 'Post Keynesian approaches to endogenous money: A time framework explanation', *Review of Political Economy*, 15(3), 291–314.

Fontana, G. (2004a) 'Hicks on monetary theory and history: money as endogenous money', *Cambridge Journal of Economics*, 1, 73–88.

Fontana, G. (2004b) 'Rethinking endogenous money: a constructive interpretation of the debate between horizontalists and structuralists', *Metroeconomica*, 55(4), 367–85.

Fontana, G. (2009) *Money, Uncertainty and Time*, Abingdon, UK: Routledge.

Fontana, G. (2011, forthcoming) 'Single period analysis and continuation analysis of endogenous money: A revisitation of the debate between horizontalists and structuralists', in Geoff C. Harcourt, *Handbook of Post-Keynesian Economics*, vol. 1, Oxford: Oxford University Press.

Fontana, G. and Gerrard, B. (2002) 'The encompassing principle as an emerging methodology for Post Keynesian economics', in P. Arestis, M. Desai and S.C. Dow (eds), *Money, Microeconomics and Keynes: Essays in Honour of Victoria Chick*, vol. 2, Cheltenham: Edward Elgar.

Fontana, G. and Palacio-Vera, A. (2002) 'Monetary policy rules: what are we learning?', *Journal of Post Keynesian Economics*, 24, 547–68.

Fontana, G. and Palacio-Vera, A. (2003) 'Modern theory and practice of central banking: an endogenous money perspective', in L.P. Rochon and S. Rossi (eds).

Fontana, G. and Realfonzo, R. (eds) (2005) *The Monetary Theory of Production: Tradition and Perspectives*, London: Palgrave Macmillan.

Fontana, G. and Setterfield, M. (2009) 'Macroeconomics, endogenous money and the contemporary financial crisis: A teaching model', *International Journal of Pluralism and Economic Education*, 1(1), 130–47.

Goodhart, C.A.E. (1989) 'Has Moore become too horizontal?', *Journal of Post Keynesian Economics*, 12, 29–34.

Harcourt, G.C. and Riach, P. (eds) (1997) *A 'Second Edition' of The General Theory*, London: Routledge.

Henry, S.G.B., Sawyer, M. and Smith, P. (1976) 'Models of inflation in the United Kingdom', *National Institute Economic Review*, 77, 60–71.

Hewitson, G. (1995) 'Post-Keynesian monetary theory: some issues', *Journal of Economic Surveys*, 9, 285–310.

Hicks, J.R. (1982, orig. 1956) 'Methods of dynamic analysis', in J.R. Hicks (ed.), *Money, Interest and Wages: Collected Essays on Economic Theory*, Oxford: Basil Blackwell, vol. 2, pp. 217–35.

Howells, P.G.A. (1995) 'Endogenous money', *International Papers in Political Economy*, 2(2), 1–41.

Howells, P.G.A. (2009) 'Money and banking in a realistic macro model', in G. Fontana and M. Setterfield (eds), *Macroeconomic Theory and Macroeconomic Pedagogy*, Basingstoke: Palgrave Macmillan, pp. 169–90.

Kaldor, N. and Trevithick, J. (1988, orig. 1981) 'A Keynesian perspective on money', in M.C. Sawyer (ed.), *Post-Keynesian Economics*, Aldershot: Edward Elgar.

Lavoie, M. (1992) *Foundations of Post-Keynesian Economics*, Aldershot: Edward Elgar.

Lavoie, M. (1996) 'Horizontalism, structuralism, liquidity preference and the principle of increasing risk', *Scottish Journal of Political Economy*, 43, 275–300.

Lavoie, M. (1999) 'The credit-led supply of deposits and the demand for money: Kaldor's reflux mechanism as previously endorsed by Joan Robinson', *Cambridge Journal of Economics*, 23, 103–13.

Lavoie, M. (2006) 'Endogenous money: accommodationist', in P. Arestis and M. Sawyer (eds).

Minsky, H.P. (1975) *John Maynard Keynes*, London: Macmillan.

Moore, B.J. (1979) 'Monetary factors', in A.S. Eichner (ed.), *A Guide to Post Keynesian Economics*, White Plains, NY: M.E. Sharpe, pp. 120–38.

Moore, B.J. (1988) *Horizontalists and Verticalists: The Macroeconomics of Credit Money*, Cambridge: Cambridge University Press.

Moore, B.J. (1991) 'Money supply endogeneity: "reserve price setting" or "reserve quantity setting"?', *Journal of Post Keynesian Economics*, 13, 404–13.

Moore, B.J. (1995) 'The exogeneity of short-term interest rates: a reply to Wray', *Journal of Economic Issues*, 29, 258–66.

Palley, T.I. (1991) 'The endogenous money supply: consensus and disagreement', *Journal of Post Keynesian Economics*, 13, 397–403.

Palley, T.I. (1994) 'Competing views of the money supply', *Metroeconomica*, 45, 67–88.

Palley, T.I. (1996) 'Accommodationism versus structuralism: time for an accommodation', *Journal of Post Keynesian Economics*, 18, 585–94.

Pollin, R. (1991) 'Two theories of money supply endogeneity: some empirical evidence', *Journal of Post Keynesian Economics*, 13, 366–96.

Pollin, R. (1996) 'Money supply endogeneity: What are the questions and why do they matter?', in G. Deleplace and E.J. Nell (eds), *Money in Motion: The Post Keynesian and Circulation Approaches*, London, Macmillan.

Rochon, L.P. (1999) *Credit, Money and Production: An Alternative Post Keynesian Approach*, Cheltenham: Edward Elgar.

Rochon, L.P. and Rossi, S. (eds) (2003) *Modern Theories of Money: The Nature and Role of Money in Capitalist Economies*, Cheltenham: Edward Elgar.

Sawyer, M. (1971) 'Concentration in British manufacturing industry', *Oxford Economic Papers*, 23, 353–83.

Sawyer, M. (1976) 'Income distribution in OECD countries', *OECD Economic Outlook*, Occasional Studies, July.

Sawyer, M. (1979) 'The variance of logarithms and industrial concentration', *Oxford Bulletin of Economics and Statistics*, 41, 165–81.

Sawyer, M. (1982) *Macro-economics in Question*, Brighton: Wheatsheaf Books and M.E. Sharpe.

Sawyer, M. (1983) *Business Pricing and Inflation*, London: Macmillan and St Martin's Press.

Sawyer, M. (1985) *The Economics of Michal Kalecki*, London: Macmillan.

Sawyer, M. (1996) 'Money, finance and interest rates', in P. Arestis (ed.), *Keynes, Money and the Open Economy: Essays in Honour of Paul Davidson*, vol. 1, Cheltenham: Edward Elgar.

Sawyer, M. (2001) 'Kalecki on money and finance', *European Journal of the History of Economic Thought*, 8(4), 487–508.

Wolfson, M. (1996) 'A Post Keynesian theory of credit rationing', *Journal of Post Keynesian Economics*, 18, 443–70.

Wray, R.L. (1992) 'Commercial banks, the central bank, and endogenous money', *Journal of Post Keynesian Economics*, 14, 297–310.

Wray, R.L. (1995) 'Keynesian monetary theory: liquidity preference or blackbox horizontalism?', *Journal of Economic Issues*, 29, 273–83.

Wray, R.L. (1998) *Understanding Modern Money: The Key to Full Employment and Price Stability*, Cheltenham: Edward Elgar.

8
Economic Growth and Income Distribution: Kalecki, the Kaleckians and Their Critics

Amitava Krishna Dutt

1 Introduction

The work of Michał Kalecki has had a major influence on heterodox theories of growth and distribution. Although heterodox theories which emphasise the role of aggregate demand are usually referred to as being 'Post Keynesian', terms such as Kaleckian, neo-Kaleckian and Kalecki–Steindl are also quite popular, and in any case the importance of Kalecki's contributions to this literature is widely acknowledged.[1] Nevertheless, Kalecki's and Kaleckian contributions have been subject to a fair amount of criticism.

The purpose of this chapter is to appraise Kalecki's and Kaleckian theories of growth and distribution in capitalist economies in the light of these criticisms. To do so, section 2 provides a brief overview of Kalecki's writings on the subject, section 3 discusses the central features of Kaleckian contributions, and section 4 examines and responds to the criticisms.

2 Kalecki on growth and distribution

Of the many aspects of Kalecki's writings related his analysis of growth and distribution we briefly discuss, in turn, his contributions closely connected to the analysis of growth and distribution, that is, on pricing, income distribution, profit and income determination, investment, business cycles and growth.[2]

Regarding pricing, after initially discussing the case of the freely competitive industry, Kalecki devoted the bulk of his career analyzing pricing behaviour in oligopolistic industries. He distinguished between sectors (mainly producing raw materials) with short-run supply limitations, in which prices are demand determined, and oligopolistic industrial sectors producing industrial goods. Kalecki (1971) assumed that in the latter firms, which normally operate with excess capacity, have constant marginal or prime costs up to the level of full capacity, after which it increases or becomes vertical. Firms set price according to

$$P = \mu\kappa,$$

where P is the price, $\mu > 1$ representing the degree of monopoly, and κ is the constant unit prime cost. Kalecki usually took labour and raw materials to be the variable inputs (and user cost in some versions), but did not formally incorporate the determination of the (demand determined) price of materials in his analysis. For simplicity, we assume that labour is the only variable input; the above equation then becomes

$$P = \mu W a \qquad (1)$$

where W is the money wage rate and a. This is the pricing assumption for the economy as a whole. Although in early presentations he tried to develop his analysis in terms of profit-maximising oligopolistic firms, he later went on to justify it in terms of the use of rules of thumb in uncertain environments. After initially focusing on the role of the elasticity of demand, he later adopted the broader approach of making it depend on the degree of concentration in industry, the extent of sales promotion and non-price competition, the size of overhead costs relative to prime costs, the power of trade unions and technological change (Kalecki, 1971). He paid some attention to aggregation issues (over firms and industries), but did not resolve these issues fully.

Concerning income distribution, the wage share in national income, using equation (1), is given by

$$\omega = 1/\mu, \qquad (2)$$

which is Kalecki's basic result that the distribution of income is determined by the degree of monopoly. If the latter is constant, the wage and profit shares in real income are constant. Kalecki (1938) argues that this theory holds not only for the short run but also for the long as long as the degree of monopoly is unaltered and the economy does not reach full capacity utilisation, which Kalecki clearly thinks not to be a necessary outcome.[3]

On the determination of profit and real output and income, Kalecki's approach may be summarised by the equilibrium condition

$$Y = C + I, \tag{3}$$

where Y, C and I denote the real level output (and income), consumption and investment. The equalisation is assumed to be satisfied through variations of real output and income since firms maintain excess capacity and change output rather than price to meet changes in demand.

Aggregate consumption is

$$C = C_W + C_c. \tag{4}$$

where C_W and C_c are consumption by workers and capitalists. Kalecki assumed, for simplicity, that workers consume what they earn, so that

$$C_W = W \tag{5}$$

where W is the real wage bill. Capitalists, who receive real profits Π, save and consume, so that

$$C_C + S = \Pi, \tag{6}$$

where S is real saving by capitalists (which includes savings done directly by firms). Since total income goes to workers or to profit, we have

$$Y = W + \Pi. \tag{7}$$

Substituting equations (4), (5) and (7) into (3) we obtain

$$\Pi = C_C + I, \tag{8}$$

which yields Kalecki's famous expression that capitalists earn what they spend and workers spend what they earn.

Kalecki assumed that current investment is given by past decisions, so that I is exogenous. Regarding the determinants of capitalist consumption he altered his views over time. If we assume, for simplicity, that it is a linear function of total profits, so that

$$C_C = C_0 + (1 - s_c)\,\Pi, \tag{9}$$

where s_c is the marginal propensity to save out profit and C_0 is autonomous consumption by capitalists, we get, by substituting equation (9) into (8), that

$$\Pi = \frac{C_0 + I}{s_c}. \tag{10}$$

Since, by definition,

$$\Pi = (1 - \omega) Y,$$

equations (3) and (10) in yield

$$Y = \frac{\mu}{\mu - 1} \frac{C_0 + I}{s_c}, \tag{11}$$

which determines the equilibrium level of output.[4]

More than any other aspect of his work, Kalecki's theory of investment underwent major changes over time. Steindl (1981) distinguishes between three versions: the first developed in the 1930s, the second in the 1940s and 1950s, and the third in the 1960s. In all, Kalecki took into account lags in investment resulting from delays between investment plans and their implementation because of the time required for the production and delivery of investment goods after orders are made. But in relation to the determinants of investment, although he consistently used linear investment functions and stressed profitability, his specific treatment underwent various changes. Version 1 takes investment plans as a ratio of capital stock to depend positively on the current rate of profit as an indicator of expected future profitability; a negative intercept on this function makes the investment plans depend negatively on the stock of capital. Version 2 replaces the profit rate as the sole determinant with two separate determinants, financial resources available to the firm (on account of his 'principle of increasing risk', according to which risk increases with the amount invested out of borrowed funds so that investment will be greater as the amount of internal funds increases), represented by the level of savings of the economy, and marketing prospects, represented by the current change in profits (Kalecki apparently believed that the level of the profit rate is too simplistic a determinant) reflecting increasing sales, and by changes in the stock of capital which has a negative effect on investment since it represents greater competition and hence more claims on available profits. Version 3, while continuing to stress savings and profitability factors, distinguishes between the returns on new capital (embodying new, efficient production methods) which affect investment decisions and the returns on old capital. Old capital retains some of its earlier markets and profits due to imperfections in competition, but new capital makes inroads due to its productivity advantage, which is assumed to be exogenously given.

Kalecki also assumed that desired investment depends on a number of other factors. Technological change begins to play an increasing role starting from version 2, where a constant positive term is added to the investment function representing it; in Kalecki (1954) its effect is taken to be proportional to capital stock. In version 3, in addition to technological change providing the stimulus incorporated into the earlier version, Kalecki tries to integrate this analysis with his theory of the distribution of profits between old and new machines. A second factor which occasionally plays a role is the interest rate. In version 1 investment plans as a ratio of capital stock depended on the nominal rate of interest (as well as the rate of profit), but its role is eliminated by making it vary proportionately with general business conditions proxied by the rate of profit. In subsequent versions it is not considered a major determinant, arguing that given the importance of internal funds, the cost of borrowed funds is not very important. Finally, the size of capital stock is at times assumed to determine investment plans. As noted earlier, in version 1 the negative intercept term in the investment–capital ratio equation implies that capital stock has a negative effect on investment. However, in version 2 the size of the capital stock implies more rapid technological change, positively affecting investment. In one version the size of capital stock is also argued to make it easier for the firm to borrow, thereby increasing investment (Kalecki, 1971, 106).

Corresponding to his three theories of investment, Kalecki's theory of the business cycle went through three phases, the other components of the theories being more or less the same. In version 1, the investment function makes investment plans depend positively on the level of profit and negatively on the stock of capital, so that, given the lag in investment, the interaction between profit and the stock of capital leads to cycles. This negative effect of capital accumulation on investment decisions is downgraded in version 2, but the role of incomplete re-investment of saving and the negative feedback from capital accumulation brings the upswing to an end. Version 3, which distinguishes between returns to old and new capital, works in a manner analogous to version 1, with the difference that investment is now affected by changes in the profit on new capital alone, rather than on changes in total profits. Mathematically, the business cycle is explained in terms of linear difference (versions 2 and 3) or mixed differential-difference equations (version 1). They result in perpetual cycles only with certain parameter values; otherwise they result in perpetual expansion or convergence to a steady growth path. Kalecki mentions that some of the parameter of his investment functions do change over the cycle, but the effects these nonlinearities is not formally examined by him.

Kalecki's analysis of macroeconomic dynamics is conducted in terms of cycles rather than in terms of equilibrium growth rates. However, Kalecki's later models, which have a growing trend, yield a quadratic equation when the condition of a constant growth rate is imposed (see Sawyer, 1996). Kalecki confined attention to what he conjectured to be the stable solutions and finds that the determinants of the equilibrium growth rate in his models are the parameters of the investment function (including the coefficients on the savings term and the past investment term), the propensity to save of the capitalists, and the parameter representing the stimulative effects of technological change (see Kalecki, 1962). Kalecki made heavy weather of the fact that outside stimuli provided the source of growth in his model, that stimulus being provided by technological change in his models. He came to this conclusion because his earlier models which did not have a growing trend due to technological change ended up in a stationary equilibrium (if stable) without positive net investment while his later models incorporated such a trend because of technological change. However, technological change, which he interpreted in a broad Schumpeterian sense to include new products, and opening up new sources of raw materials (see Kalecki, 1971, 334), did not stimulate the economy by raising the productivity of labour from the supply side, but by providing a boost to investment plans. In Kalecki's models growth is determined by demand-side factors, since the economy is not supply constrained in his models, even at the peak of the cycle.

3   The Kaleckians on growth and distribution

The theory of growth and distribution of the Kaleckians can be discussed in terms of the basic Kaleckian model used by many Kaleckians. It determines output in terms of the parameters of the model with

$$Y = \frac{\mu}{\mu - 1} \frac{I}{s_c}, \tag{11'}$$

which is simply Kalecki's equation with $C_0 = 0$, and is based on Kalecki's theories of pricing, income distribution and profit and output determination. Dividing both sides by K, the stock of capital, this equation can be written as

$$y = \frac{\mu}{\mu - 1} \frac{g}{s_c},$$ (11″)

where $u = Y/K$ is a measure of capacity utilisation and $g = I/K$ is the rate of growth of capital stock under the simplifying assumption that there is no depreciation of capital. This equation can be given a short-run interpretation in which K, and hence g, is given. But, to translate the model into a growth framework, it can be assumed that g is exogenously given, so that, when K increases, so proportionately, does investment. This assumption reflects the notion that the 'exogenous' component of investment depends on the size of the economy as measured by the stock of capital, and provides the economy with an engine of growth based on autonomous investment.

Over the long run, following Kalecki, investment is assumed to react to other economic variables. Some models assume that in the short run g is given, but in the long run it changes according to the equation

$$\dot{g} = \Theta(g^d - g)$$ (12)

where g^d is the desired ratio of investment to capital stock. The desired investment function is assumed to be given, in linear form, by

$$g^d = \gamma_0 + \gamma_1 r + \gamma_2 u,$$ (13)

which states that the desired investment–capital ratio depends on profitability as measured by the rate of profit,

$$r = \frac{\Pi}{K} = \frac{\mu - 1}{\mu} u$$ (14)

and the rate of capacity utilisation. This formulation captures both of Kalecki's main ideas on investment, that is, lags in investment and the dependence of desired investment on profitability and marketing prospects.

Equations (12) and (13), using equations (11″) and (14), imply

$$\dot{g} = \Theta\left[\gamma_0 + \left(\frac{\gamma_1}{s_c} + \frac{\gamma_2}{s_c}\frac{\mu}{\mu - 1} - 1\right)g\right],$$ (15)

which describes how g moves over time in the long run. The long-run dynamics of the model may be stable or unstable. The long-run equilibrium, at

$$g = \frac{\gamma_0}{s_c - \gamma_1 - \gamma_2 \dfrac{\mu}{\mu - 1}}, \tag{16}$$

is stable if $s_c > \gamma_1 + \gamma_2 \dfrac{\mu}{\mu - 1}$, which is the familiar condition requiring that saving adjusts more strongly than investment to changes in output and the rate of capacity utilisation. If the stability condition is satisfied, the long-run effect of a decrease in the mark-up factor μ will imply a rise in the wage share, as shown in equation (2), and the long-run rate of capital accumulation and rate of output growth of the economy, as shown in equation (16). This is the widely-discussed wage-led growth property of this model: a rise in the wage share increases output and capacity utilisation, induces an increase in investment, and therefore the long-run growth rate of the economy. If the stability condition is not satisfied, the economy exhibits knife-edge instability along Harrodian lines: an excess of desired investment over actual investment increases investment and output, and this increases desired investment sufficiently to increase the gap between desired and actual investment, leading to a cumulative expansion in investment and output.

Some Kaleckian models (see Dutt, 1984; Rowthorn, 1981) do not allow for lags in investment, assuming instead that actual and desired investment are always equal, so that

$$g = \gamma_0 + \gamma_1 r + \gamma_2 u. \tag{13'}$$

These models therefore do not distinguish between the short and long runs. As long as the stability condition noted earlier is satisfied, as far as the long-run wage-led growth result is concerned, it does not matter whether we adopt equation (13) or (13'), since in long-run equilibrium $g = g^d$ in the model in which equations (12) and (13) are used. Some other Kaleckian models, whether or not they allow for lags, remove the rate of profit as an argument in the desired investment function, that is, they set $\gamma_1 = 0$. This does not affect the conclusions of the model. Growth is still wage led, given that the stability condition is satisfied. If the stability condition is not satisfied the equilibrium will be unstable even in the short run.

The basic Kaleckian model has been extended in many directions, of which we mention a few to provide a flavour of the large Kaleckian literature. On pricing, extensions deal with the role of additional determinants of mark-ups, such as the need for financing investment (Eichner, 1976; Harcourt and Kenyon, 1976), target return considerations (Lavoie, 1992), and financial factors such as the interest rate (Dutt, 1992a; Hein, 2008). Regarding income distribution, modifications and extensions introduce: additional income groups and classes (beyond capitalists and workers), such as rentiers and financial capitalists (Dutt, 1992a; Hein, 2008), 'overhead' workers receiving salaries (Rowthorn, 1981; Lavoie, 1992) and high-skilled workers (Dutt, forthcoming); and endogenise distribution by allowing the mark-up (and possibly other parameters) to change endogenously due to changes in industrial concentration (Dutt, 1984; Lima, 2000), in the relative bargaining power of workers and firms (Dutt, 1992b), and in technology, and the interactions of these changes with growth dynamics examined (see Dutt, forthcoming). Concerning investment, financial variables such as the interest rate, the internal financial position of firms as measured by the gearing ratio (Steindl, 1952), measures of financial fragility (Taylor, 2004), technological change (Rowthorn, 1981; Dutt, 1990; and You, 1994) which is sometimes endogenised, and expected profitability as measured by the profit share and the rate of capacity utilisation (Bhaduri and Marglin, 1990) have been added, or analyzed in new ways. The last contribution shows that growth may be wage-led or profit-led: with a strong profit share effect on investment, it is possible that a rise in the wage share (or fall in the profit share) can reduce growth because of the negative effect on investment even with the positive consumption effect. Regarding business cycles, Kalecki's theory has been subject to some criticisms on account of its difference-differential structure (see Goodwin, 1989), and for generating perpetual and non-explosive cycles only under specific parameter values which meant that cycles could either require recurrent exogenous shocks or exogenous floors or ceilings, approaches criticised by Kalecki (1954) himself. Cycles have subsequently been introduced into the Kaleckian growth both by introducing additional dynamics of the real wage due to labour market conditions (Dutt, 1992b) or financial factors (Taylor, 2004), or by introducing nonlinearities in saving and investment functions (Assous, 2003). Finally, extensions have also been made to deal with more than one sector (for instance, a flexprice agricultural sector; see Taylor, 1983), government fiscal policy and debt (You and Dutt, 1996), and open economy considerations (Blecker 1999).

4   Kalecki, the Kaleckians and their critics

We saw in section 2 that Kalecki's own contributions use simple relationships between relevant distributional and growth variables, and allow aggregate demand to determine output and growth, with unemployment and excess capacity persisting along the growth path. However, he analyzes cyclical growth, rather than steady state long-run growth equilibria. We saw in section 3 that the Kaleckians draw on the former aspects of Kalecki's writings, but often examine growth in terms of long-run stable growth equilibria at which unemployment and excess capacity prevail, although they also sometimes analyze cyclical and unstable growth paths. We now turn to the critics of Kalecki and the Kaleckians, who either focus on the problems common to both, or find the latter to be at fault for departing from Kalecki's analysis.

4.1   Method

On methodology we focus on the use of the equilibrium method.[5] It has been argued that Kalecki did not use it and had doubts on its usefulness, but Kaleckians have generally adopted it in their work. Sawyer (1985: 5–6) writes that 'Kalecki made little use of (and was even hostile to) that major tool of analysis in neo-classical economics, namely equilibrium analysis. ... Kalecki viewed the capitalist economies as inherently cyclical ... Thus, for Kalecki there is no short run equilibrium position to be analyzed nor is there any long-run equilibrium to which the economy will tend.'

In defence of the Kaleckian use of the equilibrium approach, it should be pointed out that equilibrium should be thought of not as an actual state of rest, or a tranquil state, but rather as a theoretical tool of analysis. Kalecki himself was probably obsessed with cyclical behaviour in his models because he took the capitalist economy to be inherently unstable. But the equilibrium in a model does not imply a position of rest for actual economies, since in the model many things which can actually change over time are held constant in order to abstract from their influences. If these things change erratically, they need not be modelled formally. But if they do change systematically, the equilibrium model can be the basis of examining the results of the endogenous dynamics of these state variables as mentioned earlier in terms of the use of labor market and financial dynamics.

4.2   Nature of long-run equilibrium

A second set of criticisms relate to the *nature* of the long-run equilibrium position in Kaleckian models, that is, the presence of unemployment and excess capacity. Although Kalecki's own analysis did not involve the concept of such equilibrium positions, to the extent that it seems to allow for the existence of unemployment, excess capacity in the long run, they may said to implicitly apply to his work as well.

One characteristic of Kaleckian models is the persistence of unemployment in long-run equilibrium. This characteristic is clearly at odds with the conception of long-run equilibrium in neoclassical growth theory. In mainstream neoclassical models even if the economy experiences unemployment in the short run in the presence of nominal wage rigidity (a possibility not even considered in old or new neoclassical growth theory), in the long run the economy is found to converge to the natural rate path with 'full' employment (or, in some versions, at least at the natural or NAIRU rate of unemployment) in which growth is determined by the growth of labour supply and productivity growth. The mechanism by which unemployment is supposed to disappear in the long run is wage-price flexibility: unemployment in the short run leads to downward wage adjustment, which lowers the price level, reduces the real supply of money, and by reducing the interest rate or directly by increasing real balances, induces an expansion in investment and consumption demand, increasing output until 'full' employment is reached. If such market forces are insufficient, government fiscal and monetary policy can be expected to achieve this result. Kalecki's writings suggest that such forces may not take the economy to its natural rate of growth. The interest rate mechanism may not work, and a fall in money wages – if it results in a fall in the real wage and a rise in the mark-up, may depress aggregate demand because of the distributional shift away from people with a higher consumption propensity. Others, including Keynes and the post-Keynesians, have added additional reasons why the market mechanism may not operate in the presence of uncertainty, endogenous money, and debt deflation. Kalecki (1971) also argued that capitalists and other dominant classes could oppose expansionary government policies during recessions even if they increased their profits because: they could see increased government involvement as a threat to their autonomy; they have 'moral' reasons such as not spending beyond one's means, the need for sound finance, and for earning ones' living rather than receiving assistance from others; rentiers would be against any possibilities of inflationary pressures; and the captains of industry would not appreciate a fall in worker discipline resulting from low rates of unemployment. Most heterodox economists would not consider the existence of unemployment in the long run as a problem, but may still balk at the model for implying that in long-run equilibrium labour demand growth is not necessarily equal to labour supply growth, so that the unemployment rate rises or falls without bound. However, extensions of the Kaleckian model endogenise effective labour supply. For instance, in Dutt (2006) it is shown that if the rate of technological change responds endogenously to labour market conditions – that is, labour shortages spur technological change – the long-run equilibrium position of the economy implies a constant unemployment rate while maintaining the standard Kaleckian results.

A second characteristic of Kaleckian models is the existence of excess capacity in long-run equilibrium. A result common to most Kaleckian models is that in long-run equilibrium the utilisation of capacity is endogenous and can take any equilibrium value consistent with the saving and investment equations. The critics argue that such an outcome is inconsistent with a position of long-run equilibrium at which the actual level of capacity utilisation would have to be equal to the rate desired or planned by firms. Otherwise, firms would change their behaviour in an attempt to achieve their desired level (see Auerbach and Skott, 1988, Committeri, 1986).[6] If this desired level of capacity is exogenously given, the long-run equilibrium level of capacity utilisation cannot be endogenous.

The behavioural changes that firms can make include changes in the mark-up and in investment plans. The existence of excess capacity may induce firms to reduce their mark-up rates. Since this redistributes income to wages from which the propensity to spend is higher, aggregate demand increases and this increases the rate of capacity utilisation, bringing it closer to desired capacity utilisation. While this is logically unexceptionable, it is implausible. Kalecki argued that the mark-up behaves counter-cyclically and subsequent theoretical and empirical research has confirmed his idea (see Dutt, forthcoming). Moreover, to the extent that low capacity utilisation is associated with high unemployment rates, firms may be able to obtain higher mark-ups (and pay lower real wages) when capacity utilisation is low. Regarding variations in the rate of investment it is argued that if excess capacity is greater than what is desired, investment will fall. However, this fall in investment will reduce aggregate demand and result in greater excess capacity, implying Harrodian knife-edge instability. It can be argued, however, against the Kaleckian approach, that this instability result confirms the problematic nature of an investment function with capacity utilisation as a variable in the investment function. A third mechanism of adjustment is monetary policy, with the central bank pursuing expansionary (contractionary) monetary policy and stimulating (reducing) investment when actual capacity utilisation is lower (higher) than desired (Dumenil and Levy, 1999).

These criticisms have sparked a fair amount of controversy. Only a brief summary of the debates is provided here (see Skott, forthcoming; Hein, Lavoie and van Treeck, forthcoming; and Dutt, 2010). First, it is argued that the long-run equilibrium in the Kaleckian model is not actually a position of rest but, rather, a position that the economy would reach in the long run when its parameters – which in reality are subject to intermittent shocks – are notionally held constant; thus it is not appropriate to impose the condition that actual and desired capacity utilisation must be equal at that equilibrium. Second, it is argued that in a situation of uncertainty, firms may not have a precise level of desired capacity utilisation, but are likely to have a band within which they will accept any level of capacity utilisation without being surprised by the outcome and being driven to change their behaviour. Third, there is no reason for the desired degree of capacity utilisation to be exogenously given (Lavoie, 1995). Dutt (1997) shows that if one introduces strategic considerations in determining desired excess capacity, the desired degree of capacity utilization will change depending on the difference between expected growth and actual growth. Assuming adaptive expectations formation about growth, the long-run equilibrium, at which actual and expected growth are equal and desired and actual capacity utilisation rates are equal, and in which standard Kaleckian results – such as the positive relation between the real wage, the labour share, and growth, obtain. Skott (forthcoming) criticises this approach by arguing that the endogeneity of desired capacity utilisation per se does not invalidate the criticism: if the desired level of capacity utilisation depends on the profit rate, the Kaleckian results do not hold. However, if firms do not have a clear idea of their optimal desired level of capacity utilisation, but only an idea whether their desired labour is too high or low compared to what is best, and change their desired level accordingly, Kaleckian results are more plausible (Dutt, 2010). Fourth, firms may have multiple and mutually exclusive targets to achieve, of which the targeted or desired rate of capacity utilisation is only be one, so that firms have to trade-off between alternative targets and adjustment to a specific desired level of capacity utilisation need not occur. Initially proposed by Lavoie (1992), who examined conflict between firms and workers implying an additional target, Dallery and van Treeck (2010) have recently extended this argument to include conflict between shareholders and managers over the profit and growth targets, and shown that, given these conflicting objectives, the long-run equilibrium level of capacity utilisation which results from these conflicting objectives is endogenous, and produce Kaleckian results. Finally, models in which actual capacity utilisation is brought into equality with the desired rate with monetary policy, can also be shown to imply Kaleckian results because of the endogeneity of the desired rate of capacity utilisation due to the distributional effects of inflation (Hein, Lavoie and van Treeck, 2010).[7]

These criticisms are closely related to another criticism which points to the alleged empirical implausibility of the implications of long-run equilibrium positions in Kaleckian models. Skott (forthcoming), for instance, argues that with reasonable values for saving and investment parameters, the Kaleckian model implies that, starting from an initial long-run equilibrium, changes in parameters such as the saving rate result in high and unrealistic changes in levels of capacity utilisation. While this chapter is not concerned with empirical issues per se, this criticism is raised here because of the conceptual issues it raises regarding the evaluation of Kaleckian models. The criticism just discussed finds the Kaleckian model wanting by imposing additional auxiliary assumptions, such as linear saving and investment functions and abstracting from labour and asset market and open economy complications. If these assumptions are removed, the criticisms may be invalidated. For instance, if the investment function is nonlinear in the level of capacity utilisation, or if there are feedback effects from asset markets due to changes in asset prices, expectations and distribution, a change in the saving function will have a very different effect from what is implied by simple linear models.[8]

4.3   Determinants of investment

One final criticism, this time of the Kaleckians, is that they assume that investment depends on the rate of capacity utilisation, which deviates from the analysis proposed by Kalecki. Trigg (1994) argues that with this assumption, they bastardise Kalecki's contributions and do what Kalecki explicitly rejected with good reason. Although some aspects of his argument are problematic (see Dutt, 2001), Trigg is correct to note that there is a difference between Kalecki and the Kaleckians regarding this aspect of investment. He is also right in pointing out that Kalecki (1954) rejected the accelerator form of the investment function with output as an argument. However, Kalecki's rejection was actually in relation to *changes* in output, rather than the *level* of output or capacity utilisation. Moreover, Kalecki examined actual changes in output and investment to argue that the output accelerator, given appropriate time lags, was not empirically plausible. Kalecki therefore argues that it is better to introduce output considerations through its effects on profits, rather than directly.

It is another matter whether or not Kalecki is justified in his argument. First, Kalecki's empirical analysis consists only of examining time trends of two variables, one of which happens to be output *changes* rather capacity utilisation *levels*. Second, Steindl (1952), who was strongly influenced by Kalecki's writings, concludes that the rate of capacity utilisation is an important determinant of investment, and argues that this approach is supported by a careful analysis of the different versions of Kalecki's investment functions. Steindl (1981) locates two main differences between version 1 and versions 2 and 3 of Kalecki's formulations. One difference concerns whether or not investment is driven by recent changes in the relevant variables such as the change in sales or profits as in the later versions, or by integral values with result from earlier changes, such as the volume of sales and profits as in the earlier one. The later version not only leaves out changes other than the most recent changes in markets and profits, but also has the result of destabilising the model. In contrast to these problems, however, the later version has the important advantage of taking into account the separate influences of financial resources and the demand for the firm's products. To overcome the problematic aspects of the later versions but retain its positive feature, Steindl (1981) argues that it is more natural to introduce demand considerations more directly, in the form of the degree of utilisation of capacity, and suggests an investment function which depends on saving as a ratio of capital stock (to take into account financial considerations, as did Kalecki), and on the deviation of the actual rate of capacity utilisation from what he calls 'normal or desired utilisation'. Thus, the Kaleckian approach to the investment function follows the spirit, if not the letter, of Kalecki's ideas.

5   Summary and conclusions

This chapter has offered a brief discussion of Kalecki's writings on growth and distribution, examined how subsequent writers – who can be called Kaleckians – have built on his foundations, and evaluated the criticisms of the analysis of growth and distribution of Kalecki and the Kaleckians. It has argued that Kalecki and, following him, the Kaleckians have developed an internally consistent of growth and distribution which stresses the role of aggregate demand and which can address a broad range of issues related to the long-run dynamics of capitalist economies. This is not to argue that all economies will behave in the manner visualised by Kalecki and the Kaleckians, since some economies may at times reach their full employment and full capacity constraints, or be constrained by international conditions, but that it may be relevant for analyzing many economies at many times.

It has also argued that although the Kaleckians have not followed Kalecki to the letter – which can, in fact degenerate into fundamentalist idolatory – they have tried to draw from Kalecki's work his central ideas. The main aspects of Kalecki's writings from which the Kaleckians have departed are the specifics of his analysis of investment and business cycles, which underwent considerable changes over time, and which even Kalecki found to be rather mechanistic. The Kaleckians can therefore be considered justified in departing from Kalecki's specific analysis and building on his rich conceptual contributions on these issues, and on his central contributions on pricing, distribution and effective demand.

Notes

1. See, for instance, Blecker (1999), Dutt (1990) and Lavoie (1992).
2. See Sawyer for more details.
3. Kalecki also took into account materials as a variable input and overhead labour, which we ignore for simplicity.
4. Kalecki considers a number of variations, for instance incorporating multi-sector and open economy issues, which do not change the basic thrust of his analysis.
5. The use of relations between relevant variables not based explicitly on optimising underpinnings is another possible methodological criticism. Since this is a general criticism of many heterodox contributions, we do not discuss it here. Suffice it to note that many of Kalecki's relations between variables can be given optimising foundations (see Sen and Dutt, 1995), and the connection between optimisation and 'rationality' – often used as a justification for the method – is arguably tenuous at best.

   Another methodological criticism (Steedman, 1982) is the use of a macroeconomic approach which does not give attention to intersectoral linkages and the fact that production involves the use of other goods as inputs à la Sraffa. However, if the purpose of a theory of pricing is to provide microeconomic foundations of the macroeconomics of distribution and growth, it is arguable that a one-sector macroeconomic approach may be adequate, for simplicity and to avoid the contamination with 'noise' due to non-systematic differences between sectors. If there are *systematic* differences between sectors are considered relevant, then multi-sector models may be more appropriate (Dutt, 2001).
6. Indeed, some Kaleckians, starting with Steindl (1952), assume that the desired rate of investment depends on the difference between the actual rate of capacity utilisation and the planned or desired rate of capacity utilisation, but the actual and desired rates are not equalised in long-run equilibrium.
7. Kalecki and many Kaleckians both use the standard approach to the distinction between runs by allowing some variables – like output and profits – to change in the short run while holding some to be constant – like investment

and the stock of capital – which they allow to change in the long run. However, they do *not* emphasise qualitative differences between the behaviour of the economy in the two runs, consistent with Kalecki's view that 'the long-run trend is but a slowly changing component of a chain of short-run situations, it has no independent entity' (Kalecki, 1971, p. 165).

8. Another related criticism, the possible inconsistency between the Kaleckian approach and the classical-Marxian conception of the long-period position in which competition equalises the rate of profit across sectors and in which capacity utilisation is as planned by firms, is not addressed here (but see Dutt, 1995).

References

Assous, Michael (2003) 'Kalecki's contribution to the emergence of business cycle theories: An interpretation of his 1939 *Essays*', *History of Economic Ideas*, 11(1), 99–124.

Auerbach, Paul and Peter Skott (1988) 'Concentration, competition and distribution – a critique of theories of monopoly capital', *International Review of Applied Economics*, 2(1), 44–62.

Bhaduri, Amit and Stephen A. Marglin (1990) 'Unemployment and the real wage: The economic basis of contesting political ideologies', *Cambridge Journal of Economics*, 14(4), December, 375–93.

Blecker, Robert (1999) 'Kaleckian macro models for open economies', in Johan Deprez and John Harvey (eds), *Foundations of International Economics: Post-Keynesian Perspectives*, London: Routledge.

Committeri, M. (1986) 'Some comments on recent contributions on capital accumulation, income distribution and capacity utilization', *Political Economy*, 2(2), 161–86.

Dallery, T. and van Treeck, T. (2010) 'Conflicting claims and equilibrium adjustment processes in a stock-flow consistent macro model', *Review of Political Economy*, 22(2), 205–33.

Dumenil, Gerard and Levy, Dominic (1999) 'Being Keynesian in the short term and classical in the long term: The traverse to classical long-term equilibrium', *Manchester School*, 67(6), 684–716.

Dutt, Amitava Krishna (1984) 'Stagnation, income distribution and monopoly power', *Cambridge Journal of Economics*, 8(1), 25–40.

Dutt, Amitava Krishna (1990) *Growth, Distribution and Uneven Development*, Cambridge, UK: Cambridge University Press.

Dutt, Amitava Krishna (1992a) 'Rentiers in Post-Keynesian models', in P. Arestis and V. Chick (eds), *Recent Developments in Post-Keynesian Economics*, Aldershot, UK: Edward Elgar.

Dutt, Amitava Krishna (1992b) 'Conflict inflation, distribution, cyclical accumulation and crises', *European Journal of Political Economy*, 8, 579–97.

Dutt, Amitava Krishna (1995) 'Monopoly power and uniform rates of profit: a reply to Glick–Campbell and Dumenil–Levy', *Review of Radical Political Economics*, 27(2), 142–53.

Dutt, Amitava Krishna (1997) 'Equilibrium, path dependence and hysteresis in post-Keynesian models', in P. Arestis, G. Palma and M. Sawyer (eds), *Markets, Unemployment and Economic Policy*, London and New York: Routledge.

Dutt, Amitava Krishna (2001) 'Kalecki e os Kaleckianos: A relevância atual de Kalecki', in L. Pomeranz, J. Moglioli and G. T. Lima (eds), *Dinamica economica do capitalismo contemporaneo: Homenagem a M. Kalecki*, Sao Paulo: University of Sao Paulo Press, pp. 21–68.

Dutt, Amitava Krishna (2006) 'Aggregate demand, aggregate supply and economic growth', *International Review of Applied Economics*, 20(3), 319–36.

Dutt, Amitava Krishna (2010) 'Equilibrium, stability and path dependence in post-Keynesian models of growth', in Adriano Birolo, Duncan Foley, Heinz D. Kurz, Bertram Schefold and Ian Steedman (eds), *Production, Distribution and Trade: Alternative Perspectives*, London: Routledge, pp. 233–53.

Dutt, Amitava Krishna (forthcoming) 'Distributional dynamics in Post-Keynesian growth models', *Journal of Post Keynesian Economics*.

Eichner, Alfred S. (1976) *The Megacorp and Oligopoly*, Cambridge: Cambridge University Press.

Goodwin, Richard M. (1989) 'Kalecki's economic dynamics: a personal view', in Mario M. Sebastiani (ed.), *Kalecki's Relevance Today*, New York: St. Martin's Press.

Harcourt, Geoff C. and Peter Kenyon (1976) 'Pricing and the investment decision', *Kyklos*, 29, 449–72.

Hein, Eckhard (2008) *Money, Distribution Conflict and Capital Accumulation. Contributions to 'Monetary Analysis'*, Basingstoke: Palgrave Macmillan.

Hein, Eckhard, Marc Lavoie and Till van Treeck (forthcoming) 'Harrodian instability and the "normal" rate of capacity utilization in Kaleckian models of growth and distribution: a survey', *Metroeconomica*.

Kalecki, Michal (1938) 'The determinants of distribution of national income', *Econometrica*, 6, 97–112.

Kalecki, Michal (1954) *Theory of Economic Dynamics*, London: Allen and Unwin.

Kalecki, Michal (1962) 'Observations on the theory of growth', *Economic Journal*, 72(285), 134–53.

Kalecki, Michal (1971) *Selected Essays on the Dynamics of Capitalist Economies*, Cambridge, UK: Cambridge University Press.

Lavoie, Marc (1992) *Foundations of Post-Keynesian Economic Analysis*, Aldershot: Edward Elgar.

Lavoie, Marc (1995) 'The Kaleckian model of growth and distribution and its neo-Ricardian and neo-Marxian critiques', *Cambridge Journal of Economics*, 19(6), 789–818.

Lima, Gilberto T. (2000) 'Market concentration and technological innovation in a dynamic model of growth and distribution', *Banca Nazionale del Lavoro Quarterly Review*, 215, 447–75.

Rowthorn, Robert E. (1981) 'Demand, real wages and economic growth', *Thames Papers in Political Economy*, Autumn, 1–39.

Sawyer, Malcolm C. (1985) *The Economics of Michal Kalecki*, London: Macmillan.

Sawyer, Malcolm C. (1996) 'Kalecki on the trade cycle and economic growth', in J. E. King (ed.), *An Alternative Macroeconomic Theory: The Kaleckian Model and Post-Keynesian Economics*, Boston: Kluwer Academic Publishers.

Sen, Anindya and Amitava K. Dutt (1995) 'Wage bargaining, imperfect competition and the markup: optimizing microfoundations', *Economics Letters*, 48(1), 15–20.

Skott, Peter (forthcoming) 'Theoretical and empirical shortcomings of the Kaleckian investment function', *Metroeconomica*.

Steedman, Ian (1992) 'Questions for Kaleckians', *Review of Political Economy*, 4(2), 125–51.

Steindl, Josef (1952) *Maturity and Stagnation in American Capitalism*, Oxford: Basil Blackwell.

Steindl, Josef (1981) 'Some comments on the three versions of Kalecki's theory of the trade cycle', in J. Los et al. (eds), *Studies in Economic Theory and Practice: Essays*, Amsterdam: North-Holland.

Taylor, Lance (1983) *Structuralist Macroeconomics*, New York: Basic Books.

Taylor, Lance (2004) *Reconstructing Macroeconomics*, Cambridge, MA: Harvard University Press.

Trigg, Andrew B. (1994) 'On the relationship between Kalecki and the Kaleckians', *Journal of Post Keynesian Economics*, 17(1), 91–109.

You, Jong-Il (1994) 'Endogenous technical change, accumulation, and distribution', in A. Dutt (ed.), *New Directions in Analytical Political Economy*, Aldershot: Edward Elgar.

You, Jong-Il and Amitava Krishna Dutt (1996) 'Government debt, income distribution and growth', *Cambridge Journal of Economics*, 20(3), 335–51.

9
The Influence of Michał Kalecki on Joan Robinson's Approach to Economics*

G.C. Harcourt and Peter Kriesler

1 Introduction

Joan Robinson and Michał Kalecki were two of the intellectual giants of twentieth-century economics, and their contributions over a significant range of issues have had major impacts, particularly on heterodox economics. This chapter examines the significant communications between them, concentrating on the major cross-influences which were apparent from their first meeting.

In a number of places Joan Robinson describes her first meeting with Kalecki and the extraordinary impact it had on her. It marked the beginning of a life-long friendship. Joan Robinson was also the principal champion of Kalecki's independent discovery of the main propositions of Maynard Keynes's *General Theory*. Here are her accounts of their first meeting in early 1936, and of Kalecki's principled reaction to Keynes getting the lion's share of recognition. 'I well remember my first meeting with Michał Kalecki – a strange visitor who was not only already familiar with our brand-new theories, but had even invented

---

*We have chosen to write on Michał Kalecki's influence on Joan Robinson for two main reasons. First, Malcolm has made many important contributions to our understanding of Kalecki's contributions and of the theory of the firm. Secondly, both of us much admire and have been greatly influenced by Kalecki and Joan Robinson. Sadly, while we both knew Joan Robinson, neither of us ever met Kalecki – every time he was in Cambridge in the postwar period, GCH was in Australia and PK was either not born or also was in Australia. Finally, may we say how much we admire Malcolm's many contributions to post-Keynesian economics, in both his writing and teaching, and how much we value his long-sustained friendship and support? It is a privilege to contribute to this collection of essays in his honour.

some of our private jokes. It gave me a kind of Pirandello feeling – was it he who was speaking or I?' (Robinson 1964, 95).

> Kalecki did not make any public claim to his independent discovery of the *General Theory*. I made it my business to blow his trumpet for him but I was often met with scepticism … At the end of his life, Michal told me that he felt he had done right not to make any claim to rivalry with Keynes. It would only have led to a tiresome kind of argument. Perhaps scepticism about my claim for him was due to the difficulty of believing that anyone was capable of taking this high line in our degenerate age. (Robinson 1977, 186)

The only reference to this question comes in the Preface to his posthumously published essays (Kalecki 1971). He refers to three papers published in 1933, 1934 and 1935 in Polish which contained, he believed, the essentials of *The General Theory* (Robinson, 1977, 186–7).

The ongoing debates between Joan Robinson and Kalecki, although they were fundamentally in sympathy with each other, must have been extraordinarily vigorous if we may judge from their published work, what is available of their correspondence and what is known independently of their personal characteristics (see Harcourt and Kerr 2009; Steindl 1981; and Harcourt 2006, Appendix 1). An example may be found in Joan Robinson's review article of *The Economics of Full Employment* (six studies in applied economics prepared at the Oxford Institute of Statistics), published in the *Economic Journal* in 1945 and reprinted in Volume I of her *Collected Economic Papers* (*C.E.P*), 1951. She thought that overall – she exempted 'Mr Schumacher's contribution' – 'the essays [seemed] somewhat unnecessarily technical and severe in style. [Schumacher's essay provided] an interlude in pleasant pastures between the rocky uplands of Mr. Kalecki's austere exposition and the dense forest of Dr. Balogh's close-packed argument' (Robinson 1951, 99).

Kalecki and John Robinson were to spend many hours debating economic and political issues. In her published writings Joan Robinson makes frequent references to Kalecki's writings and views. In Prue Kerr and Murray Milgate's General Index to Joan Robinson's five volumes of *Collected Economic Papers* (1980), there are nearly two pages listing references by Joan Robinson to Kalecki; they cover many topics, arguments and disagreements.

Important amongst these were the discussions of Keynesian theory, and the attempt by both to extend the analysis. This is discussed in the next section. Particular emphasis is placed on Kalecki's paper on 'a theorem on technical progress' which he submitted to the *Economic Journal* under Keynes's editorship. Whereas Joan Robinson thought it an important paper extending Keynesian analysis, Keynes was contemptuous of the paper, which was eventually published elsewhere. Both Kalecki and Joan Robinson thought that one of the central issues determining the dynamic of capitalist accumulation was the role of investment and innovation. They were both critical of Keynes's analysis of investment, but disagreed about the role of 'animal spirits' as a force breaking the stagnationist tendencies of the system. This is discussed in section 3 below. The analysis of investment highlights the importance of methodological issues relating to path-dependence, which was an important area in which both Joan Robinson and Kalecki made fundamental contributions. This is discussed in section 4 below; the related methodological question of the relation between microeconomics and macroeconomics is discussed in section 5. The final section deals with their discussions of the important political constraints on full employment.

2 Keynesian debates

Sadly, Joan Robinson was never to see the translation in full into English by Ferdinando Targetti and Boguslawa Kinda-Hass of Kalecki's remarkable review of Keynes's *General Theory* which was first published in Polish in 1936. It was only published fully in English in the December 1982 issue of *Australian Economic Papers*. By the time the issue reached Cambridge, Joan Robinson had suffered the severe stroke from which she never recovered.[1] The paper provides even more conclusive evidence that Kalecki had made independent discoveries and, moreover, that his approach, coming from his understanding of Marx's schema of reproduction, was more appropriate than Keynes's Marshallian background, for a solution of the realisation problem through the role of effective demand and the provision of a theory of the trade cycle. Furthermore, Kalecki's approach provided not only a theory of the levels of activity and employment in the short period but also a theory of the distribution of the product between wages and profits, and of the determination of total profits. This analysis was built on the base of dominant market structures and individual firms' behaviour within them, as well as on the different spending and saving behaviour of the two income classes themselves. Joan Robinson's analysis in her 1977 contribution to the Kalecki Memorial issue of the *Bulletin* of the Oxford Institute is her clearest exposition of these characteristics of Kalecki's approach (see Robinson 1977, 187–96; and Harcourt 2006, 11–16). In other words, as Joan Robinson repeatedly stressed, Kalecki was able to build the theory of effective demand on the basis of foundations incorporating imperfect competition.

Kalecki's analysis of the monetary and financial aspects of modern capitalism was not as deep or subtle or sophisticated as that offered by Keynes (as Joan Robinson always acknowledged). Nevertheless, Kalecki was not handicapped by having to throw off the classical dichotomy between the monetary and the real, especially in the long period, and the accompanying quantity theory of money as a theory of the general price level, as Keynes had to, much influenced by Richard Kahn (see Harcourt 1994, 1995; and Kahn 1984), as Keynes moved from *A Treatise on Money* to *The General Theory*.

Joan Robinson always considered that Kalecki took too simplistic an approach to the term structure of interest rates by concentrating on only one short-term rate and the bond rate. Kalecki, by contrast, thought that long-term rates were 'remarkably stable' and so could not exert a great influence on the level of investment (Kalecki 1944, 370). She approved of the thrust of Kalecki's principle of increasing risk, especially its emphasis on the imperfections of capital markets, but again thought it too simple to be a comprehensive account of firm size and the rationale for the use of retained profits to finance investment. (In later life it seems that Occam's razor was not always her guiding principle.) However, Kalecki believed that Joan Robinson had not understood the basis of the argument. In one example, Joan Robinson differentiates her analysis from Kalecki's 'in respect of his treatment of finance as a bottleneck' (Robinson 1952, 129). In a letter commenting on the drafts of the book, Kalecki explicitly rejects this, arguing that 'I should like to state first that the role of finance in my theory does not correspond to what you say' (Osiatynski 1991, 538). Subsequently, in a letter to her dated 16 October 1964, Kalecki states: 'I did not ever say that the "firms invest all finance they can get". The principle of increasing risk was to show that they may not be willing to borrow as much as they could' (Osiatynski 1991, 591).

That said, it remains the case that the publication of *The General Theory*, meeting Kalecki in the mid-1930s and reading Marx systematically in the early years of the Second World War combined to bring about a sea change in her approach and in the structure of her theoretical contributions from then on, see Harcourt 1995. She stressed the importance of history while not accepting Marx's or Marxist ideology – she was basically a Left Keynesian and democratic socialist on the Left of the British Labour Party (see Harcourt and Kerr 2009, Ch. 5).

The changes may be most clearly seen if we compare her writings just before and after the publication of *The General Theory* where Marshallian method, concepts, and theory are still very much to the fore (just as they lay behind much of the structure of *A Treatise on Money* and *The General Theory* itself), with the structure of *The Accumulation of Capital* (1956) and *Essays in the Theory of Economic Growth* (1962) (see Harcourt and Kerr 2009, Chs 6–8). Thus, in her two 'interim reports', Robinson (1933a, 1933b), on the state of progress to *The General Theory*, both published in 1933 (though one was written and accepted by *Economica* in 1931; see *C.E.P.*, Vol. I, 1957, viii–ix and Harcourt and Kerr, 2009, 24–6), *A Treatise on Money*, with its Marshallian framework of short-period positions converging on the full long-period stock-flow equilibrium position, is the reference point. This is so, first, for her attempts to sort out the differences between Hayek and Keynes and, secondly, in her argument that Keynes, perhaps unknowingly or, at least, not fully realised by Keynes himself because he was writing a treatise on money, had provided the embryo of a *long-period* theory of activity and employment (see Robinson 1951, 56).

Then, in her introductory book on the new theory (1937a) and in her first attempt to extend the new theory to the long period, especially in her essay on the long-period theory of employment in (1937b), the Marshallian approach and concepts as well as Keynes's new theoretical concepts dominate. In correspondence with Joan Robinson on this paper, Kalecki insisted that the cycle was a more likely outcome than her posited long-period equilibrium. In a letter written to Joan Robinson, dated 3 October 1936, and commenting on her 'The Long-Period Theory of Employment', Kalecki argues that, as a result of a fall in the rate of interest, 'the system must not reach the new long-run equilibrium in the way described in the [last] part of your paper, or fluctuate [a]round this equilibrium, but it can also produce fluctuations [a]round the ascending curve' (Osiatynski 1990, p. 503). This denial of a position of long-period equilibrium, and the emphasis on the role of the cycle and of cyclical growth, were to prove influential in Joan Robinson's later works.

Moreover, although she argued that *The Economics of Imperfect Competition* (1933c) contained a serious critique of the application of marginal productivity theory, marginal productivity theory and the then new, 'all-the-rage' concept of the elasticity of substitution dominate the macro theory of distribution in the *Essays* volume. It is allied with the Kaleckian–Keynesian theory of the saving function which stresses the different values of the marginal propensities to save as between wage-earners and profit-receivers. But, in the postwar years – during the war she had published *An Essay on Marxian Economics* (1942) and innumerable papers and talks in a Left-Keynesian sense on Keynesian theory and its application to monetary, fiscal and incomes policy (see Harcourt and Kerr, 2009, Ch. 5), she adopted and adapted Marxian-Kaleckian constructions in her new thinking about generalising *The General Theory* to the long period as exposited in *The Accumulation of Capital* (1956) and *Essays in The Theory of Economic Growth* (1962).

At the same time, she was developing her critique of the mainstream theory of profits (or, rather, in her opinion, the absence of any such theory) and the neoclassical concept of capital, partly as a result of her need, as she saw it, to analyse the choice of technique in the economy as a whole. This was to her, a secondary, although analytically difficult, complication in her theory of long-period growth. There is little evidence that Kalecki was much interested in this aspect of her work; his emphasis was more on the analysis of technical progress in the processes of accumulation and growth, on which, of course, Joan Robinson also worked, and commented on her debt to Kalecki for his work bringing technical progress and accumulation into line with imperfect competition and the analysis of profits and employment. Indeed, she stood up for one of Kalecki's articles on the topic against the sceptical response of Keynes in his role as editor of the *Economic Journal*. Kalecki submitted 'A theorem on technical progress' to the *Economic Journal* for consideration. Keynes did not publish it, and was extremely critical of it in correspondence with Joan Robinson. From the tone of these comments there can be little doubt that Keynes would have failed these papers had he been marking them for an examination. In particular, 'Here is Kalecki's article. As I said the other night, after a highly rational introduction of a couple of pages my first impression is that it becomes high, almost delirious nonsense' (4 February 1941; Osiatynski 1991, 530).

In later letters he calls Kalecki's arguments in that paper 'esoteric abracadabra' (531) and writes of it: 'So I am of the opinion that the article is pretentious, misleading, inconclusive and perhaps wrong. I would rather have cheese to a weight equal to the paper it would occupy in 5,000 copies of the Journal' (12 March 1941; Osiatynski 1991, 535).

Keynes is particularly critical of the assumptions Kalecki makes about the generality of excess capacity in capitalist economies. For Kalecki, this was a stylised fact describing modern economies, while Keynes was extremely sceptical of it: 'Is it not rather odd when dealing with "long-run problems" to start with the assumption that all firms are always working below capacity' (4 February 1941; Osiatynski

1991, 530). Joan Robinson replied that under-capacity was a normal result of the theory of imperfect competition. This, however, did not impress Keynes:

> For I am still innocent enough to be bewildered by the idea that the assumption of all firms always working below capacity is consistent with 'a long-run problem'. To tell me that 'as for under-capacity working that is part of the usual pack of tricks of imperfect competition' does not carry me any further. For publication in the Journal an article must pass beyond the stage of esoteric abracadabra. (12 February 1941; Osiatynski 1991, 531)

Joan Robinson strongly defended Kalecki against Keynes's criticism on a number of levels. It is clear that she both supported Kalecki's arguments and thought they were important: 'In general I think Kalecki is explaining mysteries not creating them' (Osiatynski 1991, 533). 'Kalecki is on to something important' (Osiatynski 1991, 534). In particular, she defended Kalecki's use of the analysis of imperfect competition against Keynes's criticism by pointing out that 'it is in all the textbooks now', and demonstrating why, even in 'full equilibrium', there would be surplus capacity. (532).

In this correspondence we see both Keynes's scepticism in accepting the analysis of imperfect competition, and Joan Robinson's acceptance of Kalecki's version of it.

3 Investment and innovation

Kalecki wrote extensively on investment decision rules and the determination of accumulation in capitalism and subsequently in socialism. Roy Harrod and his problems influenced both Kalecki and Joan Robinson. They took rather different tacks in relation to what was central in Harrod's contributions and their own interests. In her review article of Harrod's 1948 book in the 1949 *Economic Journal* (see *C.E.P.*, Vol. I, 1951, 155–74), she writes that 'Mr. Kalecki's pioneering work ... on a system of analysis dealing with a dynamic society [had] been very little followed up [and that] Mr. Harrod [made] no reference to him' (*C.E.P.*, Vol. I, 1951, 155). Joan Robinson also gave much greater emphasis to Golden Age models than did Kalecki. She was undoubtedly influenced by Richard Kahn's insistence that Golden Age analysis was the necessary flexing of intellectual muscles before moving onto the really important and relevant development of process analysis of growth in modern developed and developing economies (see Kahn, 1959, 1972). The latter was always Kalecki's priority in these areas. He always analysed growth in terms of economic cycles, and although his analysis of the trend changed over time, it was never around a Golden Age trend (Sawyer 1985, 66–8; Nevile and Kriesler 2011).

Kalecki and Joan Robinson agreed that a thorough knowledge of 'the rules of the game' of societies, of their historical and sociological characteristics and of their inherited institutions were all necessary before any meaningful progress in understanding their behaviour and in making policy proposals would be possible. (Unlike many mainstream economists, especially those hailing from Chicago, they did not believe it was possible to give advice as they stepped off the plane because 'have model, will travel'.) In Joan Robinson's essay, 'Marx, Marshall and Keynes' (Robinson 1955) in illustrating how economists spanning the whole spectrum of views and approaches have lost sight of 'the most valuable parts of Marx's theory, she cites, as an example:

> the schema for expanding reproduction which provide a very simple and quite indispensable approach to the problem of saving and investment and the balance between the production of capital goods and the demand for consumer goods. It was rediscovered and made the basis for the treatment of Keynes's problem by Kalecki and re-invented by Harrod and Domar as the basis for the theory of long-run development. (7)

Kalecki had used the reproduction schemas in his important paper, 'Money and real wages' (Kalecki 1939) to illustrate that it was problems with effective demand, rather than the wage level which were the chief cause of unemployment, and elsewhere used them to analyse long-run capitalist growth (Kalecki 1968b).

Kalecki and Joan Robinson were critical of Keynes's theory of investment, especially as was set out in formal terms in Chapter 11 of *The General Theory* on the marginal efficiency of capital. (In recent years it has been fashionable to be particular chapters of *The General Theory* Keynesians; Joan Robinson was not a Chapter 11 Keynesian but she was very much a Chapter 12 'animal spirits' one. Kalecki, as we have noted, was his own man.) In the criticism of the formal structure of Keynes's theory, it may be surmised that Kalecki was the leader with Joan Robinson absorbing his criticism, following it and extending it, most clearly in her banana diagram (1962, 48).

As we noted, in 1936 Kalecki had written a remarkable Polish-language review article about *The General Theory* (Targetti and Kinda-Hass 1982). In this, he first set out, using his own approach, the determination of the short-period level of employment (and, explicitly, his macro theory of distribution). To do this, he provisionally took the rate of investment in the short period as a given. Then, in the second part of the article, he criticised Keynes's account of the determination of investment expenditure as being an application of static tools and concepts to what is essentially a dynamic process. In other publications in English, he elaborated his critique and Joan Robinson built on this in a number of places in her own papers – for example, in her paper on 'Keynes and Kalecki' in the *Essays* in his honour (Robinson 1964, 96–7) and in her Kalecki Memorial lecture (Robinson 1977, 193–5).[2]

Abba Lerner (1944) had made an internal critique of Keynes's theory, concentrating on Keynes's failure to distinguish between the marginal efficiency of capital (m.e.c.) and the marginal efficiency of investment (m.e.i.) in his theory of the determination of short-period investment expenditure. Lerner argued that the essence of Keynes's theory could be captured in two propositions. First, in full, stock-flow equilibrium, m.e.i. = m.e.c. = r, where r = rate of interest. Secondly, in short-period flow equilibrium, m.e.i. = r < m.e.c. (see Harcourt 2006, Ch. 4).

Kalecki's and Joan Robinson's criticism related to Keynes's arguments as to why, in a given situation, there is a downward-sloping relationship between r and planned investment expenditure in the short period. (Lerner had accepted Keynes's arguments for this – hence his was an internal critique.) Keynes usually assumed marginal cost pricing in all industries and diminishing marginal productivity of labour in the short period, so that if higher levels of output are established, prices will be higher (in the case of investment, the prices of capital goods), and so the value of the m.e.i. will be lower. But this argument only goes through (as we modern theorists say), if individual business people use in their calculations of expected rates of profit on planned investment (m.e.i.), the short-period equilibrium prices of the relevant capital goods. Otherwise, the overall outcome of individual actions will not be the level of output that establishes that equilibrium price and there-fore value of m.e.i. = r. Keynes, in effect, assumes rational expectations on the part of business people rather than the more common sense behaviour that they would use the current, existing, non-equilibrium price of capital goods in their calculations.

Keynes also proposed a second, more long-period argument, namely, that the more accumulation occurred in the present, the greater would be the future capacity of industries and so the further out to the right would be their respective short-period supply curves. He assumed that the longer-period demand curves for products could be taken as given (and downward sloping) so that expected future prices of products would be lower, the more investment is done now, and therefore the lower would be the m.e.i. as well. But as Kalecki and Joan Robinson (and also Tom Asimakopulos) pointed out, here Keynes was not being true to himself.

Usually, he argued that because the future was uncertain, the present played a large (probably too large) part in determining what would be expected to happen. Higher investment now also meant higher prices, profits, output and employment now and these events, on his usual argument, would be projected into the future. How then could the long-period demand curves be taken as givens – would they not, too, be further out to the right, the more investment that was done now? If this were the case, it was not certain that expected prices would be lower nor that the values of m.e.i. would be lower (see Harcourt, 2006, Ch. 4; Sawyer 1985, 194; and Kriesler 1997). '[T]he result of this is that, instead of Keynes providing a theory of unemployment equilibrium, Kalecki argued that it is really a theory of the business cycle' (Kriesler 1997, 311).

So both Kalecki and Robinson rebuilt Keynes's theory on the basis of the two-sided relationship between profitability and accumulation established by Kalecki (and Keynes) – that actual investment played a dominant role in determining actual profitability and actual profitability influenced expectations of what profitability would be, which in turn influenced the rate of investment that would be planned to be undertaken. Given the state of long-term expectations and financial conditions, more accumulation would be planned, the higher was expected profitability. Those two relationships constitute Joan Robinson's banana diagram, see Robinson, 1962, 48, in which the rate of accumulation and profitability are simultaneously determined at the top point of intersection of the two relationships, see Harcourt, 2006, Ch. 4. (The bottom point of intersection is a point of unstable equilibrium.)

One important area of disagreement between Joan Robinson and Kalecki was on the nature of accumulation and stagnation in capitalist economies, which represented fundamental differences on their view of the future of the system. Kalecki stressed the stagnationist tendencies of capitalist economies, believing that these could only be overcome by inventions – that is, technical progress:

'I believe that the antimony of the capitalist economy is in fact more far-reaching: the system cannot break the impasse of fluctuations around a static position unless economic growth is generated by the impact of semi-exogenous factors such as the effect of innovations upon investment' (Kalecki 1962 p. 411; see also Kalecki's letter to Joan Robinson 25 July 1951 Osiatynski 1991 539).

For Joan Robinson, by contrast, the animal spirits of capitalists would maintain investment and capitalist growth:

> This was a subject about which I was arguing with him, on and off, for many years. He maintained that inventions (technical progress) raise the prospects of profits for capitalist firms and encourage investment. I followed Keynes and Marx in regarding the desire of capitalists to expand their operations as an inherent characteristic of the system. I expressed this view in Keynes's phrase about 'animal spirits' which caused Kalecki to regard it as somehow irrational. (Robinson 1971, 90).

4   Methodological issues

Joan Robinson's construction of her banana diagram reflects two strands in the literature: Keynes's shifting equilibrium model (see Keynes 1936, 292–4), and Kalecki's never-ending search for a satisfactory theory of accumulation in capitalism. This culminated in his 1968 *Economic Journal* paper, published only two years before his death, on trend and cycle. There, he argued that the long-term trend was *not* a separate or independent entity, but the statistical outcome of happenings in successive short-term situations.[3] 'In fact, the long-run trend is but a slowly changing component of a chain of short-run situations; it has no independent entity and the [analysis] should be formulated in such a way as to yield the trend-cum business cycle phenomenon' (Kalecki 1968a, 435)

This was his version of the process of cyclical growth, ideas that had been independently developed by Richard Goodwin (see, for example, Goodwin (1967)). Joan Robinson's later writings approached agreement with Kalecki and Goodwin (see Harcourt and Kerr 2009, 96), but she did not have the formal tools that would have allowed her to set out her version of the approach, should she have wanted to (formally, we mean!).

She was very careful to point out the limited nature of the banana diagram: how even if the economy iterated onto the upper intersection point where what was expected and what happened coincided (her version of Harrod's warranted rate of growth), this was not necessarily a sustainable position. The very process of moving through historical time could change the factors determining the two relationships in any given initial situation, that is to say, path-dependence would almost certainly occur.

This highlights another important influence of Kalecki on Joan Robinson, namely in relation to the nature of the long-period analysis. For Kalecki, the concept of a long-period equilibrium was extremely problematic, as is indicated by the earlier quote. From the very beginning of their relationship, Kalecki stressed this point to Joan Robinson, insisting that the cycle was a more likely outcome than a long-period equilibrium. In a letter written to Joan Robinson, dated 3 October 1936, and commenting on her 'The Long-Period Theory of Employment', Kalecki argues that, as a result of a fall in the rate of interest, 'the system must not reach the new long-run equilibrium in the way described in [the] last part of your paper, or fluctuate [a]round this equilibrium, but it can also produce fluctuations [a]round the ascending curve' (Osiatynski 1990, 503). Throughout the later periods of her work, Joan Robinson contrasted what she called history versus equilibrium. By this she meant a rejection of the comparative static method of comparing equilibrium in favour of an analysis of the path the economy takes in historical time. In particular, she argued that equilibrium, if it existed, would always be path dependant, though, in the end she did not think that there was an equilibrium to be found or approached, or even of one waiting to be found. Already, in the early correspondence between Kalecki and Joan Robinson, we see Kalecki attempting to push her to this conclusion, in his rejection of the notion of equilibrium, and, in addition, with his rejection of the long period as having a separate identity, and in his emphasis on path determinacy: 'the rate of growth at a given time is a phenomenon rooted in past economic, social, and technological developments rather than determined fully by the coefficients of our equations as is the case with the business cycle' (Kalecki 1968a, 450).

5   Microfoundations?

Despite the fact that the distinction was suggested by Keynes (Keynes 1936, p. 293), Joan Robinson was very critical of the modern distinction between micro and macro analysis. One of the most powerful statements of her view is in 'What are the questions?' (see Robinson, 1977a, 4). One cannot exist without the other, for '[m]icro questions ... cannot be discussed in the air without any reference to the structure of the economy in which they exist [or] to the process of cyclical and secular change. Equally, macro theories of accumulation and effective demand are generalisations about micro behaviour ... If there is no micro theory, there cannot be any macro either.'

Moreover, the macro setting for orthodox micro theory is a kind of vague Say's Law world which, until very recently anyway, is *not* the macro world that is analysed in *its* own separate compartment. This implies that she would not have accepted the modern search for microeconomic foundations of macroeconomics (nor, probably, macroeconomic foundations of microeconomics, see Crotty, 1980). In this she is very close to Kalecki's view: '[t]he macro and the micro analysis each tell part of the story, and it is only through their interrelation that the whole account emerges. In this way it can be seen that the micro and the macro analyses ... lie side-by-side, existing interdependently, that is, on an equal footing' (Kriesler 1996, 66). Joan Robinson was clearly influenced by Kalecki's microanalysis, both in terms of his work on mark-up pricing, and also on the relation between microeconomic and macroeconomic aspects of the determination of output.

In a number of places Joan Robinson has argued that Kalecki's version of pricing theory is 'more robust than Keynes' and also a major improvement on her own work in *The Economics of Imperfect Competition* (Robinson 1977 p. 187). She became critical of her book due to its comparative static nature, which, she argued, ignored the fundamental issues relating to time and to the problems of getting into equilibrium discussed above. She believed that Kalecki's analysis avoided these problems. Kalecki's mark-up approach was seen as being more dynamic, and also related the pricing decision and distribution to the determination of output, while presenting an alternative theory of distribution to the neoclassical one, of which Joan Robinson was so critical. 'It was Michal Kalecki rather than I who brought imperfect competition into touch with the theory of employment' (Robinson 1933c, viii).

In Kalecki's view, in manufacturing industry, prices are set by producers as a mark-up over costs. For Kalecki, the main determinant of the mark-up was the degree of competition in the relevant market. However, Joan Robinson was unhappy with this formulation of pricing as it was strictly defined in 'short-period terms'. 'I objected that there must be some long-period element in the relation of prices to costs' (Robinson 1977, 189).

What Joan Robinson particularly appreciated in Kalecki's work was the integration of the analysis of pricing with the analysis of effective demand, which she saw as the appropriate path for future development:

> There are two elements in Kalecki's analysis, the share of profit in the product of industry is determined by the level of gross margins, while the total flow of profits per annum depends upon the total flow of capitalists' expenditure on investment and consumption... In this way, Kalecki was able to weave the analysis of imperfect competition and of effective demand together and it was this that opened up the way for what goes under the name of post-Keynesian economic theory. (Robinson 1977, 193)[4]

Joan Robinson was particularly critical of modern microeconomic theory, which, she argued, ignored important aspects of production associated with historical time and uncertainty, unlike Kalecki's analysis where both played a central role in both micro and macro analysis (Robinson 1971a 95–7).

6   The political trade cycle

Joan Robinson was also influenced by Kalecki's analysis of the political limits to full employment. As early as 1943, Kalecki was warning that there was an important distinction between achieving full employment after a slump and maintaining it. He argued that, because unemployment served important functions in capitalist economies, they were not compatible with the maintenance of full employment. Unemployment was essential for the survival of capitalism as it was the means by which the capitalist class asserted its control over the working class. Without unemployment, the system would exacerbate the underlying social and political tensions resulting in problems of discipline and instability. 'Indeed, under a regime of permanent full employment, the "sack" would cease to play its role as a disciplinary measure. The social position of the boss would be undermined, and the self-assurance and class-consciousness of the working, class would grow' (Kalecki 1943 p. 351).

Joan Robinson reinterpreted Kalecki's analysis as providing the basis of a model of the political trade cycle. According to Joan Robinson's interpretation, although governments now know how to create full employment, for the reasons discussed they would not want to do so. However, too much unemployment would have electoral implications.

'Thus [Kalecki] predicted that after the war we should experience a political trade cycle with alternating *stop* and *go*' (Robinson 1977, 195).

7 Summary and conclusions

In this chapter, we have documented the importance of the intellectual relationship between Michał Kalecki and Joan Robinson. It was a fertile relationship, one in which two great intellects influenced each other's economic ideas and thinking, to the considerable benefit of the discipline. The discussion has highlighted a number of important themes in their relationship, which their debates helped to refine. In particular, the nature of path dependence, and the interrelationship of all aspects of economic behaviour were consistent themes in their discussions. Fittingly, these are important starting points for Post Keynesian economics, not least as it has been developed by Malcolm Sawyer.

Notes

1. GCH has often written that the translated review is the most important paper published in *Australian Economic Papers* during his 20 or so years as joint editor, see Harcourt (2006, 21), for a full account of how it came to be published.
2. For a discussion of the differences between Keynes and Kalecki see Sawyer (1985, ch. 9) and Kriesler (1997).
3. Not only is this a fundamental criticism of the distinction between existence and stability of equilibrium with overall independence between the factors responsible for each, but also of the statistical procedure of breaking down time series into trends and cycles as though they too were each the outcome of separate factors independent of those responsible for the other.
4. Originally, Joan Robinson had incorrectly distinguished these two as two different theories, with the mark-up pricing theory explaining distribution in the short run, while the macroanalysis was seen as a long-run theory (Robinson 1964, 99).

References

Crotty, J. (1980) 'Post-Keynesian theory: an overview and evaluation' *American Economic Review, Papers and Proceedings*, 70, 20–5.

Goodwin, R.M. (1967) 'A growth cycle', in C.H. Feinstein (ed.), *Socialism, Capitalism and Economic Growth*. Cambridge: Cambridge University Press.

Harcourt G.C. (1994) 'Kahn and Keynes and the making of *The General Theory*' reprinted in Harcourt 1995, 47–62.

Harcourt G.C. (1995) *Capitalism, Socialism and Post-Keynesianism: Selected Essays of G. C. Harcourt*, Aldershot: Edward Elgar.

Harcourt, G.C. (2006) *The Structure of Post-Keynesian Economics: The Core Contributions of the Pioneers*, Cambridge: Cambridge University Press.

Harcourt, G.C. and Kerr, P. (2009) *Joan Robinson*, Basingstoke: Palgrave Macmillan.

Kahn, R. (1959) 'Exercises in the analysis of growth' reprinted in Kahn 1972, 192–207.

Kahn, R. (1972) *Selected Essays on Employment and Growth*, Cambridge: Cambridge University Press.

Kahn, R. (1984) The *Making of Keynes' General Theory*, Cambridge: Cambridge University Press.

Kalecki, M. (1939) 'Money and real wages', reprinted in Osiatynski 1991, 21–50.

Kalecki, M. (1943) 'Political aspects of full employment', reprinted in Osiatynski 1990, 347–56.

Kalecki, M. (1944) 'Three ways to full employment', reprinted in Osiatynski 1990, 357–76.

Kalecki, M. (1962) 'Observations on the theory of growth', reprinted in Osiatynski 1991, 411–34.

Kalecki, M. (1968a) 'Trend and the business cycle', reprinted in Osiatynski 1991, 435–50.

Kalecki, M. (1968b) 'The Marxian equations of reproduction and modern economics' reprinted in Osiatynski 1991, 459–67.

Kalecki, M. (1971) *Selected Essays on the Dynamics of the Capitalist Economy*, Cambridge: Cambridge University Press.

Kerr, P. and Milgate, M. (1980) *Collected Economic Papers, Joan Robinson 1933–1970: General Index*, Oxford: Basil Blackwell.

Keynes, J.M. (1930) *A Treatise on Money, Collected Writings, Vols. V, VI*, London: Macmillan, 1971.

Keynes, J.M. (1936) *The General Theory of Employment, Interest and Money, Collected Writings Vol. VII*, London: Macmillan, 1973.

Kriesler, P. (1996) 'Microfoundations: a Kaleckian perspective', in J. King (ed.), *An Alternative Macroeconomic Theory: The Kaleckian Model and Post-Keynesian Economics*, Boston, MA: Kluwer, pp. 55–72.

Kriesler, P. (1997), 'Keynes, Kalecki and *The General Theory*', in G.C. Harcourt and P. A. Riach (eds), *A 'Second Edition' of The General Theory*, Vol. 2, London: Routledge, pp. 300–22.

Lerner, A. (1944) *The Economics of Control: Principles of Welfare Economics*, London: Macmillan.

Nevile, J. and Kriesler, P. (2011) 'Dynamic Keynesian economics: cycling forward with Harrod and Kalecki', *Cambridge Journal of Economics*.

Osiatynski, J. (ed.) (1990) *Collected Works of Michal Kalecki, Volume I. Capitalism: Business Cycles and Full Employment* Oxford: Clarendon Press.

Osiatynski, J. (ed.) (1991) *Collected Works of Michal Kalecki, Volume II. Capitalism: Economic Dynamics* Oxford: Clarendon Press.

Robinson, J. (1933a) 'The theory of money and the analysis of output', reprinted in Robinson 1951, 52–8.

Robinson, J. (1933b) 'A parable of savings and investment', *Economica*, 13, 75–85.

Robinson, J. (1933c) *The Economics of Imperfect Competition*, London: Macmillan, 2nd edn, 1969.

Robinson, J. (1937a) *Introduction to the Theory of Employment*, London: Macmillan, 2nd edn, 1969.

Robinson, J. (1937b) *Essays in the Theory of Employment*, Oxford: Basil Blackwell, 2nd edn, 1942.

Robinson, J. (1942) *An Essay on Marxian Economics*, London: Macmillan 2nd edn, 1966.

Robinson, J. (1951) *Collected Economic Papers, Volume I*, Oxford: Basil Blackwell.

Robinson, J. (1952) *The Rate of Interest and Other Essays*, London, Macmillan, 2nd edn, 1975, *The Generalisation of The General Theory and Other Essays*.

Robinson, J. (1955) 'Marx, Marshall and Keynes', reprinted in Robinson 1960, 1–17.

Robinson, J. (1956) *The Accumulation of Capital*, London, Macmillan 2nd edn, 1965; 3rd edn, 1969.

Robinson, J. (1960) *Collected Economic Papers, Volume II*, Oxford: Basil Blackwell.

Robinson, J. (1962) *Essays in the Theory of Economic Growth* London: Macmillan.

Robinson, J. (1964) 'Kalecki and Keynes' reprinted in Robinson 1965, 92–102.

Robinson, J. (1965) *Collected Economic Papers, Volume III*, Oxford: Basil Blackwell.

Robinson, J. (1971) 'Michal Kalecki', reprinted in Robinson 1973, 87–91.

Robinson, J. (1971a) 'The second crisis of economic theory', reprinted in Robinson 1973, 92–105.

Robinson, J. (1973) *Collected Economic Papers, Volume IV*, Oxford: Basil Blackwell.

Robinson, J. (1977) 'Michal Kalecki', reprinted in Robinson 1979, 184–96.

Robinson, J. (1977a) 'What are the questions?', reprinted in Robinson 1979, 1–31.

Robinson, J. (1979) *Collected Economic Papers, Volume V*, Oxford: Basil Blackwell.

Sawyer, M. (1985) *The Economics of Michal Kalecki*, London: Macmillan.

Steindl, J. (1981) 'A personal portrait of Michal Kalecki', *Journal of Post Keynesian Economics*, vol. 3, 590–6.

Targetti, F. and Kinda-Hass, B (1982) 'Kalecki's review of Keynes' *General Theory*', *Australian Economic Papers*, 21, 244–60.

10
Shared Ideas Amid Mutual Incomprehension: Kalecki and Cambridge

Jan Toporowski

Cambridge is a very isolated place ... (Johnson 1977)

1 Introduction: the end of the Cambridge Project[1]

Discussions about the relationship between Michał Kalecki and John Maynard Keynes have rightly focussed upon the compatibility of the ideas of the two men. Interpretations of Keynes have not always found Kalecki to be complementary to Keynes. Joan Robinson famously did (Robinson 1964). But her close associate in Cambridge, Richard Kahn, did not (see, for example, Kahn 1972). Both Kahn and Robinson had worked closely with Keynes and Kalecki. Kalecki's collaboration with Joan Robinson and Richard Kahn occurred during 1939, when Robinson and Kahn supervised Kalecki's research. This chapter focuses on what the fate of that collaboration reveals about the methodological preconceptions of Keynes and Kalecki.

At the end of 1939, Kalecki learned of the termination of the project on industrial pricing, which he had been working on at Cambridge, and which was funded by the National Institute for Economic and Social Research (NIESR). Kalecki moved, with his post funded by the NIESR, to Oxford. Kalecki's relationship with Keynes does not appear to have suffered from the setback of the former's removal to Oxford. Keynes continued to support Kalecki's research through the National Institute of Economic and Social Research. Nevertheless some clash of ideas had occurred and it is useful to consider what those ideas were and why Kalecki was unable to submit his research to a standard Cambridge method of reasoning, or 'mode of thought', to use the much more vivid phrase of Sheila Dow (1996, Ch. 2). Such a consideration lies at the heart of the relationship between Kalecki and Keynes and their many

170

arguments over method. Yet it is largely missing from the extensive literature on the relationship between the theories of the two great men, drawn mainly from Joan Robinson's claim of independent discovery of common theoretical positions (Robinson 1964) and Kalecki's own claim to priority in that discovery: In a letter to T.C. Chang dated 17 February 1955, Kalecki wrote of a lecture that he gave in Cambridge in which 'they made a point of it to stress in the introduction my discovery of General Theory before Keynes' (PAN III 319/30).[2] (At the end of his life Kalecki was even more convinced of the priority of his 'discovery', refer-ring to his own papers published 'in Polish before Keynes' *General Theory* appeared and containing, I believe, its essentials'. Kalecki 1971, p. vii.)

A recent paper in the journal *History of Political Economy* on Keynes's methodological differences with Kalecki concludes correctly that Keynes's analytical methods were foreign to Kalecki but does not really explain why (De Vecchi 2008). Another paper, by Nahid Aslanbeigui and Guy Oakes, suggests that the whole Cambridge project, on the effects of the 1930–1935 depression on prices, costs, production, employment, incomes and foreign trade, was merely an elaborate ruse to remove Dennis Robertson from Cambridge as a way of obtaining the hegemony of Keynesian ideas over economics in that university (Aslanbeigui and Oakes 2002). The case put forward by Aslanbeigui and Oakes is tenuous at best. It does not explain why Robertson was the victim, rather than Arthur Pigou or Maurice Dobb, or even Piero Sraffa, none of whom were Keynesians, and confuses the style of Cambridge for its substance: Just because nothing can happen in Cambridge without a conspiracy does not mean that everything that happens in Cambridge is a conspiracy. There were other factors at work. Even if Aslanbeigui and Oakes suggest that Kalecki was dispensable after Robertson had resigned from Cambridge, Keynes certainly did not cease to support Kalecki after the project had collapsed. Robertson, in any case, returned to Cambridge as Professor of Political Economy in 1943, when Pigou retired.

The principles common to both Keynes and Kalecki were, according to their common interlocutor Joan Robinson, 'that the rate of saving is governed by the rate of investment, that the level of prices is governed by the level of money wage rates, and that the level of interest rates is governed by the supply and demand for money' (Robinson 1966). Any notion of a common monetary and financial analysis may be dismissed despite serious claims that Post Keynesian monetary principles can be detected in Kalecki's work (Sawyer 2001). Even his most sympathetic follower Joseph Steindl was moved to conclude that 'generally speaking you do not find in Kalecki very much about ... finance, debt, credit crises. I don't think Kalecki denied the importance of these factors in any way, but for him they were secondary to, and in a sense derived from, the events in the 'real' sphere of production, investment, over-capacity, and so on' (Steindl 1989, pp. 312–13). Any notion that both emphasised the importance of aggregate demand as a determinant of output and employment may also be dismissed. By the 1930s such ideas were hardly original, and could be found, for example, in Ralph Hawtrey's well-known *Good and Bad Trade*, which had been published in 1913.

In his most serious examination of the *General Theory* Kalecki himself identified 'the proposition that investment determines the global volume of production' as a principle which he had 'proved in a similar way to Keynes's in my *Essays on the Business Cycle Theory*' (Kalecki 1936). However, even among Post Keynesians, such a proposition is hardly common ground. The serious question for Keynesian economics that arises from any comparison of Kalecki with Keynes is why, if the two men had made common discoveries, their closest collaboration in Cambridge in 1939 ended in such apparent incomprehension? Part of the enigma arises because the question has always been approached from the point of view of Keynes's originality in Cambridge economics, an intellectual project to which Joan Robinson recruited Kalecki, who joined willingly because he agreed with essential elements of Keynes's ideas and had few other professional options. As she put it: 'The interesting thing is that two thinkers, from completely different political and intell-ectual starting points, should come to the same conclusion. For us in Cambridge it was a great comfort' (Robinson 1964, p. 337).

The question of the degree to which Kalecki had 'anticipated' Keynes, or shared common ground with him, is a matter of textual exegesis whose starting point has to be what Keynes really meant. The true meaning of Keynes's theory is not an issue on which his partisans themselves agree. Keynes himself sanctioned a wider discussion of his core ideas in his 1937 article in the *Quarterly Journal of Economics* in which he wrote 'I am more attached to the comparatively simple fundamental ideas which underlie my theory than to the particular forms in which I have embodied them, and I have no desire that the latter should be crystallised at the present stage of the debate' (Keynes 1937, p. 111). His most enthusiastic follower George Shackle endorsed this transcendentalist view of Keynes's ideas by referring to 'Keynes's ulti-mate meaning' (Shackle 1967, p. 129). In his last book on Keynes Alan Coddington documented the varieties of ostensibly core Keynesian ideas (Coddington 1983). Specifying the nature and significance of Keynesian ideas is therefore a major task that cannot be addressed satisfactorily in an essay that seeks to offer an intellectual biography of Kalecki. In relation to the failure of his project in Cambridge, the question 'did Kalecki anticipate Keynes?' should really be 'if Keynes and Kalecki held key ideas in common, why was the Cambridge project closed down?'

Answers to this may be found in the incompatible personal chemistry of the two men, one an urbane, 'moderately conservative' upper-class Englishman, the other a Polish Jew of pronounced left-wing and Marxist sympathies who was as socially awkward as he was confident in his views. The financially insecure Kalecki nevertheless yearned for acknowledgement from Keynes of the former's priority in discovering the principles behind the *General Theory* – another misjudgement since Keynes had little inclination to intellectual modesty. (Tadeusz Kowalik points out to me that even in Keynes's lifetime Joan Robinson promised to raise the issue of Kalecki's priority with Keynes, but procrastinated. Kalecki told Kowalik that he eventually went himself to raise the matter with Keynes. But Keynes, like Joan Robinson later, merely treated this as confirmation of the 'scientific' character of his 'discovery'.)

Nevertheless, given their own commitment to 'scientific' economic research, and to the new ideas which they espoused, personal temperament could not have been a sufficient reason for the failure of the Cambridge project. If the Keynesian revolution was the major scientific breakthrough that was claimed by Keynes's supporters in Cambridge, led by Richard Kahn and Joan Robinson, why did Kalecki, who was playing a major part in that revolution, leave the university through which passed the front line of Keynes's war with 'the Classics'?

Much of the criticism that Kalecki's research encountered in Cambridge was methodological in nature. This provides not only the rationale for his departure, but also the clue to the differences that he already had with Keynes over his publications, and which he was to have after leaving Cambridge. While the textual exegetists have pored over the two men's work in search of similarities and complementarities, the fact remains that their differences were rooted in different methodological approaches that went beyond Kalecki's class approach, and Keynes's more obvious preference for explaining economic phenomena in terms of individual choices. At the interface between Cambridge (including its most original thinker after Marshall, Keynes) and Kalecki was a much greater, even impersonal, incompatibility between the economic tradition in Cambridge that had formed Keynes, and the continental European economics from which Kalecki had emerged. Keynes's own failure to understand Kalecki is indicated in a remark that Keynes made, in parenthesis, in a letter to Kahn dated 30 April 1938 referring to the Polish economist's 'appalling method of exposition'. 'His mathematics seems to be largely devoted to covering up the premises and making it extremely difficult to bring one's intuition to bear. If only he would state his premises in the most illuminating possible manner and be perfunctory over his mathematics, instead of the other way around, one would have a better idea of what he is driving at.' Keynes's way of dealing with this, he wrote, was 'to disentangle painfully exactly what the assumptions amount to and then consider whether the conclusion appears to be correct, not bothering much about the proof which, in spite of the appearance to the contrary, obviously contains endless loopholes for introducing fresh assumptions' (Kahn Papers RFK/13/57/366). The 'appalling method of exposition' was that of Kalecki's *Econometrica* article on 'The Determinants of Distribution of National Income'; 'one's intuitions' were obviously Marshallian!

It is argued here that Kalecki's rendezvous in Cambridge was a part of a limited interchange between continental European and Cambridge economic theory. His arrival in Cambridge may be called the third emergence, or impact, of continental European economic theory, in an intellectual community made introverted by its dispersal around a federal university, and its common struggles to establish and maintain economics teaching at that university. Some of this introversion is apparent in Robert Skidelsky's generous chapter on what he called 'Cambridge Civilisation' (Skidelsky 1983). A somewhat more bilious account is provided by the otherwise judicious and scholarly Terence Hutchison in an extended essay on 'The Philosophy and Politics of the Cambridge School' (Hutchison 1981). Earlier, Harry Johnson had painted a picture of Cambridge economics that took exception, in similar terms to Hutchison, to the Marxian influence at Cambridge. However, Johnson emphasised explicitly the influence of Kalecki's ideas, through their advocacy by Joan Robinson, in the Cambridge version of Keynesian economics (Johnson 1977).

2   The Cambridge Research Project

From its very beginnings the Cambridge Project was beset by methodological issues. In the first place, and contrary to much of the subsequent reporting of the project's work, it was not a project of the University of Cambridge, or of its Faculty of Economics, but of the NIESR that was located in Cambridge because that was where Keynes was hoping to establish a permanent economic research unit that was to be the

Department of Applied Economics. This, rather than the machinations of a Keynesian faction in the Faculty of Economics, explains the peculiar administration of the project. The financing for the project came from the NIESR, managed by a Supervisory Committee consisting of Arthur Bowley and Lionel Robbins (both of whom were then working at the London School of Economics), Noel Hall of the NIESR, who was also Professor of Political Economy at University College, London, as well as Keynes and Austin Robinson.

The finance was to support a Cambridge research group that consisted of Keynes and Austin Robinson (Chairman and Secretary respectively), Richard Kahn, Joan Robinson, Piero Sraffa, David Champernowne (the University Lecturer in Statistics), and Kalecki, who was described as working for the group 'as their Statistician'. Kalecki was in fact the only member of the group who was actually engaged in project research, assisted by two research students, Brian Tew and Yu-Nan Hsu. Hence, out of the initial annual budget of £600 allocated to the project, £350 was a salary paid to Kalecki. An initial report on the work of the project referred to the 'functions' of the other members of the group as 'primarily critical and supervisory'. The actual title of the project was *The Cambridge Research Scheme of the National Institute for Economic and Social Research* and its purpose was to study 'the process of Economic Change in the United Kingdom since 1928' (Keynes Papers, King's College Cambridge N15/1/77).

The very top-heavy structures established to manage the project were in large part due to the requirements of the NIESR whose Director, Noel Hall, wanted to avoid pressure to use the Institute's funds for 'private and personal investigations'. However, by the late 1930s, there were widespread empirical investigations of the business cycle. (The best-known of these studies, and still largely underestimated among economists, was Schumpeter's massive *Business Cycles: A Theoretical, Historical and Statistical Analysis of the Capitalist Process* was published in 1939.) In a letter to Keynes, dated 22 September 1938, Hall had expressed his reservations about an earlier version of the research proposal presented by Austin Robinson, which Hall thought was 'very much too wide' and therefore likely to lead to 'overlapping and duplication' of similar work at the Institute and in universities (Keynes Papers, King's College Cambridge N15/1/17). The initial year of study was subsequently changed to 1924, and the scope of the study was narrowed to examining the relation of prices to costs in different industries; consumption and foreign trade; the relationship between foreign investment and exports; and sources of saving, bringing up to date the estimates given in the Liberal Industrial Inquiry (1928, p. 109).

At Cambridge Kalecki settled down to gathering data on industrial production by industry and the share of 'prime costs' (labour and raw materials) in the total output of the coal, cotton, steel, tobacco, shipbuilding and electricity supply industries. The result was a series of papers that have not hitherto been published but are deposited in the Keynes and Kahn Papers in the Archive Centre of King's College Cambridge. The papers are largely concerned with statistical methods to obtain consistent data series. In addition to the list given by Jerzy Osiatyński in Kalecki's *Collected Works*, derived from documents obtained from Richard Stone (Osiatyński 1991, p. 525) there is a substantial paper, *Prime Costs and Proceeds etc. in Shipbuilding*, co-authored with G.A. Bauer. This developed an ingenious method for calculating an average construction period in shipbuilding, from which a continuous series for shipbuilding construction is derived (Keynes Papers, King's College Cambridge N15/1/128).

The Kahn Papers reveal the extent of dissatisfaction among the Cambridge economists with Kalecki's research. Keynes could not understand the purpose of gathering the data and estimating gaps in it, and he worried over the aggregation of firms into industries (Kahn Papers RFK/5/1/142). He and Joan Robinson objected to Kalecki's work on the 'degree of monopoly'. Although this is not mentioned in the papers that Kalecki prepared in Cambridge, it is clear from other papers he published at the time (Kalecki 1939, pp. 23–41) that the degree of monopoly was going to feature in his explanation of different rates of profit in different industries. Kahn argued that the role of surplus capacity, associated with monopoly, was 'exaggerated'. Kahn expressed all of this in an extensive letter to Kalecki (Kahn Papers RFK/5/1/159–62). Kalecki replied with a six-page memorandum that did not mention the degree of monopoly. Point by point he dealt with the chief accusations: that his estimates had been 'manipulated'; that he did not use indices; and that his choice of industries was unclear (he had in fact chosen the industries in agreement with Richard Stone and his wife). In a letter to Kahn, dated 9 June 1939, Kalecki indicated his intention to leave Cambridge in order to write his own 'theoretical interpretation of the results' (Kahn Papers, RFK/5/1/146&147). He stayed in Cambridge until the end of 1939, when the Department of Applied Economics was ready to be set up.

3 The confrontation of methodological traditions

The confrontation over statistical method was in fact a confrontation over theory, reflecting the difficulty of incorporating Kalecki's 'degree of monopoly' analysis within a Marshallian framework. This much is clear from the excellent exposition of the dispute by Peter Kriesler (Kriesler 1987, pp. 107–11. See also Halevi 1978 and Sawyer 1985, chapter 2). Kalecki's view was derived from the discussions in Europe that followed the publication of Hilferding's *Finance Capital*, which first advanced an analysis of a capitalist economy divided into two sectors: one consisting of industries dominated by monopolies; and the other a competitive sector. However, Kalecki's was not the first confrontation between European economic theory and the tradition established by Marshall in Cambridge.

The first emergence of continental European economics in Cambridge came with Piero Sraffa's arrival there in the mid-1920s. Sraffa fired a shot across the bows of Cambridge economics by showing that Marshall's elaborate scheme of partial equilibrium in perfect competition was incompatible with increasing, or even constant, returns to scale, in a paper which his friend Keynes published in the *Economic Journal* (Sraffa 1926). Thereafter he withdrew from teaching and quietly nurtured his critique of Marshallian economics until the publication of his major reconstruction of Ricardian economics in 1960. While he participated significantly in many of the key discussions between Keynes, Joan Robinson, Kahn and Kalecki 'it remains a puzzle that the two escape routes from Marshallian orthodoxy – the one associated with Sraffa and imperfect competition, the other with Keynes and effective demand – never converged in Keynes's lifetime, though leading disciples like Kahn and Joan Robinson were heavily involved both 'revolutions' (Skidelsky 1992, p. 290). James Tobin had expressed a similar view in Tobin 1981. Even earlier, Joan Robinson admitted that the two 'revolutions' had converged in Kalecki's work: '... the two streams of thought were combined by Michał Kalecki' Robinson 1958, p. 241).

The second emergence of continental European economics at Cambridge started with the arrival of Friedrich Hayek at the London School of Economics at the beginning of 1931. He came at the behest of Lionel Robbins, who was at that time an admirer of Austrian economic theory. Hayek became the chief exponent in Britain of continental European economic ideas. But his first lectures, published as *Prices and Production*, were poorly received in Cambridge. His monetary analysis and capital theory were subjected to ferocious criticisms by Keynes, Sraffa and, subsequently, by Hayek's former student Kaldor (Keynes, 1931; Sraffa, 1932; Kaldor 1942). Hayek's own aversion to state intervention ensured that, as the Great Depression corroded established economic theory and policy, Hayek and his supporters excluded themselves from mainstream economic discussions until the 1980s. By the 1930s, and especially after the publication of his *General Theory* Keynes, with only fragmentary notions of what was being discussed among economists on the continent, but with editorial control over the *Economic Journal*, was setting the agenda for economic theory in Cambridge.

When Kalecki arrived in Cambridge, he brought with him a version of continental European analysis that was methodologically and philosophically incompatible with the Marshallian tradition. At the root of his difficulties in Cambridge lay the different approaches that had been adopted in Britain and continental Europe in answer to the most fundamental question of the scope and significance of economic analysis.

The question had been raised in the third quarter of the nineteenth century by John Stuart Mill, Auguste Comte, and Karl Marx. All of them had concluded that the economy is an abstraction from the way in which societies organise production and distribution. There were therefore no universal economic 'laws' that were not conditional upon some associated social arrangements. This view argued that economic models which claimed to represent any real situation, were always going to be under-determined because any given real situation would have, among its determinants, social, historic and cultural, as well as economic factors. In other words, economic analysis could not give rise to unambiguous conclusions, because these would always depend upon social, historic and cultural influences upon economic activity. Out of this came the notorious German *methodenstreit*, which pitched historicism against deductive analysis. But, by the early twentieth century, the discussion had moved on in Europe and in Britain, to uncover those elements of economic analysis that could be combined into determinate models, self-determinate sub-systems of evolving social systems.

4   The Cambridge peculiarity

In Britain Alfred Marshall was the major economic systems-builder who rescued academic economics from the grip of social theory. His ingenious solution to the problem of economic under-determination was established at Cambridge, and continues to hold sway throughout the English-speaking world and, increasingly, throughout the whole of mainstream economics. Marshall's solution was to divide up economic activity into discrete systems which he postulated operated in periods that allowed them to determine particular outcomes. The periods roughly coincide with observed time-periods. The basic period is a market 'day' in which the prices that bring the supply of and demand for commodities into equilibrium are fixed. During that period, firms supplying goods, and the individuals that buy them, are influenced solely by prices, and therefore can come to an agreement as to the prices that will satisfy them all. During that period too, productive capabilities do not change. Given those prices, firms then determine how much to supply. In a separate 'short-term' period, firms decide where production is most profitable, and expand into the most profitable markets, thereby eliminating excess profits. In yet a third, 'long-term' period, firms decide on what scale to produce (Marshall 1920, Book V). This, and the associated assumption that all these decisions could be made in a state of perfect competition, was the point that aroused Sraffa's criticism of Marshallian analysis (see above).

One of the difficulties with Marshall's solution to the problem of economic under-determination is that it results in an over-determined system capable of multiple equilibria. It is only useful on its own terms if the equilibrium in each period is arrived at in one period at a time. Once all things are allowed to change then it is possible to have different general equilibria in the whole system according to, for example, the different scales of production or investment in the system. Moreover, Sraffa's critique had the important methodological implication that developments in one period, such as the increasing long-term returns, may subvert the mechanisms that are assumed to bring equilibrium in other periods. Therefore it may be impossible to move through successive periods, establishing successive equilibria to the satisfaction of the analyst, in the way postulated by Marshall. Nevertheless, the Marshallian method of getting determinate solutions for particular economic subsystems defined by their periods was a way of dealing with the complexity of an economy that was otherwise under-determined. Hence, when Keynes came to consider the complexity of an economy as a whole, in his *General Theory*, it was natural to use this Marshallian method (see, for example, Keynes's definitions of income and saving in chapter 6 of the *General Theory*; Keynes 1936). As Axel Leijonhufvud noted, 'Sequential period analysis is simpler in that it substitutes step-functions for more complicated time-paths of the variables' (Leijonhufvud 1968, p. 36).

In one of her most insightful comments on the economics derived from her teacher Alfred Marshall, Joan Robinson was later to distinguish 'periods' in which all other factors are held constant, but one economic subsystem adjusts to equilibrium, from the more common time periods over which economic activity occurs, by calling the first 'logical' time and the second 'historical' time. She concluded:

> There is much to be learned from *a priori* comparisons of equilibrium positions, but they must be kept in their logical place. They cannot be applied to actual situations ... In a model depicting equilibrium positions there is no causation. It consists of a closed circle of simultaneous equations. The value of each element is entailed by the values of the rest. At any moment in logical time the past is determined as much as the future. In an historical model, causal relations have to be specified ... (Robinson 1962, pp. 25–6)

As a result, she might have added, analysis in logical time may be driven by intuitions derived from empirical observation. But such analysis has no empirical content, if only because actual economic events occur in historical time. Kalecki's empirical study of industrial prices, indeed any empirical study, could not fail to challenge the methodological preconceptions of Cambridge economics.

5   The German economic determination

By the time he came to be aware of it, continental European economic thought, which Kalecki had absorbed in the course of his economic journalism and researches at the Institute for Research in Business Cycles and Prices in Warsaw, had resolved the problem of economic under-determination in a very different way. Instead of dividing up economic decisions into discrete determinate periods, analytical economics in continental Europe identified two key systems of economic variables that were determinate. The first of these was the circular flow of income – that is, the income flows created in the process of production, as firms' expenditure which returns to them as sales revenue when those who have received incomes spend them. This economic relation may have been rooted in a social process of production, but its outcome in an identity between aggregate output, income and expenditure is obviously a logical and determinate system. Moreover, since flows occur over time, the circular flow of income offers a neat way of linking up economic activity in successive periods, as opposed to a unique equilibrium that, once obtained, disappears from history.

The origins of this analysis went back to Quesnay's *tableaux économiques*, but it had found its way into Austrian economic theory in large part through the discussions that followed the publication in

1885 of Volume II of Marx's *Capital*. It should be remembered that the 'capital' whose circulation Marx analysed in this volume consisted of the total costs of production (in aggregate total national income), that are placed into circulation in the economy by capitalist production. Thus in his first exposé of history of economic thought and economic methodology Josef Schumpeter identified the Physiocrats' circular flow of income, as a methodological cornerstone of economics that showed:

> ... how each economic period becomes the basis for the subsequent one, not only in a technical sense but also in the sense that it produces exactly such results as will induce and enable the members of the economic community to repeat the same process in the same form in the next economic period; how economic production comes about as a social process ... As long as economic periods were viewed merely as a technical phenomenon, and the fact of the economic cycle through which they move had not been recognised, the connecting link of economic causality and an insight into the inner necessity and the general character of economics was missing. It was possible to consider the individual acts of exchange, the phenomenon of money, the question of protective tariffs as economic problems, but it was impossible to view with clarity the total process which unfolds itself in a particular economic period. (Schumpeter 1912, pp. 43–4)

For Schumpeter, the other key system of determinate relations was of prices. Here he believed that the ultimate breakthrough had been achieved by Léon Walras, with all quantities supplied and demand, brought into general equilibrium by a unique system of prices. Schumpeter concluded that, along with the notion that marginal products determine the shares of 'various factors of production', '... the theory of price ... really forms the basis for the formation of incomes' (Schumpeter 1912, p. 197). Although this view fits uneasily with the circular flow of income determination of aggregate incomes, Schumpeter does not seem to have considered the approaches to be incompatible.

The circular flow of income eventually found its way into English-language economics as the identities between income, output and expenditure that are used in national income accounts. However, such accounts belong to applied economics and the circular flow of income played no part in English economic theory. Nevertheless, the idea that income depends on expenditure is the foundation of Keynes's paradox of thrift and arguably one of the key innovations in his thought that followed the publication of his *Treatise on Money*. As regards Kalecki, the circular flow of income was embedded in his ideas from at least his earliest investigations into aggregate income and expenditure. The circular flow became the foundation of the national income statistics for Poland in 1929 that Kalecki and his colleague Ludwik Landau published in 1934 (Landau and Kalecki 1934). Following his move from Cambridge, Kalecki embraced even more strongly the circular flow of income as a fundamental principle integrating economic phenomena. Using it he came to his theory of profits, on which basis he elaborated his analysis of capitalist dynamics.

6 Kalecki's economic determination

Even before Kalecki's arrival in Britain he had become aware of the methodological problems of trying to isolate economic variables and combine them into determinate systems. His excursion into this methodological territory was 'Three Systems', a rather obscure paper whose lack of immediate theoretical or practical consequence meant that it had to wait until the 1990s to be published in English (Kalecki 1934). The paper is an exercise in showing how economic variables may be combined into determinate systems under different assumptions. His first system is a two-sector (consumption and investment) barter economy with a given level of investment (corresponding to Keynes's short period) in which it is easy to show that, with flexible prices, the economy comes to a stable equilibrium at full employment. In the second system money is introduced, with an elastic supply in accordance with the demand for money. As a result the economy tends to either inflation or deflation, depending on the initial state of either over-full employment, or under-employment. However, if the interest rate is allowed to rise with inflation and fall with deflation, then a stable equilibrium at full employment may be eventually reached. In his third system investment is allowed to vary autonomously, that is, it is not fully regulated by the rate of interest. This then leads to fluctuations in economic activity until the volume and structure of the capital stock is constant.

Kalecki's conclusion underlines his methodological rather than analytical concerns:

> ... we have only examined the formation of equilibrium ... within the already existing capital equipment. ... Investment activity ... (will result in) a continual movement through a series of equilibria ... until the final equilibrium is attained. ... If we consider the time of construction of new investment goods ... it may also turn out that ...

the position of final equilibrium will never be attained ... these are proper business fluctuations. (Kalecki 1934, pp. 218–19)

In other words, there is no actual determinate equilibrium in a capitalist economy, but a series of constantly changing variables. This is reiterated in Kalecki's remarks about Keynes's analysis in the *General Theory* of movements between one short period and another (Kalecki's comments were published in Polish and hence may have been unknown to the Cambridge milieu in which he worked in 1939):

> Let us suppose that, in the original situation expected profitability was higher than the rate of interest and that investment increases. This generates such a rise in the prices of investment goods that the expected profitability, calculated on the basis of these new prices and of the expected incomes in the *initial situation*, is equal to the rate of interest. Now we must take into account the fact that the growth of investment not only generates an increase in the price of investment goods but also, according to ... Keynes's theory ... stimulates a general recovery, producing a rise in prices and output in all sectors. However, because, as Keynes holds in another part of his book, 'the facts of the existing situation enter, in a sense disproportionately, into the formation of our long-term expectations', the expectations will become more optimistic and a difference between the marginal efficiency of investment and the rate of interest will arise again. 'Equilibrium', then, is not reached, and the growth of investment will still persist (we are dealing here, as may easily be seen, with a cumulative Wicksellian process). (Kalecki 1936, pp. 230–1)

Kalecki was here clearly analysing movements in what Joan Robinson had called 'historical' time, as opposed to the 'logical' time in which Keynes had couched his *General Theory*. But Cambridge remained wedded to the Marshallian tradition of treating subsystems of variables in logical time. For Cambridge, 'dynamic' analysis in 'historical' time meant shifting from one closed subsystem of variables (with factors such as the capital stock assumed constant or irrelevant) to another closed subsystem in which the capital stock was allowed to vary, but other factors such as relative prices and competition were taken as constant (notably in Joan Robinson's 'extension of Keynes's short-period analysis to long-run development'; Robinson 1956, p. vi). This provides the clue to the methodological enigma that Keynes, Joan Robinson, Kahn, and all those Cambridge sympathisers of Kalecki found in his work. The notion of a circular flow of income integrating prices and economic decisions was as foreign to economists brought up to believe that the complexity of an economy could be made tractable or calculable by having individuals make economic decisions simultaneously in different periods, as the German economic literature was in Cambridge. Kalecki's refusal to fit price theory into Marshallian methodology condemned his Cambridge research.

7 Summary and conclusions

At the end of 1939 the research project which Keynes had set up to provide employment for Kalecki and establish applied economic research in Cambridge was discontinued. Kalecki moved from the heart of the Keynesian revolution to Oxford, where a congenial theoretical void appeared with the absence from Oxford of Keynes's chief supporters there, J.R. Hicks and Roy Harrod. Keynes continued to support Kalecki's work. But Kalecki was no longer part of the Cambridge circle that had played such an important part in the development of Keynes's ideas.

Kalecki's move from Cambridge was the result of more than just an incompatibility of personalities. The move came about as a result of a much more fundamental incompatibility of a subculture in Cambridge economics that resisted external influence and engaged with foreign ideas in order to find confirmation of its approach to economic analysis through the methodology of Alfred Marshall. That resistance is apparent from an examination of the impact of three engagements with the economic methodology that dominated central European economics in the interwar period. The first engagement, with the arrival in Cambridge of Piero Sraffa, resulted in Sraffa's diffidence towards the economic theory discussed around him, or even with him in the case of Keynes's work, and Sraffa's concentration on his Ricardian value project. The second engagement was the clash with Austrian theory, advanced by Hayek at the London School of Economics. The Austrians' policy quietism in the face of the Great Depression facilitated a successful disengagement by Keynes's Cambridge supporters.

The third engagement came with the arrival in Cambridge of Michał Kalecki. With shared elements of theory and policy it was easy at first to overlook the methodological incompatibility between the dynamic business cycle framework within which Kalecki had always worked, and Marshallian periodic equilibria. When Kalecki put forward changes in income and expenditure, rather than stylised changes in supply and demand, to explain shifts in prices and employment this proved too much for his Cambridge supporters. Cambridge was and remains resolutely hostile to business cycle analysis.

Notes

1. This chapter could not have been written without the pioneering work of Malcolm Sawyer in his *The Economics of Michał Kalecki* (Sawyer 1985) and his generous discussions with me on the meaning and significance of Kalecki's analysis.
2. References to papers in the Kalecki archives are given as PAN followed by the file and page number. The Keynes and Kahn Papers in the Archive Centre of King's College Cambridge are referred to as by their class mark (e.g., N15 or RFK) followed by their file and page number.

References

Aslanbeigui, N., and Oakes, G. (2002) 'The theory arsenal: The Cambridge circus and the origins of the Keynesian revolution', *Journal of the History of Economic Thought*, 24(1), 5–37.

Coddington, A.C. (1983) *Keynesian Economics: The Search for First Principles*, London: Allen and Unwin.

De Vecchi, N. (2008) 'Keynes on Kalecki's theory of taxation: Contents approved, method questioned', *History of Political Economy*, 40(1), 163–82.

Dow, S.C. (1996) *The Methodology of Macroeconomic Thought: A Conceptual Analysis of Schools of Thought in Economics*, Cheltenham: Edward Elgar.

Halevi, J. (1978) 'On the relationship between effective demand and income distribution in a Kaleckian framework', *Banca Nazionale del Lavoro Quarterly Review*, 125, 167–90.

Hutchison, T.W. (1981) 'The philosophy and politics of the Cambridge School', in *The Politics and Philosophy of Economics: Marxians, Keynesians and Austrians*, Oxford: Basil Blackwell.

Johnson, H.G. (1977) 'The Shadow of Keynes', *Minerva*, 15(2), 201–13, republished in Elizabeth S. Johnson and Harry G. Johnson, *The Shadow of Keynes: Understanding Keynes, Cambridge and Keynesian Economics*, Oxford: Basil Blackwell, 1978.

Kahn, R.F. (1972) 'Some notes on liquidity preference', in *Selected Essays on Employment and Growth*, Cambridge: Cambridge University Press, pp. 72–96.

Kaldor, N. (1942) 'Professor Hayek and the concertina-effect', *Economica* vol. 9, 359–82.

Kalecki, M. (1934) 'Trzy Układy', *Ekonomista*, no. 3, pp. 54–70, translated by Chester Adam Kisiel in J. Osiatyński (ed.) *Collected Works of Michał Kalecki. Volume I Capitalism: Business Cycles and Full Employment*, Oxford: The Clarendon Press, 1990.

Kalecki, M. (1936) 'Some remarks on Keynes's theory', translated by F. Targetti and B. Kinda-Hass in J. Osiatyński (ed.) *Collected Works of Michał Kalecki*

Volume I Capitalism: Business Cycles and Full Employment, Oxford: The Clarendon Press, 1990.

Kalecki, M. (1971) *Selected Essays on the Dynamics of the Capitalist Economy 1933–1970*, Cambridge: Cambridge University Press.

Kalecki, M. (1939) *Essays in the Theory of Economic Fluctuations*, London: George Allen and Unwin.

Keynes, J.M. (1931) 'The pure theory of money. A reply to Dr. Hayek', *Economica*, 11(34), 389–403. Reprinted in D. Moggridge (ed.), *The Collected Writings of John Maynard Keynes, Volume XIII: The General Theory and After Part I Preparation*, London: Macmillan for the Royal Economic Society, 1973.

Keynes, J.M. (1936) *The General Theory of Employment, Interest and Money*, London: Macmillan.

Keynes, J.M. (1937) 'The General Theory of Employment', *Quarterly Journal of Economics*, February. reprinted in *The Collected Writings of John Maynard Keynes, Volume XIV: The General Theory and After. Part II Defence and Development*, edited by Donald Moggridge, London: Macmillan for the Royal Economic Society, 1973.

Kriesler, P. (1987) *Kalecki's Microanalysis: The Development of Kalecki's Analysis of Pricing and Distribution*, Cambridge: Cambridge University Press.

Landau, L. and Kalecki, M. (1934) 'Szacunek dochodu społecznego w r. 1929', *Prace Instytutu Badania Koniunktur Gospodarczych i Cen*, no. 4, pp. 97–100, published in English as 'An estimate of social income in 1929', in Jerzy Osiatyński (ed.), *Collected Works of Michał Kalecki, Volume VI: Studies in Applied Economics 1927–1941* Oxford: The Clarendon Press, 1996.

Leijonhufvud, A. (1968) *On Keynesian Economics and the Economics of Keynes: A Study in Monetary Theory*, New York: Oxford University Press.

Liberal Industrial Inquiry (1928) *Report: Britain's Industrial Future*, London: Ernest Benn.

Marshall, A. (1920) *Principles of Economics*, London: Macmillan.

Osiatyński, J. (ed.) (1991) *Collected Works of Michał Kalecki: Volume II. Economic Dynamics*, Oxford: The Clarendon Press.

Robinson, J.V.R. (1956) *The Accumulation of Capital*, London: Macmillan.

Robinson, J.V.R. (1958) '"Imperfect competition" today', *Il Mercurio* December, reprinted in the original English in *Collected Economic Papers, Volume Two*, Oxford: Basil Blackwell 1964.

Robinson, J.V.R. (1962) *Economic Philosophy*, London: Watts & Co.

Robinson, J.V.R. (1964) 'Kalecki and Keynes', in T. Kowalik (ed.), *Problems of Economic Dynamics and Planning: Essays in Honour of Michał Kalecki*, Warsaw: Państwowe Wydawnictwo Naukowe.

Robinson, J.V.R. (1966) 'Introduction' to M. Kalecki, *Studies in the Theory of the Business Cycle 1933–1939*, Oxford: Basil Blackwell.

Sawyer, M.C. (1985) *The Economics of Michał Kalecki*, London: Macmillan.

Sawyer, M.C. (2001) 'Kalecki on Money and Finance', *European Journal of History of Economic Thought*, 8(4), 487–508.

Schumpeter, J.A. (1912) *Epochen der Dogmen- und Methodengeschichte*, Tubingen: J.E.B. Mohr (Paul Sieback) Verlag; English translation by R. Aris: *Economic Doctrine and Method: An Historical Sketch*, London: George Allen and Unwin, 1954.

Shackle, G.L.S. (1967) *The Years of High Theory: Invention and Tradition in Economic Thought 1926–1939*, Cambridge: Cambridge University Press.

Skidelsky, R. (1983) *John Maynard Keynes, Volume One: Hopes Betrayed 1883–1920*, London: Macmillan.

Skidelsky, R. (1992) *John Maynard Keynes, Volume Two: The Economist as Saviour 1920–1937*, London: Macmillan.

Sraffa, P. (1926) 'The laws of returns under competitive conditions', *Economic Journal*, 26(4), 535–50.

Sraffa, P. (1932) 'Dr. Hayek on money and capital', *Economic Journal*, 42 (March), 42–53.

Steindl, J. (1989) 'Reflections on Kalecki's dynamics', in M. Sebastiani (ed.), *Kalecki's Relevance Today*, New York: St Martin's Press.

Tobin, J. (1981) 'Review of Patinkin's *Keynes's Monetary Thought*', *Journal of Political Economy*, 89(1), 204–7.

Part III
Economic Policy

11
Is There a Role for Active Fiscal Policies? Supply-Side and Demand-Side Effects of Fiscal Policies

Jesus Ferreiro, Teresa Garcia del Valle,
Carmen Gomez and Felipe Serrano

1 Introduction[1]

There is no doubt that the subject of fiscal policy has been, is, and, with complete certainty, will continue to be a recurrent subject in Malcolm Sawyer's works. A great deal of his long-term research activity has been focused on the study of the economic impact of active fiscal economies and on the defence of the active role of fiscal policy from a double perspective. Firstly, as a tool of stabilising economic policy, correcting and compensating the disequilibrium generated by the fluctuations in economic activity, which are explained as a result of changes in the aggregate demand. Secondly, as part of an active policy aiming to reach and keep levels of economic activity, or in other words of aggregate demand, which permit reaching full employment.

In this sense, we can consider Malcolm Sawyer to be one of the most adamant defenders of the active role that can be played by fiscal policy. His work has been more than merely focused on highlighting the inconsistencies and mistakes of the analyses based on the neoclassical orthodoxy on the effects of fiscal policy. From a solid and coherent Post Keynesian foundation, with a strong Kaleckian influence, Malcolm Sawyer has shown how active fiscal policy is a useful, efficient and necessary tool to reach full employment, a target which requires coordination between fiscal and monetary policies.[2]

For Malcolm Sawyer, it is clear that fiscal policy is the main tool of the economic policy to reach the level of activity at full employment: 'The key role to the achievement of a high level of economic activity should come through fiscal policy' (Sawyer, 2009, p. 562). This prevalence awarded to fiscal policy means that, in contrast to orthodox approaches, monetary policy is seen as a tool which is subordinate to the performance of fiscal policy. In this way, monetary policy, by setting the adequate levels of interest rate, enables the implementation of fiscal policy. As Malcolm Sawyer states,

> Central Banks should be restrained from setting high interest rates (specifically above the underlying rate of growth) to make easier for the fiscal authorities to pursue 'functional finance'. The interest rate should be set in line with social objectives, and we propose in line with the rate of growth. The underlying budget deficit should be set to achieve the highest practical level of economic activity. Short-term fluctuations in economic activity can be partially addressed through a combination of automatic fiscal stabilisers, discretionary fiscal policy, and (perhaps) interest rate variations. The operation of fiscal policy should take full recognition of the effects, which the current level of economic activity has on investment and future supply capacity. (Sawyer, 2009, p. 564)

The implementation of fiscal policy is based on the handling of budget balances as a basic tool for the management of aggregate demand. With that aim, the balance between public expenditure and revenue must be managed to respond to changes in private expenditure (Arestis and Sawyer, 2010a): 'We consider the operation of fiscal policy in terms of movements in the fiscal stance in the short run and also in respect of the long-run setting. In the short term, variations in the fiscal stance can be used in conjunction with automatic stabilisers to offset fluctuations in economic activity arising from, inter alia, variations in private sector aggregate demand. In the longer term, the general fiscal stance should be set to underpin the desired level of output and employment' (Arestis and Sawyer, 2010b, pp. 96–7).

The work developed by Malcolm Sawyer over the course of a large number of years is clearly included in the traditional study developed by Post Keynesian economics on the role to be played by fiscal policy as a tool of macroeconomic policy. However, we think this study has insufficiently developed three basic elements to understand both the conditions and the institutional framework which favour the application of an active fiscal policy. It also insufficiently developed the economic effects both in the short and in the long run of fiscal policy.

In this sense, the Post Keynesian[3] traditional analysis tends to take an overly economic vision of fiscal policy. In this analysis, the budget balance is considered to be the main fiscal variable to be used in order to reach the desired level of aggregate demand. The different fiscal instruments, both on the side of expenditure and on the side of income taxes, are managed following this criterion. Consequently, all these items are identified as instruments of management of aggregate demand, apparently fulfilling only one aim. Thus, an important item is left out. This is that it leaves out the fact that income and expenditure items fulfil or may fulfil another kind of objective, different from the strictly macroeconomic goal. This may give rise to the generation of a trade-off among these objectives, as they may sometimes be contradictory.

On the other hand, Post Keynesian economics tends to focus fiscal policy exclusively on the effects caused by aggregate demand. This explains the fact that Post Keynesian treatment of fiscal policy revolves around the role to be played by budget balances in the management of aggregate demand. When we study the analysis of the particular effects of the different fiscal tools, this analysis is carried out from the study of the multipliers of the different fiscal items. This multiplier effect means quantifying the impact of the variations of the different budget items on the level of the aggregate demand.[4] The analysis of the possible effects that fiscal policy may exert on aggregate supply and the conditions of long-term production are basically excluded from this treatment.

Finally, in our opinion, Post Keynesian economics has paid little attention to the role played by public finances as a correcting element of fundamental uncertainty problems that individuals may have to confront. Usually the handling of this problem has been limited to the consideration of the role played by fiscal policy as a tool to generate and generalise the prospect of a level of aggregate demand for full employment, which favours its attainment. However, there are no studies on the extent to which particular budget items may help reduce the uncertainty agents may have about the existence of a future income and its level.

In this contribution, we try to present these aspects as research lines to be developed by heterodox economics. Obviously, we do not intend to say Post Keynesian economics or the rest of the heterodox or radical approaches do not admit the importance of these aspects. We simply want to point out that their development has been insufficient and their study may highlight how important it is to handle fiscal policy as a management tool both in the short and the long run.

2 Determinants of fiscal policy management: the existence of other objectives for public finances different from macroeconomic management

During recent decades, until the current crisis,[5] most economies, both developed and emerging markets and developing economies, have implemented an orthodox fiscal policy based on the achievement of sound public finances.[6] This label includes not only the objective of reducing fiscal imbalances (public deficits and stocks of public debt) but also the reduction of the size of public sectors, both the size of public revenues and expenditures (measured as percentages of GDP). According to the hypothesis of the expansionary fiscal consolidation, fiscal adjustment processes driven by cuts in public expenditure would have an expansionary impact on the economic activity and on the economic growth (Afonso, 2001, 2006; Alesina and Perotti, 1995, 1997; Alesina et al., 2002; Alesina, Perotti and Tavares, 1998; Briotti, 2004, 2005; European Commission, Directorate-General for Economic and Financial Affairs, 2003, 2004, 2007; Giavazzi, Japelli and Pagano, 1999, 2000; Giavazzi and Pagano, 1990; Giudice, Turrini and in't Veld, 2003, 2007; Hemming et al., 2002; Kumar, Leigh and Plekhanov, 2007; McDermott and Wescott, 1996; van Aarle and Garretsen, 2003).

Therefore, for the orthodox approach both fiscal imbalances and the size of public expenditure have a negative impact on economic growth. Thus, for those supporting the expansionary fiscal consolidation, fiscal deficits must always be reduced by cutting public expenditures regardless of the size of public expenditure.[7] This means that it is assumed, or that it is adopted as an axiom, that the size of public expenditure is always excessive, and, consequently, above that regarded as optimum.

This optimum size of public expenditure remains undetermined, although, from this orthodox perspective, it is known in terms of both its nature and its objectives. The acceptable public expenditure would be the required one to correct the potential microeconomic market failures (that is, public goods, external effects, natural or technological monopolies, and so on). We are talking of a size and kind of public expenditure that corresponds to what is usually termed the Minimum State. As is argued in the so-called public policy endogenous growth models, most items of public expenditure have a negative impact on the level of economic activity and the rate of economic growth. Only a limited number of items of public spending would have a positive effect on the long-term economic growth path. But even these items would be constrained by the existence of an optimum size, above which their impact would be negative.

Actually, despite all, the different studies do not provide us with the exact datum of the optimum size both of the whole public expenditure and of the different items individually considered. These studies take the existence of such a limit for granted but they do not clarify the size of such a limit (in absolute value or as percentage of GDP), whether that magic figure is constant or varies over time or whether that percentage has a universal validity or whether it varies from economy to economy. In this regard, it is quite illustrative what is stated by the report Public Finances in EMU 2002 of the European Commission:

> Parallel to the institutional debate, a large economic literature has explored the links between the composition of public spending and economic growth, employment, etc. (...) In general, there is no consensus as 'evidence is found to admit no conclusion on whether the relation is positive, negative or non-existent' (...) Within certain limits, public spending may have a positive impact on growth, but this trend reverses once expenditure exceeds a maximum level (...). This inverted-U shape holds for many spending items, but the reversal point differs across expenditure items. (European Commission, Directorate-General for Economic and Financial Affairs, 2002, pp. 97–8)

Below, this report divides the different items of expenditure into four categories:

- Category 1, interest payments (...) Spending always negatively affects growth and employment as these resources could be used for more productive purposes.
- Category 2 consists of old-age and survivor expenditures, collective consumption and compensation of public employees (...) Although some public spending is likely to be efficiency-enhancing, the decreasing effects arise beyond a certain level of spending.
- Category 3 includes social expenditures on disability, social exclusion, housing, family/children allowances and unemployment transfers (...) Public spending on these items can have a positive impact on efficiency provided it is kept within certain limits.
- Category 4 includes the expenditures on education, active labour market policies, health, R & D and gross fixed capital formation (...) As shown in the literature reviewed in Table III.7, they are considered to have a positive effect on economic efficiency up to a certain limit, beyond which additional spending has negative impact. However, in line with the empirical literature, it is assumed that the negative effect on growth starts at higher levels than those prevailing in EU countries. (European Commission, Directorate-General for Economic and Financial Affairs, 2002, p. 102).

Note that in no case is it explicitly stated which is the optimum size of those expenditure items and the effects arising from their 'excessive' level is always expressed in the conditional tense. The existence of this limit to the volume of overall public expenditure and to the size of each item of public spending is explained, in the mainstream tradition, by the combination of several reasons: the incrementalist bias of public expenditure, the existence of a deficit bias (and the consequent financial crowding-out effect), the crowding out of private consumption, and the negative impact generated on aggregate supply because of the (dis) incentives on the generation and optimal allocation of productive factors (capital and labour). All of these mechanisms would justify the need to reduce the size of public expenditure as an essential element to accelerate the rate of economic growth.[8]

The neoclassical analysis of public expenditure is based on the axiom that, as we have mentioned, there is only one justification for public spending: solving market failures. The analysis of public expenditure is thus made on the basis of technical criteria: those of neoclassical efficiency. Also those that need to reach a best or second-best level of activity and a best or second-best resource allocation; viewing the optimum result as one corresponding to an achievement of equilibrium or market-clearing. This reasoning is rejected by those economic approaches that we can label as radical approaches. Thus, the Marxist political economy has considered public expenditure, mainly those that are part of the Welfare States, as legitimate instruments of the capitalist system (O'Connor, 1973). In this approach, perhaps more than in any other radical approach, the relevance of political factors as determinants of the management of the size and composition of public expenditures is quite obvious.

In contrast to Marxist political economy, the Post Keynesian approach has not paid sufficient attention to the analysis of the political and institutional elements that determine the level and composition of public expenditure. We could say that the Post Keynesian analysis of public expenditure has a clear instrumental bias. The management of public spending is made from the perspective of the most general fiscal policy. Public expenditure (both as a whole and in terms of the different items of public outlays) is an instrument to manage the aggregate demand with the ultimate objective of reaching and maintaining a full employment level of economic activity.[9] This perspective assumes that the existence of other non-economic elements, like social, political or institutional ones, that could influence the size and composition of public expenditures, and, consequently, the management of public spending, is not taken into account. It is, in this sense, important to note that the traditional Post Keynesian analysis cannot explain the deep differences perceived in the size and composition of public expenditures that exist in very similar economies.[10]

Once we accept that the size and the composition of public expenditure are influenced by non-economic elements, we must reject the neoclassical arguments based on universal fiscal recipes and the simplistic Post Keynesian arguments of recommending increases (or cuts) in the overall size of public expenditures on the basis of the size of the respective multipliers of each item of public spending. Both approaches do not consider the existing constraints based on the preferences in each society about the desired level and composition of public expenditure. Besides, it is necessary to bear in mind that, as far as the economic and non-economic objectives of public expenditures are of opposite relevance, the political and social preferences of a society may act as constraints to a technical management of public expenditures as a tool of macroeconomic management. This, then, would create a sort of trade-off between the economic and the social/political objectives of public expenditure.[11]

In any case, it is striking that despite the relevance given by Post Keynesian authors to fiscal policy, and, by extension, to the role played by the public sector as the engine of economic activity and key tool to manage the aggregate demand in the short run (Arestis and Sawyer, 2004b), there are in this approach few papers dealing with the determinants of the choice of fiscal tools implemented. Actually, as Arestis and Fontana (2009) have argued in a recent paper, the Post Keynesian analysis about the role to be played by fiscal policy is quite poor:

> Post Keynesians have always been on the front line in defending a stabilisation role for fiscal policy. However, with few exceptions, the reader will look in vain for recent Post Keynesian papers on the role of fiscal policy in modern macroeconomics. It is really astonishing that the journals that typically publish contributions within the Post Keynesian tradition have few or no papers dealing with the stabilisation role of discretionary fiscal policy. (Arestis and Fontana, op. cit., p. 547)

As argued above, discretionary fiscal policy is considered a key element for the stabilisation of economic activity and for reaching a full employment level of economic activity.[12] The management of the size of public revenues and expenditures and of the size of fiscal imbalances (mainly fiscal balance) is a key element in any Post Keynesian strategy of economic policy. However, most Post Keynesian recommendations do not take into account that the characteristics of the public sector differ dramatically from country to country, and that countries manage in radically different ways not only the evolution of the overall sizes of public expenditures and revenues as a tool to reach their respective economic and fiscal objectives, but also the different kinds of revenues and expenditures.

Actually, most Post Keynesian approaches (and, indeed, other radical methodologies) analyse and identify fiscal policies with the management of the size of public expenditures and revenues, the fiscal imbalance (generating fiscal deficits during recessions and fiscal surpluses during booms) and the management of the different items of revenues and expenditures. However, in the latter case, this management of public finances is always based on the economic classification of public spending, a choice that allows the measurement of the impact of fiscal policy through the use of the respective multipliers (thus measuring the impact of fiscal policy on aggregate demand). This distinction is made at a highly aggregate level, thus distinguishing and using broad categories of public spending, mainly, current versus capital spending, transfers versus effective public expenditure, or public investment versus current expenditures.

Surprisingly, this view is very similar to that adopted by the mainstream: the management of public revenues and expenditures is carried out using strictly technical criteria – that is, the need to reach a certain macroeconomic outcome. Obviously, this outcome is differs in terms of each of the two approaches: for mainstream economics the objective is to reach an equilibrium (market-clearing) outcome, whilst in the Post Keynesian approach it is to achieve a full employment level of aggregate demand and economic activity.

Accepting the normative content of the design and implementation of public economics, macroeconomic (not only fiscal but also monetary) policies included, involves the acceptance that the existing configuration of public economic activity has a historical nature, influenced by the current set of economic, social, cultural and political elements that define not only the relationships among individuals but also the relationship and frontiers between private and public spheres. Obviously, these elements influence both the value and the evolution of the size of public revenues and expenditures. They also influence the composition of these public economic activities. In as much as these elements are different, not only the size but also the composition of public budgets will differ.

Therefore, the detected absence of convergence in the size and composition of public expenditure is related to the existence of social, cultural, demographic, political and institutional differences among countries. These differences lead to different preferences on the size, role and functions to be developed by national public sectors, something already argued by the theories of varieties of capitalism, comparative capitalism and welfare production regimes. These argue that these factors set the national-state economic policies and that a single and universal model of growth and development does not exist (Crouch and Streeck 1997; Hall and Soskice 2001).

As mentioned above, the theoretical and empirical comparative studies show that there is no single universal model of development, growth and competitiveness. Consequently, there is no single model of public sector and fiscal policy that fosters the economic growth and competitiveness, which simultaneously maximises the social welfare of a nation. Public expenditures have different purposes, not only economic growth but also, among others, income redistribution or social cohesion. Neoclassical analyses, and public policy endogenous growth models among them, take as an axiom that individual welfare is maximised when the economy reaches an equilibrium outcome. Consequently, the only purpose of fiscal policy must be economic growth, that is, to get an equilibrium outcome. However, when this analytical framework is abandoned, the notion of a single optimal composition of public spending defined in terms of its contribution to economic growth disappears. Furthermore, there can be a trade-off between the different purposes of public expenditures that can affect the size and composition of public spending.

The size and the composition of public expenditures reflect political choices about the role played by public sectors and fiscal policies. But these choices and preferences are not universal and immutable. They may vary in time and space (Ferreiro and Serrano, 2007, 2008 and 2009). Different national political choices and preferences explain the existing differences in the role, functions and size of national public sectors. However, these national preferences can also vary with time, and, consequently, optimal size and composition of public expenditure in an economy will change.

3 Fiscal policy transmission channels: the necessary integration of the effects of fiscal policy upon aggregate supply and demand

For the Post Keynesian approach, the main transmission channel to the economic activity of changes in public expenditure is the effects generated upon aggregate demand. The mechanics of this transmission channel is quite easy. Assuming that the value of the overall public expenditure multiplier is above zero, an increase in public expenditures will increase aggregate demand, thereby increasing the level of economic activity (and the level of employment) both in the short and the long run.[13]

A complementary mechanism is based on the redistributive effects of public expenditure, a transmission channel used by those economists following both the Kaleckian and the Keynesian traditions. In the former cases, if we assume the existence of groups with different marginal consumption propensities (for instance, workers versus capitalists, high-income versus low-income individuals), then if public expenditure is able to change the income distribution in an economy, it can affect the level of aggregate demand. Furthermore, and accepting that low-income individuals have higher marginal consumption propensities, policies that contribute to a more egalitarian income distribution, for example, a composition of public expenditures favouring low-income individuals, will increase aggregate demand and stimulate economic growth (Keynes, 1936).

The Kaleckian approach emphasises the redistributive effects of public expenditure. Public expenditure would influence economic activity by fostering or disciplining, depending on the fiscal stance (expansive or restrictive, respectively), wage claims, thereby affecting the profit rate and the functional income distribution between wages and profits, and, consequently, the level and evolution of the spending on private consumption and investment (Kalecki, 1943).

As mentioned above, most of the analyses of the impact of public expenditures on economic activity focus only on the effects generated on aggregate demand. Implicit in this view we find the assumption of an adaptive demand-driven aggregate supply. It is aggregate demand that determines, in both the short and the long term, the levels of economic activity and employment and their respective rates of growth. Very few papers analyse the relevance of supply-side factors in the determination of employment, economic activity and growth (Arestis, Baddeley and Sawyer 2007 is one such exception). However, in almost all papers analysing the impact of fiscal policy on aggregate demand, it is the overall stance of fiscal policy the element that generates these consequences, and no or little attention is paid to single types of public expenditure.

It is hard to accept the assumption that the public expenditure has only a minimal impact on aggregate supply. This is like arguing that public spending has no impact on capital stock accumulation, on labour supply, on human capital, or on the generation and assimilation of knowledge and innovation. As far as the nominal and real effects of fiscal policy are concerned, they are determined by the dynamic interaction between aggregate demand and supply. If the composition (and not only the level) of public expenditures affects aggregate supply then the nominal (inflation) and real (real economic activity and employment) effects of fiscal policy depend not only on the evolution of the total volume of public revenues and expenditures and on the sign and evolution of public balances but also on the composition of public spending.

With all this, we are not defending the neoclassical approaches based on what is known as public policy endogenous growth models. According to these models, fiscal policy can accelerate the long-run rate of economic growth by shifting the revenue stance away from distortionary forms of taxation and towards non-distortionary forms; it can also switch expenditures from unproductive to productive forms (Angelopoulos et al., 2007; Aschauer, 1989; Barro, 1990, 1991; Barro and Sala-i-Martin, 1995; Devarajan et al., 1996; Gemmel and Kneller, 2001; Gupta et al, 2005; Irmen and Kuehnel, 2009; King and Rebelo, 1990; Kneller et al., 1999, 2001; Romero de Avila and Strauch, 2003). In these models, only certain items of expenditure, through their effects on aggregate demand, are considered to be stimulating for economic activity. This happens as long as the volume of these items (and of the total spending) is lower than a fixed figure or the budget balance is in equilibrium. What we are suggesting is the need to make a more thorough analysis of the possible effects that the different items of expenditure may exert on the aggregate demand. Above all, and in the long run, combining these results with the effects exerted more directly and immediately on aggregate demand is such a possibility.

4   Fiscal policy, public finances and uncertainty

Although a distinctive feature of the Post Keynesian approach is the relevance given to expectations and to uncertainty as key determinants of the economic activity (Keynes, 1936, 1937; Davidson 1991, 2002, 2007), this approach has not paid any attention to how public expenditure can directly reduce the fundamental uncertainty about the future. This analysis is only developed as far as public expenditures are interpreted as a tool of the more general fiscal policy in order to reach and keep a full employment level of aggregate demand. But, again, there is no differential treatment given to the different kinds of public expenditure.

If we assume that consumption and savings propensities depend on the long-term expectations about income, then changes in these expectations will also affect consumption and savings decisions.

Consequently, the level of aggregate demand and economic activity will be affected even more substantially. The existence of a public expenditure that warrants individuals the possibility of a future flow of income, regardless of the amount of these flows, helps to stabilise expectations about the future. It, thus, stabilises private spending and aggregate demand. In other words, public expenditure stabilises consumption propensities. This, in turn, allows implementing macroeconomic policies that manages to achieve the objective of a full employment economic activity.

However, for individuals not all items of public expenditure have the same stabilising impact on long-term expectations about their future incomes. Social expenditures in cash, like unemployment compensation benefits or retirement pensions, warrant individuals that in certain situations, such as foreseeable (like the retirement) or uncertain (like the unemployment), they will maintain a certain level of income, what in turn stabilises and smooths the life path of consumption and saving. This, depending of the sizes of these expenditures, favours the maintenance of a full employment level of economic activity (Ferreiro and Serrano, 2008 and 2009). From this perspective, the contribution of public expenditures to getting full employment is not only related to the volume of public expenditures but also to their composition.

5   Summary and conclusions

The present economic crisis, which is currently having an impact on large parts of the world economy, has once again highlighted the need and capacity of performance of fiscal policy as a tool for macroeconomic management. In contrast to what economic orthodoxy proposes, massive fiscal stimulus packages have allowed, in some cases, a curbing of the economic slump. In other instances they have allowed some economies, especially the emerging ones, to achieve record macroeconomic results similar to those existing before 2008.

This performance and its results have allowed countersigning the proposals defended by numerous non-orthodox economists such as Malcolm Sawyer for whom active fiscal policy must play the main role in the framework of an economic strategy oriented to full employment. Works developed by Malcolm Sawyer provide us with the essential theoretical and (empirical) support to endorse the proposals made by different approaches, such as the Post Keynesian, about the role to be played in modern economics by fiscal policy.

In our opinion, obviously, this is not a closed task. In the study of the effects of fiscal policy and of the management of public finances there are still several elements to be developed, such as the ones mentioned here. These elements will improve our knowledge not only of the short- and long-term effects of fiscal policy but also of the capacity to implement fiscal policy and the restrictions existing on that implementation.

Notes

1. This work was supported by the University of the Basque Country (Research Project EHU09/33) and the Basque Government (Consolidated Research Group GIC10/153).
2. It is an almost impossible task to sum up in a few works the publications on fiscal policy by Malcolm Sawyer, whether on his own or with other authors, especially with the collaboration of Philip Arestis. We can mention, if we just take into account his most recent works, the following: Arestis and Sawyer (2010a, 2010b, 2008, 2006, 2004a, 2004b, 2003, 2001, 1998), Arestis, McCauley and Sawyer (2001), Creel and Sawyer (2008), Sawyer (2009, 2007), among many others.
3. It is also comparable to most non-neoclassical 'radical' analyses.
4. Nevertheless, in practice, it implies measuring the multiplier effect of a reduced number of fiscal tools, such as taxes, transfers, expenditure on public investment, or public consumption, among others.
5. The implementation of counter-cyclical active fiscal policies during the present crisis has been rather the result of the need to prevent a collapse both of the economy, in general, and of financial sectors, in particular, than the result of a process of reflection and reorientation of active fiscal policy. In this sense, and on neoclassical economics reasoning, there is still a defence of the application of fiscal measures addressed to reduce, as fast as possible, the present levels of deficit and public debt as essential tools for the economic recovery, even though it is admitted they have a negative potential effect in the short run. See the following works: International Monetary Fund (2010), European Commission, Directorate-General for Economic and Financial Affairs (2010), Blanchard and Cottarelli (2010), and Blanchard, Dell'Ariccia and Mauro (2010), among others.
6. Probably, the most extreme case of this fiscal strategy is the fiscal policy implemented in the countries, which make up the European Monetary Union or wish to do so in the future. Both the convergence criteria established in the Maastricht Treaty and the arrangements established in the Stability and Growth Pact determine a fiscal policy strategy completely subordinated to the 'anti-inflation' monetary policy defined and implemented by the European Central Bank. This strategy of fiscal policy is limited to the fulfil-ment of strict fiscal rules regarding both the maximum admissible size of public deficits and the size of the outstanding public debt.
7. It is rather odd that the empirical evidence is far from being conclusive on the expansionary effects of fiscal consolidation. The studies only manage to conclude that *under certain circumstances some* episodes of fiscal consolidation *may* have a stimulating effect on economic growth, at least, in the *short term*. See on this score Briotti (2005).

8. Although this is not the focus of our work, from the neoclassical perspective the reduction of public spending must come with a simultaneous reduction of public income, especially, reducing the weight and importance of those tax figures, which would have a negative effect on the generation and allocation of productive factors (capital and work). This means reducing direct taxation (income tax, corporation tax and social security contributions, basically), making up for such reduction by means of an increase of indirect taxation.

9. It is common knowledge that the concept of full employment of Post Keynesian economics and all radical approaches is substantially different from the neoclassical concept of full employment, according to which this would be the existence of an equilibrium market wage where unemployment is always voluntary (that is, for the existence of a real wage higher than the marginal productivity of work).

10. For an analysis of the differences in the size and composition of public expenditures in the European Union, see Ferreiro et al. (2008, 2009 and 2010).

11. This same restriction may work when determining the choice of a fiscal tool to be used to handle aggregate demand; that is, taxes or public expenditures.

12. A few words that are more illustrative in this sense can be gauged from the abstract of a recent article by Paul Davidson in the Editor's Corner of the Journal of Post Keynesian Economics: 'This paper explains why, given Keynes's General Theory, worries over the size of the government's national debt per se are foolish. It is more important to educate politicians and the public that government fiscal policy should be designed to make sure that aggregate market demand will produce sufficient profits so that entrepreneurs will hire all domestic workers willing and able to work. Empirical evidence is provided to demonstrate the correctness of this concept of fiscal policy of the balancing wheel for full employment effective demand' (Davidson, 2009, p. 661).

13. A multiplier of public expenditure between 0 and 1 involves a partial crowding-out of private expenditure (in a closed economy) and/or a fall in the net exports (in an open economy). A value of the multiplier above 1 involves that both public and private expenditure increase (or fall).

References

Afonso, A. (2001) 'Non-Keynesian effects of fiscal policy in the EU-15', *Working Paper, Department of Economics*. Institute for Economics and Business Administration (ISEG), Technical University of Lisbon, WP 2001/07.

Afonso, A. (2006) 'Expansionary fiscal consolidations in Europe', *Working Paper Series European Central Bank*, 675.

Alesina, A., Ardagna, S., Perotti, R. and Schiantarelli, F. (2002) 'Fiscal policy, profits and investment', *American Economic Review*, 92, 571–89.

Alesina, A. and Perotti, R. (1995) 'Fiscal expansions and adjustments in OECD countries', *Economic Policy*, 21, 205–40.

Alesina, A. and Perotti, R. (1997) 'Fiscal adjustments in OECD countries: composition and macroeconomic effects', *IMF Staff Papers*, 44, 297–329.

Alesina, A., Perotti, R. and Tavares, J. (1998) 'The political economy of fiscal adjustments', *Brooking Papers on Economic Activity*, 1, 197–248.

Angelopoulos, K., Economides, G. and Kamman, P. (2007) 'Tax-spending policies and economic growth: theoretical predictions and evidence from the OECD', *European Journal of Political Economy*, 23(4), 885–902.

Arestis, P., Baddeley, M. and Sawyer, M.C. (2007) 'The relationship between capital stock, unemployment and wages in nine EMU countries', *Bulletin of Economic Research*, 59(2), 125–48.

Arestis, P. and Fontana, G. (2009) 'Special symposium of discretionary fiscal policy: fiscal policy is back!', *Journal of Post Keynesian Economics*, 31(4), 547–8.

Arestis, P., McCauley, K. and Sawyer, M. (2001) 'An alternative stability pact for the European Union', *Cambridge Journal of Economics*, 25(1), 113–30.

Arestis, P. and Sawyer, M. (1998) 'Keynesian economic policies for the New Millenium', *Economic Journal*, 108, 181–95.

Arestis, P. and Sawyer, M. (2001) *The Economics of the Third Way*, Cheltenham: Edward Elgar.

Arestis, P. and Sawyer, M. (2003) 'Reinventing fiscal policy', *Journal of Post Keynesian Economics*, 26(1), 3–25.

Arestis, P. and Sawyer, M. (2004a) 'On the effectiveness of monetary policy and of fiscal policy', *Review of Social Economy*, 62(4), 441–63.

Arestis, P. and Sawyer, M. (2004b) *Re-examining Monetary and Fiscal Policies in the Twenty First Century*, Aldershot: Edward Elgar.

Arestis, P. and Sawyer, M. (2006) 'Fiscal policy matters', *Public Finance*, 54(3–4), pp. 133–53.

Arestis, P. and Sawyer, M. (2008) 'A critical reconsideration of the foundations of monetary policy in the new consensus macroeconomic framework', *Cambridge Journal of Economics*, 32(5), 761–9.

Arestis, P. and Sawyer, M. (2010a) 'The return of fiscal policy', *Journal of Post Keynesian Economics*, 32(3), 327–46.

Arestis, P. and Sawyer, M. (2010b) '21st Century Keynesian economic policies', in P. Arestis and M. Sawyer (eds), *21st Century Keynesian Economics*, Basingstoke: Palgrave Macmillan, pp. 81–119.

Aschauer, D. (1989) 'Is government spending productive?', *Journal of Monetary Economics*, 23(2), 177–200.

Barro, R.J. (1990) 'Government spending in a simple model of endogenous growth', *Journal of Political Economy*, 98 (S5), s103–17.

Barro, R.J. (1991) 'Economic growth in a cross-section of countries', *Quarterly Journal of Economics*, 106(2), 407–44.

Barro, R.J. and Sala-i-Martin, X. (1995) *Economic Growth*, New York: McGraw Hill.

Blanchard, O. and Cottarelli, C. (2010) 'Ten commandments for fiscal adjustment in advanced economies', *VoxEU.org*, 28 June.

Blanchard, O., Dell'Ariccia, G. and Mauro, P. (2010) 'Rethinking macroeconomic policy', *IMF Staff Position Note*, SPN/10/03.

Briotti, M.G. (2004) 'Fiscal adjustment between 1991 and 2002: stylised facts and policy implications', *Occasional Paper Series, European Central Bank*, 9.

Briotti, M.G. (2005) 'Economic reactions to public finance consolidation: a survey of the literature', *Occasional Paper Series, European Central Bank*, 38.

Creel, J. and Sawyer, M. (eds) (2008) *Current Thinking on Fiscal Policy*, Basingstoke: Palgrave Macmillan.

Crouch, C. and Streeck, W. (eds) (1997) *Political Economy of Modern Capitalism*, London: Sage.

Davidson, P. (1991) 'Is probability theory relevant for uncertainty? A Post Keynesian perspective', *Journal of Economics Perspectives*, 1, 129–43.

Davidson, P. (2002) *Financial Markets, Money and the Real World*, Cheltenham: Edward Elgar.

Davidson, P. (2007) 'Strong uncertainty and how to cope with it to improve action and capacity', in J. McCombie and C. Rodriguez Gonzalez (eds), *Issues in Finance and Monetary Policy*, Basingstoke: Palgrave Macmillan, pp. 8–27.

Davidson, P. (2009) 'Editor's corner: Making dollars and sense of the US government debt', *Journal of Post Keynesian Economics*, 32(4), 661–5.

Devarajan, S., Swaroop, V. and Zou, H-F. (1996) 'The composition of public expenditure and economic growth', *Journal of Monetary Economics*, 37(2), 313–44.

European Commission, Directorate-General for Economic and Financial Affairs (2002) 'Public finances in EMU 2002', *European Economy*, 3/2002, Brussels: European Commission.

European Commission, Directorate-General for Economic and Financial Affairs (2003) 'Public finances in EMU 2003', *European Economy*, 3/2003, Brussels: European Commission.

European Commission, Directorate-General for Economic and Financial Affairs (2004) 'Public finances in EMU 2004', *European* Economy, 3/2004, Brussels: European Commission.

European Commission, Directorate-General for Economic and Financial Affairs (2007) 'Public finances in EMU 2007', *European* Economy, 3/2007, Brussels: European Commission.

European Commission, Directorate-General for Economic and Financial Affairs (2010) 'Public finances in EMU 2010', *European Economy*, 4/2010, Brussels: European Commission.

Ferreiro, J., Garcia del Valle, M. and Gomez, C. (2008) 'Fiscal adjustment and composition of public expenditures in the EMU', in J. Ferreiro, G. Fontana and F. Serrano (eds), *Fiscal Policy in the European Union*, Basingstoke: Palgrave Macmillan, pp. 84–108.

Ferreiro, J., Garcia del Valle, M. and Gomez, C. (2009) 'Is the composition of public expenditures converging in EMU countries?', *Journal of Post Keynesian Economics*, 31(3), 459–84.

Ferreiro, J., Garcia del Valle, M. and Gomez, C. (2010) 'Social preferences and fiscal policies: an analysis of the composition of public expenditures in the European Union', *Journal of Post Keynesian Economics*, 32(3), 347–71.

Ferreiro, J. and Serrano, F. (2007) 'New institutions for a new economic policy', in E. Hein and A. Truger (eds), *Money, Distribution and Economic Policy. Alternatives to Orthodoxy*, Cheltenham: Edward Elgar, pp. 141–57.

Ferreiro, J. and Serrano, F. (2008) 'Institutions, welfare state and full employment', in P. Arestis and J. McCombie (eds), *Missing Links in the Unemployment Relationship*, Basingstoke: Palgrave Macmillan, pp. 182–99.

Ferreiro, J. and Serrano, F. (2009) 'Institutions, expectations and aggregate demand', in G. Fontana and M. Setterfield (eds), *Macroeconomic Theory and Macroeconomic Pedagogy*, Basingstoke: Palgrave Macmillan, pp. 309–22.

Gemmel, N. and Kneller, R. (2001) 'The impact of fiscal policy on long-run growth', *European Economy. Reports and Studies*, 1, 97–129.

Giavazzi, F., Japelli, T. and Pagano, M. (1999) 'Searching for non-Keynesian effects of fiscal policy', *Working Paper Centro Studi in Economia e Finanza*, 16.

Giavazzi, F., Japelli, T. and Pagano, M. (2000) 'Searching for the non-linear effects of fiscal policy: Evidence for industrial and developing countries', *NBER Working Paper Series*, 7460.

Giavazzi, F. and Pagano, M. (1990) 'Can severe fiscal contractions be expansionary? Tales of two small European countries', *NBER Macroeconomics Annual*, 5, 75–111.

Giudice, G., Turrini, A. and in't Veld, J. (2003) 'Can fiscal consolidation be expansionary in the EU? Ex-post evidence and ex-ante analysis', *Economic Papers* 195, European Commission, Directorate-General for Economic and Financial Affairs.

Giudice, G., Turrini, A. and in't Veld, J. (2007) 'Non-Keynesian fiscal adjustments? A close look at expansionary fiscal consolidations in the EU', *Open Economics Review*, 18(5), 613–30.

Gupta, S. et al. (2005) 'Fiscal policy, expenditure composition and growth in low-income countries', *Journal of International Money and Finance*, 24(3), 441–63.

Hall, P.E and Soskice, D. (eds) (2001) *Varieties of Capitalism: The Institutional Foundations of Comparative Advantage*, Oxford: Oxford University Press.

Hemming, R., Kell, M. and Mahfouz, S. (2002) 'The effectiveness of fiscal policy in stimulating economic activity. A review of the literature', *IMF Working Paper*, WP/02/208.

International Monetary Fund (2010) *World Economic Outlook April 2010: Rebalancing Growth*, Washington, DC: International Monetary Fund.

Irmen, A. and Kuehnel, J. (2009) 'Productive government expenditure and economic growth', *Journal of Economic Surveys*, 23(4), 692–733.

Kalecki, M. (1943) 'Political aspects of full employment', *Political Quarterly*, 14(4), 322–31.

Keynes, J.M. (1936) *The General Theory on Employment, Interest and Money*, Cambridge: Macmillan Cambridge University Press, for Royal Economic Society.

Keynes, J.M. (1937) 'The General Theory of Employment', *Quarterly Journal of Economics*, 51, 209–33.

King, R.G. and Rebelo, S. (1990) 'Public policy and economic growth: developing neoclassical implications', *NBER Working Paper*, 3338.

Kneller, R., Bleaney, M.F. and Gemmell, N. (1999) 'Fiscal policy and growth: evidence from OECD countries', *Journal of Public Economics*, 74(2), 171–90.

Kneller, R., Bleaney, M.F. and Gemmell, N. (2001) 'Testing the endogenous growth model: public expenditure, taxation and growth over the long-run', *Canadian Journal of Economics*, 34(1), 36–57.

Kumar, M.S., Leigh, D. and Plekhanov, A. (2007) 'Fiscal adjustments: determinants and macroeconomic consequences', *IMF Working Paper*, WP/07/178.

McDermott, C.J. and Wescott, R.F. (1996) 'An empirical analysis of fiscal adjustments', *IMF Staff Papers*, 43, 725–53.

O'Connor, J. (1973) *The Fiscal Crisis of the State*, New York: St Martin's Press.

Romero de Avila, D. and Strauch, R. (2003) 'Public finances and long-term growth in Europe: Evidence from a panel data analysis', *European Central Bank Working Paper*, 246.

Sawyer, M. (2009) 'Fiscal and interest rate policies in the "new consensus" framework: a different perspective', *Journal of Post Keynesian Economics*, 31(4), 549–65.

Sawyer, M. (2007) 'Fiscal policy under new labour', *Cambridge Journal of Economics*, 31(6), 885–99.

Van Aarle, B. and Garretsen, H. (2003) 'Keynesian, non-Keynesian or no effects of fiscal policy changes? The EMU case', *Journal of Macroeconomics*, 25(2), 213–40.

12
Fiscal Policy and Private Investment in Mexico

Emilio Caballero U. and Julio López G.

1 Introduction

Throughout the mid-1980s Mexico embarked on a complete renewal of its economic strategy by aligning with the so-called 'Washington Consensus'. This renewal led to many changes in the structure and functioning of the economy.

Within such changes there is one in particular we would like to high-light: the drastic reduction of the government's role in the economy. At least four phenomena illustrate this: the fall of public expenditure as a share of gross domestic product (GDP); the dismantling of a great part of the institutions and enterprises through which the state exerted its direct intervention in the economy; the quasi-disappearance of the public deficit in the governmental accounts, going as far as having established a constitutional law which in principle rejects the use of the deficit as a policy instrument; and the transfer of the responsibility of the monetary policy entirely to an independent central bank.

Although these phenomena have been global in nature, in the case of Mexico they have been more worrying than in other countries. On the one hand, because in Mexico income distribution is extremely unequal, and redistributing income through social expenditure is of the utmost importance. But without additional resources coming from higher taxes levied on the richer strata of the population, the redistribution of income cannot be carried too far. On the other hand, the weight of the state in the economy is already very low, and the tax rate is one of the lowest among middle-income countries. In 2008 taxes[2] stood at about 11 per cent with respect to GDP, while the Latin American average was about 17 per cent, and the OECD average was around 40 percent. In the same year the share of government consumption expenditure with respect to GDP was around 15 per cent; seven percentage points below the Latin American average (22.15 per cent), and about only one-third of the European average (43 per cent).

Now, despite the expectations of supporters of the new strategy, the macroeconomic evolution of the country has been disappointing. This is particularly apparent when we contrast Mexico's 'golden' years of growth, which lasted *grosso modo* from the 1940s until the mid-1970s, with what has been taking place in the recent past. In particular, Mexico suffered two important crises in the 1980s and another deep crisis in the mid-1990s; of all the Latin American economies it has been the most badly affected by the current world crisis (experiencing a fall of output of about 6.5 per cent in 2009); and, more generally, the average growth rate of the economy during the last three-odd decades has been very low.

Many authors have argued that the poor economic performance of the country can be explained by either one of the two following factors, or perhaps the two working in combination: a slow capital accumulation and a reduced government presence in the economy. However, some observers see here a fundamental incompatibility. The increasing participation of the state in the economy requires higher taxes, necessary to finance the rising government expenditures; while, they argue, raising taxes could discourage private investment.

The purpose of this work is to analyse the relationship between fiscal policy and private investment in Mexico. We try to prove the hypothesis that government expenditure stimulates private investment; for income taxation does not discourage it, as long as income from such tax contribute to finance a public spending that, at the same time, generates new demand.

This is a topic which can be identified within the current debate about the type of tax policy that is required in Mexico, because there are certain positions, included the official one, which hold the opposite hypothesis, that is, that higher public expenditure does not stimulate demand nor private investment, especially when such higher expenditure is financed by increasing the income tax. In order to carry out our work, we make use of econometric techniques.

This chapter is made up of three parts, plus this introduction. In the following section we will refer to the macroeconomic debate on this topic. In the third section we present some general background about the evolution of investment, and of some of its possible determinants. We then carry out an econometric study on the topic. In the last section we draw our conclusions.

2   The contemporaneous macroeconomic debate

Before carrying out our empirical work, it is worth revisiting the theoretical and applied literature on the effects of fiscal policy on the macroeconomy. As we know, in the last few decades a sort of consensus about it was generated, at least amongst mainstream economists and many governments. In this consensus fiscal spending is considered as, in the best-case scenario, neutral with respect to its effects on aggregate demand and production, for it crowds out private demand; and, in the worst-case scenario, it has negative effects. As we know, the recent crisis forced virtually every government in the developed countries, as well as many of the semi-industrialized ones, to abandon such a vision and apply expansionary fiscal policies. Even then, despite the fact that the crisis has not yet been overcome, there is a powerful current of opinion that does not recognise the beneficial effects fiscal expansion has had in moderating the intensity of the recession, and that advocates for a return to 'sound finance'.

In the context of this debate, it seems useful to take as a starting point the work by Arestis and Sawyer (2003), in which the authors evaluate the theoretical and empirical evidence on the issue. On the theoretical side, they demonstrate that the alleged crowding-out effect of government spending on private spending is not inevitable because of, among others, the following reasons:

- An adequate monetary policy could avoid the increase in the interest rate that may come along with fiscal expansion.
- Domestic saving is not reduced at the expense of investment, given that government spending raises output and savings.
- The substitution effect that imports exert on private spending (international crowding-out) will not necessarily occur.
- The argument that in the long run fiscal expansion leads to an increase in prices and wages, and to a reduction of private spending, is based on a supposed negative association between prices and private demand that is not necessarily valid.
- The objection to a fiscal expansion, based on a supposedly existing natural rate of unemployment that does not allow increasing demand without igniting inflation, assumes a supply-side equilibrium in which demand always adjusts to be consistent with such supply equilibrium. But this assumption is not necessarily valid.
- The Ricardian equivalence theorem between taxes and debt, which also denies the expansionary effects of fiscal policy, arguing that it

reduces private spending because the public anticipates higher taxes in the future, is based on extremely unrealistic assumptions.

Arestis and Sawyer (2003) also analyse the so-called 'institutional aspects of fiscal policy', which would allegedly render fiscal policy largely ineffective. They consider, among others, the following aspects:

- Fiscal policy is pro-cyclical. However, this effect can be reduced if, for instance, fiscal rules based on precise objectives are established.
- The idea that tax rate volatility provokes inefficiency on the supply side due to its interference on the labour supply, saving and investment, is not supported empirically.
- The thesis that fiscal policy is more effective in developed countries than in developing countries because the latter are frequently subject to supply shocks does not consider that a supply shock can have no effect on the level of economic activity if it also brings about changes in aggregate demand which compensate it. However, in developing countries the availability and cost of internal and external financing is the main restriction of the fiscal deficit.
- Finally, Arestis and Sawyer (op. cit.) analyse the empirical evidence obtained in different studies about the effectiveness of fiscal policy in both developed and developing countries. They conclude that there is no empirical support for the claim that fiscal expenditure crowds out private spending:[3]

Let us now consider a few studies dealing with the Mexican case. For instance, López (1994) conducted an empirical estimation of the determinants of private consumption and private investment for the period 1980–1994. With respect to the effect of public expenditure on private expenditure, he found (1) that government expenditure and the budget deficit stimulate consumption and private investment; (2) the existence of an accelerator effect in the Mexican case; (3) that the recovery of private investment (which started in 1987 and lasted until 1994) did not seem to have been due to the spontaneity of market forces, it was rather the consequence of the application of a moderately expansive fiscal policy and a revaluation of the Mexican peso; and (4) that the reduction of government spending and its subsequent stabilisation at a low level played a decisive role in the contraction and the consequent stagnation of domestic expenditure. Also under an effective demand approach, Guerrero de Lizardi (1996) studied private investment in Mexico for the period 1980–94, reaching similar results.

In later work, Lachler and Aschauer (1998) tested the hypothesis that the reduction of the growth rate of output in Mexico, which began in 1981, had been the consequence of the fall of public spending in infrastructure, observed since that time. With respect to the effect of public on private spending, they used a simple OLS model with annual data of private investment, government spending (in consumption and investment), public sector income and GDP, for the period 1970–96. On this specific issue, they found that to a certain extent the hypothesis of the fall of the growth rate of output (due to the fall of public expenditure on infrastructure) is valid. With a similar approach, Ramírez (2004) found, through a logarithmic Cobb–Douglas production function, that both private investment and public spending on infrastructure have a strong and statistically significant positive effect on the growth rate of the Mexican economy, and that there is a strong attraction effect on private capital from public capital in infrastructure. His main conclusions, in addition to the one already mentioned, are that: (1) output increases do not seem to induce high levels of public spending in infrastructure; (2) the latter explains a significant percentage of variation of private investment but the inverse does not happen; (3) when introducing the public industrial capital stock (excluding capital in infrastructure), a positive and significant effect on output and private investment is found, though quantitatively smaller than in the previous case.

In a more recent study, Castillo and Herrera (2005) studied the effect of public spending on private spending in Mexico for the period 1980–2002. Their objective was to evaluate if, indeed, there have been crowding-out effects of private consumption and investment as a result of the increase in public expenditure. They find that an increase in public spending leads to a permanent diminution of private consumption. In addition, they concluded that the short-run impact of increases in public investment induces reductions in private investment, possibly because of the lack of financial resources to induce capital formation. But the long-run impact of public investment on private investment is positive. They argue that this is as a result of the fact that government capital formation projects usually translate into infrastructure that render support to the participation of the private sector in productive activities which are linked to its utilisation.

With the previous antecedents in mind, let us now examine the evolution of private investment in Mexico's recent experience, and see whether, and how, it is associated with the fiscal policy stance.

3 Evolution of private investment in Mexico, 1980–2007

The purpose of this section is to describe the evolution of private investment; and to contrast this evolution with that of some variables which
are of particular interest for our work, especially fiscal variables. Our aim
is to make a first approach to the problem, in order to determine later,
through econometric methods, the existence, the direction and the size
of the possible economic relations among such variables. In this way,
we will be able to identify the determinants of private investment in the
case of Mexico, and the influence that fiscal variables exert on it.

Between 1980 and 1981 total investment in Mexico represented
23.5 per cent of aggregate demand, but by 2006–07 the situation had
changed significantly, and the proportion had declined to 22.1 per cent.
This fall was associated with an increase in private investment from
13.1 per cent to 18.3 per cent of GDP.[4] This occurred at the same time as a
decrease of government spending from 20.9 per cent to 12.6 per cent of
GDP. Finally, the share of exports increased from 15.9 per cent to 41.3
per cent of GDP during that period. In fact, the openness and deregulation process of the Mexican economy, which began in the first half of
the 1980s, provoked, on the one hand, the more-than-proportional
increase in imports (from 15.9 per cent of GDP to 45.9 per cent. The
net result of this process has been the worsening of the balance of payments' current account and the increase in the component of imports
in demand and domestic production. This is how the reduction of the
multiplier and the investment accelerator effects are explained (Ibarra,
2008, 2009). Also, this is the main factor behind the poor growth performance of the economy.

At a greater level of disaggregation one can observe that between
1981 and 1987, the period that witnessed the beginning of the so-called
debt crisis (end of 1982), total investment in Mexico shows a decreasing
trend, albeit with a slight recovery between 1983 and 1985. By contrast,
from 1998 and up to 2007 there is an increasing trend. But such an
increase is interrupted by two falls. The first one in 1995, a single year;
while the second fall began in 2001 and lasting until 2003.

On the other hand, it must be noted that during the period under
consideration the performance of private investment has conditioned
the evolution of total investment, due to the fall in public investment,
in both absolute and relative terms. As stated earlier, private investment
increased its share in total investment at the expense of public investment. The rather modest growth rate of private investment (annual
average: 3.72 per cent), along with the decrease in public investment,

214

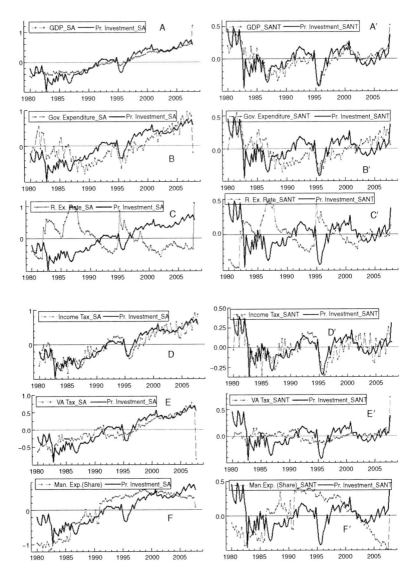

Figure 12.1 Private investment and selected fiscal and external variables in Mexico
Source: INEGI, (Sistema de Cuentas Nacionales and Secretaría de Hacienda y Crédito Público),
Secretaría de Hacienda y Crédito Público and Banco de México, authors' calculations.

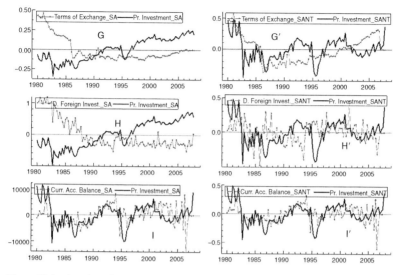

Figure 12.1 (*continued*)

give as a result the low growth rates of total investment (2.08 per cent) and of output (2.38 per cent).

We will now discuss the possible association between a series of variables that might be related to private investment, for which it is useful to look at Figure 12.1. Apart from the fiscal variables, which are crucial for the present research, we have included some other variables because in some theoretical approaches, or in other studies, they are considered to influence private investment. To have a better intuition of the possible associations, in the leftward panel we plot private investment and a selected variable, both seasonally adjusted, while in the rightward panel we also remove the trend from the two variables.

Let us now consider in the first place the possible association between private investment and GDP. In this regard, it can be observed (see Figure 12.1, panels A and A') that there is a strong direct relation between the two, with a very high correlation coefficient. This close association is observed for the variables in levels, as well as for the seasonally adjusted and detrended series. All of which suggests the possible presence of strong investment multiplier effects on output, as well as accelerator effects of output on investment.

We will now consider the association between public spending and private investment. It is convenient to bear in mind that in our case budget public spending is basically determined by current spending, for in average during the whole period this represented 85.8 per cent of total budget spending, whereas capital spending contributed only with the remaining 14.2 per cent. Note also that in the first two business downswings (1981–87 and 1994–95), a pro-cyclical fiscal policy can be observed, for the growth rates of public investment in both periods were also negative. On the other hand, in the period 2000–02, the greater oil-related federal government receipts allowed the growth of public investment in the middle of the downswing.

Anyway, the correlation coefficients between total and current expenditure, on the one hand, and private investment, on the other, are also quite similar (around 0.32; see Figure 12.1 panels B and B'). By contrast, the relationship between capital spending and private investment is weaker. Nevertheless, the fall in the rate of private productive accumulation is accompanied by a fall in the several types of public expenditure as a share of GDP.

Finally, let us point out that primary spending, which does not include interest payments on public debt, follows a similar evolution to that of private investment, with a high correlation coefficient between both. Additionally, it can also be seen as a pro-cyclical performance, for it contracts along with private investment in 1995 and 2001. Incidentally, the latter confirms the theoretical approach whereby primary spending, and not public debt interest payments, is the one that really contributes to the expansion of effective demand and thus the enhancement of economic activity and employment. Keynes (1997: 95) expressed it as follows:

> We must also take account of the effect on the aggregate propensity to consume of government sinking funds for the discharge of debt paid for out of ordinary taxation. For these represent a species of corporate saving, so that a policy of substantial sinking funds must be regarded in given circumstances as reducing the propensity to consume. It is for this reason that a change-over from a policy of government borrowing to the opposite policy of providing sinking funds (or vice versa) is capable of causing a severe contraction (or marked expansion) of effective demand.

Let us now consider the evolution of tax receipts, and let us see how these have been associated with private investment (see Figure 12.1, panels D and D', as well as E and E'). As mentioned, Mexico's share of total tax receipts in GDP is extremely low (around 10–11 per cent). In 2008 just four types of taxes contributed 95.3 per cent of total Federal Government tax revenue: Income Tax, 56.4 per cent; Value Added Tax,

46.0 per cent; Special Taxes on Production and Services, –10.7 per cent; and Import Tax, 3.6 per cent.[5]

However, it does not seem to be the case that taxation had a negative influence on the level of private investment. For example, while the rate of productive accumulation was reduced by two percentage points in 2006–07 with respect to 1980–81, the tax load (Income Tax/GDP) remained constant. Moreover, it can be observed that, while VAT had almost doubled its share in the total between both periods, the Income Tax rate remained constant; which could be interpreted as the intention of the Federal Government adopting the idea that the latter discourages private investment. It is also worth pointing out that the growth rate of total taxation in the period of analysis was 2.5 per cent (annual average), more than double the growth rate of public spending during the same period. It can also be observed that the VAT increases its share in taxation because the annual average growth rate of its collection was 4.5 per cent, almost double the corresponding Income Tax for the same period (2.5 per cent). Moreover, it must be noted that, besides its regressive character, the VAT follows a rather more procyclical evolution than the Income Tax. Indeed, VAT collection increases between 1981–87 and 2000–02 and contracts only in 1995; whereas Income Tax contracts in 1981–87 and notably more than VAT in 1995, increasing less than VAT in 2000–03 (Secretaría de Hacienda y Crédito Público).

On the other hand, the empirical evidence for Mexico indicates that total taxation, which includes both income and consumer taxes, has a close positive relation to private investment. In the same sense, and contrary to what could be assumed a priori, the relation between private investment and Income Tax collection is direct and not inverse, with a high correlation coefficient. Furthermore, the share of Income tax with respect to GDP, and the share of private investment in GDP has a higher correlation coefficient (0.596) when compared to Income Tax load; that is, according to this seemingly paradoxical result, the greater the average Income Tax rate the larger the proportion of GDP private agents assign to investment.

The relation between private investment and VAT is also positive, with a high correlation coefficient (see panels E and E'). At the same time, the relation between private investment and tax load on VAT (that is, the variable's share of GDP) is positive and high. Moreover, in comparing the evolution of the rate of productive accumulation (the share of private investment on GDP) and the tax load of VAT (share of VAT on GDP), a positive relation can be observed. Lastly, there exists no definite relation between the tax ratio and private investment, whose correlation coefficient is negative and very low. In other words, whenever the coefficient of the tax ratio is low, both low and high values of private investment are found. This last result is reinforced when the evolution of the private productive accumulation rate and the tax ratio are compared; the correlation coefficient is negative, though very low.

There is consensus between the different schools of economic thought in the sense that a negative relationship exists between interest rates and private investment. With respect to this point, let us first observe that the idea that public spending substitutes private investment through the raising of the interest rate does not hold for Mexico. For example, between 1980 and 1995, the budget public spending and the interest rate moved more or less in the same direction, but from 1995 up to 2007 such variables moved in opposite directions. Moreover, the empirical evidence suggests that the interest rate has not been very important in the determination of private investment.

Finally, let us now study the association of investment with some external-related variables, which are of special importance within the framework of an increasingly globalized economy, as Mexico is nowadays.

In the first place, the real exchange rate[6] has been a very important variable in explaining the evolution of private investment, although in the case of Mexico different studies have provided controversial results with respect to the sign of the reference relation. For instance, Ibarra (2008, 2009) presents a set of private investment regressions with quarterly data for the period 1988–2008, and finds a positive association between real exchange rate and private investment. In the same vein, Blecker (2009) shows that the lagged real exchange rate explains most of the fluctuations in Mexico's annual growth by using different univariate and multivariate econometric techniques. Among his most remarkable conclusions, the author mentions that the real value of the peso (that is, the inverse of the real exchange rate) has a positive direct effect on investment, which is roughly cancelled out by the negative indirect effect via the output growth rate. However, as can be shown in Figure 12.1 (panels C and C'), the raw figures suggest a negative association between real exchange rate and private investment; in fact, between both variables we find a negative correlation coefficient (–0.62) for the period under study.

Some of the additional external-related variables that may influence private investment appear in panels F to I. Thus, we may think that the share of manufacturing exports in total exports (F), or Foreign Direct Investment (H), may tend to stimulate private investment, because they open up new investment possibilities. And in fact, in the two cases we see a certain degree of association between the corresponding variable and private investment. Also, one could presume that, since Mexico is a foreign-exchange constrained economy, an improvement in the real terms of exchange (relative price of exports vis-à-vis imports), or in the current account balance (I), could ease investment, by lifting the exchange constraint upwards. However, the correlation coefficients of these two variables with private investment, appears to be very low (see panels G and I).

To summarise, the statistical description of the evolution of private investment in Mexico, on the one hand, and some other relevant domestic variables, shows firstly a positive relationship between private investment and GDP, suggesting the possible presence of strong multiplier and accelerator effects. On the other hand, we find an inverse relation of interest rate with private investment.

On the other hand, the association between private investment in Mexico and different types of tax receipts and public spending during the period 1987–2007 shows interesting results. In the first place, primary spending seems to have a direct and significant impact on private investment. This is probably because such spending is assigned to important government activities, excluding debt payments, which do not necessarily contribute to the increase in effective demand and thus do not stimulate profits and investment. Moreover, the Income Tax seems to have a direct relation (not inverse) with private investment.

Finally, let us look at the association of private investment with some international-related variables. We find, in the first place, a negative association of investment with the real exchange rate; while private investment's association with foreign direct investment, with the real terms of exchange, or with the current account balance, is less clear.

Keeping in mind the previous findings, we turn now to the econometric analysis.

4 Econometric analysis

As a preliminary step, we consider it useful to say a few words about the econometric methodology we shall adopt, in particular because there is an important controversy amongst econometricians about the most adequate procedure to carry out empirical modelling. Colander (2009), for example, contrasts two alternative perspectives in empirical macroeconomics. He distinguishes on the one hand what he calls the 'European perspective', based on 'the general-to-specific Cointegrated Vector AutoRegressive (CVAR)' approach; and on the other the currently dominant 'Dynamic Stochastic General Equilibrium (DSGE) models'. However, as has been pointed out by Spanos (2009), the latter one can be

> ... better described as a Pre-Eminence of Theory standpoint, where the data are assigned a subordinate role broadly described as quantifying theories presumed adequate. In contrast, the European general-to-specific CVAR perspective attempts to give data a more substantial role in the theory-data confrontation and is more accurately described as endeavoring to accomplish the goals accorded by sound practices of frequentist statistical methods in learning from data.[7]

Here we shall follow the 'CVAR perspective' to econometrics. Accordingly, we emphasise the use of *statistically adequate* models as the basis of drawing reliable inferences, where the term *statistically adequate* refers to the validity of the probability and the statistical assumptions underlying the estimated model. The foundation of this approach is a purely probabilistic construal of the notion of a statistical model, considered to be a set of internally consistent probabilistic assumptions aimed to capture the statistical information in the data (chance regularity patterns). Thus, we distinguish between the structural model, which is based on substantive (theoretical) subject matter information, and the statistical model, which is chosen to reflect the systematic statistical information contained in the particular data. The way in which the two sources of information can be blended together harmoniously is to embed the structural model into a statistically adequate statistical model (Spanos 1999). The structural and statistical models will coincide when we can give an adequate, and sufficient for the purpose at hand, economic rationalisation to the latter one. When this is not the case, we will need to reformulate (reparameterise/restrict) an estimated well-defined statistical model in order to arrive at a structural model.

Accordingly, one important feature of our empirical modelling is that we subject all of our estimates to a battery of misspecification tests to secure the *statistical adequacy* (the validity of its probabilistic assumptions vis-à-vis the data in question) of the model and thus the reliability of our results. In addition, we use system-based cointegration methods in an attempt to capture the interdependencies in the economy. This procedure allows for an appropriate econometric analysis in the presence of non-stationary time series and endogeneity among the relevant variables.

We first estimate a VAR(4) with quarterly data for the period 1985(3)–2007(4). The model we show below included the following variables (lower-case letters denote logarithms): private investment (i); output (y); real exchange rate (e);[8] government primary spending (g); income tax revenue (t) and VAT revenue (v).[9] According to unit root tests (not shown here), all variables are nonstationary (I(1)). We subjected our estimated VAR model to a series of misspecification tests, and none of the tests rejected the null hypothesis of no misspecification. The results of the tests are in Table 12.1.

We then carried out cointegration analysis and found the presence of three possible equilibrium long-run relations among the variables. The results of the Trace values for the cointegration test are shown in Table 12.2.

Table 12.1   Single-equation VAR misspecification tests

Variables	Name of test	Statistic	Probability
i	AR	0.83341	[0.5320]
y	AR	0.4365	[0.8210]
g	AR	0.1617	[0.9754]
e	AR	0.65099	[0.6620]
t	AR	0.4038	[0.8440]
v	AR	0.41288	[0.8377]
i	Normality	1.2168	[0.5442]
y	Normality	4.2856	[0.1173]
g	Normality	0.96852	[0.6162]
e	Normality	0.77286	[0.6795]
t	Normality	0.59229	[0.7437]
v	Normality	1.5784	[0.4542]
i	ARCH	0.58352	[0.6760]
y	ARCH	1.6028	[0.1885]
g	ARCH	0.87161	[0.4877]
e	ARCH	0.65211	[0.6282]
t	ARCH	0.36302	[0.8337]
v	ARCH	0.74668	[0.5650]
i	Hetero	0.26366	[0.9984]
y	Hetero	0.23867	[0.9993]
g	Hetero	0.22729	[0.9995]
e	Hetero	0.21248	[0.9997]
t	Hetero	0.35341	[0.9882]
v	Hetero	0.14779	[1.0000]

Vector misspecification tests

Test	Test	Statistics	Probability
Normality	Normality test	6.6856	[0.8777]
Autocorrelation	AR	1.2283	[0.1022]
Hetero test	hetero test	1025.4	[0.3445]

Table 12.2 Trace test

H0:rank <=	Trace test	[Prob]
0	142.98	[0.000]**
1	86.961	[0.001]**
2	49.539	[0.033]*
3	20.841	[0.378]
4	7.9942	[0.473]
5	0.21532	[0.643]

We also imposed the restriction that one of these relations characterizes private investment, and the corresponding statistical test did not reject this restriction.[10] The long-run equilibrium relation for private investment can be expressed as follows (standard errors below the estimated values of the parameters):

$$i = 0.93107y + 0.77901g - 1.6563e - 0.63767t - 0.033002v$$

$$\text{SE} \quad [0.107] \qquad [0.278] \qquad [0.181] \qquad [0.136] \qquad [0.021]$$

We finally estimated an equilibrium correction model with a twofold objective. Firstly, in order to establish the short-run impacts of the variables under study in their transit from one equilibrium point to another, which is expressed, in theory, by the process described by the multiplier. Secondly, in order to verify that the variables we assume determine private investment actually Granger-cause it. This model is presented next. Note, the letter D before a variable indicates that we take its first difference; u is the error correction mechanism. In Table 12.3 we show the results of the Equilibrium Correction Model with the corresponding misspecification tests.

We have thus been able to identify the long- and the short-run determinant of private investment for the Mexican economy; and we could establish that the right-hand side variables do Granger-cause the left-hand side variable. Let us now analyze the economic meaning of our econometric results.

The equation indicates that the GDP elasticity of private investment is positive in both the long run and the short run, in accordance with the multiplier and accelerator principles. It is quite high, and in the long run for each 10 per cent increase in output, private investment increases by 9.3 per cent.

Second, the reference equation indicates that the elasticity of private investment with respect to primary expenditure is positive, of the

Table 12.3 Equilibrium correction mechanism

	Coefficient	Std.Error	t-value	t-prob
Di_4	0.2521	0.0863	2.92	0.0046
De_1	–0.3736	0.1071	–3.49	0.0008
Dy_2	0.6735	0.2269	2.97	0.0040
Dg_3	0.1028	0.0389	2.65	0.0099
u_1	–0.0066	0.0019	–3.51	0.0008
dummy96I	0.3231	0.0761	4.25	0.0001
Seasonal	0.1630	0.0313	5.21	0.0000

Misspecification tests		
Variables	Coefficient	t-prob
AR	1.1626	[0.3358]
ARCH	0.89683	[0.4706]
Normality	0.40471	[0.8168]
Hetero	1.0327	[0.4307]
Hetero-X	1.2143	[0.2710]
RESET	0.28333	[0.5961]

order of 0.78 in the long run, and of 0.10 after three periods, whereas income tax (t) and VAT (v) exert a discouraging effect on investment, with long-run elasticity coefficients of –0.63 and –0.03, respectively. This implies a positive net balance for the fiscal variables considered on private investment. We can then conclude that, if income tax receipts are used in order to finance primary spending then private investment is stimulated.

A corollary of the latter statement is that, at least in Mexico, the conventional hypothesis, which holds that income tax always discourages private investment, should be rejected. On the contrary, when the tax is used to spend it stimulates demand and investment. Incidentally, this result is compatible with two ideas originally formulated by Kalecki. The first is that profits retained by firms are one of the main determinants of their investment decisions; and the second is that profits increase whenever deficit spending increases.[11]

Lastly, we observe that the real exchange (e) rate exerts a strong negative effect on private investment, in that when it increases by one percentage point private investment is reduced 1.7 per cent in the long run; with a negative impact after one period of –0.37 per cent. Note, our result is contradicted by the findings in Ibarra (2008, 2009), who found a positive long-run effect of the real exchange rate on private investment.

It is worth mentioning that this result is, at first sight, surprising. Indeed, when the so-called Marshall–Lerner condition[12] holds, a higher real exchange rate is likely to boost profits in the short run. This is because it improves the position of the trade balance (X increases in Kalecki's profit equation), which should stimulate investment. However, the reader must recall two additional consequences associated with a rise in the real exchange rate. These exert a negative effect – something that is quite significant in an economy such as Mexico. On the one hand, an increase in the real exchange rate (the consequence of a depreciation of the peso, for instance) increases the value of the debt of firms indebted in foreign currency. In the second place, such an increase also raises the price of capital goods. According to our econometric results, the negative impact of both effects would be stronger than the stimulating effect.

To summarise, in the specific case of Mexico and in the period under consideration, the neoclassical postulate whereby an increase in the income tax (which reduces after-tax marginal physical capital productivity) and an increase of public expenditure (which under certain circumstances raises the interest rate) jointly affect negatively private investment decisions does not hold. On the contrary, it strengthens the Kaleckian hypothesis that an increase of the income tax does not discourage private investment if it is used to finance primary spending.

5   Summary and conclusions

In this chapter, we have discussed the effects of fiscal policy on private investment, and have carried out an applied study for the Mexican economy to conduct an empirical assessment of these effects. Generally speaking, according to a first (classical/neoclassical) view, increasing taxation, and especially the income tax, will discourage private investment, and raising government expenditure simply crowds out private spending. On the other hand, Kalecki and Keynes, as well as their followers, consider that under the conditions of less-than-full-employment, which normally prevail under capitalism, when taxes are spent by the government, they expand demand. Thus, an appropriate fiscal policy may contribute to stimulate, rather than discourage, private investment.

If the dispute were exclusively amongst theoretical paradigms, perhaps the debate would not be too relevant. However, as Keynes (1997, p. 383) phrased it so aptly:

> the ideas of economists and political philosophers, both when they are right and when they are wrong, are more powerful than is commonly understood. Indeed the world is ruled by little else. Practical

men, who believe themselves to be quite exempt from any intellectual influence, are usually the slaves of some defunct economist.

Now, during recent decades different Mexican governments, which allegedly do not share the same outlook, have insisted on shrinking the state's role in the economy. This stance probably took place because, under the new consensus now ruling the world, the reduction of the government's role would stimulate a higher level of activity from the private sector. In its fiscal policy, the recipe has been *grosso modo* to maintain Mexico's low level of taxation, while simultaneously substituting value added tax for income tax (because of the alleged perverse effects the latter has on private investment).

In our applied study we have specified a rather general model where the two main alternative theoretical views on fiscal policy can be nested. The conclusions of our applied study confirm, in the case of Mexico, the arguments and policy advice of Kalecki and Keynes and their followers; and they reject the hypothesis of the classical/neoclassical outlook.

Our results also support the demand, voiced from many quarters, to carry out ambitious fiscal reform in Mexico, raising the tax rate. Radical reform in this area would be socially just, given the extreme levels of income inequality that exist in the nation. Furthermore it would also give the government the requisite revenues to fulfil its social and economic responsibilities.

Moreover, a larger tax base would not discourage private investment. On the contrary, if the state spends the supplementary resources sensibly, private investment will be stimulated thanks to the improved material and institutional infrastructure provided by the state, and also the additional demand forthcoming from government spending. The private and the public sector in Mexico can, and should, work in unison, as they did during its 'golden' period of growth.

Notes

1. The authors would like to thank DGAP-Papiit, Proyecto IN-303609 for its support in carrying out this research. They also thank Elizabeth Martínez, Guillermo Arenas, Pamela Soria and Cynthia Sosa for their excellent research assistance. Last, but not least, they are grateful to Philip Arestis, the editor of this volume, for his extremely thoughtful suggestions. Any remaining errors are our own responsibility.
2. Oil taxes represent about 9 per cent of GDP; but then, taxes on oil are not paid by the domestic sector.

3. On this point Arestis and Sawyer (2003) rely essentially on the works of Hemming et al. (2002a, 2002b).
4. The negative association between private and public investment was the consequence of the privatisation of many state-owned firms.
5. We do not consider here the Single Rate Entrepreneurial Tax (IETU for its Spanish acronym), which came into force that year and for which 4.7 per cent of total tax receipts was estimated.
6. The concept of real exchange rate (RER) we use here is: RER = E (P_f/P_d), where E is the nominal exchange rate, P_f is the Consumer Price Index of the foreign country (that is, that of the USA), and P_d is domestic CPI (Mexico's).
7. See also Juselius (2006).
8. The real exchange rate was previously defined. An increase in the nominal exchange rate means a higher competitiveness of domestically produced goods.
9. We started with a larger information set, but in our final model we included only the statistically significant variables, ensuring that the model was not rejected by any of the different misspecification tests used to check the statistical properties of our estimates. The number of lags was chosen according to statistical adequacy grounds.
10. The values for the test for this restriction are the following:

    LR test for over-identification: squared [1] = **0.27697**, p-value = **0.59869**

11. Readers, and especially Malcolm Sawyer's students, surely recall Kalecki's extended formula for profits, which reads:

    $$P = Ck + I + X + B - Sw$$

    where Ck and I are capitalists' consumption and investment, respectively, X is the trade balance (net exports), B the budget deficit and Sw workers' savings.
12. Several studies indicate that this condition holds for Mexico; see for instance López and Sánchez (2008).

References

Arestis, P. and Sawyer, M. (2003) 'Reinventing fiscal policy', *Journal of Post Keynesian Economics*, 26(13), 3–25.

Banco de México. Estadísticas, finanzas públicas, ingresos y gastos del sector público. www.banxico.gob.

Blecker, R. (2009) 'External shocks, structural change, and economic growth in Mexico, 1979–2007', *World Development*, 37(7), 1274–84.

Castillo, R. and Herrera, J. (2005) 'Efecto del Gasto Público sobre el Gasto Privado en México', *Estudios Económicos*, 20(2), 173–96.

Colander, D. (2009) 'Economists, incentives, judgement, and the European VAR approach to macroeconometrics', *Economics. The Open-Access, Open-Assessment E-Journal*, vol. 3, 2009–9.

Guerrero de Lizardi C. (1996) 'La Inversión: Teoría y Comportamiento en México 1981–1995', Tesis de Maestría en Ciencias Económicas UACPyP. Mexico: UNAM.

Hemming, R., Mahfouz, S. and Schimmelpfennig, A. (2002a) 'Fiscal policy and economic activity in advanced economies', IMF Working Paper 02/87, Washington, DC: IMF.

Hemming, R., Kell, M. and Mahfouz, S. (2002b) 'The effectiveness of fiscal policy in stimulating economic activity: A review of the literature', IMF Working Paper 02/208, Washington, DC:IMF.

Ibarra, C. (2008) 'Mexico's slow growth paradox', *Cepal Review*, 95, 93–102.

Ibarra, C. (2009) 'Capital flows, preemptive policy, and the external constraint in Mexico'. Working paper. Department of Economics Universidad de las Américas Puebla.

INEGI, Sistema de Cuentas Nacionales. www-inegi.gob.

Juselius, K. (2006) *The Cointegrated VAR Model: Methodology and Applications*, Oxford: Oxford University Press.

Keynes, John Maynard, (1997) *The General Theory of Employment, Interest, and Money*, New York: Prometheus Books.

Lachler U. and Aschauer, D. (1998) *Public Investment and Economic Growth in Mexico*, Policy Research Working Paper 1964, Washington, DC: World Bank.

López, J. (1994) 'Los problemas del ajuste en una economía abierta: una interpretación de la evolución reciente de la economía mexicana', in J. López (ed.), *México: La Nueva Macroeconomía*, Mexico: Ed. Nuevo Horizonte Editores.

López, J. and Sánchez, A. (2008) 'Short-run macroeconomic effects of trade liberalization in Latin America', *Economie Appliquée*, 56(3), 5–34.

López, J., Spanos, A. and Sánchez A. (unpublished) 'Macroeconomic linkages Mexico'. UNAM, Facultad de Economía. Processed.

Ramirez, Miguel D. (2004) 'Is public infrastructure investment productive in the Mexican case? A vector error correction analysis', *Journal of International Trade and Economic Development*, 13(2), 159–78.

Secretaría de Hacienda Crédito Público. Sistema de Finanzas Públicas. Dirección General Adjunta de Estadística de la Hacienda Pública. www.hacienda.gob.

Spanos, Aris (1999) 'The pre-eminence of theory versus the European CVAR perspective in macroeconometric modeling', *Economics: The Open-Access, Open-Assessment E-Journal*, Vol. 3, 2009–10.

13
A Keynes–Kalecki Model of Cyclical Growth with Agent-Based Features

Mark Setterfield and Andrew Budd

1 Introduction*

Throughout his career, Malcolm Sawyer has maintained an active interest in the development and promulgation of Kaleckian macroeconomics. In *Macro-Economics in Question* (Sawyer, 1982), he advocated a Kaleckian alternative to mainstream Keynesianism and monetarism, featuring: (i) explicit description of cost-plus pricing by firms and wage bargaining by workers in a non-marginalist theory of value and distribution; and (ii) the importance of both accelerator effects and (following Kalecki's principle of increasing risk) the rate of profit for the determination of aggregate investment. Both of these are now staple features of the canonical Kaleckian model of growth and distribution.[1]

At the turn of the millennium, Malcolm drew attention to various changes in the structure of capitalist economies to which Kaleckians needed to pay attention (Sawyer, 1999). These included changes in the relationship between finance and industry, a topic to which Kaleckians have since devoted considerable energies.[2] More recently, Malcolm has contributed to the analysis of the interaction of demand and supply in the Kaleckian approach to growth and distribution (Sawyer, 2010), an approach that, since its inception, has also been refined and extended to include analyses of the interaction of growth, distribution and inflation (Dutt, 1987; Lavoie, 2002; Cassetti, 2002), and even to

---

*Earlier versions of this paper were presented at the Analytical Political Economy Workshop, Queen Mary University of London, 16–17 May 2008 and at the University of Technology, Sydney, Australia. We would like to thank, without implicating, workshop and seminar participants for their helpful comments.

incorporate the effects of advertising and conspicuous consumption (Dutt, 2007).

Despite these various developments and Malcolm's contributions to them, one theme has received scant attention in Kaleckian macrodynamics: the role of historical time and uncertainty in shaping the economy's growth path. Under conditions of uncertainty, economic outcomes (including growth) are affected by changes in the 'state of long run expectations' (SOLE) – second-order features of the decision-making process, such as confidence and animal spirits, that impinge on behaviour independently of the best forecast of actual future events that decision makers can procure (Gerrard, 1995; Dequech, 1999).[3] Explicit acknowledgement that historical time and uncertainty are part of the fabric of the economy can be found in the Kaleckian literature (see, for example, Lavoie, 1992, pp. 282–4). But by and large, Kaleckians have adopted the modelling strategy of Keynes (1936) who, according to Kregel (1976), sought to 'lock up without ignoring' the effects of uncertainty on behaviour by assuming a *given* SOLE. In analytical terms, this provides a form of model closure that has, in turn, permitted the use of an equilibrium methodology in Kaleckian analysis. This, together with the attendant method of comparative statics (or dynamics), has been used to good effect to demonstrate the main results of the Kaleckian theory of growth and distribution.

From a Post Keynesian perspective, however, permitting variability in the SOLE is a necessary and important step in the development of Keynesian macrodynamics (Kregel, 1976). In what follows, we take up this challenge in the confines of an otherwise canonical Kaleckian growth model. The paper builds on Setterfield (2003), in which variations in the SOLE affect investment behaviour. Setterfield's model is formally open and hence admits no closed form solution, but is shown to suggest the possibility of cyclical growth. In this chapter, we: (a) extend the analysis of Setterfield (2003) by permitting heterogeneity amongst firms (in particular, with respect to changes in their SOLE), thus introducing agent-based features into the analysis; (b) simulate the resulting model to show more clearly the aperiodic growth cycles to which Setterfield alludes; and (c) explore other features of the model economy (including the size distribution of firms) that are not obvious from its basic construction, and that might be considered emergent properties of its operation.

The remainder of the paper is organised as follows. Section 2 describes the basic model, paying particular attention to its incorporation of agent-based features into what is initially an aggregate structural model. Section 3 reports simulation results and section 4 concludes.

2   A Keynes–Kalecki model of cyclical growth

(i)   An initial structural model

We begin with the following structural model:

$$g_t^i = \alpha_t + g_r r_t^e + g_u u_t^e \tag{1}$$

$$g_t^s = s_\pi r_t \tag{2}$$

$$r_t = \frac{\pi u_t}{v} \tag{3}$$

$$g_t^s = g_t^i \tag{4}$$

$$r_t^e = r_{t-1} \tag{5}$$

$$u_t^e = u_{t-1} \tag{6}$$

$$\alpha_t = \alpha_t(u_{t-n}, u_{t-n}^e), \quad n = 1, 2 \tag{7}$$

where g^i is the rate of accumulation and g^s is the rate of growth of savings, α denotes the SOLE, r^e and r are the expected and actual rate of profits, respectively, u^e and u are the expected and actual rates of capacity utilisation, respectively, π is the profit share and v is the fixed full capacity capital–output ratio. The model stated above is replicated from Setterfield (2003), and comprises what Lavoie (1992, Ch. 6) describes as the canonical Kaleckian growth model (equations [1]—[6]) augmented by a SOLE reaction function (equation [7]). Hence equation [1] is a standard Kaleckian investment function, equation [2] is the Cambridge equation, and equation [3] is true by definition. Note that, since v is fixed by assumption, the rate of accumulation described in equation [1] is equivalent to the economy's rate of growth at any given rate of capacity utilisation. Equation [4] insists that the growth of savings adjusts to accommodate the rate of accumulation in each period, whilst equations [5] and [6] describe the adjustment of expectations between periods. Finally, equation [7] states that the SOLE – which includes the confidence that firms place in their expectations and their animal spirits, and hence the willingness of firms to act on the basis of their expectations – depends on expected and actual events in the recent past.[4]

Combining equations [1]–[6] to produce reduced-form expressions for g^i and u and combining these expressions with equation [7], we arrive at:

$$\alpha_t = \alpha_t(u_{t-1}, u_{t-2}, u_{t-3}) \tag{7}$$

$$g_t^i = \alpha_t + \left(g_u + \frac{g_r \pi}{v}\right)u_{t-1} \tag{8}$$

$$u_t = \frac{v}{s_\pi \pi}g_t^i \tag{9}$$

In Setterfield (2003), the implicit function in [7] is rendered explicit in the manner described in Table 13.1, with c constant and:

$$\varepsilon_t \sim (\mu_{\varepsilon t}, \sigma_{\varepsilon t}^2)$$

The idea in Table 1 is that firms revise their SOLE in a manner that depends on: (i) comparison of the difference between actual and expected events to the value of a conventionally determined 'acceptable' margin of expectational error, c; and (ii) the adjustment parameter (ε) that is influenced by the convention $\mu_{\varepsilon t}$, from which decision makers can deviate at will (hence $\sigma_{\varepsilon t}^2 \neq 0 \; \forall \; t$).[5]

Outcomes in the model described above result from the recursive interaction of equations [7]–[9]. Using conventional analytical techniques, Setterfield (2003, 327–31) shows that the model has the capacity to produce cumulative increases (or decreases) in the rates of growth and capacity utilisation, that may occasionally be punctuated by turning points. He thus alludes to the capacity of the model to produce growth

Table 13.1 Revisions to the state of long-run expectations

Nature of disappointment	Value of α_t
$u_{t-1} - u_{t-2} \geq c$	$\alpha_t = \alpha_{t-1} + \varepsilon_t$
$u_{t-1} - u_{t-2} > -c$ And $u_{t-2} - u_{t-3} \leq -c$	$\alpha_t = \alpha_{t-1} + \varepsilon_t$
$u_{t-1} - u_{t-2} \leq -c$	$\alpha_t = \alpha_{t-1} - \varepsilon_t$
$u_{t-1} - u_{t-2} < c$ And $u_{t-2} - u_{t-3} \geq c$	$\alpha_t = \alpha_{t-1} - \varepsilon_t$

cycles, that are aperiodic and of no fixed amplitude. Part of the purpose of this paper is to more clearly demonstrate the existence of these cycles by utilising simulation techniques.

(ii)   Introducing agent-based features into the model

One advantage of simulation is that it eliminates the need for simplifying assumptions designed to permit the derivation of a tractable analytical solution to a model. Models designed for simulation can be as complicated as available computing capacity allows. In what follows, we use this advantage to introduce 'agent-based features' into our model. Specifically, we replace the single representative firm implicit in the structural model developed thus far with a multiplicity of heterogeneous firms.

Agent-based computational economics (ACE) is a fast growing sub-field in economics.[6] A basic ambition of ACE is to construct dynamic models that feature multiple, heterogeneous agents. In some quarters, the impetus for this ambition derives from a desire for a 'second-generation' micro-foundations project in macroeconomics – one that properly recognises the substance of the SDM theorems in Walrasian economics and thus eschews the representative agent construct (see, for example, Kirman, 1989, 1992).[7] As such, the ACE project is avowedly 'bottom up' in its approach to model building, beginning with (heterogeneous) individual agents and looking for macroscopic phenomena – at whatever level of aggregation – to arise from their interaction (see, for example, Markose et al. 2007, p. 803). The approach taken in this paper is, however, rather different. It involves disaggregating certain features of an aggregate structural model in order to incorporate agent heterogeneity. For this reason, we refer to the model as having 'agent-based features', rather than as an ACE model per se.

Our introduction of agent-based features into the model described earlier focuses exclusively on firm behaviour, with respect to the revision of the SOLE in response to expectational disappointment. We distinguish between different types of firms along two broad dimensions. First, we differentiate between 'aggressive adapters' and 'cautious adapters'. Aggressive adapters revise their SOLEs in response to small discrepancies between u and u^e. In terms of Table 13.1, they set a low value of the convention c. Aggressive adapters are also characterised by short reaction periods. In other words, there need only be a discrepancy between u and u^e for a brief period of calendar time to trigger a change in the SOLE.[8] Cautious adapters, meanwhile, display the opposite characteristics: they revise their SOLE only in response to large discrepancies between

u and u^e (i.e., they set high values of c) observed over longer intervals of calendar time (i.e., they have long reaction periods).

Second, we differentiate between firms that are more and less sensitive to macroeconomic events in their evaluation of the business climate. Specifically, we envisage all firms as revising their SOLEs in response to a mixture of *both* their own individual experience *and* aggregate economic outcomes. The more sensitive to macroeconomic events a firm is, the greater will be the weight it attaches to aggregate economic outcomes (relative to individual experience) in the process of revising its SOLE. In this way, our model resembles a *blackboard system*, in which individual agents' behaviour is affected by both their own proprietorial knowledge (of their own economic performance), and shared information (about macroeconomic outcomes) derived from the 'blackboard' (see, for example, Wooldridge, 2002, pp. 301–9). Note that this blackboard structure creates feedback from macroeconomic outcomes to microeconomic (firm) behaviour. This avoids the 'one way street' favoured by reductionist approaches to macroeconomics, according to which macro outcomes are affected by micro behaviour, but the converse does not apply. The blackboard is also central to the conception of agent interaction in our model, as explained below.

Based on these considerations, we replace equations [7]—[9] of the structural model above with:

$$\alpha_{jt} = \alpha_j(u_{jt-n}, u_{t-n}), \quad n = 1, 2, 3 \qquad [7a]$$

$$g_{jt}^i = \alpha_{jt} + \left(g_u + \frac{g_r \pi}{v}\right) u_{jt-1} \qquad [8a]$$

$$u_{jt} = \frac{v}{s_\pi \pi} g_{jt}^i \qquad [9a]$$

for $j = 1, ..., 100$, and with [7a] rendered explicit as in Table 13.2.

In Table 13.2, $\varepsilon_{jt} \sim (\mu_{\varepsilon t}, \sigma_{\varepsilon t}^2) \, \forall j$, and the conventions c_j are now modelled as:

$$c_j = \beta_j \sigma_u$$

where $0 < \beta_j \leq 1$ and σ_u is the standard deviation of the aggregate capacity utilisation rate. We then use the values of β_j, k_j and κ_j to distinguish between the different types of firms outlined above – aggressive adapters (low β_j and k_j), cautious adapters (high β_j and k_j), firms that are more sensitive to aggregate economic outcomes (low κ_j) and firms that

Table 13.2 Agent-based revisions to the state of long-run expectations

Nature of disappointment	Value of α_{jt}
$\dfrac{\kappa_j}{k_j}\displaystyle\sum_{i=1}^{k_j}(u_{j,t-i}-u_{j,t-1-i})+\dfrac{(1+\kappa_j)}{k_j}\displaystyle\sum_{i=1}^{k_j}(u_{t-i}-u_{t-1-i})\geq c_j$	$\alpha_{jt}=\alpha_{jt-1}+\varepsilon_{jt}$
$\dfrac{\kappa_j}{k_j}\displaystyle\sum_{i=1}^{k_j}(u_{j,t-i}-u_{j,t-1-i})+\dfrac{(1-\kappa_j)}{k_j}\displaystyle\sum_{i=1}^{k_j}(u_{t-i}-u_{t-1-i})>-c_j$ And $\dfrac{\kappa_j}{k_j}\displaystyle\sum_{i=1}^{k_j}(u_{j,t-k_j-i}-u_{j,t-k_j-1-i})+\dfrac{(1-\kappa_j)}{k_j}\displaystyle\sum_{i=1}^{k_j}(u_{t-k_j-i}-u_{t-k_j-1-i})\leq -c_j$	$\alpha_{jt}=\alpha_{jt-1}+\varepsilon_{jt}$
$\dfrac{\kappa_j}{k_j}\displaystyle\sum_{i=1}^{k_j}(u_{j,t-i}-u_{j,t-1-i})+\dfrac{(1-\kappa_j)}{k_j}\displaystyle\sum_{i=1}^{k_j}(u_{t-i}-u_{t-1-i})\leqslant -c_j$	$\alpha_{jt}=\alpha_{jt-1}-\varepsilon_{jt}$
$\dfrac{\kappa_j}{k_j}\displaystyle\sum_{i=1}^{k_j}(u_{j,t-i}-u_{j,t-1-i})+\dfrac{(1-\kappa_j)}{k_j}\displaystyle\sum_{i=1}^{k_j}(u_{t-i}-u_{t-1-i})<c_j$ And $\dfrac{\kappa_j}{k_j}\displaystyle\sum_{i=1}^{k_j}(u_{j,t-k_j-i}-u_{j,t-k_j-1-i})+\dfrac{(1-\kappa_j)}{k_j}\displaystyle\sum_{i=1}^{k_j}(u_{t-k_j-i}-u_{t-k_j-1-i})\geq c_j$	$\alpha_{jt}=\alpha_{jt-1}-\varepsilon_{jt}$

are less sensitive to aggregate economic outcomes (high κ_j). The precise values of these parameters and their correspondence to the types of firms discussed above is described in detail in section 2(iii)c below.[9]

Before proceeding, several remarks on the model described above are in order. First, note that equation [9a] results from the solution of firm-specific versions of equations [2]–[4] (featuring the variables g_{jt}^s, r_{jt}, u_{jt} and g_{jt}^i), and therefore embodies the equality $g_{jt}^s = g_{jt}^i$ for all *j*. This means that in every period, each individual firm generates (from its profits) sufficient saving to exactly fund the investment that it (independently of saving behaviour) chooses to undertake. In other words, firms are akin to city states that either engage in strictly balanced trade with one another, or else practice autarky. Since the Kaleckian model requires only that saving equals investment in each period *in the aggregate* (as in equation [4]), $g_{jt}^s = g_{jt}^i$ is sufficient but not necessary for our model to remain faithful to the features of the underlying structural model on which it is based. The condition could, therefore, be relaxed (on which see Gibson and Setterfield, 2010). It is retained in what follows, however, so as to maintain a narrow focus on the psychological interaction of agents via revision of the SOLE, this having been identified as the central 'driver' of aggregate fluctuations.

Second, notice that k_j, β_j, κ_j, and ε_j are the only agent-specific parameters in our model. Parameters such as g_u and g_r in equations [7a]—[9a] are common to all firms. Ultimately, then, we retain many features of the single representative firm implicit in our original aggregate structural model, introducing agent heterogeneity only into the SOLE reaction function. We focus on equation [7a] as the essential basis for distinguishing between agents of different types because, once again, revisions to the SOLE have been identified as the key 'driver' of aggregate fluctuations.

Finally, note that the recursive interaction of [7a]—[9a] is subject to an important constraint that is not considered by Setterfield (2003), but that must inform our simulations. Specifically, since $u \in [0\ 1]$, we can identify from equation [9a] upper and lower bounds to the growth rate, given by:

$$g^i_{max} = \frac{s_\pi \pi}{v}$$

for $u_j = 1$, and:

$$g^i_{min} = 0$$

for $u_j = 0$. These 'limits to growth' can be incorporated into our simulation model by insisting, following the calculation of g^i_{jt} during each iteration, that:

$$g^i_{jt} > 0 \Rightarrow g^a_{jt} = \min[g^i_{jt}, g^i_{max}]$$

$$g^i_{jt} < 0 \Rightarrow g^a_{jt} = \max[g^i_{jt}, g^i_{min}]$$

where g^a_{jt} denotes the rate of growth that is actually used in the calculation of u_{jt}. To ensure that our simulations are consistent with $u \in [0\ 1]$, we therefore add to our model the equation:

$$g^a_{jt} = \max\left[0, \min\left(g^i_{jt}, \frac{s_\pi \pi}{v}\right)\right] \qquad [10]$$

and replace [9a] with:

$$u_{jt} = \frac{v}{s_\pi \pi} g^a_{jt} \qquad [11]$$

Ultimately, then, our simulations are based on the recursive interaction of equations [7a], [8a], [10], and [11].

(iii)   Setting parameter values and initial conditions

In order to proceed, we need to establish the values of the parameters in equations [8a], [10] and [11], set the initial values of certain variables, and operationalise equation [7a].

(a)   Setting parameter values

Referring first to equations [8a] and [9a], and drawing on Lavoie and Godley (2001–02) and Skott and Ryoo (2008), we set:[10]

$$g_r = 0.49 \qquad g_u = 0.025$$

We also set:

$$\pi = 0.33 \qquad v = 3.0$$

which, together with their implications for the rate of profits, are broadly congruent with the stylised facts of long-run growth, as originally identified by Kaldor (1961).

This leaves us with the parameter s_π. Lavoie and Godley (2001–02) set the corporate retention rate at 0.75, and (on p. 291) the household saving rate (regardless of the form of household income) at 0.2. Total saving out of profit income, S, is therefore given by the sum of corporate retained earnings and household saving out of distributed earnings, or in other words:

$$S = 0.75\Pi + (0.2)(0.25\Pi)$$

where Π denotes total profits. The propensity to save out of profits $s_\pi = S/\Pi$ is therefore given by:

$$s_\pi = 0.75 + 0.25(0.2) = 0.8$$

(b)   Initial conditions

Note that if we replace equation [7] with:

$$\alpha = \bar{\alpha} \qquad\qquad [7b]$$

equations [1]–[6] can be solved for the steady-state rates of growth and capacity utilisation:

$$g^* = \frac{s_\pi \pi \bar{\alpha}}{\pi(s_\pi - g_r) - g_u v} \qquad [12]$$

$$u^* = \frac{v \bar{\alpha}}{\pi(s_\pi - g_r) - g_u v} \qquad [13]$$

Skott and Ryoo (2008) set $\bar{\alpha} = 0.0075$. Using this parameter value, together with those noted earlier, we can numerically evaluate equations [12] and [13] to get:

$$g^* = 0.0725$$

$$u^* = 0.8242$$

The computed value of u^* reported above can now be used as a reference point for setting the initial values of u and u_j that we require for our simulation exercise. Hence we set:

$$u_{jt-1} = u_{t-1} = u^* = 0.8242$$

and:

$$u_{jt-2} = u_{t-2} = u_{t-1} - \sigma_u = 0.6857$$

where $\sigma_u = 0.1385$ is the standard deviation of u calculated from US capacity utilisation data.[11]

(c)   Operationalising equation [7a]

As intimated above, equation [7a] is rendered explicit by Table 13.2, with:

$$c_j = \beta_j \sigma_u = 0.1385 \beta_j$$

Consistent with our setting $u_{jt-1} = u_{t-1} = u^* = 0.8242$, we set $\alpha_{jt-1} = \bar{\alpha} = 0.0075$ (which is the value of α consistent with our computed steady-state value of u). The variables ε_{jt} are set as random draws from a normal distribution with mean $\mu_\varepsilon = 0.0015$ and variance $\sigma_\varepsilon^2 = 0.0005$, moments that have been chosen in accordance with the magnitude of the parameter $\bar{\alpha}$. Note the system closure implicit in this formulation: for the sake of simplicity, both the mean and the variance of ε_j $\forall_j$ are treated as time-invariant, unlike their original formulation in Setterfield (2003). Finally, we choose the values of β_j, k_j and κ_j to distinguish between the different types of firms described earlier, as follows:

- $\beta_j = 0.5$ and $k_j = 1$ denotes 'aggressive adapters' – firms with a greater inclination to be encouraged/discouraged by short-term results, and a shorter reaction period.
- $\beta_j = 1$ and $k_j = 3$ denotes 'cautious adapters' – firms that are less inclined to be encouraged/discouraged by short-term results, and that have longer reaction periods.
- $\kappa_j = 0.9$ denotes firms whose psychology is less affected by macroeconomic events, and who therefore attach less weight to aggregate outcomes when revising their SOLEs.
- $\kappa_j = 0.5$ denotes firms whose psychology is more affected by macroeconomic events, and who therefore attach more weight to aggregate outcomes when revising their SOLEs.

Ultimately, then, our model distinguishes between the following four different types of firms:[12]

$$j = 1, ..., 25: \quad k_j = 1, \quad \beta_j = 0.5, \quad \kappa_j = 0.9$$

$$j = 26, ..., 50: \quad k_j = 1, \quad \beta_j = 0.5, \quad \kappa_j = 0.5$$

$$j = 51, ..., 75: \quad k_j = 3, \quad \beta_j = 1, \quad \kappa_j = 0.9$$

$$j = 76, ..., 100: \quad k_j = 3, \quad \beta_j = 1, \quad \kappa_j = 0.5$$

Recall that the value of ε_{jt} will vary even within these types of firms. Hence our model ultimately features a population of one hundred different firms, its dynamics depending on the heterogeneous behavioural responses of these firms to disappointed expectations.

(iv) Determining aggregate outcomes

Simulating equations [7a], [8a], [10], and [11] produces one hundred different values of g_{jt}^i and u_{jt} at the end of each period. But of course our interest is ultimately in g_t^i and u_t – and in fact, we *need* to know the latter in order make the calculations described in Table 13.2 and thus continue with the next iteration of our simulation. As such, we proceed to calculate the aggregates g_t^i and u_t as follows. We begin by assuming that all firms start with the same capital stock, which we normalise so that $K_j = 1 \, \forall \, j$ initially. Then for any subsequent period t:

$$K_t = \sum_{j=1}^{100} (1 + g_{jt}^i) K_{jt-1} \qquad [14]$$

and:

$$g_t^i = \frac{K_t - K_{t-1}}{K_{t-1}} \qquad [15]$$

Finally, the value of u_t is then calculated from equation [9].

(v) Summary

Our simulations proceed as follows. Given the initial conditions and parameter values outlined above, every k_j periods we establish the value of ε_{jt} for each individual firm and, using α_{jt-1}, calculate α_{jt} in accordance with the criteria in Table 13.2. Next, we numerically evaluate equations [8a], [10] and [11] to produce growth and utilisation rates for each of our individual firms. Finally, we numerically evaluate equations [14], [15] and [9] to produce the growth and capacity utilisation rates for the aggregate economy. The simulation then moves forward one period and the process described above starts again.

Before discussing our simulation results, it is worth drawing attention to one final feature of our model: the nature of agent interaction. Agent-based simulations are typically dependent on the notion of locality. That is, one agent must be within a certain proximity of another agent in order for the two agents to interact. This notion of locality is usually conceptualised in terms of a grid of cells. Our model, however, does not depend on proximity to facilitate the interaction of agents. Instead, each firm engages in its own individual decision-making process, through which it revises its SOLE for the next period (or set of periods) based on its own past performance and the performance of the aggregate economy, derived from the 'blackboard'. It is each firm's reference to the latter (in the form of the aggregate rate of capacity utilisation, and as a result of $\kappa_j \neq 1 \, \forall j$ in Table 13.2) that causes individual agents to interact with one another in our model. Put differently, instead of the 'direct' interaction between individual agents typical of ACE models, our model exhibits 'indirect' agent interaction, resulting from the sensitivity of individual firm behaviour to aggregate economic outcomes that are a product of the actions of *all* agents.

3   Results and discussion

Our simulation was implemented using the open source Recursive Porous Agent Simulation Toolkit (Repast), developed at the University of Chicago. The version of Repast used was written in Java. More information about Repast is available at http://repast.sourceforge.net.

(i)   Aggregate outcomes

Figures 13.1 and 13.2 illustrate the aggregate rates of growth and capacity utilization from a representative run of our model. After about 50 periods, the behaviour of the model stabilises, the economy experiencing aggregate fluctuations about average rates of growth and capacity utilisation of 7.5 per cent and 83.4 per cent, respectively.[13] This is the behaviour anticipated by Setterfield (2003, 327–31). Recall that there are no (fixed) equilibrium rates of growth or capacity utilisation towards which the economy is automatically drawn (or that it is compelled to orbit). Instead, 'the long-run trend is but a slowly changing component of a chain of short-period situations: it has no independent identity' (Kalecki, 1968, p. 263).[14] Note also that the behaviour of the

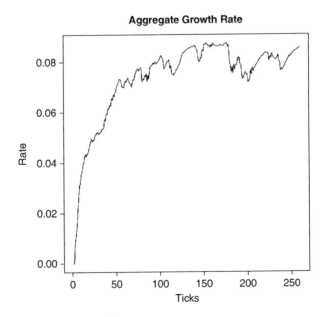

Figure 13.1   Aggregate growth

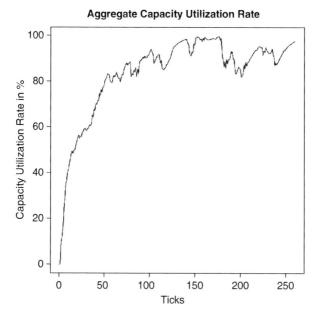

Figure 13.2   Aggregate capacity utilisation

economy in Figures 13.1 and 13.2 bears out Keynes's (1936) claim that even in the absence of such equilibrium 'anchors', a capitalist economy in which expectations are formed under conditions of fundamental uncertainty is likely to fluctuate for long periods of time at levels of economic activity that are below potential, but without the system ever collapsing completely. Put differently, rather than displaying classical stability, the economy displays *resilience* (Holling, 1973).[15]

The fluctuations depicted in Figures 13.1 and 13.2 are aperiodic and their amplitude is non-constant. The longest peak-peak cycle depicted in Figures 13.1 and 13.2 lasts for about 25 periods. If we interpret each period as a calendar year,[16] then the cycles depicted in Figures 13.1 and 13.2 are analogous to Kuznets swings.

(ii)   Firm-specific outcomes and the size distribution of firms

The aggregate regularities noted above are, however, not typical of the experience of all individual firms. Figure 13.3, which shows the total number of idle firms, provides the first indication of this. Figure 13.3 draws attention to an important feature of our model. Although it does not formally involve firm exit, the model does provide for the possibility

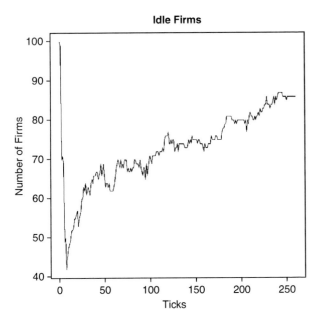

Figure 13.3   Number of idle firms

of 'pseudo exit' in the sense that firms can become idle (their rate of capacity utilisation falling to zero) at any point in time. By the same token, although the model does not formally involve firm entry, it provides for 'pseudo entry', since the SOLE reaction function in Table 13.2 allows for the possibility of currently idle firms becoming economically active again in the future. In this way, although the population of firms in our model is fixed, the ability of firms to transition into and out of a state of economic activity provides for pseudo entry and exit. And as is illustrated in Figure 13.3, this type of behaviour is actually observed over the course of our simulations.

Indeed, Figure 13.3 shows an *increasing* number of firms becoming inactive over time, providing prima facie evidence that the aggregate economy is becoming dominated by an ever smaller number of firms over time.[17] This is borne out by Figure 13.4, which illustrates the size distribution of firms (as measured by the quantity of capital that firms own) near the mid-point of our representative simulation.[18] The distribution in Figure 13.4 is suggestive of a power law of the form:

$$p(x) \sim x^{-\beta} \qquad [16]$$

where x denotes the size of the capital stock owned by firms. Power laws (and in particular, the Pareto distribution) are thought to characterise numerous size distributions in economics (Reed, 2001; Gabaix, 2009).[19] They are empirically well established as features of the size distribution of firms (Steindl, 1965; Ijiri and Simon, 1977) and the size distribution of wealth (Pareto, 1897) – both of which are effectively represented in Figure 13.4.

In order to subject the power law hypothesis to further scrutiny, we first estimate the scaling parameter β in equation [16] for the size distribution of firms in each period of our representative simulation, using the maximum likelihood technique outlined by Clauset et al (2007, pp. 4–6).[20] We then determine the goodness of fit of our estimated power law to the original data by computing the Kolmogorov–Smirnov (KS) statistic:

$$D = \max_{x \geq x_{min}} |S(x) - P(x)|$$

where $S(x)$ is the cumulative distribution function (CDF) of the data for all observations that satisfy $x \geq x_{min}$, $P(x)$ is the CDF of our estimated power law for $x \geq x_{min}$, and x_{min} is the lower bound of the estimated

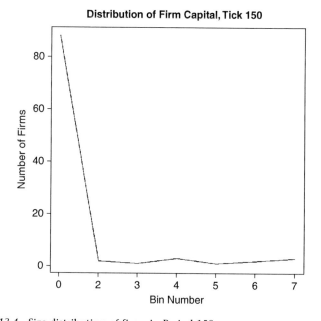

Figure 13.4   Size distribution of firms in Period 150

power law (Clauset et al., 2007, pp. 8, 11). The KS statistic measures the maximum distance between the CDFs of the data and our estimated power law relationship – so the higher is D, the worse is the goodness of fit of the power law. Bearing this in mind, the KS statistics for each of the 250-plus periods of our representative simulation are illustrated in Figure 13.5.

Excluding the first few periods, the values of the KS statistics in Figure 13.5 appear uniformly low throughout our representative simulation. This supports the claim that the size distribution of firms generated by our model conforms to a power law. Of course, this does involve a value judgement: there is no established critical value of the KS statistic above which it is conventional to reject the hypothesis that the power law fits the data. It is possible to calculate a p-value, quantifying the probability that a data set was drawn from a particular (estimated) power law distribution. As Clauset et al. (2007, pp. 11–12) explain, this involves a Monte Carlo procedure in which $1/4\varepsilon^2$ synthetic data sets are generated, where ε is the difference between the estimated and true p-values that we are willing tolerate. While this is well within the possibilities of modern High Performance Computing,

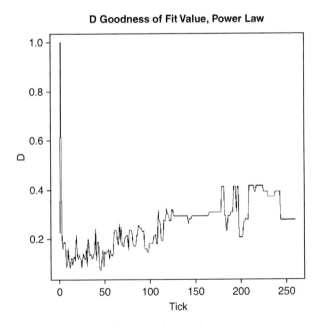

Figure 13.5   Goodness of fit of estimated power laws

it still requires that we choose a critical *p*-value in order to reject the hypothesis of a power law. Moreover, it is important to bear in mind that the evidence that real-world size distributions conform to power laws is not incontrovertible. For example, Clauset et al. (2007, pp. 16–20) *reject* the hypothesis that the size distribution of wealth (specifically, the aggregate net worth of the richest individuals in the USA in 2003) conforms to a power law. It seems, then, that the best we will ever be able to say is that there is some evidence that the size distribution of firms generated by our model conforms to a power law, just as there is some evidence that this same size distribution conforms to a power law in real-world data.

Nevertheless, even this tentative result is interesting in the present context. The cyclical behaviour of the growth and utilisation rates discussed in the previous sub-section is more or less predictable based on the underlying structure of our model (see, for example, Setterfield, 2003, pp. 327–31). The process of simulation serves to better illustrate a property of the model that is already understood to (potentially) exist. However, nothing in the structure of our model suggests we should observe a size distribution of firms conforming to a power law. This feature of our model emerges spontaneously from our simulation results.

One final feature of Figure 13.5 that merits discussion is the tendency of the value of the KS statistic to drift upwards. This suggests that the goodness of fit of the power law declines over time. However, there may be a simple explanation for this. The increasing value of the KS statistic may be explained by the decreasing number of 'bins' into which firms are sorted as our simulation progresses. In order to properly estimate a power law, there can be no empty bins in the histogram in Figure 13.4. It is therefore necessary to choose the largest number of bins that will result in each of the individual bins containing at least one firm. But as the number of small firms grows, and the gap between very large and very small firms increases, it is necessary to use fewer and larger bins to prevent the occurrence of empty bins. This reduces the number of data points that we have, resulting in a poorer quality fit for the power law. If this explanation is correct it suggests we should use more firms in future simulations, to improve the spectrum or breadth of our data and so increase the accuracy of our analysis of the size distribution of firms.

4 Summary and conclusions

Inspired by Malcolm Sawyer's long-standing interest in the development of Kaleckian macroeconomics, this chapter constructs and simulates a

Keynes–Kalecki model of cyclical growth with agent-based features. Based on the propensity for decision makers confronted by fundamental uncertainty to revise their 'state of long-run expectations' in response to short-run events, it has been shown that the economy can experience aggregate fluctuations in its rate of growth that are aperiodic and of no fixed amplitude. While this observation merely corroborates and better illustrates the results of an earlier study based on a similar model, the incorporation of agent heterogeneity into our model permits exploration of other features of the economy – most notably, the size distribution of firms. Evidence suggests that the size distribution of firms produced by our simulation model – like the size distribution of firms in real-world economies – conforms to a power law. Unlike the observation of cyclical growth, this outcome is not obvious from the model's basic construction, and might be considered an emergent property.

Perhaps the most interesting feature of our model, however, is methodological. Markose et al. (2007, p. 1803) list four prominent features of the 'ACE revolution' in economics, two of which ('heterogeneous (instead of homogenous) decision processes as a characteristic of socioeconomic systems and the statistical non-Gaussian properties of their macro-level outcomes; [and] adaptive and evolutionary dynamics under limited information and rationality') are exhibited by the model developed above. And yet ours is not an ACE model per se, but rather an aggregate structural model with 'agent-based features'. It involves disaggregating a structural model, rather than the 'bottom-up' approach characteristic of ACE; and it involves indirect interaction (which does not depend on locality) rather than direct, locality-dependent interaction amongst heterogeneous agents. The methodological question that these observations prompt is: are aggregate structural models with agent-based features a potentially useful but relatively under-exploited frontier of the increases in computing power that have facilitated the development of ACE? Our tentative answer to this question is affirmative. First, the results presented in this chapter suggest that exploitation of this frontier offers advantages for aggregate structural modellers. Specifically, it presents the opportunity to generate results (regarding the size distribution of firms, for example) that conventional aggregate structural models cannot, by their very nature, produce. Second, exploitation of the same frontier may be advantageous to the development of ACE. This claim stems from observations such as that of Tesfatsion (2006, p. 845), that 'it is not clear how well ACE models will be able to scale up to provide empirically and practically useful models of large scale systems with many thousands of agents'.[21] The point is that the approach taken in this paper – which *does* yield recognisable macroeconomic results – may represent a useful compromise between aggregate structural modelling and 'bottom-up' ACE modelling, either at this particular stage in the latter's development or even in the long term.

Notes

1. See, for example, Blecker (2002).
2. See Hein and van Treeck (2010) for a recent survey, and Dutt (1992), Dutt and Amadeo (1993), and Lavoie (1992, 1995) for earlier contributions that incorporate financial variables into the Kaleckian model.
3. See, for example, Taylor and McNabb (2007) and Starr (2008) for recent empirical assessments of the impact of (respectively) business confidence and consumer sentiment – both components of the SOLE – on growth and fluctuations. See also Stockhammer and Grafl (2010) for a related analysis.
4. See Kregel (1976). The way that equation [7] produces parametric variation in equation [1] that is induced by the effect on animal spirits of recent experience is reminiscent of one of the approaches to modelling cycles taken by Kalecki himself. See Sawyer (1996, pp. 100–1).
5. The convention μ_ε is described as time-dependent because, although conventions are relatively enduring, they can (and do) change, and in novel ways. It is this latter feature (novelty) that explains the absence of any equation of motion that purports to explain *how* μ_ε changes over time. See Setterfield (2003, pp. 326–7) for further discussion of the process of revising the SOLE.
6. See Tesfatsion (2006) for an overview of this sub-field.
7. It can be argued that this second-generation microfoundations project shares certain ontological affinities with aggregate structural modelling in macroeconomics. See Setterfield (2006).
8. The concept of a reaction period is due to Harrod (see Asimakopulos, 1991, ch. 7). The concept is not formally represented in Table 13.1.
9. It is possible that in any period t, *none* of the conditions described in the first column of Table 13.2 will be satisfied. Specifically, we might find that:

$$\left| \frac{\kappa_j}{k_j} \sum_{i=1}^{k_j} (u_{j,t-i} - u_{j,t-1-i}) + \frac{(1-\kappa_j)}{k_j} \sum_{i=1}^{k_j} (u_{t-i} - u_{t-1-i}) \right| < |c_j|$$

having previously observed:

$$\left| \frac{\kappa_j}{k_j} \sum_{i=1}^{k_j} (u_{j,t-k_j-i} - u_{j,t-k_j-1-i}) + \frac{(1-\kappa_j)}{k_j} \sum_{i=1}^{k_j} (u_{t-k_j-i} - u_{t-k_j-1-i}) \right| < |c_j|$$

In such cases, the SOLE is randomly seeded to prevent it from becoming completely inert. Experiments with optimism and pessimism bias in this random seeding (where either $\alpha_{jt} = \alpha_{jt-1} + \varepsilon_{jt}$ or $\alpha_{jt} = \alpha_{jt-1} - \varepsilon_{jt}$, respectively) reveal that such biases have no substantive effect on the results reported below.

10. The values taken from Lavoie and Godley (2001–02) are not reported in the article itself, but were provided in a private correspondence. Note that the value of g, in both Lavoie and Godley (2001–02) and Skott and Ryoo (2008), is 0.5. We have adjusted this parameter value very slightly to better calibrate our model (which is different from theirs) to the stylised facts of growth and capacity utilisation.

11. As will become clear in the discussion of operationalising equation [7a] below, this will ensure that $u_{jt-1} - u_{jt-2} = u_{t-1} - u_{t-2} = \sigma_u \geq c_j \ \forall j$ initially.

    We used monthly data on total industry capacity utilisation in the US 1967–2007 taken from the Board of Governors of the Federal Reserve System to compute the standard deviation of u.

12. With reference to the calculations in Table 13.2, for $j = 51, ..., 100$ (i.e., firms for which $k_j = 3$) we set $\alpha_{jt} = \alpha_{jt-1}$ for: (i) any value of t that is not a multiple of 3; *and* (ii) in early iterations of the model, any value of t that *is* a multiple of 3 but for which none of the conditions of expectational disappointment in Table 13.2 are fully satisfied. The latter is necessary to prevent a behavioural 'black hole', given that we have only specified the values of $u_{jt-1} = u_{t-1} = 0.8242$ and $u_{jt-2} = u_{t-2} = 0.6857$ in the process of specifying initial conditions.

13. The latter is close to the average rate of capacity utilisation in the US over the past 60 years (82.4 per cent).

14. On the interpretation of this statement as a rejection of traditional equilibrium analysis, see Sawyer (1996, pp. 103–4).

15. The concept of resilience focuses on the *durability* of a system and hence its capacity for longevity. The key question posed by this concept is: can the system under scrutiny reproduce itself in a sufficiently orderly manner to ensure that it persists over time?

16. This interpretation is plausible given that the capital stock – which is constant in the short run, an interval of less than one year – changes between periods in our model.

17. Note that, although economically inactive firms retain their capital (which does not depreciate), their inactivity means that their (constant) stock of wealth will become progressively smaller as a proportion of the aggregate capital stock.

18. In order to construct the size distribution in Figure 13.4, several functions were written to automatically 'bin' all firms during each period based on the relative size of their capital stocks and the maximum number of bins permitted. The maximum number of bins was set to 12 for the purposes of this analysis.

19. The Pareto distribution is sometimes referred to as the '80–20 rule', according to which 20 per cent of the population owns 80 per cent of society's wealth.

20. The actual relationship estimated is $p(x) = Bx^{-\delta}$ where B is a constant. The power law analysis was executed using the plfit.r library, written by Aaron Clauset of the Santa Fe Institute and University of New Mexico. This library, and more information about it, is available at http://www.santafe.edu/~aaronc/powerlaws/.

21. Similar reservations are expressed by Hartley (2001) who, in his review of Gallegati and Kirman (1999), questions 'whence comes our certainty that it is possible to build tractable models of the macroeconomy from the ground up? Maybe the real lesson of the book is that it may not be possible to build such models, that we can certainly build better microeconomic models than those used in the representative agent literature,

but that such models do not directly translate into macroeconomics' (Hartley, 2001, pp. F146–7).

References

Asimakopulos, A. (1991) *Keynes' General Theory and Accumulation*, Cambridge: Cambridge University Press.

Blecker, R. (2002) 'Distribution, demand and growth in neo-Kaleckian macro models', in M. Setterfield (ed.), *The Economics of Demand-Led Growth: Challenging the Supply-Side Vision of the Long Run*, Cheltenham: Edward Elgar.

Cassetti, M. (2002) 'Conflict, inflation, distribution and terms of trade in the Kaleckian model', in M. Setterfield (ed.), *The Economics of Demand-Led Growth: Challenging the Supply-Side Vision of the Long Run*, Cheltenham: Edward Elgar.

Dequech, D. (1999) 'Expectations and confidence under uncertainty', *Journal of Post Keynesian Economics*, 21, 415–30.

Dutt, A.K. (1987) 'Alternative closures again: a comment on "Growth, distribution and inflation"', *Cambridge Journal of Economics*, 11, 75–82.

Dutt, A.K. (1992) 'Rentiers in post-Keynesian economics', in P. Arestis and V. Chick (eds), *Recent Developments in Post-Keynesian Economics*, Aldershot: Edward Elgar.

Dutt, A.K. (2007) 'The dependence effect, consumption and happiness: Galbraith revisited'. Paper presented at the Analytical Political Economy Workshop, Queen Mary and Westfield College, University of London, June.

Dutt, A.K. and E. Amadeo (1993) 'A post-Keynesian theory of growth, interest and money', in M. Baranzini and G.C. Harcourt (eds), *The Dynamics of the Wealth of Nations: Growth, Distribution and Structural Change*, London, Macmillan.

Gallegati, M. and A. Kirman (eds) (1999) *Beyond the Representative Agent*, Cheltenham: Edward Elgar.

Gerrard, B. (1995) 'Probability, uncertainty and behaviour: a Keynesian perspective', in S. Dow and J. Hillard (eds), *Keynes, Knowledge and Uncertainty*, Aldershot: Edward Elgar.

Gabaix, X. (2009) 'Power laws in economics and finance', *Annual Review of Economics*, 1, 295–318.

Gibson, B. and M. Setterfield (2010) 'Real foundations of financial crisis'. Paper presented at the Analytical Political Economy Workshop, Queen Mary University of London, May.

Hartley, J.E. (2001) 'Review of *Beyond the Representative Agent* edited by Gallegati (Mauro) and Kirman (Alan)', *Economic Journal*, 111, F145–7.

Hein, E. and T. van Treeck (2010) 'Financialization in post-Keynesian models of distribution and growth: a systematic review', in M. Setterfield (ed.), *Handbook of Alternative Theories of Economic Growth*, Cheltenham: Edward Elgar.

Holling, C.S. (1973) 'Resilience and stability of ecological systems', *Annual Review of Ecology and Systematics*, 4, 1–23.

Ijiri, Y. and H. Simon (1977) *Skew Distributions and the Sizes of Business Firms*, Amsterdam: North-Holland.

Kaldor, N. (1961) 'Capital accumulation and economic growth', in F.A. Lutz and D.C. Hague (eds), *The Theory of Capital*, London: Macmillan.

Kalecki, M. (1968) 'Trend and business cycle reconsidered', *Economic Journal*, 78, 263–76.

Keynes, J.M. (1936) *The General Theory of Employment, Interest and Money*, London: Macmillan.

Kirman, A. (1989) 'The intrinsic limits of modern economic theory: the emperor has no clothes', *Economic Journal*, 99 (Supplement), 126–39.

Kirman, A. (1992) 'Whom or what does the representative agent represent?', *Journal of Economic Perspectives*, 6, 117–36.

Kregel, J. (1976) 'Economic methodology in the face of uncertainty: the modelling methods of Keynes and the Post Keynesians', *Economic Journal*, 86, 209–25.

Lavoie, M. (1992) *Foundations of Post-Keynesian Economic Analysis*, Aldershot, Edward Elgar.

Lavoie, M. (1995) 'Interest rates in Post-Keynesian models of growth and distribution', *Metroeconomica*, 46, 146–77.

Lavoie, M. (2002) 'The Kaleckian growth model with target return pricing and conflict inflation', in M. Setterfield (ed.), *The Economics of Demand-Led Growth: Challenging the Supply-Side Vision of the Long Run*, Cheltenham: Edward Elgar.

Lavoie, M. and W. Godley (2001–02) 'Kaleckian models of growth in a coherent stock-flow monetary framework', *Journal of Post Keynesian Economics*, 24, 277–311.

Markose, S., J. Arifovic, and S. Sunder (2007) 'Advances in experimental and agent-based modelling: asset markets, economic networks, computational mechanism design and evolutionary game dynamics', *Journal of Economic Dynamics and Control*, 31, 1801–7.

Pareto, V. (1897) *Cours d'Economique Politique*, vol. 2, Lausanne: F. Rouge.

Reed, W.J. (2001) 'The Pareto, Zipf and other power laws', *Economics Letters*, 74, 15–19.

Sawyer, M.C (1982) *Macro-Economics in Question: The Keynesian-Monetarist Orthodoxies and the Kaleckian Alternative*, Armonk, NY: M.E. Sharpe.

Sawyer, M. (1996) 'Kalecki on the trade cycle and economic growth', in J.E. King (ed.), *An Alternative Macroeconomic Theory: The Kaleckian Model and Post-Keynesian Economics*, London: Kluwer Academic.

Sawyer, M. (1999) 'The Kaleckian analysis and the new millennium', *Review of Political Economy*, 11, 303–19.

Sawyer, M. (2010) 'The Kaleckian analysis of demand-led growth', Leeds University Business School, mimeo.

Setterfield, M. (2003) 'Neo-Kaleckian growth dynamics and the state of long run expectations: wage- versus profit-led growth reconsidered', in N. Salvadori (ed.), *Old and New Growth Theories: An Assessment*, Cheltenham: Edward Elgar, pp. 321–39.

Setterfield, M. (2006) 'The case for macroeconomics', Trinity College, mimeo.

Skott, P. and S. Ryoo (2008) 'Macroeconomic implications of financialization', *Cambridge Journal of Economics*, 32, 827–62.

Starr, M. (2008) 'Consumption, sentiment, and economic news', American University Department of Economics Working Paper No. 2008–16.

Steindl, J. (1965) *Random Processes and the Growth of Firms*, New York: Hafner.

Stockhammer, E. and L. Grafl (2010) 'Financial uncertainty and business investment', *Review of Political Economy*, 22, 551–68.

Taylor, K. and R. McNabb (2007) 'Business cycles and the role of confidence: evidence for Europe', *Oxford Bulletin of Economics and Statistics*, 69, 185–208.

Tesfatsion, L. (2006) 'Agent-based computational economics: a constructive approach to economic theory', in L. Tesfatsion and K.L. Judd (eds), *Handbook of Computational Economics, Volume 2: Agent-Based Computational Economics*, Handbooks in Economic Series, Amsterdam: North-Holland.

Wooldridge, M. (2002) *An Introduction to Multi Agent Systems*, Chichester: Wiley.

14
Unsurprising to Keynes, Shocking to Economists: The Normalisation of Capital Controls in the Global Financial Crisis

Ilene Grabel

1 Introduction*

Malcolm Sawyer's illustrious career is marked by his profound engagement with Keynesian and Kaleckian macroeconomic theory and by his critically important interventions in debates over economic policies, particularly in the European context. He has been a leading force in the revitalisation and increased professional standing of heterodox economics research around the world. This immense contribution to our profession has been manifest in many different ways: through his enormously important body of published research over wide-ranging topics, and through his ceaseless energy for providing opportunities for heterodox economists around the world to enter into conversation with one another and with the mainstream of the profession through the many projects, journals, and edited books that he has initiated (often with his collaborator and dear friend, Philip Arestis).

This chapter very much reflects the interest that Malcolm has long had in heterodox, Keynesian-inspired approaches to macroeconomic policy. I address here the matter of capital controls, the support for

*I am grateful for the very useful reactions to this research offered by Jim Boyce, James Crotty, Mwangi wa Githinji, Jonathan Kirshner, and especially George DeMartino, and participants at conferences or seminars at the Central Bank of the Argentine Republic, Federal University of Rio de Janeiro, the Political Economy Research Institute of the University of Massachusetts-Amherst, the New School for Social Research, the IDEAs conference in Muttukadu, India, and Cornell University. I benefited immensely from the research assistance of Stu Thomas and Jesse Golland.

which stems from Keynes's own work and from the broad traditions in which Malcolm's work is rooted.

The last several decades of neoliberalism have had many pernicious effects on policy choices in the developing world. One of the consequences of neoliberalism was that capital controls were delegitimised as a policy tool. I argue here that the current global financial crisis has had one silver lining in connection with policy space for development – this is the normalisation of capital controls in developing countries. I suggest that this may represent the beginning of what may very well turn out to be the most significant expansion of policy space in the developing world of the past several decades.

2   Capital controls: the 'new normal'

The current crisis has achieved in a hurry something that heterodox economists have been unable to do for a quarter-century. It has provoked policy makers around the world to impose capital controls as a means to protect domestic economies from the ravaging effects of liberalised financial markets. What is perhaps more surprising and hopeful is that the new controls have been met variously with silence on the part of the International Monetary Fund (IMF) and the international business community and tacit acceptance of their necessity and prudence. This reception contrasts sharply with the IMF and investor condemnation that was provoked when Malaysia imposed stringent capital controls during the East Asian financial crisis. At the time the IMF called these controls on capital outflows a 'step back' (Bloomberg, 6 May 2010), and a representative article in the international business press stated that 'foreign investors in Malaysia have been expropriated, and the Malaysians will bear the cost of their distrust for years' (cited in Kaplan and Rodrik, 2001: 11). More recently, capital controls in Thailand were reversed by the Central Bank within a few days after their implementation in December 2006 (following a coup) after they triggered massive capital flight (Bloomberg, 6 May 2010).

The IMF's inconsistent stance on and response to the new capital controls makes it easier for other countries to follow suit, and it appears that they are doing so (DeMartino, 1999). In my view, the normalisation of capital controls is the single most important way in which policy space for development has widened in several decades.

Capital controls were the norm in developing and wealthy countries in the decades that followed the Second World War (Helleiner, 1996).[1] At that time, they were widely understood by academic economists, policy makers and officials at multilateral institutions to be an essential tool of economic management. Policy makers deployed capital controls in order to enhance macroeconomic policy autonomy, promote financial and currency stability, protect domestic industries/sectors from foreign control or competition, and ensure the provision of adequate credit to favoured sectors and firms at the right price (Epstein, Grabel, Jomo KS, 2004).

The reception that greeted Malaysia's capital controls during the East Asian crisis was unremarkable inasmuch as it was consistent with the view of neoliberal economists and policy makers at the time. Indeed, up until the East Asian crisis the Fund was poised to modify its Articles of Agreement to make the liberalisation of all international private capital flows a central purpose of the Fund and to extend its jurisdiction to capital movements. But despite the neoliberal tenor of the times, some developing countries nevertheless maintained capital controls – most famously, Chile and Malaysia, but also China, India, Colombia, Thailand, and a few others.

Then a notable development occurred. In the wake of the East Asian crisis, IMF research staff started to change their views of capital controls – modestly and cautiously to be sure. In the post-Asian crisis context, the centre of gravity at the Fund and in the academic wing of the economics profession shifted away from an unequivocal, fundamentalist opposition to any interference with the free flow of capital to a tentative, conditional acceptance of the macroeconomic utility of some types of capital controls. Permissible controls were those that were temporary, market-friendly, focused on capital inflows, and introduced only when the economy's fundamentals were mostly sound and the rest of the economy was liberalised (Prasad et al., 2003; Ariyoshi et al., 2000). Academic literature on capital controls in the decade that followed the East Asian crisis reflected this view: as Gallagher (2010a) points out, cross-country empirical studies (many of which are reviewed in Magud and Reinhart, 2006) offered strong support for the macroeconomic achievements of controls on inflows. (See also David, 2008; Coelho and Gallagher 2010; Epstein et al. 2004 on inflow and outflow controls in seven countries; Chwieroth, 2010: ch. 8.) Evidence supporting the achievements of outflow controls remains far more scant. Research on Malaysia by Kaplan and Rodrik (2001) finds strongly in favor of the achievements of Malaysia's controls on outflows. They find that compared to other countries in the region that had IMF programs during this period, Malaysian policies produced faster economic recovery, smaller declines in employment and real wages, and more rapid turnaround in the stock market. Magud and Reinhart's review (2006) bears out this view of Malaysia's outflow controls as well, although their survey also concludes that outflow controls had inconclusive effects in other countries.

The IMF itself took note of its own change in stance. A 2005 report by the IMF's internal watchdog, the Independent Evaluation Office (IEO, 2005: 48), finds that during the 1990s the IMF 'displayed sympathy with some countries in the use of capital controls and ... even suggested that market-based measures could be introduced as a prudential measure'. The report then finds that the IMF's support for capital controls increased after the East Asian crisis. That said, the report acknowledges (correctly) that there was a lack of consistency in the IMF's advice on this matter during the post-Asian crisis period. Thus began the tepid, gradual and uneven practical and ideational process by which some types of capital controls came to be normalised conditionally by the IMF and by academic economists after the East Asian crisis.

Although the seeds of an intellectual evolution had been planted in the post-Asian crisis context, there was a push back in this period from stalwarts in the academic wing of the profession (for example, Forbes, 2005; Edwards, 1999). In addition, there was a curious disconnect between the research of IMF staff, on the one hand, and advocacy for capital account liberalisation by the institution's economists when they worked in the field with particular countries, on the other.[2] Hence, despite the modest intellectual progress on capital controls that began after the East Asian crisis, capital controls were still largely viewed as an exceptional measure that could achieve desirable outcomes only where state capacity was high and/or where investors were undeterred by controls because opportunities in the country were so attractive.

But something happened in the midst of the current global financial crisis. Policy makers quietly began to impose a variety of capital controls, often framing them simply as prudential policy tools (akin to what Epstein et al. 2004 termed 'capital management techniques'). These controls are now becoming a part of the global financial landscape for several reasons that we will explore below. At the same time we see that the ideas of economists at the Fund on capital controls have continued to evolve with the consequent effect of now normalising this policy instrument.

The case of Iceland is particularly interesting for the discontinuity that it demonstrates in connection with the IMF's view of capital controls.[3] Iceland was the first country to sign a Stand-By Arrangement (SBA) during the current crisis, and it was the first financial rescue in Western Europe since Britain's in 1976. The country originally went to its Nordic neighbours for assistance, and then to Russia in early October 2008. When these negotiations failed other European countries refused to lend unless Iceland negotiated an arrangement with the IMF, which it ultimately did in the fall of 2008. What is most interesting about the Icelandic SBA is that it includes provisions regarding the need for stringent capital controls, something that we do not find in earlier SBAs that the IMF signed in connection with East Asian countries or in other crises during the neoliberal era. Even more surprising, the SBA provided for controls even on outflows. In the words of the IMF's Deputy Managing Director, Murilo Portugal, Iceland's capital controls are 'an essential feature of the monetary policy framework, given the scale of potential capital outflows' (cited in Krugman, 2010).

Iceland's controls were initially imposed prior to the signing of the SBA in October 2008, although the agreement with the Fund made a very strong case for their necessity and maintenance as means of restoring financial stability. The central bank formalised the capital control regime in November 2008, and then modified it via the issuance of new rules the next month. The December rules prohibited foreign exchange related to capital transactions and required domestic parties to submit all foreign currency that they acquired either from the sale of goods and services or in another manner to a domestic financial institution. These capital controls were designed to protect the Icelandic krona from collapsing due to capital outflows from the country. (As soon as the crisis emerged, the krona depreciated by 70 per cent and the stock market lost more than 80 per cent of its value. Since most of Iceland's debt is denominated in foreign currency, the large currency depreciation had severe spillover effects on debt-service abilities.) Unsurprisingly, given the IMF's long-held allergy to capital controls, IMF staff were questioned repeatedly in news conferences on what seemed to be an abrupt about face. Fund staff repeatedly said the capital controls in the country were crucial to prevent a free fall of the currency, that they were explicitly temporary, and that it was a priority of the Fund to end all restrictions as soon as possible. Indeed, the country's central bank began a sequenced removal of its capital controls in November 2009.

Although the IMF's stance with respect to Iceland's capital controls initially appeared anomalous, it soon became clear that it marked a dramatic precedent. For example, the SBA with Latvia of December 2008 allowed for the maintenance of pre-existing restrictions arising from a partial deposit freeze at Parex, the largest domestic bank in the country (IMF, 2009a). Soon thereafter, a joint World Bank–IMF report (2009: Table 1.4) on the current crisis notes without evaluation that six countries (namely, China, Colombia, Ecuador, Indonesia, the Russian Federation, and Ukraine) all imposed some type of capital control during the crisis.[4] Another Fund report acknowledges that Iceland, Indonesia, the Russian Federation, Argentina and Ukraine all put capital controls on outflows in place to 'stop the bleeding' related to the crisis (IMF, 2009b). These reports offer neither details on the nature of these controls nor commentary on their ultimate efficacy, something that further suggests that capital controls – even on outflows – have a kind of 'taken for granted' aspect at the Fund these days.

The Brazilian case is also notable since it illustrates both the evolution and the continued equivocation in the views of Fund staff on the matter of capital controls. Moreover, it illustrates the policy space that is increasingly being appropriated by policy makers in developing countries that remain independent of the Fund. In late October 2009, Brazil imposed capital controls via a tax on portfolio investment. The controls were self-described as modest, temporary and market-friendly, and were aimed at slowing the appreciation of the currency in the face of significant international capital inflows to the country. Initially they involved a 2 per cent tax on money entering the country to invest in equities and fixed income investments, while leaving foreign direct investment untaxed. Once it became clear that foreign investors were using purchases of American Depository Receipts (ADRs) issued by Brazilian corporations to avoid the tax, the country's Finance Ministry imposed a 1.5 per cent tax on certain trades involving ADRs.

The IMF's initial reaction to Brazil's controls on capital inflows was one of mild disapproval. A senior official said: 'These kinds of taxes provide some room for maneuver, but it is not very much, so governments should not be tempted to postpone other more fundamental adjustments. Second it is very complex to implement those kinds of taxes, because they have to be applied to every possible financial instrument', adding that such taxes have proven to be 'porous' over time in a number of countries. In response, no less than John Williamson (with Arvind Subramanian) indicted the IMF for its doctrinaire and wrong-headed position in relation to the Brazilian capital controls, taking the institution to task for squandering the opportunity to think reasonably about the types of measures that governments can use to manage surges in international private capital inflows (Subramanian and Williamson, 2009). But Williamson's criticism misses the point that in fact the IMF reaction was quite muted, especially in comparison with its unequivocal reaction to Malaysia's capital controls during the East Asian crisis, and likely intended not to deter Brazil (a new lender to the IMF) from its strategy but to warn other developing countries against following Brazil's lead down a policy path that the IMF views as a last resort. A week later the IMF's Strauss-Kahn reframed the message on Brazil's capital controls. The new message was, in a word, stunning: 'I have no ideology on this'; capital controls are 'not something that come from hell' (cited in Guha, 2009).

As the crisis progressed, other developing countries have implemented capital controls. Many of these are aimed at controlling capital inflows so as to reduce speculative or inflationary pressures and/or pressures on the currency to appreciate, while some target outflows. In December 2009 Taiwan imposed new restrictions on inflows that aim to reduce speculative pressures from overseas investors. The controls preclude foreign investors from placing funds in time deposits (Brown, 2010). Around the same time, China added to its existing controls on inflows and outflows. Then, in June 2010, Indonesia announced what its officials awkwardly term a 'quasi capital control' that governs short-term investment. Indonesia's new inflow controls seek to dampen speculation in the country via a one-month holding period for central bank money market securities, the introduction of longer maturity instruments, and new limits on the sales of central bank paper by investors and on the interest rate on funds deposited at the central bank (Wagsty, 2010). In the same month, South Korea also announced controls on inflows. These controls seek to reduce the risks associated with a possible sudden reversal of inflows, rising short-term foreign borrowing and the use of derivative instruments. The controls limit the amount of currency forward and derivatives trading in which financial institutions can engage, and limit the foreign currency loans extended by banks to local companies (*Economist*, 16 June 2010). Also in June, Argentina and Venezuela implemented controls on outflows: in Argentina they involve stricter limits on US dollar purchases (Webber, 2010), and in Venezuela they involve new restrictions on access to foreign currency (Mander, 2010).[5] The response of investors (and credit rating agencies) to these initiatives is silence and, in some cases, tacit approval. The response by economists at the IMF has been the same.

Ambivalence and inconsistency in IMF practice are echoed in its research and in the public statements of leading Fund officials. These evidence both a much more explicit and far-reaching acceptance of capital controls than we saw prior to and following the East Asian crisis. In the raft of reports that the IMF has issued in the context of the crisis, we find frequent mention of the protective role of capital controls. For example, an IMF report on low-income countries states that the impact of the crisis on banking systems in these countries has been modest insofar as '[t]he existence of capital controls in several countries and structural factors have helped moderate the direct and indirect effects of the financial crisis' (IMF 2009c, 9, fn. 9).

That said, the IMF is trying to avoid going too far in embracing this policy instrument. One Fund report warns that capital controls should be considered only as a last resort. The costs of even temporary capital controls are enumerated with great care; for example, a country 'could as a last resort regulate capital transactions – though these carry significant risks and long term costs'. Later on the report argues that 'even temporary standstills will have long-lasting legal implications' (IMF 2009d, 8–9, fn. 5, fn. 8). A joint report by the Bank and Fund discusses capital controls in the same cautionary vein, though the brief discussion concludes that 'nonetheless, capital controls might need to be imposed as a last resort to help mitigate a financial crisis or stabilise macroeconomic developments' (WB–IMF 2009, 65).

In February 2010 IMF economists (Ostry et al.) reached far beyond the Fund's public statements or practice to date in regards to controls on inflows. Ostry et al. (2010) commend controls on capital inflows for preventing economic contraction in countries that relied on them; reducing financial instability; and reducing financial fragility by lengthening the maturity structure of countries' external liabilities and improving the composition of capital inflows. These findings pertain to capital controls that were in place prior to and after the East Asian crisis, as well as during the current crisis. The report also indicates that 'such controls, moreover, can retain their potency even if investors devise strategies to bypass them … the cost of circumvention strategies acts as "sand in the wheels"' (p. 5) The paper argues that 'policymakers are again reconsidering the view that unfettered capital flows are a fundamentally benign phenomenon. … even when flows are fundamentally sound … they may contribute to collateral damage …'. Not exactly your grandfather's IMF!

Other parts of the Ostry et al. policy note qualify this new openness towards controls on inflows, however. The report hedges in the expected ways – identifying the restrictive conditions under which capital controls can work (or be justified). But in comparison with earlier reports by the IMF the qualifications are just that – they are not offered as insuperable obstacles to the use of controls. And that, in itself, represents a major advance, as many observers have acknowledged. After the Ostry et al. (2010) policy note was released, several prominent IMF watchers praised the Fund for finally embracing a sensible view of capital controls. For example, Ronald McKinnon stated 'I am delighted that the IMF has recanted' (cited in Rappeport, 2010); the former IMF official Eswar Prasad states that the paper represented a 'marked change' in the IMF's advice (cited in Wroughton, 2010), and Dani Rodrik stated that the 'the stigma on capital controls [is] gone' and the (Ostry et al. 2010) 'policy note is a stunning reversal – as close as an institution can come to recanting without saying, "Sorry, we messed up"' (Rodrik, 2010). No less telling is the sharp rebuke to the empirical work in Ostry et al. by noted economist William Cline, which is illustrative of the discomfort that 'true believers' in capital account liberalisation have with what they see as the Fund's troubling and wrong-headed embrace of capital controls (Cline, 2010).

In the lead up to the spring 2010 IMF–World Bank meetings, the IMF's Global Financial Stability Report (GFSR, IMF 2010a) also dealt with capital controls in surprising ways. Many analysts responded to the GFSR (one of the Fund's most important regular publications) by indicating that the Fund is already renouncing what seems to be a new openness to capital controls. It is certainly true that the discussion in the GFSR contains more caveats than we find in the other recent studies of controls discussed here. But the basic and very important message that appears in Ostry et al. (2010) and elsewhere that 'capital controls may have a role in the policy toolkit' is retained in the GFSR (see also IMF, 2010b). It is also notable that the GFSR acknowledges conflicting empirical findings on capital controls among empirical researchers, and even acknowledges empirical work on the achievements of capital controls by heterodox economists, such as Coelho and Gallagher (2010).

Recent statements by top officials at the Fund (and the Bank) further illustrate a general normalisation of capital controls as a policy tool. For example, the IMF's First Deputy Managing Director, John Lipsky, in an address to the Japan Society in December 2009 stated that '[c]apital controls also represent an option for dealing with sudden surges in capital flows'. In this address he makes clear that controls should be used when the surge in capital inflows is temporary (though we have to wonder when sudden surges would not be temporary?), and that the controls themselves should be temporary. Despite these caveats, he argues that 'Above all, we should be open-minded.' The same views are articulated in a speech made in Moscow in June 2010 (Lipsky, 2010). After the Governor of the Bank of Thailand made a speech in the summer of 2010 embracing the rise of capital controls in Asia, the IMF's Strauss-Kahn stated that he was 'sympathetic' to emerging countries embracing controls as a last resort to counter foreign investors' inflating asset bubbles, but warned that '[y]ou have to be very pragmatic … long-term capital controls are certainly not a good thing … But short-term capital controls may be necessary in some cases: it is matter of balancing the costs of different options' (cited in Johnston, 2010). He argued in July 2010 that 'it is just fair that these [developing] countries would try to manage the inflows' as a last resort against a flood of investors pumping up inflation and asset values (cited in

Oliver, 2010). Top officials at the World Bank have also gone on record in support of capital controls. For example, Bank president Robert Zoellick had this to say of the re-emergence of capital controls in Asia: 'it's not a silver bullet but it doesn't surprise me that people are trying them and they may help at the margin' (cited in Gallagher, 2010b).

Given the inertia at the IMF, its actions during the current crisis mark a minor revolution. Change at the Fund has been uneven, however, with one step back for every two steps forward. In the growing pile of reports that the Fund (and the World Bank) have issued in the context of the current crisis, we find positive statements about the protective role of capital controls followed immediately by warnings about their use only as a temporary, last resort, and an enumeration of the significant risks and potential long-term costs of capital controls. This should not be surprising. We would expect that long-held ideas – especially those that have hardened to the level of ideologies and been codified in institutional practices – have long half-lives (Grabel 2003). The process of changing these ideas and practices is necessarily uneven; moreover, progress will inevitably generate push back from within the institution itself. Hence we should expect to find continuing evidence of tension and equivocation in future IMF reports that preclude a clear and decisive Fund verdict on capital controls.

This new intellectual openness towards capital controls on the part of the IMF is about to be tested in practice. Asset bubbles are continuing to emerge in many rapidly growing developing countries as private capital flows are flooding the most dynamic of these markets. This is largely due to the low interest rates and dismal prospects in the USA and the countries of the Euro zone. It is quite likely that some of these countries (and perhaps others) will soon find it necessary to expand or introduce additional capital controls. It will be important to watch the IMF closely as it tries to figure out just how to respond. This will be the real test of the Fund's new 'open-mindedness' regarding capital controls. It may be that the patience of economists at the Fund will be severely taxed as other countries test the limits of the developmental policy space that has arisen as a consequence of the crisis. What is clear from the foregoing is the tenuous situation in which the IMF now finds itself, as it has begun to acknowledge the reality of its diminished influence across the developing world and the necessity of capital controls in cases of financial disruption, while not wanting to lose control over just when, how and by whom this policy instrument is employed.

One important caveat is in order before we conclude. The above should not be read to suggest that the IMF has conducted itself in an exemplary and entirely new fashion during the current crisis. In other work, I argue that in several important respects the Fund's conditionality programmes during the current crisis evidence strong continuity with the policy adjustments that the institution put in place during the East Asian and the Mexican financial crises of the 1990s. Today, the IMF continues to apply pressure to secure compliance with stringent, pro-cyclical fiscal and monetary policy targets.[6] Moreover, despite rhetoric by Fund staff to the contrary, expansive forms of conditionality (that involve, for example, privatisation, market liberalisation, land, labour market and pension system reform) have also returned as a key feature of recent Fund programmes. Finally, the greater degree of fiscal flexibility granted by the Fund in some country contexts (particularly on the Eastern side of the European periphery) has little to no practical significance. (See Grabel (2010) for discussion of both the continuities and the discontinuities in Fund practice during the current crisis.)

3 Summary and conclusions

The story of the ultimate effects of the current crisis on policy space for development cannot yet be written insofar as the crisis is continuing to unfold. But at this point we can see that the crisis has had one beneficial effect, and this is the normalisation of capital controls. This development would no doubt be pleasing and unsurprising to Keynes since the turbulence of the interwar period created the intellectual and policy space for capital controls after the Second World War.

Like that earlier normalisation of capital controls, the normalisation of capital controls has come about for many complementary reasons. Here I list some of these reasons. First, the views of IMF staff on capital controls appear to be continuing the evolution that began after the East Asian crisis. Second, IMF leadership and staff may be driven by a pragmatic recognition that the institution has no effective choice but to amend its policy prescriptions, owing to the diminution of its influence in the developing world since the East Asian financial crisis. Relatedly, there may be concern at the IMF about existing and future competition with other institutions (such as the World Bank, the Asian Development Bank, Brazil's national development bank) and regional financial arrangements (such as the Chiang Mai Multilateralisation agreement involving members of ASEAN, and South Korea, China and Japan, the Latin American Reserve Fund, the Bank of the South, and so on) in the area of crisis management. Third, the plasticity of IMF staff views on capital controls may well reflect the influence of leading academic economists, who themselves have come to question – and in some respects reject – the traditional neoliberal prescription for development. Fourth, the current global financial crisis, coming just a decade after the East Asian crisis, may be having the effect of encouraging those economists at the IMF (and the World Bank) who have long had reservations about the neoliberal model to give voice to their concerns and to assert themselves more effectively. It is important to keep in mind in this connection that like any complex organisation, the IMF comprises diverse constituencies that may very well disagree among themselves about some fundamental matters pertaining to the institution's strategies. And fifth, policy makers in developing countries that are independent of the Fund are utilising their policy autonomy and are experimenting, among other things, with diverse types of capital controls.[7]

Of course, the ultimate outcome of this expansion of policy space is uncertain. It is possible that the neoliberal worldview may re-establish itself, not least because advocates of this view have proven remarkably adept at 'paradigm maintenance' over the last three decades as Wade (1996) has noted and as Polanyi (1944: 143) suggested long ago. Mirowski (2010) and Hodgson (2009) are pessimistic about the economics profession's ability to learn from its mistakes. And it might be that the centre of the battle over policy space has shifted from the IMF to other arenas. As Gallagher (2010a) has shown, for example, there are powerful restrictions on the right to impose capital controls embodied in US trade and investment agreements.

At the present time we can say that heterodox economists have reason to maximise the policy and intellectual space that seems to have been created by the global financial crisis. We can be sure that our colleague Malcolm Sawyer will be a tenacious and efficacious participant in this critically important project.

Notes

1. Capital controls refer to a range of policies that are designed to manage international capital flows. They can and have taken many forms in various countries over time. For example, they have involved restrictions on foreign investment in certain sectors or assets, minimum stay requirements on foreign investment, restrictions on capital outflows, taxes on foreign investment, restrictions on access to the domestic or to foreign currencies or to holding bank accounts outside the country, and so on.
2. Although the matter is outside the scope of this paper, the disconnect between IMF research and advocacy work might be explained by the relative

autonomy of different departments at the IMF, a lack of leadership from the top on capital controls, and the internal entrepreneurship of mid-range IMF staff when working in different contexts. The latter two issues are examined in Chwieroth (2010).

3. See the discussion of Iceland in Wade (2009).

4. See Reuters.com (2009) for a brief description of Ukraine's controls and also those imposed by Nigeria during the crisis. An IMF report (2009a) notes in passing that in Ukraine and Pakistan it 'encouraged timely elimination of exchange restrictions on current payments.' If this is code for stronger opposition it would suggest the existence of a greater degree of continuity between the IMF's current view of capital controls and the view that it held during the Asian crisis. But no further details are provided in Fund reports on the negotiations involving Pakistan or Ukraine's capital controls. Weisbrot et al. (2009b) mention that there was conflict between Pakistan and the IMF over capital controls, but information on the content of these discussions or any conflict is unavailable at this time.

5. There have also been reports of new capital controls under discussion in India and in China (on India, Economic Times, 2010; on China, Bloomberg, 8 June 2010). The rumoured new controls in China will seek to deter investors from betting on an end to its peg to the US dollar.

6. A large number of recent studies of the SBAs (and other assistance programmes) negotiated during the current crisis have established that the IMF has promoted pro-cyclical macroeconomic policy adjustments or targets (UNICEF, 2010; Van Waeyenberge, Bargawi and McKinley, 2010; UN, 2010; Muchhala, 2009; Eurodad, 2009; Solidar, 2009; Cordero, 2009; Weisbrot et al., 2009b). Indeed, only two studies conclude otherwise, and both are self-congratulatory reports by the Fund (IMF 2009a, 2009e). The evidence overwhelmingly supports the conclusion that current IMF conditionalities are similar to those during the Asian (and previous) crises. For example, a study by Van Waeyenberge et al. (2010) of 13 low-income countries with IMF programmes in place prior to and during the current crisis concludes that they preclude countries from utilising counter-cyclical policies and public investment programmes. Similarly, a study by Weisbrot et al. (2009b) of 41 countries that had Fund programmes in 2009 finds that 31 of these agreements involve tightening fiscal or monetary policy or both. Fund programmes across the European periphery are also illustrative of the pro-cyclical policy adjustments that we have seen in previous crises. Interestingly, in cases involving European countries, the EU and the German government appear to be going even further than the IMF in regard to demands for fiscal austerity. (See discussion of this dynamic in the cases of Hungary, Romania and Latvia in Lütz and Kranke, 2010).

7. I note here that Russia, China, Brazil, India and South Korea became the first developing countries to lend money to the IMF. In April 2009 they collectively committed to lend the Fund $90 billion.

References

Ariyoshi, A., Habermeier, K., Laurens, B., Otker-Robe, I., Canales-Kriljenko, J.I., and Kirilenko A. (2000) 'Capital controls: Country experiences with their use and liberalization', *IMF Occasional Paper no. 190,* Washington DC: International Monetary Fund.

Best, J. (2005) *The Limits of Transparency,* Ithaca, NY: Cornell University Press.

Bloomberg (2010) 'Asia should consider capital controls to stem asset-bubble risks'. Obtainable from http://www.bloomberg.com/news/2010-05-06/asia-should-consider-capital-controls-to-stem-asset-bubble-risks-un-says.html.

Bloomberg (2010) 'China said to consider controls on yuan forward transactions'. Obtainable from http://www.businessweek.com/news/2010-06-08/china-said-to-consider-controls-on-yuan-forwards-update1-.html.

Bretton Woods Project (2009) *Bretton Woods Update, No. 67,* London: Bretton Woods Project. Obtainable from http://www.brettonwoodsproject.org/update/67/bwupdt67.pdf.

Bretton Woods Project (2010) *Bretton Woods Update, No. 71,* London: Bretton Woods Project. Obtainable from http://www.brettonwoodsproject.org/update/71/bwupdt71.pdf.

Brown, K. (2010) 'Asia toys with introducing capital controls', Financial Times. Obtainable from: http://www.ft.com/cms/s/0/feb03e14-828b-11df-85ba-00144feabdc0.html.

Chang, H.J. and Grabel, I. (2004) *Reclaiming Development: An Alternative Economic Policy Manual,* London: Zed Books.

Chwieroth, J. (2010) *Capital Ideas: The IMF and the Rise of Financial Liberalization,* Princeton, NJ: Princeton University Press.

Cline, W. (2010) 'The IMF staff's misleading new evidence on capital controls', *Peterson Institute for International Economics.* Obtainable from: www.piie.com/realtime/?p=1351.

Coelho, B. and Gallagher, K. (2010) 'Capital controls and 21st century financial crises: Evidence from Colombia and Thailand', *Political Economy Research Institute Working Paper No. 213,* Amherst: University of Massachusetts-Amherst.

Cordero, J.A. (2009) 'The IMF's Stand-by Arrangements and the economic downturn in Eastern Europe: The cases of Hungary, Latvia, and Ukraine', *Center for Economic and Policy Research,* Washington DC, Obtainable from: www.cepr.net.

David, A. (2008) 'Controls on capital inflows and the transmission of external shocks', *Cambridge Journal of Economics,* 32(5), 887–906.

DeMartino, G. (1999) 'Global neoliberalism, policy autonomy, and international competitive dynamics', *Journal of Economic Issues,* 33(2), 343–9.

Economic Times (2010) 'RBI hints at curbs on capital inflows'. Obtainable from http://economictimes.indiatimes.com/news/economy/finance/RBI-hints-at-curbs-on-capital-inflows/articleshow/5525961.cms.

Economist (2010) 'The won that got away'. Obtainable from http://www.economist.com/blogs/newsbook/2010/06/south_koreas_currency_controls16.

Edwards, S. (1999) 'How effective are capital controls?', *Journal of Economic Perspectives,* 13(4), 65–84.

Epstein, G., Grabel, I. and Jomo, K.S. (2004) 'Capital management techniques in developing countries: An assessment of experiences from the 1990s and lessons for the future', *G24 Discussion Paper No. 27,* New York and Geneva: United Nations.

Eurodad (2009) 'Bail-out or blow-out? IMF policy advice and conditions for low-income countries at a time of crisis'. Obtainable from http://www.eurodad.org/uploadedFiles/Whats_New/Reports/Bail-out%20or%20blow-out.pdf.

Forbes, K. (2005) 'Capital controls: mud in the wheels of market efficiency', *Cato Journal*, 25(1), 153–66.

Gallagher, K (2010a) 'Policy space to prevent and mitigate financial crises in trade and investment agreements', *G-24 Discussion Paper No. 58*, New York and Geneva: United Nations.

Gallagher, K. (2010b) 'Obama must ditch Bush-era trade deals', guardian.co.uk. Obtainable from: http://www.guardian.co.uk/commentisfree/cifamerica/2010/jun/30/obama-bush-us-trade.

Grabel, I. (2003) 'Ideology, power and the rise of independent monetary institutions in emerging economies', in J. Kirshner (ed.), *Monetary Orders: Ambiguous Economics, Ubiquitous Politics*, Ithaca, NY: Cornell University Press.

Guha, K. (2009) 'IMF refuses to rule out use of capital controls', Financial Times. Obtainable from: http://www.ft.com/cms/s/0/e3fd1610-c818-11de-8ba8-00144feab49a.html.

Helleiner, E. (2010) 'A Bretton Woods moment? The 2007–2008 crisis and the future of global finance', *International Affairs*, 86(3), 619–36.

Helleiner, E. (1996) *States and the Reemergence of Global Finance*, Ithaca, NY: Cornell University Press.

Hodgson, G. (2009) 'The Great Crash of 2008 and the reform of economics', *Cambridge Journal of Economics*, 33, 1205–21.

Independent Evaluation Office (IEO), International Monetary Fund (2005), "Evaluation Report: The IMF's Approach to Capital Account Liberalization", *Independent Evaluation Office*, Washington DC: International Monetary Fund.

International Monetary Fund (2005) 'Evaluation report: The IMF's approach to capital account liberalization', *Independent Evaluation Office*, Washington DC: International Monetary Fund.

International Monetary Fund (2009a) 'Review of recent crisis programs', *Strategy, Policy and Review Department*. Obtainable from http://www.imf.org/external/np/pp/eng/2009/091409.pdf.

International Monetary Fund (2009b) *Annual Report on Exchange Rate Arrangements and Exchange Restrictions*, Washington, DC: International Monetary Fund.

International Monetary Fund (2009c) 'The implications of the global financial crisis for low-income countries', Washington DC: International Monetary Fund. Obtainable from https://www.imf.org/external/pubs/ft/books/2009/globalfin/globalfin.pdf.

International Monetary Fund (2009d) 'Coping with the crisis: Policy options for emerging market countries", *IMF Staff Position Note, No. 8*, Washington DC: International Monetary Fund. Obtainable from http://www.imf.org/external/pubs/ft/spn/2009/spn0908.pdf.

International Monetary Fund (2009e) 'Creating policy space – responsive design and streamlined conditionality in recent low-income country programs', *Strategy, Policy and Review Department*. Obtainable from http://www.imf.org/external/np/pp/eng/2009/091009A.pdf.

International Monetary Fund (2009f) *Factsheet on IMF Conditionality*, Washington DC: International Monetary Fund.

International Monetary Fund (2010a) *Global Financial Stability Report*, Washington DC: International Monetary Fund.

International Monetary Fund (2010b) 'How did emerging markets cope in the crisis?', *Strategy, Policy and Review Department*. Obtainable from http://www.imf. org/external/np/pp/eng/2010/061510.pdf.

Johnston, T. (2010) 'Thailand joins Asian central bankers taking on Greenspan', Financial Times. Obtainable from http://blogs.ft.com/beyond-brics/2010/07/21/asian-central-banks-continue-to-challenge-western-status-quo/.

Kaplan, E. and Rodrik, D. (2001) 'Did the Malaysian capital controls work?', *NBER Working Paper No. 8142*, Cambridge, MA: National Bureau of Economic Research.

Krugman, P. (2010) 'The conscience of a liberal', *New York Times*. Obtainable from http://krugman.blogs.nytimes.com/.

Lipsky, J. (2009) 'Building a post-crisis global economy – An address to the Japan Society', New York: IMF External Relations Department, Obtainable from http://www.imf.org/external/np/speeches/2009/121009.htm.

Lipsky, J. (2010) 'The road ahead for central banks: Meeting new challenges to financial stability', Moscow. Obtainable from http://www.imf.org/external/np/speeches/2010/061810.htm.

Lütz, S. and Kranke, M. (2010) 'The European rescue of the Washington Consensus? EU and IMF lending to Central and Eastern European Countries', *LEQS Paper*, No. 22, London: London School of Economics.

Magud, N. and Reinhart, C. (2006) 'Capital controls: An evaluation', *NBER Working Paper No. 11973*, Cambridge: National Bureau of Economic Research.

Mander, B. (2010) 'Venezuela begins anti-inflation plan', Financial Times. Obtainable from http://www.ft.com/cms/s/0/ff0eeb3c-7294-11df-9f82-00144 feabdc0.html.

Mirowski, P. (2010) 'The great mortification: Economists' responses to the crisis of 2007–and counting', *Hedgehog Review*, 12(3). Obtainable from: http://www.iasc-culture.org/publications_article_2010_Summer_mirowski.php.

Muchhala, B. (2009) 'The IMF's financial crisis loans: No change in conditionalities', *Third World Network*. Obtainable from http://www.twnside.org.sg/title2/par/IMF.Crisis.Loans-Overview.TWN.March.2009.doc.

Oliver, C. (2010) 'IMF warns on emerging market currency controls', Financial Times. Obtainable from http://www.ft.com/cms/s/0/5ba241aa-8ce9-11df-bad7-00144feab49a.html.

Ostry, J., Ghosh, A., Habermeier, K., Chamon, M., Qureshi, M., and Reinhardt, D. (2010) 'Capital inflows: The role of controls', *IMF Staff Position Note No. 4*. Obtainable from http://www.imf.org/external/pubs/ft/spn/2010/spn1004.pdf.

Prasad, E., Rogoff, K., Wei, S.J., and Kose, M.A. (2003) 'Effects of financial globalization on developing countries: Some empirical evidence'. Obtainable from http://www.imf.org/external/np/res/docs/2003/031703.htm.

Rappeport, A. (2010) 'IMF reconsiders capital controls opposition', *Financial Times*, 22 February.

Reuters.com. (2009) 'Factbox – recent capital controls in emerging markets'. Obtainable from http://in.reuters.com/article/governmentFilingsNews/idINLK53166920090520.

Rodrik, D. (2010) 'The end of an era in finance', Project syndicate. Obtainable from http://www.project-syndicate.org/commentary/rodrik41/English.

Solidar (2009) 'Doing a decent job? IMF policies and decent work in times of crisis'. Obtainable from http://www.eurodad.org/uploadedFiles/Whats_New/Reports/Doing%20a%20decent%20job.pdf.

Subramanian, A. and Williamson, J. (2009) 'The Fund should help Brazil to tackle inflows', Financial Times. Obtainable from: http://www.ft.com/cms/s/0/0fb77bf6-c1cf-11de-b86b-00144feab49a.html.

United Nations (2010) *World Economic Situation and Prospects 2010*, New York: UN Department of Economic and Social Affairs.

UNICEF (2010) 'Prioritizing expenditures for a recovery with a human face: Results from a rapid desk review of 86 recent IMF country reports', *Social and Economic Policy Working Brief*, April. Obtainable from: www.unicef.org.

Van Waeyenberge, E., H. Bargawi, and T. McKinley (2010) 'Standing in the way of development? A critical survey of the IMF's crisis response in low-income countries, Eurodad and Third World Network'. Obtainable from http://www.eurodad.org/whatsnew/reports.aspx?id=4083.

Wade, R. (1996) 'Japan, the World Bank, and the art of paradigm maintenance: The East Asian Miracle in political perspective', *New Left Review*, 217, 3–36.

Wade, R. (2003) 'What strategies are viable for developing countries today? The WTO and the shrinking of "development space"', *Review of International Political Economy*, 10, 627–44.

Wade, R. (2007) 'The aftermath of the Asian financial crisis: From "liberalize the market" to "standardize the market" and create a "level playing field"', in B. Mucchala (ed.), *Ten Years After: Revisiting the Asian Financial Crisis*, Washington, DC: Wilson Center Press, pp. 173–94.

Wade, R. (2009) 'Iceland as Icarus: From "miracle" to crash, and beyond', *Challenge*, May–June, 5–33.

Wagsty, S. (2010) 'Indonesia: Controls or quasi-controls on capital inflows?', Financial Times. Obtainable from http://blogs.ft.com/beyond-brics/2010/06/16/indonesia-controls-or-quasi-controls-on-capital-inflows/.

Webber, J. (2010) 'Argentina unveils tighter controls on US dollar buys', Financial Times. Obtainable from http://blogs.ft.com/money-supply/2010/06/08/argentina-unveils-tighter-controls-on-dollar-buys/.

Weisbrot, M., Cordero, J. and Sandoval, L. (2009a) 'Empowering the IMF: Should reform be a requirement for increasing the Fund's resources?', Center for Economic and Policy Research. Obtainable from http://www.cepr.net/documents/publications/imf-reform-2009-04.pdf.

Weisbrot, M., R. Ray, J. Johnston, J. A. Cordero, J. A. Montecino (2009b) 'IMF-supported macroeconomic policies and the world recession: A look at forty-one borrowing countries', *Center for Economic and Policy Research*, Washington DC, October. Obtainable from www.cepr.net.

Weisbrot, M. and Johnson, J. (2009) 'IMF voting shares: No plans for significant changes', *Center for Economic and Policy Research Issue Brief*, Washington, DC: Center for Economic and Policy Research.

World Bank–IMF (2009) 'Global monitoring report 2009: A development emergency', Obtainable from http://siteresources.worldbank.org/INTGLOMONREP2009/Resources/5924349-1239742507025/GMR09_book.pdf.

Wroughton, L. (2010) 'IMF endorses capital controls as temporary measure', reuters.com. Obtainable from http://www.reuters.com/article/idUSN1912428020100219.

15
Regulating Wall Street: Exploring the Political Economy of the Possible

Gerald Epstein and Robert Pollin

> The world can be and has been changed by those for
> whom the ideal and real are dynamically contiguous.
> – William James

1 Introduction

US President Barack Obama signed into law the Dodd–Frank Wall Street Reform and Consumer Protection Act in July 2010. Dodd–Frank is the most ambitious measure aimed at regulating US financial markets since the Glass–Steagall Act was implemented in the midst of the 1930s Depression. However, it remains an open question whether or not Dodd–Frank is capable of controlling the wide variety of hyperspeculative practices that produced the near total global financial collapse of 2008–09, which in turn brought the global economy to its knees, with the Great Recession.

Of course, Dodd–Frank would not have been necessary in the first place, and the Great Recession itself would not have occurred, had US politicians – Democrats and Republicans alike – not chosen to dismantle the Glass–Steagall system step by step, beginning in the 1970s. The basic argument on behalf of deregulation that began emerging in the 1970s, advanced by an overwhelming majority of mainstream economists, was that Glass–Steagall was designed in reaction to the 1930s Depression and was no longer appropriate under contemporary conditions. This chorus of politicians and economists was correct that the financial system has become infinitely more complex since the 1930s and that Glass–Steagall had become outmoded. But it never followed from this that financial markets should operate unregulated, as opposed to renovating the regulatory system to address the most recent developments.

Dodd–Frank is a massive piece of legislation, 875 pages in length, that covers a wide range of issues. These include coordinating the management of the Federal Reserve and other financial regulatory agencies around issues of systemic risk; bringing hedge funds and derivative markets under regulatory supervision; creating effective prohibitions on proprietary trading by investment banks; establishing new oversight over public credit rating agencies; and creating a consumer financial protection bureau.

It is inevitably difficult to fully anticipate the effects over time of any major piece of economic legislation, since economic conditions and institutions are always evolving, including as a result of the regulatory environment. But such challenges are especially great in trying to forecast the likely impacts of Dodd–Frank. This is because the legislation itself, despite its enormous length, mainly lays out a broad framework for a new financial regulatory system. It leaves the details of implementation to ten different regulatory bodies in the USA. These include the US Treasury, Federal Reserve, Securities and Exchange Commission, and Commodities Futures Trading Commission, in addition to requesting action from overseas agencies such as the Basil Committee on Banking Reform. Dodd–Frank calls on these agencies to set down 243 separate rules, and to undertake 67 separate studies to inform the rule-making process. The final set of rules under Dodd–Frank are designed to be implemented only over a number of years, up to 12 years in some areas.

The lack of specificity in setting down new financial regulations was widely viewed as a victory for Wall Street, and, equally, as a defeat for proponents of a strong new regulatory system. This is because both Wall Street lobbyists and also advocates of strong regulation anticipate that the lobbyists will be able to dominate the process of detailed rulemaking to a greater extent than they managed in establishing Dodd–Frank's broad guidelines during Congressional deliberations.

It is clear that Wall Street is moving into the phase of regulatory rule making with a strong hand. First, the major Wall Street firms have huge budgets at their disposal to intervene at will during the process of detailed rule-setting. By contrast, the supporters of strong regulations operate with budgets that are minuscule by comparison. The Wall Street firms also have a direct and intense level of self-interest tied up in the details of specific rulings. For reformers, the level of direct connection, and thus direct interest, is likely to be far less on any given detailed matter. Finally, there is the matter of pure regulatory capture. Regulators understand that they can burnish their future private sector career opportunities if they are solicitous to the concerns of Wall Street while still employed on the public payroll.

These are all unavoidable realities. However, it is still the case – and indeed the central premise of this chapter – that dominance by Wall Street in implementing Dodd–Frank is not a foregone conclusion. Rather, Dodd–Frank remains a contested terrain – supporters of financial regulation can still achieve significant victories within the regulatory framework created by Dodd–Frank.

The political ammunition on behalf of a strong regulatory system begins with a simple fact – the overwhelming evidence provided by the financial meltdown itself that weakly regulated financial markets will produce economic disasters. The final version of Dodd–Frank that was passed into law testifies to the force of this factor. Despite the weaknesses and ambiguities included the final law, many features of the measure did become stronger through the drafting process, as lobbying efforts by Americans for Financial Reform and other citizens' groups effectively exerted influence over many areas of the debate. Americans for Financial Reform (AFR) describes itself as follows on its website: 'We are a coalition of more than 250 national, state and local groups who have come together to reform the financial industry. Members of our coalition include consumer, civil rights, investor, retiree, community, labor, religious and business groups as well as Nobel prize winning economists.' The voices of the people did end up mattering in the debate.

But there is also a second crucial factor. This is that it is unnecessary for the supporters of effective regulations to win victories on all 243 rules that need to be decided, or to have their positions incorporated into all 67 studies mandated by the legislation. Rather, a great deal can be achieved through achieving effective rules in a few key areas within the full expanse of Dodd–Frank.

The focus of this chapter is to explore three central areas of Dodd–Frank where we think effective regulations can be established. These are: (1) proprietary trading by banks and other financial institutions; (2) oversight of credit rating agencies such as Moody's and Standard & Poors'; and (3) the markets for commodities futures derivative contracts. In each of these areas, we address the question: under what conditions are some of the basic features of Dodd–Frank capable of succeeding in controlling hyper-speculation and promoting financial stability?

In pursuing these questions, we are guided by the formidable body of research in the areas of macroeconomics, finance and policy making by Professor Malcolm Sawyer. Over the course of nearly 40 years, beginning with such important early works as *Macroeconomics in Question: The Keynesian-Monetarist Orthodoxies and the Kaleckian Alternative* (1982), Professor Sawyer has made major contributions to developing a Post

Keynesian heterodox tradition, and more precisely a framework that builds from Kalecki, Marx and others as well as Keynes. Professor Sawyer's work has been crucial in enabling those of us willing to learn from him to both understand the severe deficiencies of orthodox macroeconomics as well as advance a positive agenda for explaining the world and changing it for the better. Indeed, among Post Keynesian macroeconomists, Sawyer's contributions have been unique through their insistence on attacking fundamental questions rigorously at both the levels of theory and policy.

By taking seriously the analytical questions connected to the specifics of designing economic policies, Sawyer has also been able to bring remarkable depth to exploring the most pressing questions in macroeconomics today. This quality of Sawyer's work is dramatically evident in, for example, his 2005 survey paper with Philip Arestis 'Financial Liberalization and the Finance–Growth Nexus: What Have We Learned?' Reading this paper five years after it was published – that is, three years prior to the global financial collapse and the Great Recession – Sawyer and Arestis could not have been more prescient in exposing as fraudulent both the theoretical and empirical cases for financial deregulation. Sawyer and Arestis wrote this paper at a time when the overwhelming majority of mainstream economists still clung fiercely to both their theoretical and empirical claims in behalf of financial deregulation. Yet Sawyer and Arestis concluded their paper as follows:

> It is clear from this excursion in the literature that no convincing evidence has been provided in support of the propositions of the financial liberalization hypothesis. On the contrary, the available evidence can be interpreted as indicating that the theoretical propositions of the thesis are at best weak, and as such they ought to be abandoned. (p. 33)

Our aim here is to work within this analytic tradition advanced by Malcolm Sawyer. The next three sections of the chapter consider, respectively, questions regarding the regulations of proprietary trading and related matters; the credit rating agencies; and the commodities futures derivative market. The paper then concludes with some brief general observations.

2 Prohibitions on proprietary trading

One of the most important provisions of Dodd–Frank is the so-called 'Volcker rule'. This is actually not one rule, but a series of measures, which were strongly supported by former Federal Reserve Chair Paul Volcker, to prevent proprietary trading and related highly risky and destabilising activities by banks. The Volcker rule aims to also impose limits and large capital charges on proprietary trades by non-bank financial intermediaries, such as hedge funds and private equity firms.

Proprietary trading and related activities by large banks and other major financial firms was a primary cause of the financial bubble as well as the collapse of the bubble and near total global meltdown in 2008–09. This was due to the fact that proprietary trades by the banks was a key force in sustaining upward pressure on security prices, thereby feeding the bubble. The banks ran large trading books – inventories of securities that they themselves own – ostensibly to operate as market makers only for their clients. But maintaining large trading books enabled them to operate with inside information on their clients' trading patterns to stay ahead of market movements, i.e. to 'front run'.

In addition, these activities were funded mainly with short-term borrowing and backed up with questionable collateral. The banks were able to operate in this way because the accounting standards for such activities were weak, enabling the banks to operate free of public scrutiny. The proprietary trades were also closely intertwined with hedge funds, insurance companies and private equity funds, often involving credit default swaps and other opaque financial instruments. For example, a large investment bank, such as Goldman Sachs, could sell bundles of mortgage-backed securities to private investors, and these clients could purchase insurance on these securities, in the form of credit default swaps from, say, AIG. All of these transactions could then be debt-financed to an unlimited degree, raising the level of risk exposure to all the parties to each level of transaction – that is, to the private investors, Goldman Sachs and AIG. It was precisely such series of interconnections, formed on the basis of high levels of leveraging, that fuelled the credit market bubble, which in turn led to the crash.[1]

It is difficult to know for certain the extent of the banks' proprietary trading activities. Within days of the announcement of the proposed Volcker rules to limit proprietary trading, the business press reported that proprietary trades were actually only a small part of the major banks' overall operations. For example, the *Wall Street Journal* reported on 21 January 2010 that proprietary trades made up about 10 per cent of Goldman Sachs revenue, 5 per cent for Citibank, less than 5 per cent for Morgan Stanley and less than 1 per cent for Bank of America and J.P. Morgan.[2]

However, there is strong evidence that these figures are much too low. This is because it is difficult to separate out proprietary trading from trading for clients and market making. Working with the available data, Crotty, Epstein and Levina (2010) found that as of mid-2008, large banks had lost roughly $230 billion – about one-third of their value at the 2006 market peak – on their proprietary holdings of what were presumed to have been low-risk AAA-rated assets. The banks were holding little or no reserve funds to support these assets in the event of a market downturn. Regulators thought that these were simply inventories of assets held to facilitate client trading. But Crotty et al. show that this proprietary portfolio constituted roughly one-third of the total trading portfolio, including assets managed for clients and those available for the banks' use as market makers. Crotty et al. go on to show that as of 2006, prior to the crisis, proprietary trading accounted for a very high proportion total net revenue for the major investment banks – that is, 64 per cent or more for Goldman Sachs and 43 per cent for Morgan Stanley.

2.1 How Dodd–Frank could control proprietary trading

Dodd–Frank includes four major features intended to dramatically reduce the risks associated with proprietary trading by banks as well as the highly risky interconnections between banks and other intermediaries, such as hedge funds.

First, the legislation includes a blanket prohibition against banks engaging in transactions involving material conflicts of interest or highly risky trading activities. The precise language in Dodd–Frank reads as follows:

> No transaction, class of transactions, or activity may be deemed ... permitted ... if it (i) would involve or result in a material conflict of interest ... (ii) would result, directly or indirectly in material exposure by the banking entity to high-risk assets or high-risk trading strategies ... (iii) would pose a threat to the safety and soundness of such banking entity; or (iv) would pose a threat to the financial stability of the United States. (Dodd–Frank Act, Section 619(2)((A)(i–iv)

In principle, these are very strong regulatory standards. However, to implement these standards in practice, regulators will need to establish clear definitions for the concepts of 'material conflict of interest', and 'high-risk trading strategy'. Without clear and workable definitions of these terms, these provisions of Dodd–Frank cannot possibly succeed in achieving their intended purpose.

In addition to these outright prohibitions, Dodd–Frank also establishes that regulators impose capital requirements or other quantitative limits on trading, such as margin requirements, on banks or significant non-bank financial firms engaged in risky trading activities. Moreover, the Volcker rule regulations also restrict interactions between banks and non-bank affiliates that are engaged in high-risk trading and investing.

Capital requirements entail that traders maintain a minimal investment of their own cash relative to the overall size of their level of asset holdings, while margin requirements require traders to use their own cash reserves, in addition to borrowed funds, to make new asset purchases. There are two interrelated purposes to both capital and margin requirements. The first is to discourage excessive trading by limiting the capacity of traders to finance their trades almost entirely with borrowed funds. The second is to force the banks to put a significant amount of their own money at risk when undertaking new asset purchases – that is, to 'put skin in the game'.

Here again, in principle, these measures can be highly effective at reducing excessively risky practices by banks and other intermediaries. But whether they will succeed in practice will depend on the specific decisions undertaken by the relevant regulatory agencies. As the law in this section is written, the regulatory agencies have full discretion to establish whether and to what extent 'additional capital and quantitative limitations are appropriate to protect the safety and soundness of banking entities engaged in such activities'. For the regulatory agencies to make these decisions will require clarity as to the processes which create fragile financial structures and how to apply the regulatory tools most effectively to prevent excessive risk-taking and fragility.

More generally, even while Dodd–Frank establishes strong general principles for regulation, it also allows for exemptions from regulations as well as various ambiguities that could be readily exploited by the banks. For example, Dodd–Frank allows banks to own some shares in hedge and private equity funds. This could make it easier for banks to hide proprietary trading in the deals executed through hedge funds. Dodd–Frank also allows for proprietary trading as long as such activities support 'market-making activities' and 'risk-mitigating hedging activities' (from Section 619(d)). It will be difficult for regulators to distinguish these activities from front-running proprietary trading by the banks and other activities entailing conflicts of interest. Such exemptions from the strong regulatory principles articulated within Dodd–Frank are exactly what Stiglitz was referring to in writing that 'unfortunately, a key part of the legislative strategy of the banks was to get exemptions so that the force of any regulation passed would be greatly attenuated. The result is a Swiss cheese bill – seemingly strong but with large holes' (2010, p. 335).

In short, Dodd–Frank does provide sufficiently strong regulatory tools for controlling proprietary trading. The real question is whether these tools will be permitted to operate effectively, or whether, alternatively, the Swiss cheese features of the law become predominant over time.

3 Public and private credit rating agencies

The major private credit rating agencies – Moody's, Standard & Poors, and Fitch – were significant contributors to the creation of the financial bubble and the subsequent financial crash of 2008–09. The rating agencies were supposed to be in the business of providing financial markets with objective and accurate appraisals as to the risks associated with purchasing any given financial instrument. Instead, they consistently delivered overly optimistic assessments of assets that either carried high, or at the very least, highly uncertain risks.

Moreover, the reason these agencies consistently understated risks was not simply that they were relying on economic theories that underplay the role of systemic risk in guiding their appraisals, although this was a contributing factor. The more significant influence was the market incentives themselves, which pushed the agencies towards providing overly favourable appraisals. That is, giving favourable risk appraisals was good for the rating agencies' own bottom line, and the rating agencies responded in the expected way to these available opportunities.

The Dodd–Frank Act contains a provision addressing this question, written by Senator Al Franken, based on a proposal from James Lardner of the Demos Institute (2009). The Franken provision calls on the SEC to create a ratings oversight board with investor representatives in the majority. This board will choose a rating agency to conduct the initial evaluation of each new set of structured finance products. Securities issuers would not be allowed to participate in the assignment of raters, and the assignments would be based on an evaluation of accuracy of ratings over time. In addition, under this approach, the SEC will have an Office of Credit Ratings with the authority to write rules and levy fines. Investors will now be able to recover damages in private anti-fraud actions brought against rating agencies for gross negligence in the rating. Rating agencies are also required to establish their ratings on a consistent basis for corporate bonds, municipal bonds, and structured finance products and instruments.

The rating agencies and banks fought hard to weaken this Franken amendment. The final outcome was that Dodd–Frank requires the SEC to undertake a two-year study, and on the basis of the study to implement either the Franken proposal or an alternative that eliminates the conflict of interest problem with rating agencies. Given that Dodd–Frank remains open in terms of adopting either the Franken proposal or an alternative, we describe here what we believe would be the most effective approach. This is to create a public credit rating agency that operates free of the same perverse incentive system that distorts the work of private agencies. We then compare the strengths of this proposal relative to the Franken approach.

3.1   Public credit agency as corrective[3]

The fundamental contribution of a public credit rating agency would be to offer a counterforce to the perverse incentive system facing private agencies. It is true that providing accurate risk appraisals has become increasingly challenging as securitised markets have deepened. There may well be situations in which the staff of the public agency concludes that an instrument is too complex to provide an accurate risk appraisal. In such situations, it would be the obligation of the public agency to be open with such an assessment – that is, to assess an instrument as 'not ratable'. Financial market participants could then decide the degree to which they might wish to take a gamble with such an instrument.

The public credit rating agency operating in this way would bring about a dramatic change in the incentives for the private rating agencies as well as the broader array of financial market participants. It would weaken the biases in favour of greater risk and complexity, and lead the financial system to operate with a higher level of transparency. The private agencies would be free to continue operating as they wish. But when their appraisals differ significantly from those provided by the public agency, the private agencies would be forced to explain the basis for their divergent assessments.

Market participants would thus be free to evaluate the full range of information and assessments available to them, from the public agency, the private agencies, and elsewhere. It is useful to recall that in the 1980s, Michael Milken of the now defunct firm Drexel Burnham Lambert created the 'junk bond' market precisely by insisting that the traditional rating agencies were overly cautious in their appraisals of corporate bonds. Market participants could make comparable assessments on their own with respect to the appraisals of the public rating agencies.

3.2   How the agency could operate

We propose that all private businesses issuing securities that are to be traded publicly in US financial markets would be required to seek a rating by the public agency before any trading could be conducted legally. The security could be legally traded after the public agency had issued its appraisal, even if the appraisal ended up being 'not ratable'.

The new agency could be organised to operate through procedures that borrow from existing regulatory agencies in the United States, including the Food and Drug Administration (FDA) as well as the SEC. Just as the FDA assesses health risks associated with new pharmaceuticals before the drugs can be marketed, the public rating agency would assess the riskiness of financial assets before the securities could be publicly traded. Unlike the FDA, the public rating agency would not have the authority to prevent securities from being marketed, but only to offer their independent risk assessment. Similar to the SEC, which is financed largely through a low-level securities transactions tax and registration fees, the public ratings agency could be financed by cost-recovery fees.

The staff of the public agency would be compensated as high-level civil servants. They would receive no benefits as such from providing either favourable or unfavourable ratings. Indeed, a compensation system could be established whereby the professional staff is evaluated on the basis how well their risk assessments of given assets end up comporting with the market performance of these assets over time. Safeguards would be put in place to dismiss any professional staff members who have conflicts of interest that could compromise the integrity of their ratings.

3.3 Comparing a public rating agency with the Franken proposal

The key difference between the two approaches is that with the public rating agency, a new independent source of market information will have been established. The explicit and only mandate of this agency will be to serve the public interest in conducting ratings. Under the Franken proposal, the private agencies would still be the only entities which are operating with adequate staffing levels to conduct appraisals of new financial market products. The SEC would be contracting with the private agencies on an individual basis to produce appraisals under the Franken proposal. However, the private agencies would still be primarily in the business of providing ratings for private-sector firms that hire the agencies to conduct appraisals. The profits of the private agencies would therefore still be coming mainly from the major Wall Street firms, and this central fact will not be lost on the private agencies. And even when a given agency is providing a rating under contract with the SEC as opposed to a private Wall Street firm – for example, Moody's has been hired by the SEC to evaluate a new credit default swap being issued by AIG – the market will have to be clear that this particular rating by Moody's was based on a different contractual arrangement than its normal operating procedure.

It is true that, under the Franken proposal, the private rating agencies will become more vulnerable legally should they be found guilty of 'gross negligence' in producing excessively optimistic ratings. But legal correctives of this sort can only be applied years after the compromised rating have been issued. In the meantime, the private ratings agencies could have provided their seal of approval to a new financial bubble. Moreover, even in attempting to apply this legal remedy years after a bubble has inflated and collapsed, it will be very difficult to prove 'gross negligence' in a court of law. This is because the rating agencies could accurately claim that their ratings were only reflecting the views of the vast majority of other market analysts at that time. On this point, it is important to underscore that a financial bubble expands precisely because lots of people are receiving huge financial rewards through rapidly rising asset values. These people naturally want the bubble to continue for as long as possible. Former Federal Reserve Chair Alan Greenspan himself used the evocative terms 'irrational exuberance' and 'infectious greed' to describe the self-feeding momentum that drives financial bubbles.

Given these incentives among private parties in financial markets, what becomes clear is the importance of creating at least one rating agency operating unambiguously in the public interest. This agency, moreover, needs to be held accountable contemporaneously, indeed on a day-to-day basis, just as financial firms issue new securities on a day-to-day basis. Such an arrangement is not possible under the Franken proposal. As such, creating a public agency with such a straightforward mission would actually be easier to administer than the Franken proposal. It would entail far less ambiguity in terms of the source of any given rating, since the public would know that the rating came from the public agency, not a private agency operating on a part-time basis under an SEC contract. Creating a public agency would also mean far fewer opportunities for distorting the intentions of the regulations through legal challenges and manipulation.

4   Commodities futures market speculation

Financial deregulation, particularly from the late 1990s onwards, led to other economic malignancies in addition to being the primary cause of the financial bubble and subsequent financial crash and Great

Recession of 2008–09. Dodd–Frank offers an opportunity to address these matters as well.

First on this list of additional malignancies was that the commodities futures derivative markets – including the markets for futures contracts in energy and food commodities – became new venues for Wall Street hyper-speculation.[4]

Futures markets for food, oil and other commodities have long been used by farmers and others to maintain stability in their business operations and plan for the future. For example, under a 'plain vanilla' wheat futures contract, a farmer could spend $50,000 planting her crop now, and agree now with a commodities futures trader to sell the crop at a fixed price when the crop is harvested. But such simple agreements became increasingly overwhelmed by big-time market speculators in 2000 when the markets were deregulated, along with the rest of the US financial system. Deregulation produced severe swings in the global prices of food and oil. The most severely impacted victims of commodity price volatility are people in developing countries, where it is common for families to spend 50 per cent or more of their total income on food. The United Nations found that sharp price increases in 2008 – a 40 per cent average increase across a range of different food items – led to malnourishment for 130 million additional people.[5]

Provisions of Dodd–Frank offer the opportunity for meaningful control of these markets. Moreover, the regulations that will apply to the commodities futures market will also extend to the trading of derivatives instruments more generally. Our discussion here will focus only on commodities futures derivatives.

Dodd–Frank establishes four basic tools for regulating commodity futures markets: an outright prohibition of agricultural swap markets; capital requirements for organisers of all derivative exchanges, along with margin requirements and position limits for traders on these exchanges. In addition, Dodd–Frank stipulates that most trading be conducted on exchanges as opposed to unregulated over-the-counter (OTC) markets. If implemented effectively, these tools can provide a viable framework for promoting stability in derivative markets.

We have already discussed how capital and margin requirements can be used effectively to dampen excessively risky arrangements between traditional banks and shadow banks. This same tool can also be effective in dampening speculation on commodities futures markets. We therefore focus here on position limits and on the issue of granting exemptions to the regulations, which are permitted in principle under Dodd–Frank.

4.1 Position limits

Dodd–Frank requires the Commodities Futures Trading Commission (CFTC) to establish limits on contracts for physical commodities. The purpose of position limits is to prevent large speculative traders from exercising excessive market power. That is, large traders can control the supply side of derivative markets by taking major positions, either on the short or long side of the markets. Once they control supply, they can then also exert power in setting spot market prices.

A useful starting point for analysing where to set the position limits would be with the experiences in food commodities futures during the huge price run-up in the period 2006–08. Table 15.1 shows the position limits at that time for corn, soybeans and wheat, along with the average position size for three types of long traders, as defined by the CFTC, that is, commercial, non-commercial, and index traders. 'Commercial traders' are producers or consumers of commodities, such as farmers, oil companies or airlines who wish to hedge against future market risks; 'non-commercial traders' are brokerage houses or hedge funds that will sell futures or swap contracts to commercial traders; and 'index traders' are those holding positions in an basket – that is index fund – of commodities. They trade based on the movements of this index fund relative to movements in other asset markets, such as stocks, bonds, and real estate. The index traders are generally large hedge funds or equity holding companies.

To begin with, the figures in Table 15.1 show clearly that the position limits that operated in 2006–08 were relevant only for index traders. The average position sizes for both commercial and non-commercial traders were far below the stipulated limits.

In terms of the index traders, with corn, the position limit was 22,000 contracts, a figure well above the average position of index traders of

Table 15.1 Futures and options market long positions by trader group, January 2006–December 2008

	Position limit (# of contracts)	Average position size (no. of contracts)		
		Commercial traders	Non-commercial traders	Index traders
Corn	22,000	1,499	1,134	16,260
Soybeans	10,000	1,052	590	6,500
Wheat	6,500	964	553	8,326

Source: UNCTAD Trade and Development Report 2009, p. 64.

16,260. These figures suggest that the stipulated position limit was not likely to be binding on the behaviour of most index traders, although there may have been some cases of very large index traders holding positions well above the average. A similar story holds with soybeans, where the position limit was 10,000 contracts, while the average position size for index traders was 6,024. However, the situation is different with wheat. The position limit there was 6,500, but the average index trader held 8,326 contracts. These figures for wheat futures suggest two things: (1) the position limits were set at a level that would have been binding for a significant share of index traders; but (2) the limits were not binding in fact, since the average trader held nearly 30 per cent more contracts than the position limits permitted. Obviously, large index traders in wheat futures were granted exemptions from the stipulated position limits (UNCTAD 2009, p. 65).

The contrasting experiences with the corn, soybeans and wheat markets over the period 2006–08 could thus shed light on how to effectively use the tool of position limits in preventing index traders from exercising excessive market power. One approach would be to set position limits based on the actual position levels of commercial traders, as opposed to index traders, assuming that the distinctions between these can be clearly established through the data. For example, one could set the position limits as one standard deviation greater than the median position levels for commercial traders.

However, the most serious problem here is that as trading practices have become more complex, it becomes increasingly difficult to clearly establish distinctions between 'commercial' and 'index' traders, certainly for purposes of writing regulations that could hold firm against legal challenges. This point was illustrated well in a paper by Silber, 'On the Nature of Trading: Do Speculators Leave Footprints?', which was published in 2003, years before index trading exploded in commodities futures markets. Silber describes how two types of traders, what he terms 'market-makers' and 'speculators', establish their positions and manage their risk exposure. Market-makers are customer-based traders, corresponding closely to what we have termed 'commercial traders', who earn money on the bid/ask spread without speculating on future prices. His category of 'speculators', corresponding to the category of 'index traders', are those who earn money trying to anticipate the direction of future price movements. The key relevant point here is that Silber's discussion makes clear that balance sheets are insufficient to determine whether a trader is a market-maker or a speculator. This means that speculators can readily engage in activities that, at least through examining their balance sheet, would make them appear to be market-makers.

Given this difficulty in distinguishing categories of traders in commodities futures markets, the simplest solution for establishing position limits is to develop an approach that does not rely on making such distinctions. In fact, this can be accomplished readily, by generalising from the idea of defining position limits relative to the median trading levels of commercial traders. That is, we can simply set limits relative to the median trading level of *all* traders in the market. The total number of index traders is small relative to other traders, even though their average positions are much larger. As such, to set position limits relative to the *median* for the overall market will accomplish the same outcome as attempting to set limits only after having distinguished commercial from index traders. In addition, to prevent the position limits from moving excessively based on possible large swings in the levels of market activity, this approach could be adjusted by, for example, defining the median position as a moving average of actual positions over, say, a three-year period.

4.2   Scope of coverage and exemptions

The expansion in regulatory coverage through Dodd–Frank for derivative markets, including the commodities futures markets, includes some potentially significant exemptions. The first is the commercial end-user exemption to clearing. This provides exemptions to any swap counterparty that (1) is not a financial entity; and (2) is using the swap to hedge or mitigate commercial risk. But even more generally, the CFTC may grant any exemptions it deems appropriate from the prescribed position limits.

The aim in offering such exemptions is to prevent the Dodd–Frank regulations from imposing excessive burdens on derivative market participants who are legitimate hedgers, and are thereby not contributing to destabilising the markets. This may be a desirable goal in principle. But in practice, it will be difficult for the CFTC to sort out which market participants truly merit exemptions by the standards established. As such, the effectiveness of the entire regulatory framework around derivative markets will hinge on the CFTC proceeding with great caution in offering exemptions. The only way to insure that the Dodd–Frank regulations are implemented effectively is to allow no exemptions at all.

4.3   How to prevent regulatory arbitrage

For traders to shift the physical or, more importantly, legal venue of trading activity to minimise regulations – that is, to engage in regulatory arbitrage – is a real concern with the Dodd–Frank derivative regulations, but it is hardly a new problem. Indeed, a parallel situation arose with US derivative regulations beginning with the so-called 'Enron loophole' in 2000. The Enron loophole exempted over-the-counter energy trading undertaken on electronic exchanges from CFTC oversight and regulation. Enron quickly seized this market opportunity to create an artificial electricity shortage in California in 2000–01, which led to multiple blackouts and a state of emergency, and, finally, the collapse of Enron itself and its once-'Big 5' accounting firm, Arthur Andersen. Nevertheless, following Enron's example, the big market players subsequently took advantage of similar major loopholes – the 'London loophole' for nominally foreign market trading and the 'Swap dealer loopholes', which permitted all swap trading to move into OTC markets. The overall effect was to enable the OTC markets to flourish alongside the regulated markets (UNTCAD 2009, pp. 76–7).

There are no definitive solutions to regulatory arbitrage, which means, to begin with, regulators must remain fully conscious of the problem and vigilant in pursuing solutions that maintain the integrity of the regulatory system. The most effective starting point would be for all major trading platforms to agree to implement complementary regulations. However, even with serious international efforts at regulatory harmonisation, the whole point with traders intent on avoiding regulation is to find trading platforms anywhere that will enable them to operate as they wish, regardless of whether there is a major market already established at that setting.

As such, the most reliable approach for the US market would be to establish a straightforward rule, whereby the trading of derivative instruments would need to be conducted within the standards of the US regulatory system in order for such transactions to have legal status in the United States. If such a rule were established, we would envision few instances in which derivative traders would be willing to forego the protections of the US legal system simply to avoid regulations.

5 Summary and conclusions

Financial deregulation in the United States – which begin in the 1970s but became formally codified with the repeal of the Glass–Steagall Act in 1999 – has proven disastrous to human well-being both within the USA. and globally, just as Post Keynesians and allied heterodox economists had long admonished. For more than a generation, Malcolm Sawyer has been a leading voice making the case against neoliberal economic policies in general and financial deregulation in particular.

But how do we move forward, digging out of the wreckage created by financial deregulation and building an effective new regulatory framework? Most progressives in the United States regard the new Dodd–Frank regulatory law as offering little promise, because the 'Swiss cheese' features of the law offer Wall Street lobbyists a multitude of opportunities to water down the regulations to their liking, operating in conjunction with sympathetic regulators at the major government agencies. This remains a serious possibility, but, as we try to show, it is not a foregone conclusion.

Rather, we try to show how Dodd–Frank can be used as a framework for building effective regulations. We concentrate on three crucial areas in this chapter – proprietary trading, the credit rating agencies, and the commodities futures derivative markets. Similar possibilities also exist in other areas. In our three chosen areas, we argue that some fairly straightforward regulatory tools can accomplish a great deal. These include capital and margin requirements, position limits, a public credit rating agency, and, most generally, enforcing the principles set down within Dodd–Frank, such as banks being prohibited from engaging in activities that 'would pose a threat to the financial stability of the United States'.

We are not so naïve as to assume that because these regulatory standards will be enforced effectively simply because they are written down on paper within Dodd–Frank. But the fact that they are indeed written down on paper does offer real opportunities for serious political engagement and positive outcomes. Capturing these opportunities will require insightful economic analysis in the Malcolm Sawyer tradition in combination with effective political mobilisations, recalling, as we proceed, the William James epigram which begins this paper, that 'the world can and has been changed by those for whom the ideal and real are dynamically contiguous'.

Notes

1. One excellent and relatively brief discussion within an already extensive literature on these issues is Jarsulic (2010).
2. This *Wall Street Journal* article and related references are presented in Crotty, Epstein and Levina (2010).
3. The following discussion draws on the more fully developed proposal in Diomande, Heintz and Pollin (2009).
4. Ghosh (2010) offers an excellent overview of this development.
5. This figure was cited by Sheeran (2008), Executive Director of the UN World Food Programme.

References

Arestis, P. and M. Sawyer (2005) 'Financial liberalization and the finance–growth nexus: What have we learned?', in P. Arestis and M. Sawyer (eds), *Financial Liberalization: Beyond Orthodox Concerns*, London: Palgrave Macmillan, pp. 1–43.

Crotty, J., G. Epstein and I. Levina (2010) 'Proprietary trading is a bigger deal than many bankers and pundits claim', SAFER Policy Brief #20, 18 February 2010, Political Economy Research Institute, http://www.peri.umass.edu/fileadmin/pdf/other_publication_types/SAFERbriefs/SAFER_issue_brief20.pdf.

Diomande, M.A., J. Heintz and R. Pollin (2009) 'Why U.S. Financial Markets Need a Public Credit Rating Agency', *The Economists' Voice*, June, http://www.bepress.com/cgi/viewcontent.cgi?article=1507&context=ev.

'Dodd–Frank Wall Street Reform and Consumer Protection Act', *Public Law* 111–203, Washington, DC: Government Printing Office, 2010.

Ghosh, J. (2010) 'Unnatural coupling: Food and global finance', *Journal of Agrarian Change*, January, 72–86.

Jarsulic, M. (2010) *Anatomy of a Financial Crisis: A Real Estate Bubble, Runaway Credit Markets, and Regulatory Failure*, New York: Palgrave Macmillan.

Lardner, J. (2009) 'Reforming the rating agencies: A solution that fits the problem', Demos Briefing Paper, http://www.demos.org/pubs/reforming_ratingagencies.pdf.

Sawyer, M. (1982) *Macroeconomics in Question: The Keynesian–Monetarist Orthodoxies and the Kaleckian Alternative*, Armonk, NY: M.E. Sharpe.

Sheeran, J. (2008) Testimony before the US Senate Committee on Foreign Relations, 14 May.

Silber, W. (2003) 'On the nature of trading: Do speculators leave footprints?', *Journal of Portfolio Management*, 29(4), 64–70.

Stiglitz, J. (2010) *Freefall: America, Free Markets, and the Sinking of the World Economy*, paperback edition, New York: Norton.

United Nations Conference on Trade and Development (UNCTAD) (2009) *Trade and Development Report, 2009*, Chapter 2, 'The financialization of commodity markets', Geneva: United Nations, pp. 52–84.

Index